Love of QUILTS

A Treasury of Classic Quilting Stories

Compiled by Cuesta Ray Benberry and Carol Pinney Crabb
Time line by Cuesta Ray Benberry

whitecap

Originally published in 1993 by the American Quilter's Society as A *Patch-work of Pieces: An Anthology of Early Quilt Stories, 1845–1940*. Published in 2004 in the United States by Voyageur Press, Inc., Stillwater, MN 55082

This edition published in Canada in 2004 by
Whitecap Books Ltd.
For more information, contact
Whitecap Books,
351 Lynn Avenue,
North Vancouver, British Columbia, Canada, V7J 2C4

Edited by Margret Aldrich
Designed by Maria Friedrich
Printed in China

ISBN 1-55285-584-8

Dedication

This book is dedicated to Bill Crabb whose generous assistance and active participation enabled us to reach our goal.

Acknowledgments

We gratefully acknowledge those publishers who granted permissions to include the short stories in this quilt fiction anthology.

Some of the original sources for the stories were: Hearst Magazines, Inc., New York, *Good Housekeeping Magazine*, "Blazing Star" by MacKinlay Kantor and "Missouri Rose" by Martha Cheavens; Crowell Publishing, New York, *Woman's Home Companion*, "The Orange Quilt" by Della T. Lutes and "The Horoscope" by Eliza Calvert Hall; *The Home Circle*, "What Letty's Quilt Told" by Bessie Barber; *The Youth's Companion*, "The Quilt-of-the-Cloth-of Gold" by Anne McQueen, "The Ashley Star" by Marjorie Hill Allee, "The 'Rose and Lily' Quilt" by Elsie Singmaster, and "Mrs. Hannah" by F. Roney Weir; *Argosy*, "Quilt Scraps" by Louise Platt Hauck; *Ladies' Home Journal*, "The Best Housekeeper in Banbury" by Edith Robinson; *Harper's Monthly Magazine*, "The Bedquilt" by Dorothy Canfield.

We appreciate the generosity of Virginia Gunn, Dorothy Cozart, Shirley McElderry, and the late Sally Garoutte, who sent us quilt stories to add to our cache.

For typing our entire introduction, time line, and bibliography on floppy discs and acting as advisor, Bill Crabb has earned our eternal thanks.

Our editor, Victoria Faoro, maintained an ideal mixture of professionalism and patience with this long distance, three-city operation, and we admire her very much.

To our families who have endured the entire project with good humor, your funny remarks were true stress relievers, and we thank you.

Contents

INTRODUCTION

From the mid nineteenth century to the early twentieth century short stories about quilts reflected social awareness and concerns, served as moral guidance for young girls, defined the tastes in needlework of the time or the fads of the moment. They revealed regional differences in taste in quilts and differences in customs. The stories disclosed the popular perceptions of quilts in the nineteenth century and in a larger sense, popular attitudes toward the persons who made the quilts. Frequently, there were both subtle and overt distinctions of class in the portrayal of quiltmakers.

The common thread running through this collection of short stories is the humble bed quilt.

Plays, songs, poems, and a myriad of short stories have been written about the patchwork quilt. No other handmade textile has been the cause of so much inspiration. Woven coverlets, blankets or crochet work have not aroused the musician or author to sing their praises or to weave a story around them. Those textile skills are single-handed projects; solo performances. There is not the interaction with friends or neighbors in weaving that there is in making quilts.

One person can make a quilt from start to finish, or as many as fifteen or twenty people can be involved. Friendship quilts have the greatest number of participants as each block is made by a different person. When the quilt top is ready to be quilted the maker can quilt it alone, or she may choose to ask others to help.

Settings
The authors of these short stories usually did not locate the stories in a particular town, city or state. Some locations, however, are mentioned in a general way, such as The South, The Deep South, and Texas. One story was set in Boston. In another story an old mother left her small town to take a long trip by train into

New York City to deliver a quilt to her son and his new wife. The literary ladies of New England, Mary E. Wilkins, Harriet Beecher Stowe, Dorothy Canfield, and Louisa May Alcott, as might be expected, placed their stories in small New England towns most familiar to them. Locations of the rest of the stories are left to the reader's imagination.

Occasionally a man ventured into the female-dominated field of quilt fiction. A Methodist Bishop, John Heyl Vincent, wrote of a quilt that had a story to tell. T. S. Arthur, a publisher, tried his hand at quilt fiction when he wrote "The Quilting Party" for *Godey's Lady's Book*.

Crazy Quilts

A phenomenon in the quilt world was the crazy quilt, as it excited the interest of writers more than any other kind of quilt. In this collection are pieces of fiction employing the crazy quilt as a theme. The crazy quilt sky-rocketed to fame in the early 1880s and gradually disappeared by the turn of the century. Most of the crazy quilt stories were written during their ascendancy in popularity, 1882 to 1890.

While the crazy quilt was the pivot around which the stories were told, their plots differed. One story described at what great lengths two girls would go to obtain fabrics for their crazy quilts. They even resorted to dishonest means! A young lady, Bessie, tried to live a better life and she was helped while working on her crazy quilt. Bessie concentrated on the quilt's designs, which kept her from fretting about things over which she had no control.

In one quilt story young lovers were separated, almost permanently, because the young man put his love note in with her crazy quilt scraps, and she did not take her work out of its bag for almost a year.

Although in the early 1900s Mary E. Wilkins wrote a children's story about a scarecrow that wore a crazy quilt to keep warm, it was rare after that time to see a crazy quilt story. Authors as well as numerous quiltmakers lost their interest in crazy quilts.

Scrap Quilts

There are almost as many different story plots as there are patterns for quilts, yet several themes appear repeatedly. The earliest published quilt story we know was titled "The Patchwork Quilt," published in 1845 in Massachusetts. The idea behind the story was that when a woman looked at her quilt, the fabrics reminded her of the people who had worn the clothing, and of occasions long past.

Nearly a century and a half have passed since that piece was written, but the plot is still a favorite. Almost every general interest periodical or quilt publication has printed stories about scrap quilts made of fabrics from garments worn by friends and relatives.

Aunt Bina made quilts from scraps given to her only by people she liked. She did not want any pieces from people who were stingy or snobbish, meddlesome or cruel. Aunt Bina wanted her quilt to be like fresh air and sunshine. Young girls made scrap quilts, too. In the story "Quilt of Happiness" the girls made a quilt from scraps of clothing worn only when they were happy.

This theme of making memory quilts from scraps of clothing strikes a responsive chord in people's hearts, and continues to give pain and pleasure when they see the quilt.

Quilting Bees

When a quiltmaker finished piecing a quilt top but didn't want to quilt it alone, she invited ladies in to help her. A group work session was called a bee, so a joint effort on a quilt was known as a quilting bee. Stories about quilting bees give us information about quilt pattern names and techniques, such as marking quilts. We also read of local customs. If a girl became engaged in the spring, she would probably marry in the fall. In the summer her pieced tops were quilted for her by neighbors. The ladies complained both about the oppressive heat and the number of quilt tops waiting to be quilted for the bride-to-be. The hostess couldn't slack off in the summer, and so it was difficult for her to prepare food in a hot kitchen.

In these stories the bees were held in homes, in a cabin, in a parlor, or in a bedroom with enough space to contain the large rectangular quilting frame. Chairs were placed around the frame for the quilters. As the quilters worked, side by side and across from each other, the conversation flowed. Sometimes the author had the characters gossiping about everybody in town. The minister was a frequent target, and if he had a wife, she was scandalized, too. A popular perception was that the minister was always poor, especially if he had a rural pastorate.

Refreshments invariably followed a quilting, and varied from a "light" summer tea with seven kinds of cakes and five different pies to a full course meal. Frequently bees were held in the fall or winter to insure a longer evening for merriment. Men and boys came to the dinner and they ate heartily. Afterwards the young people danced or played parlor games. The elders sat out and kept a watchful eye on the young ones. According to the authors, some young couples often courted on the way home.

Quilt Pattern Names

In recent years controversy has arisen among quilt history researchers as to the validity of names assigned to early American quilts. Some scholars deny the existence of names for early quilt patterns. Instead, they maintain the quilt naming process was essentially a twentieth century practice that commercial and print sources used to make their quilt patterns more attractive to the buying public by imbuing the patterns with contrived historical connotations and faux charm. A good place to gain insight as to whether American quilts did or did not have names in the early part of the nineteenth century is to consult quilt fiction of that era. As early quilt fiction authors were not usually quiltmakers, it is evident when quilt names appeared in their stories, those names were in common usage at the time. The non-quiltmaking authors did not invent names for the quilts. They utilized names familiar to themselves and to their readers.

Quilts were considered to be only practical household items. Even if a quilt were of rare beauty, it was not regarded as being commensurable with an art object such as a painting. A painting was given a title with capitalized proper nouns. Quilt names were often written in lowercase letters: "beggar's patchwork," instead of "Beggar's Patchwork," or "oak leaves," "star quilt," "nine-patch," "evening star," "log cabin," or "honeycomb." Written in lowercase letters, the words become simply descriptive terms, not proper names or titles. That quilts were largely women's work may have also contributed to the popular perception that the names given by women to their quilts were generic ones.

The practice of writing quilt names in lowercase letters in stories indicates the status of quilts in the minds of the nineteenth-century quilt fiction writers. The quilt naming process was so pervasive that authors were compelled to acknowledge the names; however, they seemingly believed these ordinary household objects were not worthy of having formal titles. It should be noted that there were exceptions; a few writers of early quilt fiction did use capitalized titles for quilts in their stories. "Irish Chain" and "Job's Troubles" are capitalized in the 1846 story "The Quilting Party," while "rising star" and "block work" are not. It must also be stated that early quilt fiction writers were not the sole practitioners of writing quilt titles so they looked like generic names. Quilt names written in lowercase letters, such as "link and chain" or "goose chase," also occurred in later non-fiction articles in magazines, farm journals, and newspapers. When we consider nineteenth-century females' subservient roles, it is not surprising that some women's letters, diaries, and wills reflected their acceptance of the common belief that the names they gave their quilts were not titles. Women wrote "tree of life" and "eagle quilt" in their various documents, accepting the popular perception that quilts were not important enough to merit titles.

Whether quilt fiction authors wrote "rising star" or "Rising Star," it is apparent that American quiltmakers, quite early on, did assign their quilts names that were widely known and used by both quilters and the general public.

Moralizing

Moralizing, a favorite ploy in quilt fiction, was usually directed at young girls who were in the care of elderly spinsters or grandmothers. The elders kept a tight rein on their young charges, making sure they completed their sewing stint for the day, and that it was well done. If not, the work must be redone until it passed inspection before the child could play. Sewing a certain number of pieces together was a discipline which helped build moral fiber in the young. Duty before pleasure was a very strong principle at that time. Independent, strong-willed children sometimes rebelled but in the stories they were always found out. Disclosure of the disobedience usually resulted in a softening of the adult's attitude. Did the child learn her lesson? More important, did the young reader grasp the object lesson the author tried to convey?

Presentations of African-Americans

In early quilt fiction, African-Americans were portrayed in the stereotypical manner common in the nineteenth century. Prior to the providing of any physical description, the reader was frequently signaled as to the black character's color by written speech patterns—invariably dialect. The phonetic spellings of the exaggerated dialect were often unreadable.

In quilt fiction that had black characters, a central figure was usually an obese black Mammy. In some stories the black Mammy was the quiltmaker or the quilt owner. In other stories the black woman was a servant assigned to work during the white women's quilting session, but not participate in the actual sewing. In "The Minister's Wooing," the black servant, Candice, delivered baskets of food as well as gossip to the gathering. In another story the black Mammy was commanded by her master to go to the home of what she considered "po white trash," where a quilting was being held. Mammy became agitated, and she was described as "arrogant, aggressive in her exclusiveness." The descriptions of the black female characters range from indulgently negative to pejorative, as in an 1846 story "Patch-Work," where the elderly quiltmaking servant, Lilly, who was devoted "to her white people," was termed " . . . the very incarnation of hilarity . . . and her morals are not of the sternest. . . ." Or the non-quiltmaking Mammy Hester, in a later story "The Quilting at Old Mrs. Robertson's," who was portrayed as " . . . old Hester, black and greasy as pots and skillets could make her. . . ." Although Lilly's devotion to her white folks seemed unquestioned, the Mammy in the story "Mammy Hester's Quilt," showed visible devotion only to the quilts she made, and is pictured as a mean-spirited, selfish old woman.

The presence of a beautiful all-silk pieced quilt in the home of a poor black family is a subject of wonder in the story "Viney's Conversion and Courtship." The quilt's owner, Ally, was a slave child who was piecing the quilt when Union soldiers came to her mistress's house. The child fled in terror, but not before snatching up the silk quilt top and patches. In the ten years since that incident, Ally had been collecting silk scraps to complete the beloved quilt. Two other stories give vivid and detailed descriptions of black-made Bible quilts made on Southern plantations. In one story in *Black April*, eight women came to quilt two tops, and the hostess brought out her awe-inspiring Bible quilt to explain the symbolism of each block. In "The Bible Quilt: Plantation Chronicles," the washerwoman quiltmaker comments, " . . . I got a log cabin quilt an' a sunrisin' quilt, but my Bible quilt tecks de shine off dem." About the quilting party she stated, "A quiltin' is mos' as good fun as a funeral or a stracted meetin' or a baptizin'. . . ."

None of the early quilt stories collected were written by black people. Thus these tales of the period reflect white Americans' negative perceptions of blacks as ignorant, servile, clownish people. As we moved beyond the racist caricatures and comic-derogatory images, searching for quilt information in these stories, we found that African-Americans held communal quilting parties, that some quiltmakers worked alone during the entire process, that pride was taken in exceptional quilts, and that quiltmaking generally flourished in Southern black communities.

Periodicals

Almost every type of literary journal or magazine published short stories about quilts. In the nineteenth century, the three eminent women's magazines—*Godey's Lady's Book*, *Peterson's Magazine*, and *Arthur's Home Magazine*—all published quilt fiction. Quilt fiction seemed to be an open field in the nineteenth and early twentieth centuries as famous, non-famous, and even unsigned anonymous writers produced quilt-themed stories in numerous periodicals. Quilt stories appeared in *Harper's Monthly*, *Harper's Weekly*, and *Harper's Bazar*. Stories on this topic were published in literary journals such as *Living Age*, *Atlantic Monthly*, *The Outlook*, *Granite Monthly*, and *Metropolitan Magazine*. Youths were not forgotten, either. *Aunt Jo's Scrapbag*, *The Youth's Companion*, *Harper's Young People*, and *St. Nicholas Magazine* featured quilt stories of interest to juveniles and young adults. Farm journals such as *The Country Gentleman* and *Ohio Farmer*, general interest magazines, and even the pulps have published quilt fiction. It does seem that quilt stories have appealed to a broad range of readers over many years.

The Patchwork Quilt

**Harriet Farley or Rebecca C. Thompson, *The Lowell
Offering: Writings by New England Mill Women* (1840–
1845)**

*An old maid tells of a patchwork quilt begun during her child-
hood, worked on during adolescence, and completed when
she became a young adult. As she views the various patches
in the quilt, she recalls memories of her family life, including
her chagrin when her younger sister married first, thus rel-
egating the narrator to the status of being an old maid.*

There it is! in the inner sanctum of my "old-maid's hall"—as cosy
a little room as any lady need wish to see attached to her boudoir,
and gloomy only from the name attached to it—for there is much
in a name; and the merriest peal of laughter, if echoed from an
"old-maid's hall," seems like the knell of girlhood's hopes.

Yes, there is the Patchwork Quilt! looking to the uninterested
observer like a miscellaneous collection of odd bits and ends of
calico, but to me it is a precious reliquary of past treasures; a
storehouse of valuables, almost destitute of intrinsic worth; a her-
barium of withered flowers; a bound volume of hieroglyphics,
each of which is a key to some painful or pleasant remembrance,
a symbol of—but, ah, I am poetizing and spiritualizing over my
"patchwork quilt." Gentle friends! it contains a piece of each of
my childhood's calico gowns, and of my mother's and sisters';
and that is not all. I must tell you, and then you will not wonder
that I have chosen for this entertainment my patchwork quilt.

It is one of my earliest recollections, and that of the memorable period when I emerged from babyhood to childhood—the
commencement of this patchwork quilt. I was learning to sew! O,
the exultations, the aspirations, the hopes, the fears, the mortifi-
cations, the perseverance—in short, all moral emotions and valu-

able qualities and powers, were brought out in this grand achievement—the union of some little shreds of calico. And can I ever
forget the long-suffering, patience and forbearance of my kind
mother?—her smiles and words of encouragement and sympathy; her generosity in the donation of calico bits; her marvellous
ingenuity in joining together pieces of all shapes, so that they
would result in a perfect square! Parents, never purchase for your
children mathematical puzzles—you can teach them and amuse
them by making patchwork.

Nor must I forget the beautiful brass thimble that my father
gave me, with the assurance that if I never would lose it he would
one day give me one of silver! Nor, the present of the kind old
lady who expressed her gratification over my small stitches by a
red broadcloth strawberry, which was introduced to me as an
emery-bag. An emery-bag! its office and functions were all to be
learned! How much there was that I did not know. But when I
had so far learned to sew that five minutes' interval of rest and
triumph did not occur between every two stitches, the strenuous
application, by which I drove the perspiration from every pore of
the hand, soon taught me the value of the emery-bag. O what a
heroine was I in driving the stitches! What a martyr under the
pricks and inflictions of the needle, which often sent the blood
from my fingers but could not force a tear from my eyes! These
were the first lessons in heroism and fortitude. How much, too, I
learned of the world's generosity in rewarding the efforts of the
industrious and enterprising. How many pieces in that quilt were
presented because I "could sew," and *did sew*, and was such an
adept in sewing. What predictions that I should be a noted
sempstress; that I should soon be able to make shirts for my father, sheets for my mother, and nobody knows what not for little
brothers and sisters. What legends were told me of little girls who
had learned patchwork at three years of age, and could put a shirt
together at six. What magical words were *gusset, felling, button-
hole-stitch*, and so forth, each a Sesame, opening into an arcana

of workmanship—through and beyond which I could see embroidery, hem-stitch, open-work, tambour, and a host of magical beauties. What predictions that I could some day earn my living by my needle-predictions, alas! that have most signally failed.

Here, also, are the remembrances of another memorable period—the days when the child emerged into girlhood!—when the mind expanded beyond the influence of calico patchwork, and it was laid aside for more important occupations. O what a change was there! Once there could have been nothing more important—now the patchwork was almost beneath my notice. But there was another change. Muslin and lace, with cloths of more common texture, had long occupied my attention when my thoughts and efforts were returned to my patchwork quilt. Well do I remember the boy who waited upon me home from singing-school "six times running." I do not mean that he *waited* "*running*," but that he escorted me home six times in succession. What girl would not under such circumstances have resumed her patchwork quilt? But how stealthily it was done. Hitherto the patchwork joys had been enhanced by the sympathy, praises and assistance of others; but now they were cherished "in secrecy and silence." But the patchwork quilt bears witness to one of the first lessons upon the vanity of youthful hopes—the mutability of earthly wishes; and—and—any body might accompany me home six hundred times now, and such attentions would never be succeeded by a renewal of those patchwork hopes. Well do I remember the blushes of painful consciousness with which I met my sister's eye, when she broke into my sanctuary, and discovered my employment. By these alone might my secret have been discovered.

But how many passages of life seem to be epitomized in this patchwork quilt. Here is the piece intended for the centre; *a star* as I called it; the rays of which are remnants of that bright copper-plate cushion which graced my mother's easy chair. And here is a piece of that radiant cotton gingham dress which was purchased to wear to the dancing school. I have not forgotten the almost supernatural exertions by which I attempted to finish it in due season for the first night; nor how my mantua-maker, with pious horror, endeavored as strenuously to disappoint me; but in spite of her it was finished, and she was guiltless—finished, all but the neck-binding, and I covered that with my little embroidered cape.

Here is a piece of the first dress I ever saw, cut with what were called "mutton-leg" sleeves. It was my sister's, and what a marvellous fine fashion we all thought that was. Here, too, is a remnant of the first "bishop sleeve" my mother wore; and here is a fragment of the first gown that was ever cut for me with a bodice waist. Was there ever so graceful beautiful pointed a fashion for ladies' waists before? Never, in my estimation. By this fragment I remember the gown with wings on the shoulders, in which I supposed myself to look truly angelic; and, oh, down in this corner a piece of that in which I first felt myself a woman—that is, when I first discarded pantalettes.

Here is a fragment of the beautiful gingham of which I had so scanty a pattern, and thus taxed my dress-maker's wits; and here a piece of that of which mother and all my sisters had one with me. Wonderful coincidence of taste, and opportunity to gratify it! Here is a piece of that mourning dress in which I thought my mother looked so graceful; and here one of that which should have been warranted "not to wash," or to wash all white. Here is a fragment of the pink apron which I ornamented so tastefully with "tape trimming;" and here a piece of that which was pointed all around. Here is a token of kindness in the shape of a square of the old brocade-looking calico, presented by a venerable friend; and here a piece given by the naughty little girl with whom I broke friendship, and then wished to take it out of its place, an act of vengeance opposed by my then forbearing mother—on this occasion I thought too forbearing. Here is a fragment of the first dress which baby brother wore when he left off long clothes; and here are relics of the long clothes themselves. Here a piece of that pink gingham frock, which for him was so splendidly decked with pearl buttons; and here a piece of that for which he was so unthankful, for he thought he was big enough to wear something more substantial than calico frocks. Here is a piece of that calico which so admirably imitated vesting, and my mother—economical from necessity—bought it to make "waistcoats" for the boys. Here are pieces of that I thought so bright and beautiful to set off my quilt with, and bought strips of it by the cent's worth—strips more in accordance with the good dealer's benevolence than her usual price for the calico. Here is a piece of the first dress which was ever earned by my own exertions! What a feeling of exultation, of self-dependence, of self-reliance, was created by this effort. What expansion of mind!—what awakening of dormant powers! Wellington was not prouder, when he gained the field of Waterloo, than I was with that gown. The belle, who purchases her dresses with the purse her father has always filled, knows not of the triumphant beatings of my heart upon this occasion. And I might now select the richest silk without that honest heart-felt joy. To do for myself—to earn my own living—to meet my daily expenses by my own daily toil, is now a task quite deprived of its novelty, and Time has robbed it of some of its pleasure. And here are patterns presented by kind friends, and illustrative of their tastes; but enough for you.

Then was another era in the history of my quilt. My sister— three years younger than myself—was in want of patchwork, while mine lay undisturbed, with no prospect of being ever called from its repository. Yes, she was to be married; and I not spoken for! She was to be taken, and I left. I gave her the patchwork. It seemed like a transference of girlish hopes and aspirations, or rather a finale to them all. Girlhood had gone, and I was a woman. I felt this more than I had ever felt it before, for my baby sister was to be a wife. We arranged it into a quilt. Those were pleasant hours in which I sympathized so strongly in all her hopes that I made them mine. Then came the quilting; a party not soon to be forgotten, with its jokes and merriment. Here is the memento of a mischievous brother, who was determined to assist, otherwise than by his legitimate occupation of rolling up the quilt as it was finished, snapping the chalk-line, passing thread, wax and scissors, and shaking hands across the quilt for all girls with short arms. He must take the thread and needle. Well, we gave him white thread, and appointed him to a very dark piece of calico, so that we might pick it out the easier; but there! to spite us, he did it so nicely that it still remains, a memento of his skill with the needle—there in that corner of the patchwork quilt.

And why did the young bride exchange her snowy counterpane for the patchwork quilt? These dark stains at the top of it will tell—stains left by the night medicines, taken in silence and darkness, as though to let another know of her pains and remedies would make her sickness more real. As though Disease would stay his hand if met so quietly, and repulsed so gently. The patchwork quilt rose and fell with the heaving of her breast as she sighed in the still night over the departing joys of youth, of health, of newly wedded life. Through the bridal chamber rang the knell-like cough, which told us all that we must prepare for her an early grave. The patchwork quilt shrouded her wasted form as she sweetly resigned herself to the arms of Death, and fell with the last low sigh which breathed forth her gentle spirit. Then settled upon the lovely form, now stiffening, cold and lifeless.

And back to me, with all its memories of childhood, youth, and maturer years; its associations of joy, and sorrow; of smiles and tears; of life and death, has returned to me THE PATCHWORK QUILT.

—Annette

THE PATCH-WORK QUILT

Miss C. M. Sedgwick, *The Columbian Lady's and Gentleman's Magazine*, March 1846

A wealthy white woman visits Lilly, a black former servant of her family who is now taking care of Hector the fiddler, a dying black man. Lilly shows the visitor a "beggar's Patchwork" quilt, one that contains numerous memories of the white woman's family. Interwoven in the story are many of the stereotypical portrayals of black people which were common in nineteenth-century American literature.

The Germans are the best economists in all the small details of life. They have the true husbandry of social means. Their faculties as well as their outer world are under the dominion of a wise economy. They carry it into the work of their imaginations. An every-day household circumstance, a piece of rustic furniture or a common domestic event will supply them warp and woof for a complicated fabric, which they adorn with quaint or, it may be, brilliant fancies. In their illustrations of homely domestic life, they have the great advantage of awakening general sympathy and appealing to universal experience. Rare events and great deeds are for the few, while all share in the family history—the daily bread of life. The furniture and utensils of our childhood's home are idealized by affection and consecrated in after life. Poetry may chance or be written about them, but if it be not, they are poetry to us. They have life and a living agency. In the German fable "needles and pins come out of the tailor's shed and lose themselves in the dark, and the shovel and the broom stand upon the step and quarrel and fight." Our fancies are more subdued, but still old household things are instinct with our early lives. They embody hopes and memories long ago faded; laughs that rang out in merrier days, forgotten like the thrush's song, or the summer's rose. What woman but can recall some bundle-drawer, or piece-bag, into which, as a girl, she was permitted to dive when a new doll was to be dressed, to explore its rolls of chintz and silk, and to gather up bits of fringe and fragments of lace, muslin and embroidery: and in long after years when the chapter of life is nearly read out, when the eye is dim and the hand tremulous, a fragment of these stuffs, made to perish in the using, which, nevertheless, have survived the frames fearfully and wonderfully made, meets the eye and unseals the fountains of emotion. A piece of puttied china will recall the family gathering and the festive dinner, and the whole array of the pantry to which the hungry school-child was admitted for the bit of pudding that thoughtful kindness had set aside.

I went, a few mornings since, to see an old family servant who had passed her childhood and youth in the service of my parents. M__, 'Little Lil' as she was called, and is even now, though a bulky old woman, was not born to serve, but to enjoy. She is the very incarnation of hilarity. She has floated down the current of life without dread, anxiety, or regret. Not *sans reproche,*' for Lilly lives in a strict community, and her morals are not of the sternest, but feeling no responsibility (that she evidently looks upon as the exclusive privilege of "white folks") she has escaped anxiety and remorse. She is the most vivacious of that race whom God seems to have endowed with cheerfulness, as a divine armor against the evils of man's infliction. Lil, at three score and ten, has a face as smiling as a child's—not a mark of time or sorrow upon it. One of the boasted Saxon race, one of our New England matrons, who had met with a tithe of the dark events of Lilly's life would never smile again. She lives in a wretched hut where food and clothing seem to come to her by happy chances. She is the survivor of nearly all her contemporaries; she has buried parents, children, grandchildren, and great-grandchildren, and has lost some half dozen husbands, by death or desertion, yet, I doubt not, she would dance like a girl of eighteen to a merry measure. She is as earnest and indefatigable as she ever was in all good natured gossiping, and if, by any chance, she sheds a tear, it is like the rain when the sun shines—a smile chases it. She loves her old friends, but when they drop off she turns to new ones. Like most of the colored people she is fond of merry-making and all social cheerfulness— all gatherings of human beings together, except in churches or at funerals. Solemnity is night and darkness to Lilly. She likes the excitement of a camp-meeting, but she likes it not for its religious purposes, but for any little chance crumb of folly or absurdity that may be dropped there. She can even tolerate a funeral if there is a gleam of fun upon it. I once saw her at one where her side glances and stolen gesticulations were subjects of Wilkie, or Mount, the true painter of our home humorous scenes. The chief mourner, being of our Saxon race, Lilly pointed out to me as the white widow. The ceremony was marshaled by a servant of a militia colonel, and the procession of wretched one-horse-vehicles, equestrians mounted on broken-down hacks, and pedestrians scrambling after, was arranged with as much show of ceremony as a Roman ovation. Our master of ceremonies—being mounted on a black steed of "the colonel's"—calling out, as if he were commanding forces at a battle of Waterloo, now "to the right!" and now "to the left!" and now "close your ranks, gentlemen and ladies!"—himself, sometimes a hundred yards in advance of the procession, and then curveting and galloping among the old women and children to their infinite dismay. "It is as good as 'lection-day," said Lilly, aside, to me.

Though Lilly is a precious element in our country contentments, I rarely visit her. She saves her friends the trouble of looking after her, by dropping in once or twice a week, with an ample basket on her arm, which goes much heavier than it comes, for Lilly is in good fellowship with the servants, and she pays the heads of the house in sunshine (the best of coins) for all she gets. She is to the kitchen what the newspaper is to the parlor, and better, inasmuch as the spoken is better than the written word.

I met Lilly outside her door, and without her wonted smile, and on my asking her why she had been absent for a week, she answered:

"Why Miss__, don't you know Hector is dying!" Hector was a fiddler by profession, and was dying, as most of our colored people do, of a galloping consumption. After adding a few particulars of his illness, Lilly led the way in and I followed. Her little room, its rafters blackened with smoke, was darker than usual, being filled with men, women and little children of her own color. Any occasion, it matters not much what, calls these social people together. A mess was boiling over the fire for their future cheer, the only future they look to, and the dying man was very gently sinking away. He was bolstered with pillows on a chair, and he kindly nodded to me as his friends, with their customary civility, fell back to give me a view of him. He beckoned to Lilly and said something to her, but so faintly that I did not hear him. She gave me a significant glance, and going to the other side of the room took Hector's fiddle from the case in which it was hanging and brought it to him. He dimly smiled and took the bow—he could not hold the fiddle—Lilly held it for him. He essayed a last tune, and, the ruling passion strong in death, attempted a lively one, but he was too far gone: the notes were few and solemn—the bow fell from his hand and he breathed his last. There was one moment of death-stillness, then Lilly taking up the instrument as reverently as if it contained a living spirit, replaced it in its case and, brushing away a tear, said:

"I wish you all to take notice that Hector said to me last night, 'Lilly,' says he, 'do you keep my violin as long as you live'—and I will, and let the select men and Deacon Bates talk!"

She then went into her bed-room, beckoning to me to follow her. She selected in a hurried and troubled manner the articles necessary to the last offices for Hector, and having given them to his friends in the next room, she said to me:

"This is the worst of taking boarders, having them die, and

seeing to things. It's a chore I don't like, but then I ought not to complain, for Hector was lively as long as he lived. Its only a week ago he played for our folks to dance, and come what would, there was always a pleasant tune in Hector's fiddle! We shall be lonesome now. He's gone—he drew company as the sun draws water, and shone on them when they came. It was always bright where Hector was!"

"Has he saved anything," I asked her, "to pay the expenses of his sickness?:

"Saved, Miss__! Fiddlers never save—they enjoy themselves—and what's the use of saving? What would he be the better for it now if he had gold in his trunk and two full suits? He was welcome every where, and the best was set before him. Nobody grudged Hector, and why should they? He paid in fiddling; he was the best fiddler that ever walked the country, and if he had laid up clothes, as some foolish folks do, what good would they do him now? A very little serves now, you see, and while he wanted it he had enough. Major Smith gave him that military coat he died in. The collar was silk velvet and the old epaulette kept bright to the last. That red and yellow plaid handkerchief round his neck was given to him by a New York lady at the Pittsfield Hotel. Old Aunt Esther wanted me to take them off from him this morning. She said they did not seem suitable for a dying man to die in. 'Pooh!' says I, 'what's that to Hector? He likes to look lively as long as he lives.' 'Lilly,' she whined out, 'it will be a solemn change to his winding-sheet!' 'Never mind, Aunt Esther,' says I, 'he won't see that, and you can enjoy it as much as you please.' You are thinking I am wicked, Miss__, but white folks does enjoy such things! I heard old Aunt Esther say to Miss Babcock the other day:—'Sally,' says she, 'you and I have enjoyed a great many sicknesses and a great many deaths together,' says she."

The difference in the spirit of the two races as elucidated by Lilly is certainly striking. Those who look farthest back and forward may be most exalted in the intellectual scale, but there is a blessed compensation for a lower graduation, in the buoyant, cheerful, enjoying spirit, that gilds the dark cloud, makes pleasant waters to spring from rocks, and plucks away flowers from thorns.

It was evident that Lilly was ingeniously prolonging our conversation to escape from the solemnities of death in the next room, and I smiled at the eagerness she betrayed when having, as I fancied, listened, to the last thing she could have to say, she cut short my leave—taking by "Oh! Miss__, don't you want to see that quilt I told you about, that's made of pieces of all our folks gowns?" "Our folks" is, you know, Lilly's designation for my own family, of which she was a member for the first thirty years of her life. I did wish to see the quilt. It was one of those memorials that in a German household would have been held a sacred history. Lilly produced it from among a store of quilts which she has been her whole life amassing, not as property—no saint or hermit was ever freer from the desire of accumulation than Lilly. Diogenes himself had not a truer contempt for it. Her instincts are limited to the present. She has not the power of forecast. She is grateful to any one who will give her a present pleasurable sensation, but she would not thank her best friend for an ample annuity to become due a year hence. The quilts are not in her eye property. They are not the means of warmth and comfort—they are never used as such—they are story-books—family legends—illustrated traditions. Lilly reverses the French maxim, *"I'l n'ya a rien de beau que l' 'utile;"* with her there is nothing useful but the beauty that touches the spring of her imagination. The Italians have a saying that a transplanted tree will not take root till it has been danced around. The merry gathering that forms the quilt perpetuates its pleasant associations to Lilly.

The quilt in question is what is called a beggar's-patch-work, formed of hexagonal bits of calico and silk. Being originally made of unwashed materials and wisely kept for show, it has preserved its original gloss. Yes, these base, perishable materials have remained unchanged, when those of whose garments they were the fragments, have long ago, played out their parts in life, and are now clothed in the white robes of the saints. In these little bits of silk and cotton is stored the memory of many a tear or smile.

"There, Miss___," said Lilly, "there is a bit of your mother's wedding-gown, worn long before you were born, of course, or I either, as to that matter; but I have heard my mother say there was not such another this side of Boston.

"Woman, or gown, Lilly?"

"Either, Miss___, either, but I mean gown. Gowns was gowns then, that could stand alone. It was a merry time they had, ma'am." Thus, Lilly, always calls her beloved mistress. "Ma'am's grandmother, old as the hills, she came over from Hampshire, came to the wedding—riding all the way on a pillion behind her grandson—a deal pleasanter that, than railway-ing. That is a bit of the old lady's chintz. Mother has told me how straight she stood in it, and how she curtsied to show your mother and Miss Susan—Kin-Ken-Kemp—Oh, I forget her name. The young folks learned manners in her day. The old lady did not live to mount her pillion again. She died soon after the wedding and was buried here, and her tombstone is one of the oldest in the burying-ground. It does not stand as straight as the old lady did. Is not that square pretty? pink shot on white. That was a bit of Miss Susan's dress. She came all the way from New York to be your mother's bride's-maid. She was the beauty of the city, and gay as a bird, or butter-fly. She sang, and danced and frolicked, but for all that, she gained the old lady's heart and her son's too. Your uncle, he was a young minister then—a missionary to the Stockbridge Indians. They were here yet, and he had them all dressed up in the fine scarlet and purple broadcloths Queen Anne sent them, to show off to Miss Susan. But the old lady was the master hand, she did the court-ing, and one bright day she had two horses brought for them to ride together. She had given him a hint to tell his love-tale, as they rode up the hill and through the woods by the green pond.

But when the horses came, the one for the minister was prancing and gay, and when he would have mounted he could not or dared not. So Miss Susan, a little fear-nought she was, ordered the saddles changed, and rode away laughing and cheering, and he, poor creature, after her. But they were not to hitch their horses together, for as often as he began to hem and ha, and stammer and so on, Miss Susan's horse would get the deuce into him and off he would go, and at last it got through poor Mr. John's hair, that for love of his kin, she did not want to say him no and she could not say yes. Now, Miss__, can't you see her in that silk square? so rosy and so lively!"

I wiped away a tear that Lilly's bright vision had called forth. I saw this "Miss Susan" a few weeks since, now, herself, a granddame past ninety and blind! But that precious oil of a glad disposition that burned so brightly in her youth still burns cheerily on; and though the fire of her earlier days be somewhat diminished, she is till the central light of her home circle.

"That's a piece of ma'am's dressing-gown," resumed Lilly, "that your father brought her from Philadelphia. It was handsome enough to wear to meeting, but m'am always took most pains to look well at home. Your father's eyes was her looking-glass. She had it on when the little girl you were named for died. I can see her now as she bent down over the dead child, and I heard her soft voice saying 'The Lord gave and the Lord hath taken away, blessed be his name.' I had heard the minister preach from that text a thousand times, but it seemed to me then that I heard those words for the first time, as they rose out of her heart. She was bending over—that was the way she always took trouble—rising up against it only makes the blow the harder you know. They named you after her, but I minded it was long and long before ma'am called your name. It was Russy, or Rosy, or any thing but that name. All the children had frocks like that," she continued, pointing to a pink and green plaid; "I can see them all now. One running out to feed the chickens, another bringing in eggs, one dressing dolls, and little Harley telling how many lions and tigers he had killed. Oh, dear, dear! Miss____, can it be they have all grown up, men and women, and are dead, gone forever? but that," she added, turning instinctively from these sad thoughts, "that is a bit of the gown your cousin Olive wore when the French Doctor came to court her, and slipped into the saddle-room to put on his nankins. Ben, unknowingly locked the door, and when the poor little fellow was let out he was as blue as indigo, and his teeth chattered so that Miss Olive could not tell whether he talked French or English."

"He got his answer in the shortest of all English words, did he not, Lilly?"

"Why, yes, he was French," reason enough, Lilly would have thought, had he issued from a Parisian dressing-room instead of a country saddle-house. "Miss Olive was odd," continued Lilly. "she kept on saying, no, no, to every one that came. I used to say, its just like winding a tangled skein, Miss Olive: if you begin with putting through your thread, so you will do to the end. But that Miss Olive did not mean, for she vowed if she lived to turn the old maid's corner she would kill herself. She did for all go fairly round it, and married a widower at last, who was looking out, as he said, for a permanent housekeeper. Even ma'am could not help smiling when she heard that. There's a season for all things," wisely added Lilly, though she had herself, tried the conjugal experiment at all seasons. Lilly now came down to the epoch of my own memories, and visions of the past crowded upon me. My school-days, our breakfasts and dinners, our meetings and partings at the old home, our merry-makings and our tragedies, my school-mates, the partners of my life, the partners of my hoped-for immortality, all were brought forth into actual presence and glowing life by these little talismans! My blinding tears fell thick and heavy over them. Lilly dashed off the great drops that came in spite of her, and rolling up the quilt thrust it back into the old cupboard, muttering something about there being no use in crying. We parted without exchanging another word.

As I retraced my way to the village I marked the changes since this patchwork history was constructed. The Indians that figured in Queen Anne's broadcloths have been driven from their loved homes here farther and farther into the shadowy West and are melted away. The wooded sides of our mountains have been cleared to feed yonder smoking furnace. Those huge fabrics for our friend H.'s chemical experiments indicate discoveries in science that have changed the aspect of the world. The whistle reached my ear from the engine plying over the very track where our good old granddame found but a bridle-path. The meadows enriched by the overflowings of the river, and ploughed by the sun-beams remain, much as they were, when the Indians planted their corn here; but the white man has let the sun in upon the hill-side, has made his plantations and his drainings. Churches have been built and decayed and built again. The Bishop visits his Diocesan where 'Miss Susan's' missionary lover preached in an Indian dialect, and Puritanism holds kindly fellowship with the church. Houses have decayed and new ones have been built over the old hearthstone. New friends almost as good as the old have come among us. Families have multiplied, and sent forth members to join the grand procession towards the Oregon, and at this very moment the bell is ringing for a meeting of the town to extend the limits of our burying-ground, it being full!

All these changes, and the patch-work-quilt remains in its first gloss!

THE QUILTING PARTY

T. S. Arthur, *Godey's Lady's Book and Magazine*, September 1849

A man recalls a quilting party held twenty years earlier for the local beauty, Amy Willing. He laments that his contemporaries are no longer familiar with the "Irish Chain," "Rising Sun," "Brick Work" and "Job's Troubles" quilts of yesteryear. This story of unrequited love, set against the dynamics of the quilting party, was written by T. S. Arthur for Godey's Lady's Book and Magazine. It is somewhat ironic that this story was written by T. S. Arthur, the man who later published Peterson's Magazine, a women's magazine which was quite similar to Godey's and became its chief rival in the women's magazine field.

Our young ladies of the present generation know little of the mysteries of "Irish chain," "rising star," "block work," or "Job's trouble," and would be as likely to mistake a set of quilting frames for clothes poles as for anything else. It was different in our younger days. Half a dozen handsome patchwork quilts were as indispensable then as a marriage portion; quite as much so as a piano or guitar is at present. And the quilting party was equally indicative of the coming-out and being "in the market," as the fashionable gatherings together of the times that be.

As for the difference in the custom, we are not disposed to sigh over it as indicative of social deterioration. We do not belong to the class who believe that society is retrograding, because everything is not as it was in the earlier days of our life history. And yet—it may be a weakness; for early associations exercise a powerful influence over us. We have never enjoyed ourselves with the keen zest and heartiness, in any company, that we have experienced in the old-fashioned quilting party. But we were young then, and every sense perfect in its power to receive enjoyment. No care weighed down the spirit; no grief was in the heart; no mistakes had occurred to sober the feelings with unavailing regrets. Life was in the beauty and freshness of its spring time; in the odor of its lovely blossoms. We had but to open our eyes—to touch, to taste—to find an exquisite delight. Of the world we knew nothing beyond the quiet village; and there we found enough to fill the measure of our capacity. In a wider sphere we have not found greater social pleasures; though in a more extended usefulness there has come a different source of enjoyment—purer, and more elevating to the heart.

But this is all too grave for our subject. It is not the frame of mind in which to enjoy a quilting party. And yet, who can look back upon the early times without a browner hue upon his feelings?

There was one quilting party—can we ever forget it? Twenty years have passed since the time. We were young then, and had not tarried long at Jericho! Twenty years! It seems but yesterday. With the freshness of the present it is all before us now.

In our village there dwelt a sweet young girl, who was the favorite of all. When invitations to a quilting party at Mrs. Willing's came, you may be sure there was a flutter of delight all around. The quilting was Amy's, of course, and Amy Willing was to be the bright, particular star in the social firmament. It was to be Amy's first quilting, moreover; and the sign that she was looking forward to the matrimonial goal, was hailed with a peculiar pleasure by more than one of the village swains, who had worshiped the dawning beauty at a respectful distance.

We had been to many quilting parties up to this time; but more as a boy than as a man. Our enjoyment had always been unembarrassed by any peculiar feelings. We could play at blind man's buff, hunt the slipper, and pawns, and not only clasp the little hands of our fair playfellows, but even touch their warm lips with our own, and not experience a heart-emotion deeper than the ripple made on the smooth water by a playful breeze. But there had come a change. There was something in the eyes of our young companions, as we looked into them, that had a different meaning from the old expression, and particularly was this true with Amy. Into her eyes we could no longer gaze steadily. As to the reason we were ignorant; yet so it was.

The invitation to attend her quilting was an era; for it produced emotions of so marked a character, that they were never forgotten. There was an uneasy fluttering of the heart as the time drew near, and a pressure upon the feelings that a deep, sighing breath failed to remove. The more we thought about the quilting, the more restless did we grow, and the more conscious that the part we were about to play would be one of peculiar embarrassment.

At last the evening came. We had never shrunk from going alone into any company before. But now we felt that it was necessary to be sustained from without; and such sustentation we sought in the company of the good-natured, self composed bachelor of the village, who went anywhere and everywhere freely, and without apparent emotion.

"You're going to Amy Willing's quilting?" said we to L__, on the day before the party.

"Certainly," was his reply.

"Will you wait until we call for you?"

"Oh yes," was as good-naturedly answered.

"So much gained," thought we, when alone.

In the shadow of his presence we would be able to make our debut with little embarrassment. What would we not have then give for L__'s self-possession and easy confidence!

When the time came we called, as had been arranged, upon L__. To our surprise, we found no less than four others, as bashful as we, waiting his convoy. L__very good-humoredly—he never did an ill-natured thing in his life—assumed the escort, and we all set off for the cottage of Mrs. Willing. How the rest felt, we know not, but as for our own heart, it throbbed slower and heavier at each step, until, by the time the cottage was reached, the pulses in our ears were beating audibly. We could not understand this. It had never been so before.

The sun still lingered about the horizon when we came in sight of the cottage—fashionable hours were earlier then than now. On arriving at the door, L__ entered first, as a matter of course, and we all followed close in his rear, in order to secure the benefit of his countenance. The room was full of girls, who were busy in binding Amy's quilt, which was already out of the frame, and getting all ready for the evening's sport. There was no one equal to L__ for taking the wire edge from off the feelings of a promiscuous company, and giving a free and easy tone to the social intercourse, that would otherwise have been constrained and awkward. In a little while the different parties who had entered under his protection, began to feel at home among the merry girls. It was not long before another and another came in, until the old-fashioned parlor, with its old-fashioned furniture, was filled, and the but half-bound quilt was forcibly taken from the hands of the laughing seamstresses, and put "out of sight and out of mind."

The bright, particular star of that evening was Amy Willing—the gentle, quiet, loving Amy Willing. There was a warmer glow upon her cheeks, and a deeper tenderness in her beautiful eyes, than they had ever worn before. In gazing upon her, how the heart moved from its very depths! No long time passed before we were by the side of Amy, and our eyes resting in hers with an earnestness of expression that caused them to droop to the floor. When the time for redeeming pawns came, and it was our turn to call out from the circle of beauty a fair partner, the name of Amy fell from our lips, which were soon pressed, glowing, upon those of the blushing maiden. It was the first warm kiss of love. How it thrilled, exquisitely, to the very heart! Our lips had often met before—kissing was then a fashionable amusement—but never as at this time. Soon it became Amy's place to take the floor. She must "kiss the one she loved best." What a moment of suspense! Stealthily her eyes wandered around the room; and then her long, dark lashes lay quivering on her beautiful cheeks.

"Kiss the one you love best," was repeated by the holder of the pawns.

The fringed lids were again raised, and again her eyes went searching around the room. We could see that her bosom was rising and falling more rapidly than before. Our name at length came, in an undertone, from her smiling lips. What a happy moment! The envied kiss was ours, and we led the maiden in triumph from the floor.

And, to us, the whole evening was a series of triumphs. Somehow or other, Amy was by our side, and Amy's hand in ours oftenest of any. We did not talk much—delicious feeling sealed our lips. It was our first, sweet dream of love. But we knew little then of human nature, and less of woman's human nature. And as little of all this knew a certain young man, who was present, and who, more sober and silent than any, joined in the sports of the evening, but with no apparent zest. Amy never called him out when she was on the floor; nor did he mention her name when the privilege of touching some maiden's lips with his own was assigned him.

He was first to retire; and then we noticed a change in Amy. Her voice was lower, her manner more subdued, and there was a thoughtful, absent expression in her face.

A few weeks later, and this was all explained. Edward Martin was announced in the village as Amy's accepted lover. We did not, we could not, we would not, accredit the fact. It was impossible! Had she not called us out at the quilting party, as the one she "loved best?" Had not her hand been oftenest in ours, and our lips oftenest upon hers? It could not be! Yet time proved the truth of the rumor—ere another twelvemonth went by, Amy Willing was a bride. We were at the wedding; but as silent and sober as was Edward Martin at the quilting. The tables were turned against us, and hopelessly turned.

Ah, well! More than twenty years have passed since then. The quiltings, the corn huskings, the merry-makings in the village of M__ are not forgotten. Nor is Amy Willing and the party forgotten, as this brief sketch assuredly testifies. Twenty years. How many changes have come in that period! And Amy, where is she? When last at M__ we saw a sweet young maiden, just in the dawn of womanhood, and, for the moment, it seemed as if we were back again in the old time—the intervening space but a dream. Her name was Amy. It was not our Amy. She had passed away, leaving a bud of beauty to bloom in her place.

Our sketch of a merry-making has turned out graver than was intended. But it is difficult for the mind to go back in reminiscence, and not take a sober hue. We will not attempt to write it over again, for, in that case, it might be graver still.

THE QUILTING AT MISS JONES'S
Josiah Allen's Wife, *Godey's Lady's Book*, July 1868

Josiah Allen's Wife (a pseudonym for Marietta Holley) became a popular author of fiction in the nineteenth century. This story recounts the overwhelming amount of gossip that occurred at a village quilting party held to complete the minister's bed quilt. Each woman had pieced a calico quilt block; the group had jointly purchased the batting and the lining, set the quilt with turkey red strips, and decided to quilt it in the herringbone pattern. At the quilting frames, the quilters in turn scandalized the "path-master," the school mistress, the Ripley's party, Mrs. Brown's "idiot" baby and all neighbors who were absent from the quilting party. Finally the minister's young wife became the target of their gossip. The story's surprise ending points up the serious misinterpretations gossip can generate.

Our minister was married a year ago, and we hev been piecing him a bed-quilt; and last week we quilted it. I always make a pint of going to quiltings, for you can't be backbited to your face, that's a moral sertenty. I know wimmen jest like a book, for I hev been one a good while. I always stand up for my own sect, still I know sertin effects follow sertin causes, to wit, and namely, if two bricks are sot up side by side, if one tumbles over on to the other one, the other one can't stand, it ain't natur'. If a toper holds a glass of liker to his mouth, he can't help swallerin', it ain't natur'. If a young man goes a slay-riding with a pretty girl, and the buffelo robe slips off, he can't help holdin' it round her, it ain't natur'. I might go on illustratin', but enuff; quiltin' jest sets wimmen to slanderin' as easy and beautiful as enything you ever see'. So I went. There wasn't anybody there when I got there. For reason, I always go early.

I hadn't been there long before Miss Deacon Graves came, and then the Widder Tubbs, and then Squire Edwardses wife, and Maggie Snow, and then the Dobbs girls (we call 'em *girls*, though it would be jest as proper to call mutton lamb, for forty summers hev gilded their heads if one has gilt 'em). They was the last that come, for Miss Brown's baby had the mumps, and otherwise couldn't leave; and the Ripleys had unexpected company. But with Miss Jones, where the quiltin' was held, and her girls, Mary Ann and Alzina, we made as many as could set round the quilt comfortable.

The quilt was made of different kinds of calico; all the wimmen round had pieced a block or two, and we took up a collection to get the batten and linin', and the cloth to set it together with, which was turkey red, and come to quilt it it looked well; we quilted it herrin'-bone, and a runnin' vine round the border. After the path-master was demorelized, the school-mistress tore to pieces, the party to Ripleys scandelized, Miss Brown's baby voted a unquestionable idiot, and the rest of the unrepresented neighborhood dealt with, Lucinder Dobbs spoke up, and sez she:—

"I hope the minister will like the bed-quilt" (Lucinder is the one that studies mathematics to disipline her mind, and has the Romen nose).

"It ain't noways likely he will," sez her sister Ophelia (she is the one that has her hair frizzled on top, and wears spectacles). "It ain't noways likely he will—he is a cold man, a stone statute."

Now, you see, I set my eyes by the minister, he is always doin' good to somebody, besides preachin' more like a angel than a human bein'. I can't never forget—nor I don't want to—how he took hold of my hand, and how his voice trembled and the tears stood in his eyes, when my little Joe died; pretty little lamb, he was in his infant class, and he loved him; you see such things cut deep, and there is some lines you can't rub out, if you try ever so hard. And I wasn't goin' to set still and hear him run down; you see it riled up the old Smith blood, and when that is riled, Josiah says he always takes his hat and leaves till it settles. And I spoke up, and sez I:—

"Lucky for him he was made of stone before he was merried, for common flesh and blood, sez I, would have gin out a hundred times, chaste round by the girls as he was" (you see it was the town's talk how Ophelia Dobbs acted before he was married, and she almost went into a decline, and took heaps of mother wort and fetty).

"I don't know what you mean, Miss Allen," sez she, turning red as a brick. "I never heard of his bein' chaste; I know I never could bear the sight of him."

"The distant sight," sez Mary Ann Jones.

Ophelia looked so mad at that, that I don't know but she would have pricked her with her quiltin' needle, if old Miss Graves hadn't spoke up. She is a fat old lady with a double chin, "mild and lovely" as Mount Vernen's sister. She always agrees with every-body; Thomas Jefferson, Josiah's boy by his first wife, calls her "Woollen Aprons," for one day he sez he heard her say to a neigh-bor, "I don't like woollen aprons, do you?" "Why, yes, Miss Graves, I do." "Wall, so do I." But good old soul, if we was all such peace-makers as she is, we should be pretty sure of Heaven, though Thomas J. said that if Saten should ask her to go the other way, she would go rather than hurt his feelings; I jest told him to shet up his weekedness, and he shet up.

As I said, she looked mildly up over her spectacles and nod-ded her purple cap ribbons two or three times, and said, "Yes," "Jest so," to both of us; and then she was so afraid that we wouldn't think she was jinein' with both of us, sez she, "Yes, Miss Allen," "Jest so, Ophelia." And then to change the subject, sez she, "Has the minister's wife got home yet?"

"I think not," said Maggie Snow, "I was to the village day before yesterday, and she had not come then."

"I suppose her mother is well off," sez the Widder Tubbs, "and as long as she stays there she saves the minister five dollars a week. I should think she would stay all summer."

The widder is about as savin' a woman as belongs to the meetin'-house.

"It don't look well for her to be gone so long," sez Lucinder Dobbs, "I am very much afraid it will make talk."

"Mebby it will save the minister five dollars a week," sez

Ophelia, "as extravagant as she is in dress—as many as four silk dresses she has got, and folks as good as she is in the congregation hain't got but one, and a certain person *full* as good as she is, that hain't got any" (Ophelia's best dress is poplin), "it won't take her long to run out the minister's salery."

"She had her silk dresses before she was married, and her folks was wealthy," said Miss Squire Edwards.

"As much as we have done and are still doing for them, it seems ungrateful in her," sez Lucinder, "to wear such a bonnet as she wore all last summer—a plain white straw with a little bit of white ribbon on it; it looked so scrimped and stingy. I have thought she wore it on purpose to mortify us before the Baptists, jest as if we couldn't afford to dress our minister's wife as good as they did theirs."

Maggie Snow's cheeks was gettin' red as fire and her eyes begun to shine jest as they did that day we found some boys stonin' her cat. You see she and the minister's wife are the greatest friends that ever was. And I see she couldn't hold in much longer; she was just openin' her mouth to speak, when the door opened, and in walked Betsy Babbet.

"Why, it seems to me you are late, Betsy," said Miss Jones, "but walk rite into the spare bed-room and take off your things."

"Things!" said Betsy, "who cares for things?" And she dropped into the nearest rockin'-chair and commenced rockin' violently.

Betsy Babbet was a humbly critter. But we hadn't no time to meditate on her, for as Miss Jones asked her agin to take off her things, she broke out:—

"Would that I had died when I was an infant babe!"

"Amen!" whispered Mary Ann Jones and Maggie Snow.

"Do tell us what is the matter, Betsy," said Miss Jones.

"Yes, do," said Miss Deacon Graves.

"Matter enuff!" sez she; "no wonder there is earthquakes and jars! I heard the news jest before I started, and it made me weak as a cat; I had to stop to every house on the way down to rest, and not a soul had heard of it till I told 'em. Such a turn as it give me,

I sha'n't get over it for a week; but it is jest as I always told you; I always said the minister's wife wasn't any *too good*. It didn't surprise me—not a bit."

"You can't tell me one word against Mary Linden that I will believe," said Maggie Snow.

"You will admit that the minister went North last Tuesday, won't you?"

Seven wimmen spoke up to once, and said, "Yes, his mother was took sick, and they telegraphted for him."

"So he said," sneered Betsy Babbet, "so he said; I believe it's for good."

"Oh, dear!" shrieked Ophelia Dobbs, "I shall faint away; ketch hold of me, somebody."

"Ketch hold of yourself," said I, severely, and then sez I to Betsy, "I don't believe he's run away any more than I believe I am the next President of the United States."

"Well, if he hain't, he'll wish he had," sez she. "His wife came night before last on the cars."

Four wimmen said "Did she?" two said, "Do tell?" and three opened their mouths and looked at her speechless; amongst the last was Miss Deacon Graves. I spoke in a kolected manner, and sez I, "What of it?"

"Yes, what of it?" said she. "I believe the poor man mistrusted it all out, and run away from trouble and disgrace."

"How dare you!" sez Maggie Snow, "speak the word disgrace in connection with Mary Linden?"

"How dare I?" sez Betsy Babbet. "Ask Jake Coleman, as it happened I got it from his own mouth, it didn't come through two or three."

"Get what?" sez I; "if you can speak the English language, Betsy Babbet, and have got sense enuff to tell a straight story, tell it and be done with it," sez I.

"Well, jest as I come out the gate to our house," sez she, "Jake Coleman came along, and sez he, 'Betsy, I have got something to tell you,' sez he; 'I want to tell somebody that can keep it; it ought to be kept,' sez he, and then he went on and told; sez he, 'Miss

Linden has got home, and she didn't come alone, neither.' Sez I, 'What do you mean?' He looked as mysterious as a ghost, and sez he, 'I mean what I say,' sez he, 'I drove the carriage home from the depot,' and sez he 'as sure as my name is Jake Coleman, I heard her talking to somebody she called Hugh (you know her husband's name is Charles); I heard her tell this Hugh that she loved him, loved him better than the whole world.' And then he made me promise not to tell; but he said he heard not only one kiss, but fourteen or fifteen. Now," sez Betsy, "what do you think of the minister's wife?"

"Good heavens!" cried Ophelia Dobbs, "am I deceived? is this a phantagory of the brain, or have I got ears? Have I got ears?" she kontinude, wildly glaring at me.

"You can feel and see," said I, shortly.

"Will he live with the wretched creature?" kontinude Ophelia. "No, he will get a divorcement from her; such a tender-hearted man as he is too. If ever a man wanted a comforter in a tryin' time he is the man, and tomorrow I will go and comfort him."

"I guess you will find him, first," said Betsy Babbet. "And I guess if he was found, there is a certain person he would be as glad to see as he would another certain person."

"There is some mistake," said Maggie Snow. "Jake Coleman is always joking."

"It was a male," said Lucinder Dobbs, "else why did she call him Hugh? You have all heard the minister say his wife hadn't a relative on earth except her mother and a maiden aunt; it couldn't have been her mother, and it couldn't have been the maiden aunt, for her name was Martha instead of Hugh. Besides," she kontinude, for she had so hardened her mind with mathematics, that she could grapple the hardest fact and floor it, so to speak. "Besides," sez she, "the maiden aunt died a year and a half ago, that settles the matter conclusively it was not the maiden aunt."

"I have thought something was on the minister's mind all the spring," said the Widder Tubbs, "I have spoken to sister Ann about it a number of times." Then she kinder rolled up her eyes, jest as she does in class-meetin', and sez she, "It is an awful dispensation, but I hope he'll turn it into a means of grace; I hope his speritooil strength will be renewed. But," sez she, "I have borryed a good deal of trouble about his bein' so handsome; I have noticed that handsome ministers don't turn out well, they most always have somethin'; happen to 'em sooner or later; but I hope he'll be led."

"Well, I never thought that Miss Linden was any too good," said Betsy Babbet.

"Neither did I," said Lucinder Dobbs.

"She has turned out jest as I always thought she would," said Ophelia, "and I have jest as good an opinion of her has I have for them that stand up for her."

Maggie Snow spoke up then; jest as clear as a bell her voice sounded; she ain't afraid of anybody, for she is Lawyer Snow's only child, and has been to Boston to school. Sez she, "Aunt Allen" (she is a little related to me on her mother's side), "Aunt Allen, why is it that, as a generel rule, the very worst folks are the first ones to suspect other folks of being bad?"

Sez I, "Maggie, they draw their pictures from memory." And sez I, "They want to pull down other folkses reputations, for they feel as if their own goodness is in a totterin' condition, and if they fall, they want something to fall on, so as to come down easier like."

Maggie Snow laughed, and so did Miss Edwards, and the Joneses, but Betsy Babbet and the Dobbs' girls looked black as Erobious. And, sez Betsy Babbet to me, sez she: "I shouldn't think, Josiah Allen's wife, that you would countenance such conduct."

"I will first know there is wrong conduct," sez I. Sez I, "Miss Linden's face is jest as innocent as a baby's, and I ain't a-goin' to mistrust any evil out of them pretty brown eyes till I am obleeged to."

Jest at this minute the hired girl came in and said supper was ready, and we all went out to eat it. Miss Jones said their wasn't anything on the table fit to eat, and she was afraid we couldn't make out, but we did have a splendid supper, good enough for the Zero of Rushy.

We hadn't more 'n got up from the supper table and got back into the parlor when we heard a knock onto the front door. Miss Jones went and opened it, and who, for all the live world, should walk in but the minister! The faces of the wimmen as he entered would have been a study for Michael Angelico, or any of the old painters. Miss Jones was so flustrated that she asked him the first thing to take his bonnet off, then she bethought herself, and sez she, "How's your mother?" before she had sot him a chair or anything. But he looked jest as pleasant and composed as ever, though his eyes kinder laughed. And he thanked her and told her he left his mother, the day before, a good deal better; and then he turned to Maggie Snow, and sez he:—

"I have come after you, Miss Maggie," sez he. "My wife come home night before last, and wanted to see you so bad, that I told her as I had business past your house I would call for you as I went home, and your mother told me you was here. I think I know," sez he, "why she wants to see you so very much now, she is so proud of our boy she can't wait till"—

"Your boy!" gasped nine wimmen to once.

"Yes," sez he, smilin' more pleasant than I ever see him. "I know you will all wish me joy. We have a nice little boy, little Hugh, for my wife has named him already for her father. He is a fine, healthy little fellow—almost two months old."

"It wouldn't have done any good for Michael Angelico to have been there then, nor Mr. Ruben, nor none of the rest of them we read of, for if they had their paletes and easelses all ready they never could have done any justice to the faces of Betsy Babbet and the Dobbs girls, and, as for Miss Deacon Graves, her spectacles fell off unnoticed, and she opened her mouth so wide that it was very doubtful to me if she could ever shet it agin. And, as fer me, I was truly happy enuff to sing the Te Deus.

Maggie Snow flew out of the room to put on her bonnet, with her face shinin' like a cherubin, and, as I lived half a mile on the road they was goin', and the quilt was most off, and he had two horses, and insisted, I rode with 'em, and I haint seen none of the quilters sense.

BUSY BEES, STINGING BEES, FEEDING THE BEES

Excerpt from: "The Shadow of Moloch Mountain"
Mrs. Jane G. Austin, *Hearth and Home*, 1870

*One of the most amazingly detailed accounts of a quilting
bee appeared in three chapters of the serialized story "The
Shadow of Moloch Mountain," published in the magazine
Hearth and Home in 1870. Very few other mid-nineteenth
century fictional accounts described as completely the tech-
nical aspects of "putting in," "snapping the cord" for marking, and the differences between shell quilting and wave quilting. Unusual, also, are the uses of the singular term "bee" to
mean a quilting party, and the plural term "bees" to refer to
the women attending the affair. Social and skill levels of "the
bees" were indicated by the areas of the home to which the
women were assigned, whether to the front parlor, the front
guest chamber, or the upstairs room. Those women assigned
to the latter room, being the least proficient quiltmakers, were
only allowed to make the tacked comforters. Very specific information was included, almost a manual of directions for
such topics as the process of tying comforters, and the writing
of examples—supplied verses to be written on an album quilt
meant to be a wedding gift.*

Chapter XXVII—Busy Bees

The morning proved Jacob a true prophet, for it broke with a
steady downpour of rain, of the soft, quiet description as little
likely to change as the will of those smiling, serene women, than
whom the mountains are less obstinate.

"Now, Mr. Monckton," said Aunt Rachel, as the traveller after breakfast approached the window, "you might as well consent
to what you can't help. The going will be miserable today, and
the rain will soak through that coat of yours like brown paper.

Send back your sleigh to Bloom and make yourself contented here until to-morrow, when you can take the stage. We are going to have a bee today, and there will be some gentlemen to tea; and Beatrice, she isn't of much account for quilting, and she will keep you company through the day. You'd better stay."

"I think so too, sir, and I should be glad of some one to keep me in countenance among so many of the more powerful sex," said the deacon, with the quiet smile that always suggested a little good-humored satire in his remarks upon womankind, and re-minded his hearers that the opinions formed sixty years ago were less liberal in their appreciation of the fairer half of mankind that those of today.

"Oh! yes, he'll stay," chimed in grandmamma. "There'll be a plenty of pretty girls here, even if we hadn't one of our own."

"And we shall be edified in watching some new proofs of uni-versal adaptiveness," said Beatrice softly.

"How can I choose but stay with so many temptations, even if my own wishes were not too powerful to be denied?" said Monckton gayly; and Miss Rachel slipped out of the room to give the stable lad from Bloom a substantial breakfast, and bid him make ready to depart alone.

A few hours later the bees began to arrive in spite of the con-tinued and increasing bad weather.

"I told you how it'd be," said Jacob, as he approached the doorstep where Beatrice was lingering to enjoy the soft, moist air, while the guests she had just welcomed were piloted up-stairs by Miss Rachel.

"Yes, but how will they get home again?" murmured the young lady, as Jacob took the horse by the head and began to lead him toward the barn.

"Oh! that's of no account," replied he scoffingly. "They're here, and they a'n't to home, and that's all they care for."

"How unlikely such a servant would be in England!" said Mr. Monckton, who had quietly approached the open door.

"So familiar, and yet so truly respectful," said Beatrice.

"Yes. Here in New-England, a servant is merely a man who

for wages consents to perform certain service for another man. He retains his self-respect and commands the respect of his employer, and both of them tacitly confess that some day the employed may become employer, and even rise to a rank far above that of his present master. There is nothing servile, nothing presuming in this man's manners, but a servant who is born and will die a servant cannot cease to be servile without becoming presuming."

" 'My country 'tis of thee, Sweet land of liberty,' " sung Beatrice with a smile; and as another sleigh, heavily loaded with women, old and young, one small boy and several umbrellas toiled up to the door, the friends, now really friends once more, withdrew to the east room, which was to be left undisturbed for the occupancy of the old people, and whoever chose to join them.

"Maybe, Mr. Monckton, if you are not wanted at the quilting, you would like to look over some old records and curious papers saved through two hundred years in our family," said the deacon, feebly rising and unlocking the great brass-bound secretary, whose deep drawers and pigeon-holed recesses contained antiquarian wealth enough to set a whole college mad.

Mr. Monckton, who had the taste to relish and the training to appreciate these treasurers, accepted the offer with a cordiality which evidently raised him in the opinion of the old man, who seldom vouchsafed such an offer to a stranger, and who valued his family treasures to their full extent.

With a smile of quiet amusement, Beatrice watched the preparations of the two convives as they seated themselves to their feast, and so soon as they were fairly engrossed, left the room and joined the throng of workers already busy in the great parlor.

"How d'y do, Beatrice? How's your health since you've been to the city?" asked Mrs. Green, the sturdy, comfortable wife of Doctor Bliss's rival in Milvor.

"Very good, thank you, Mrs. Green. Let me help you with that bar."

"Thanky. You see we thought we'd set up the best quilt in this room, because it's the parlor, and birds of a feather had oughter flock together—don't you see?"

And Mrs. Green looked round upon her co-adjutors for the approving laugh, of which they did not disappoint her, it being a fortunate illustration of the law of demand and supply, that to any persons of small intellectual average a very little wit goes a great way, or even no wit at all supplies the place of that stimulant better than the genuine article.

Beatrice politely joined in the laugh, and also with more interest in the labor of raising the heavy quilting—bars upon the backs of four chairs, and securing them in the form of a hollow square by means of gimlets kept for that purpose. Next, the lining of the quilt—economically composed of a worn and faded counterpane—was sewed to the border of cloth tacked to the inner edges of the bars; then the rolls of cotton-wool were laid upon it, and a warm discussion as to the proper amount to be used went round the circle of ladies gathered about the frame like a congress of crows considering a prey fallen into their midst.

"Well, every body has their own notions; but for my part, I don't never want more than two pound of cotton in a quilt that's going to lay over me. If you get in more, it's more heft than warmth," said Mrs. Green.

"What I say is, if you're going to have a quilt, why have it, and let it be of some use. I don't think four pound of cotton a mite too much, and I haven't got a quilt in the world with less in, and one I've got for the boys' bed has got six in it."

"I should think your boys would be smashed down flat under it, Miss Williams," suggested another matron, slightly flushed with the heat of argument; and at this moment, fortunately for the harmony of her party, Miss Rachel entered the room. The question was at once referred to her, and decided with a dove-and-serpent wisdom which excited the admiration of her niece, who had become a little alarmed.

"Why, to my mind, it depends altogether on where the quilt is to be used," said Miss Rachel. "For a cold, windy room—up garret, say—I like a good thick quilt, or maybe a comforter, and if the wool is good and clean, I don't believe four or five pounds would be too heavy; but in a warm room, I think it is better to have your quilts lighter an more of them, so that you can throw them off and put them on, as you like. My mother, now has four quilts on her bed besides the blankets, and I don't believe there is more than a pound apiece in them. So, seems to me, I wouldn't put more than two pounds in this quilt, and after we get it out, we'll tack a comforter, and put five pounds in. Then they could go on one bed together, and whoever slept there could turn one or the other off as they were a mind to."

"Yes, it's well to suit all tastes when you can; and some folks like to lie warm, and some not so warm" said an old lady soothingly. And the two pounds of cotton were laid in, with no more discussion.

The next operation was to adjust the cover or upper crust of this cotton-wool pie. This was patchwork, composed of small octagonal squares of brightly-colored calico, alternated with large octagons of solid-colored cambrics, and had been Miss Rachel's fancy-work during the last month.

It now received many encomiums and a minute examination, sweet to the vanity of the laborious artist.

"There's a piece of your lilac calico," and "Where did you get that rosy piece?" or "These pretty cambrics was your morning gowns, Beatrice, wasn't they?" and "What a lot of work to get them all together, and how nice you set off the colors one against another!" were some of the ejaculations. And Miss Rachel modestly deprecating the praise she felt richly merited, helped to lay the cover evenly upon the cotton, and to sew it to the edges of the bars.

"Now, what pattern be we going to do it in?" asked Mrs. Green, producing a ball of hard white cord and a piece of chalk from her pocket.

"Herring-bone is about as pretty as any way, a'n't it?" asked Mrs. Williams.

"I like di'monds, inch-square di'monds," said another lady positively.

"Shell-pattern is pretty," remarked one.

"Waves are prettier," suggested another.

"How do you do waves?"

"Why lay down a small plate or a saucer, if you want them small, and chalk round half the edge. Just like shell-pattern, only you do that with a teacup."

"It's pretty to have double parallel lines, each pair about ten inches from the next, and then waves in between each pair," said quiet Mrs. Phelps, the minister's wife.

"Like skeins of yarn drying on a clothes-horse," whispered Mrs. Green, who never approved any other person's suggestion, and yet dared not openly contradict the minister's wife, whose proposed pattern was at once adopted by Miss Rachel.

"First we must mark out the lines," said Mrs. Phelps, looking about her. "Mrs. Green, will you chalk your cord, and lay it on where you think it ought to go?"

Mrs. Green thus called to the front, graciously obeyed, and first drawing the cord over the lump of chalk, laid it across one side of the quilt, and held it firmly at one end, while Mrs. Phelps drew the other tight.

"Now, Miss Rachel, you must snap it, for the sake of the sign," said Mrs. Green; and Rachel, with a prim smile, took the middle of the cord between her thumb and forefinger, raised it a little, and let it fall with a smart snap striking out a line of chalk-dust.

"What is the sign?" asked Beatrice.

"Why, the one that snaps the first line on a bed-quilt will lay under a wedding bed-quilt first of any one in the room," said Mrs. Green mysteriously, as she and the minister's wife moved their chalked cord about an inch, had a line snapped there, and then removed it ten inches further inlaid, and chalked another pair of parallel lines, while Mrs. Bruce, with an inverted breakfast-plate and a piece of chalk sharpened to a crayon, proceeded to draw the "waves" between the two.

Leaving them thus engaged, Beatrice stole away and up-stairs, where in the room overhead she found another group of ladies similarly employed over a "comforter," already in the frame, and ready to be "tied" in diamonds, a process effected by pushing a needle filled with soft thread down through cover, cotton, and lining and drawing it up again nearly in the same place, a little bunch of bright colored wools being tied into the knot thus formed. But in the other front chamber, the guest-chamber, a knot of matrons, working in secret conclave, were preparing the crowning glory of the day—Miss Rachel herself being rigidly excluded from the room, and Beatrice only allowed to enter under promise of inviolable secrecy.

This was an album bed-quilt, the gift of Miss Barstow's widest circle of Milvor acquaintance, each octagon composed by a different person—the point of harmony insisted upon being the size, and a small white square in the middle, bearing the name of the donor either written in indelible ink, or fairly wrought in cross stitch, according to her taste or ability. Below the name was generally a date, and frequently a couplet, either original or selected—as:

"When this you see,
Remember me."

"The rose is red, the violet blue,
Pinks are pretty, and so are you"
"Of your dreams just when you wake,
Special notice you should take."

"Your hand and heart
Shall never part."

"I send this square to Miss Rachel,
to show that I wish her well."

"As soon as you're married, dear Miss,
You'll surely be living in bliss."
"This pretty piece of bedding
Is to grace Miss Barstow's wedding."

Beatrice gravely read these and many similar effusions, admired the taste displayed in the various squares, some of which were very pretty, and was just about to assume her place among the needle-women already busily at work, when her aunt's voice summoned her into the hall, and she obeyed, first renewing her promise of secrecy.

Chapter XXVIII — Stinging Bees

"Beatrice, it's just struck twelve, and don't you think we'd better call 'em out to luncheon?" whispered Miss Barstow, drawing her niece into her own chamber, at the moment deserted, although the bed was piled up with outer garments, and a small baby slumbered peacefully in a basket upon the hearth.

"Why, aren't we going to have dinner pretty soon?" asked Beatrice, stooping to touch the velvety check of the little sleeper with her lips.

"Dinner! Why, Trix, have you forgotten? We are going to give them luncheon now, and by and by, about five o'clock, when it gets too dark to quilt, and the gentlemen come, we're going to have dinner and supper all in one."

"Oh! yes, I remember, aunty. They must have some tea with their luncheon, mustn't they? Old ladies always like tea when they are at work, I notice."

"Yes, they will have tea, and coffee, and bread, and butter, and cake, and cheese, and apple-tarts," said Miss Rachel, checking off each article upon her fingers. "And I want you to carry round the cream and sugar on that little silver waiter that brother Israel gave me last New Year's, and just see that every body is getting enough to eat, and sort of urge them to take more, or something else, you know. Some people always say no the first time, and mean yes all the while."

"I know it, aunty. Yes, I will see that they are all properly urged. Where shall I find the salver?" asked Beatrice, smiling roguishly at her aunt's directions.

"It's in the buttery, with the silver cream-pot and sugar-bowl on it, all ready. You needn't put any napkin over the waiter, Beatrice. I am going to carry in a little hot dinner to grandpa and grandma in the east room, because they hate to be put out of their ways, you know, and I suppose Mr. Monckton will eat with them. I'm afraid he's dreadful lonesome, Beatrice."

"Not a bit, aunty. He is having the nicest time you can imagine, with grandfather and the old records. I peeped in there just now."

"I dare say you did," said Miss Rachel grimly, touching her niece's rosy cheek with her forefinger. "Well, Trix, I think he is as nice a man as I have seen for a great while. I like him ever so much."

"So do I, aunty; but don't go to building air-castles with me for Chatelaine; although it is natural enough that your thoughts should run on matrimony."

"You saucy girl—" began Miss Rachel; but Beatrice with a merry laugh was already running down stairs to look for the silver salver.

Long afterward, both she and her aunt remembered that merry laugh and that lighthearted audacity, and wondered that no shadow of the clouds sweeping across that brilliant sky should have warned them of its coming.

The luncheon was served, and Beatrice, flitting from group

to group, the pretty salver, with its cream-ewer and sugar-basin, in her hand, and her face bright with cordial interest in those whose wants she supplied, presented a more attractive picture to the eyes of a reasonable man than even Beatrice in all the luxury of her gala robes, and the plenitude of her social power.

So thought at least Mr. Monckton, standing unobserved in the hall of the old house, sipping his coffee, and watching the groups in the various rooms with the attentive eye of a practiced observer. As Beatrice approached, he, wishing her to remain unconscious of his presence, lest she should lose the simple earnestness which charmed him so much in her present manner, seated himself quietly behind a group of thick-set matrons close at hand, and so became most unintentionally auditor of their conversation.

"Zilpah says she's real comfortable," pursued Zilpah's sister-in-law. "They don't have no great variety, nor no company, and it's so seldom that they any of them go out of the woods, that she hadn't had a chance to write before, since they got there; and I don't believe she'd have written now, only she wanted to tell about some things that Marston Brent gave her when he broke up here, and she left them with Samooel to sell for her, and I suppose she thought it was time to hear from them. She was always dreadful sharp after money, Zilpah was, and that's a complaint folks don't get better of as they get older."

"Marston Brent and his folks thought a sight of Zilpah," said another matron meditatively.

"Yes, and she of them. She has a lot to say about Marston in her letter. He's going to be married."

"Is? Why, who to, up there in the woods?"

"Well, a girl that's living with him some way now. Zilpah don't say much about it; only that evenings, they all sit round, and he teaches Comfort all sorts of things. Zilpah says that nobody here needn't think he's feeling any way bad about what's past and gone, for she never see a man more taken up in a girl than he is in this Comfort, and they'll be married soon."

"He's got over the breaking off with—"

"S—h! here she is," whispered another voice; and between the portly forms of the matrons, Monckton saw the glitter of the silver salver, and heard a low voice saying:

"Will you have some more sugar or cream, ladies?"

It was not five minutes since he had heard that voice so free, so sweet, so ringing with innocent mirth, and hardly his own eyes or ears could persuade him that this was the same. He stole a look at Beatrice, more careful now than before not to let her perceive him. Yes, face as well as voice had met a change so great as to be almost incredible. Those blanched cheeks—those lips, straight, hard, and colorless—those eyes, vacant, yet burning—that constrained, mechanical manner! Ah! was this the light hearted Beatrice he had stolen away from his appointed place to admire?

And then he fell to speculating upon the sudden change. The talk of those women—it must be that; and this Marston Brent was the man she had loved, and from whom she had been separated. A lover's quarrel, which she had thought some day to reconcile, and now he loved another woman! And she, so proud, so sensitive, so—yes, she was jealous in her friendship, as their late difference proved; and still more would she be jealous in her love— not meanly jealous, not desiring to harm or wound either faithless lover or successful rival, but disdaining a divided reign, resigning all without a struggle the moment a struggle became necessary. This was the temper of the woman whom Monckton read as easily as that morning he had read the old Saxon Bible brought from England by her ancestor.

Passing quietly behind the matrons, and out of the room, he waited in the hall until she should come out, meaning he knew not what, but to comfort her in some way. Presently she came; and even Monckton, practiced societist as he was, stood confounded before her. The change wrought by those idle words was not more absolute than this—so different from both the other moods; and who but he, who knew the whole, could have distinguished between the girlish glee of the first and the practiced persiflage of the present manner?

He looked at her curiously. Yes, her eyes were bright, her lips smiling, her cheeks flushed, her tone gay and unconcerned, and the slight pallor about her mouth and the slighter tremor of the jesting voice were so faintly marked that no observer less acute than he could have distinguished them.

"And she could hardly forgive me for the transparent lie told in self defence. That is woman," said he softly to himself. Beatrice paused before him.

"Why, Mr. Monckton! A drone among the bees! Aren't you afraid of being stung to death?"

"Not while the queen-bee is my friend," said Monckton significantly, and making a show of helping himself from the salver, he detained her long enough to see that the allusion had shaken somewhat her desperate mood.

"I am glad that we were reconciled last night," said she, suffering her face to fall for one moment into an expression of such piteous suffering that all the manhood of Monckton's heart was stirred.

"So am I. I want to see you alone, when all these people are gone," said he.

"For what?"

"I will tell you then. Nothing that will trouble or annoy you— be sure of that."

"Sure? I am sure of nothing now." And with this one cry, wrung from the sharp agony of her heart by his sympathetic tone, Beatrice passed quickly on.

Chapter XXIX—Feeding the Bees

The afternoon passed much as the morning—the usual conversation, varied by occasional remarks upon the weather, which continued "soft" and threatening for the homeward flight of the bees. Needles, however, flew as actively as tongues, and by five o'clock three bed-quilts, including the famous album-quilt, and four comforters lay completed upon the floor of the guest-chamber; the frames were rapidly dismembered and taken to the garret, the rooms cleared of litter, and the ladies requested to amuse themselves for half an hour, when supper would be served. Complying with this invitation, the elders, after smoothing their black silk or alpaca dresses, and adjusting their cap-ribbons, repaired in squads of two and three to the east room to pay their respects to the patriarchs, while the younger women, after devoting a little more time and pains to the renovation of their toilets, collected in groups, gossiping in low voices and with much-supressed giggle, or hanging around the window to watch the arrival of the gentlemen who had been invited for the supper and evening frolic offered to the bees by way of recompense for the toils of the day.

This supper, as it was justy styled—for certainly it was neither breakfast, dinner, nor tea—was a feast such as never perhaps is spread out of New-England, and, alas! is rarely seen in these degenerate days even in that favored region.

It was spread upon two extempore tables extending the length of the dining room, and crowded upon both sides with plates; for Miss Rachel strongly condemned the inhospitable fashion of "stand-up teas," and declared that if she was to have any thing to eat, she also wished a comfortable place to eat it in, or wanting that, had rather go unfed. Upon these tables, then, were set the dishes, including an enormous round of spiced beef at either end, roasted turkeys and geese as central ornaments, and such trifles as roasted and boiled fowls, hams, tongues, headcheese, and smoked beef between. Varying these meats were plates of smoking-hot fried doughnuts, hot biscuit, brown bread, dipped toast, and short-cakes, and to succeed them upon the bill of fare came pies of every imaginable variety, cake of every hue and description, sweet-meats, pickles, cheese, custards, and fruit.

At a smaller table acrosss the head of the room stood Miss Barstow and Beatrice pouring cups of coffee and tea, which Nancy smilingly distributed; while Dr. Bliss, Mr. Monckton, and a few other gentlemen, waited upon the fair guests at the tables, carving the pieces de resistance, and urging them upon the delicate creatures whose creed of manners peremptorily inculcated resistance to all such overtures, however much exhausted nature might crave support. This point, however, being thoroughly understood among the jocund swains of these shy Daphnes, was easily disposed of, and somewhat in this fashion:

"Have a piece of the turkey, Miss Welch?"

"No; I'm obliged to you, Mr. Snell; I can't get through what I've got on my plate."

"You ha'n't got nothing but a piece of bread, as I see. Better have some turkey, it's first-rate."

"La! no, I couldn't eat it if I was to take it."

"Well, if you don't maybe it'll eat you, for one of you's got to suffer, and there it is."

"O my! Mr. Snell, what be you doing? Well, then I shall leave it on my plate."

Which she did not do.

Mr. Monckton, everywhere at once, attentive to every one, rather preferring the older and less attractive of the guests to the younger and prettier ones, proved an invaluable auxiliary, and won for himself more golden opinions than have often crowned more real self sacrifive.

The admiration excited by his fine face and polished manner among the younger ladies might, indeed, have become dangerous to the peace of their respective swains, had it not been tempered by the information dropped early in the day by Miss Rachel, and industriously circulated ever since, to the effect that this was "Beatrice Wansted's beau," and therefore not available for any other aspirant. At a later day, Miss Barstow defended herself with considerable skill from the charge of setting a false rumor in circulation, with the remark:

"Well, if he wasn't he ought to have been unless my eyes deceived me when I came in with that loaf of cake."

But with all Mr. Monckton's efforts, he never lost sight or thought of the friend whose grief was to him as his own. He saw that the exertions she forced herself to make were too great to be sustained; he was sure that presently she must fail utterly, either in muscle or nerve—must faint or burst into hysterical weeping; and he well knew how cruelly she would afterward reproach herself for either betrayal.

Watching her with ever increasing anxiety, he saw her eyes glazing with the inward fever that burned upon her cheeks and lips, wander about the room with the appealing gaze of some timid creature trapped and doomed to death, yet seeking despairingly an impossible escape. He saw her totter and grasp at the back of a chair for support, and in the next moment he was at her side, her hand within his arm.

"One last effort—look about you and try to smile—don't fail now—remember all these people!" murmured he in her ear, supporting her as well as he could without attracting attention, and leading her rapidly from the room. In the hall she tottered, and would have fallen, but with his arm around her waist, he raised and carried her into the deserted parlor and laid her upon a sofa. The cool air and tender twilight of the place revived her, and opening her eyes, she whispered:

"Thank you. I am so glad —"

"I did not mean to let you spoil all your effort by breaking down at the last. You have done nobly."

Beatrice opened her eyes more consciously, and fixed them upon his face. The she said half defiantly:

"Yes, I have been growing tired for some time."

Mr. Monckton bowed with a face which neither denied nor accepted the proposition, and Beatrice blushed scarlet.

"You should teach me how to say those things better," said she bitterly.

"You need first some food; then warmth and rest," replied Monckton quietly. "Go to your own room, and I will send you something to eat and drink. You have taken nothing since breakfast."

"How do you know?"

"Am I not your friend?"

"I do not like surveillance."

"You like nothing to-night; but after eating you will wrap yourself very warmly, and go to sleep—to oblige me."

"Why should I?"

"Because I cannot be happy unless you are at least physically comfortable—because I am your friend."

"Ah!" shivered Beatrice, as if the word had hurt her; and with a sudden, uncontrollable impulse, she laid both her hands in his, and fixed those piteous, eloquent eyes upon his face.

"My friend! Are you indeed my friend?" moaned she. "Then pray that I may die tonight."

"Beatrice! No, child, you shall not be alone through the sharpness of this agony—you could not bear it yet. Come into the other room, and sit beside that saintly old man; the peace and perfectness of his calm will soothe you, and the thought of the battles he has fought and conquered will give you strength for your own. Come."

She suffered him to raise and lead her from the room, just as the advance guard of the devastating army in the dining-room appeared at the lower end of the hall, returning upon their footsteps. Monckton quickly opened the door of the east room, entered with Beatrice, and closed it behind them. The grandparents, sitting placidly at either side the fire, with a little tea-table between them, looked up and smiled.

"Miss Wansted is so much fatigued with her hospitable efforts that I persuaded her to come in and rest a little, and, if I might venture, I should suggest to Mrs. Barstow to make her drink a cup of tea."

So speaking, with the easy manner of one who knows his presence and his proposition sure to be favorably received, Mr. Monckton seated Beatrice in a comfortable chair near her grandmother, left the room in search of a cup and saucer, and brought back with them a plate containing some bits of chicken and a piece of bread.

"Now, Miss Beatrice, if you will allow me, I shall recommend as much chicken and bread as you can possibly dispose of; and to show that I really believe in my own prescriptions, I shall go and bring yet another plate, cup and saucer, and set you a good example. You see, Mrs. Barstow, we have been so busy in waiting upon other people that we have as yet done nothing for ourselves, and I fear this young lady is quite exhausted."

"I haven't a doubt of it," replied the old lady, with emphasis. "It was always the way with her from a child; if she got excited, or tired, or any thing, she wouldn't eat perhaps not a mouthful in a day, and then, of course, she'd break down. She isn't very rugged at the best of times, nor her mother wasn't before her. Some how, these pretty creters don't seem to wear so well as the plain, home spun ones—like Rachel, say."

"My wife probably wishes to say, sir, that, without unnaturally giving the preference to either of her daughters, she valued each for her own peculiar gifts," said the patriarch, somewhat severely; and his wife, stirring her tea, vehemently exclaimed:

"Certain, certain; that is what I meant."

Mr. Monckton, replying to both with a smile that conveyed everything or nothing, as the receiver chose, left the room, and presently returning with his own supper, drew a chair to the table; and while eating and drinking with unfeigned relish, contrived to insist upon Beatrice's doing the same. When she would take no more, he contrived that her grandmother should suggest her reclining upon the soft, old-fashioned couch, and himself threw a shawl across her feet. Then, returning with a smile her look of gratitude, he set aside the little tea-table, and devoted himself to conversation with the deacon and his wife upon topics which he knew to be especially interesting to his silent auditor.

Thus was he still engaged when the jingle of sleigh-bells announced that the guests were about to depart; and Mr. Monckton feeling that he also owed a duty to Miss Rachel, rose to fulfil it, seeing, with quiet satisfaction, as he passed the couch, that Beatrice had fallen fast asleep.

"Ef there a'n't some hosses' legs broke 'fore we all get home, why I lose my guess," remarked the father of a family, standing rather discontentedly upon the doorstep, and examining the gray, watery sky, the plashy and uneven road, and the erractic movements of the sleigh just driving from the door.

"Now, look out, girls, for some fun. If you don't get upset before you reach Four Corners, it won't be my fault!" exclaimed a jolly young farmer, escorting a bevy of shrieking, exclamatory girls to the same point. And half an hour later the last guest had said goodnight, and the Old Garrison returned to its usual condition of quiet and repose.

HANNAH'S QUILTING

Anonymous, *Harper's Bazar*, March 5, 1870

*In the pre-telephone days of nineteenth-century rural America,
handwritten and hand-delivered invitations to quiltings were
an important facet of the local social scene. One special invitation written by young Hannah for her upcoming quilting
inadvertently went awry. The resultant mix-up almost had a
disastrous effect on Hannah's love life.*

Hannah thought she knew the state of Aleck Freeman's heart.
She had trifled with him a little, and her own mind was not quite
made up.

She was sitting now in her chamber, sweet and clean with
whitewash and new buff paper, and bowery with green light which
fell from the pear-tree boughs through freshly-starched muslin
curtains. Hannah was a nice-looking blonde maiden, dressed in
a tidy chocolate print, with a blue bow nestling in her thick, wavy
hair. She had been writing a note by the stand, and was sealing it
with one of the motto seals then in fashion. This one said, "Come;"
and it was easy to see that it indorsed a note of invitation.

She ran down stairs into the fresh morning air, where her
father, Deacon Ashley, was just ready to head old Charley toward
the village. Her mother, a buxom matron, was standing bareheaded beside the democrat wagon, handing up the molasses jug,
and charging the Deacon not to forget that pound of Castile soap
and the lamp-wicks. Hannah tucked up her trim skirts, and ran
out through the dewy grass.

"See here, father," she called, in her pleasant voice, "you must
stop at the school-house and give this note to Andy Freeman. It's
for Jane, you know, asking her and Miss Lang to come to the
quilting."

"Ain't there one for Aleck, too?" inquired the good-natured
old Deacon, with a wink.

"I told Jane he could come in the evening, if he chose," returned Hannah, with slightly heightened color. "Doctor Bingham will be here," she added, "and some other young men."

"Aleck Freeman is worth the whole kit," responded the Deacon; "and that young pill-box, according to my way of thinking, runs too much to hair-ile and watch-chains; but Aleck has got good hard sense and first-rate learning. He can appear with any of 'em. If you don't look out, Han, he'll be shining round that pretty girl from Hillsdale."

"It makes no difference to me, who he shines round," returned Hannah, with a slight shade of offense; but, nevertheless, there was a little pang at her heart as she turned back toward the house. Hannah's mind was not quite easy about Jane Freeman's visitor, the pretty girl from Hillsdale, but she thought if she could see Aleck and Mary Lang together, she would know in just what quarter the wind was setting.

The Deacon tucked the note into his breast-pocket, took the molasses jug between his feet, and gave old Charley a cut with the lines preparatory to making him begin to move, an operation of some length, as Charley believed the Deacon to be under his orders. At last, however, the two were trotting and rattling past the goose-pond, and the big barns, and the tall elms that cast some very cool shadows across the brown dust of the road, until with a kind of mutual understanding and sympathy they came out against a stretch of post and rider fence, inclosing a field of the biggest kind of clover. It looked like good farming to the Deacon's eyes. He could calculate pretty closely the number of tons of sweet, juicy feed there would be to the acre; and yet this morning the fragrance and the rosy bloom and the hum of insects among the thick heads brought him a different kind of pleasure.

With the long sight of age he could see the cows grazing in the back pasture, and he thought of the "cattle on a thousand hills," and whose they are. His gaze wandered back lovingly even to the old stone-walls with mulleins growing beside them, and the shadows of birds flitting over them, and everything seemed good, even the May-weed and daisies and Canada thistles that farmers hate by instinct. He felt a gush of childlike thankfulness, because "the earth is the Lord's, and the fullness thereof."

Presently the Deacon and Charley came across a group of school-children—brown, freckle-faced little urchins, in calico shirts, tow trowsers, and shilling hats much the worse for wear. Then there was a tall red-headed girl who had outgrown all the tucks in her dress, and had torn her apron in following the boys over the wall after a chipmunk, and one or two little tots, with very flappy sun-bonnets, whose short legs would not allow them to keep up. They all carried dinner-pails and dog's-eared spelling-books, and at the very end of the string there was a low-spirited yellow dog.

"Whoa!" cried the Deacon, setting his two boot-soles, which resembled weather-beaten scows, against the dash-board, and pulling in hard—an operation Charley did not at all relish, although he at last yielded, with a shake of his homely head, which intimated it was done by special favor, and could not be repeated.

"Jump in, children!" cried the good-natured old man; "I'll give ye a lift as far as the schoolhouse. Beats all how much little shavers think of ketchin' a ride. There, don't crowd, boys. Let the girls in first, and mind your manners;" and he lifted in a little roly-poly maid, with pincushion hands and a very suggestive stain of wild cherries around her dimpled mouth, and seated her on the buffalo beside him. The others all tumbled in in a trice.

" 'Pears to me I wouldn't eat them puckery things," said the Deacon, in his grandfatherly fashion, pointing to some suggestive smears on the little maid's high gingham apron. "They'll give you the colic."

"Yes, Sir," replied the child, folding her funny little hands contentedly in her lap. "Sissy had the measles and I didn't, and my mother said I might have the colic if I wanted to."

The Deacon leaned back and laughed, and Charley shook his ears and turned up at him an eye of mild reproach.

"What a little goose you are!" said a bright-faced boy, who had been very much squeezed in the legs, and had just administered several sharp punches in the side of the squeezer, as he leaned over the back of the seat to pinch the little girl's ear.

"Bless me! there's Andy Freeman, and I had like to have forgot the what-d'ye-call-it—billy-do—my Hannah sent to the girls up at your house."

The Deacon veered half round, and checked Charley, who by this time began to consider the whole thing disgusting, especially as the low-spirited dog had mixed himself up with his feet.

"This must be it," he went on, fumbling in his pocket. "You see I've left my best eyes at home; the old pair I carry in my head don't amount to much."

Andy took the folded paper, and promised to be careful of it; and by that time Charley and his load had arrived at the stone school-house, which looked very much like a juvenile penitentiary. The school mistress was standing in the door ringing the bell; and the children scrambled down the side of the wagon, and scampered off, to save their marks for punctuality.

Jane Freeman had been busy all day with her friend Mary Lang, the pretty girl from Hillsdale. There is nothing, at first, so engrossing to the mind of a country girl as the stylish clothes of her city visitor. Mary had a number of fashionably-made dresses, and, as old Mrs. Freeman remarked, she had got the "very latest quirk" in her pretty hair. She was a good-natured girl, and had let Jane cut the pattern of her visite and her tabbed muslin cape, and had shown her just how to do the captivating twist. Now the two girls were bending out of the sitting-room window, which looked upon the orchard, with its gnarled boughs, and cool green lights, and white clover-heads dropped upon the grass like unstrung pearls. Aleck had come up from the garden, and was leaning on his hoe-handle, talking to them. He was a muscular, well-made young fellow; and the fact that he had once passed three years in a city, and had rubbed off his rustic bashfulness, told upon him well. Now there was a half-quizzical, half-pleased look peeping out from under his dropped eyelids; and old Mrs. Freeman, sitting on the back porch, with her glasses in the fold of a magazine story, and the toe of one of her husband's socks covering her knobby finger-ends, glanced at the group, and thought to herself that Mary Lang, with all her finery, wouldn't be sorry to catch Aleck. Then at the memory of Hannah Ashley there came a little twinge of anxiety; for Hannah was her prime favorite; and, after the manner of substantial matrons, she desired her boy to marry a practical wife, who knew how to cook his dinner and make him comfortable. The sight of Mary Lang's white nerveless hands, with their pretty rings, caused the old lady to shake her head, and mutter something about "dolls and poppets."

Andy had come home from school, and had let the low-spirited dog out into the back lot to bark at the hens a little while by way of wholesome recreation. He was preparing to go down to his squirrel-trap in the woods; and as he sat fussing away and whistling on the porch step, suddenly he pulled a paper out of his jacket pocket, and scampered off with it to the window.

"Here's something Deacon Ashley told me to give you, Sis. He called it a billy."

"You mean a William," put in Mary, chucking him under the chin.

"Why it's nothing but that advertisement of Puffer's Pills the Deacon promised father! I thought Hannah would be sure to invite us to her quilting," said Jane, in a disappointed tone. "Say, Aleck, have you and Han been quarreling?" and she gave him a provoking little thrust, such as sisters are wont to administer.

Aleck turned round, and set his elbows squarely against the window-sill, and began to whistle low to himself.

"Let's take that ride over Saddleback Hill I promised to give you tomorrow afternoon, Mary," said he, veering back again and chewing an end of grass.

Miss Lang expressed herself delighted to take the ride; and every body appeared satisfied but Jane, who now would have no opportunity to display the new twist to the girls before Sunday.

Hannah's quilt had been put on the frames the day before, up in the spare chamber—a large apartment with a carpet in Venetian stripe, a high-post bedstead draped in the whitest dimity, a heavy mahogany bureau with respectable brass knobs, and an old-fashioned glass adorned with festoons of pink and white paper. There were faded foot-stools, worked by Mrs. Ashley when a girl, in chain-stitch embroidery; and framed samplers and silhouette portraits upon the wall of a cappy old lady and a spare old gentleman and matronly bunches of life-everlasting and crystallized grasses filling the plethoric vases upon the mantle-piece. Every thing was in apple-pie order, from kitchen to parlor. A pleasant, moist odor of Hannah's sponge-cake clung to the walls; and if you don't know what Hannah's sponge-cake was like, it is useless for me to describe it.

Hannah had put on her prettiest lawn dress—a pale green that became her blonde beauty, and touched it up here and there with a bit of pink ribbon. Mrs. Ashley was pinning on her false puffs before the glass, and fastening her collar with a brooch adorned with a daguerreotype likeness of the Deacon, which looked as if it had been taken in a particularly bad fit of dyspepsia. She dearly loved young company; and there was a bright twinkle in her eye, and a pucker about her mouth provocative of jokes.

When the girls had assembled, and the kissing and taking off of things was well through with, the grand business of the afternoon began. Every body praised Hannah's pretty quilt—pink stars dropped on to a white ground. Miss Treadwell was champion quilter. She understood all the mysteries of herrin'-bone and feather patterns; and, with a chalk-line in her hand, as the Deacon's wife expressed it, "ruled the roost." Miss Treadwell was a thin-faced, precise old maid, with a kind of withered bloom on her cheek-bones, and a laudable desire to make the most of her few skimpy locks.

"Beats all how young Salina Treadwell appears," whispered the Deacon's wife to her next neighbor. "She's as old as I be, if she's a day, and here she goes diddling round with the girls."

"Hannah, you ought to give this quilt to the one that gets married first," put in Susan Drake, threading her needle.

"I know who that will be," said Mrs. Ashley, winking hard toward Hetty Sprague, a pretty soft-headed little maiden, with cheeks of the damask-rose and dewy dark eyes.

"Oh, Miss Ashley!" cried Hetty, simpering sweetly, "how can you talk so? You know I never mean to get married all my born days. Men are such deceitful creatures!"

Miss Treadwell heaved a deep sigh, and snapped the chalk-line sentimentally, as if she too could a tale unfold that would tell of the perfidy of the male sex.

"I don't, for my part, see why every thing should be given to the married folks," returned Hannah, tapping lightly on the frame with her thimble, and feeling annoyed because Jane Freeman and her friend had not yet put in an appearance. "When I get to be an old maid I'll stuff every thing soft with feathers and wool, and keep sixteen cats, like Aunt Biceps."

"You an old maid!" cried merry little Nancy Duffy. "That's a likely story. I guess Aleck will have a word or two to say about it."

"It looks as if Aleck had got a new string to his bow," remarked Miss Treadwell, who knew how to give a sharp little thrust of her own. "He appears to be mighty thick with that girl from Hillsdale."

"Why, there goes Aleck now!" cried Hetty Sprague; and the girls ran to the window, upsetting one end of the quilt, just in time to see Aleck's sleek chestnut mare trot past, with Aleck himself so absorbed in the companion by his side that he did not appear to remark the battery of bright eyes under which he was passing.

Hannah colored and bit her lips, but she recovered herself with a light laugh.

"Never mind, girls," said she; "there are as good fish in the sea as ever have been caught. I'll show you Doctor Bingham to-night, and you'll all say he is perfectly splendid."

Then began a little mild gossip over the Doctor, as to who he was, and what had brought him to out-of-the-way Drastic—for the young man was only a visitor in the neighborhood—and in the clatter of tongues, before the second rolling, Hannah had slipped out to get tea. At first she did a very curious thing for a sensible young woman to do. She got behind the buttery door and hid her face in the roller-towel, and something very like a genuine sob shook her bosom, while some bitter tears were absorbed into the crash. The truth is, Hannah was jealous. The sight of Aleck devoting himself to that girl from Hillsdale, whom she had begun to detest, woke her up to the state of her own feelings, and perhaps nothing but that would ever have done the work.

Nevertheless, there was the sponge-cake to cut, and the best doyleys to be got out, and the ivory-handled knives to be taken down from the top shelf of the closet. She had to calculate how much of the strawberry preserves it would take to go round and not look skimpy, and who should sit by the glass dish, and how many custard-cups would be required to fill the middle of the table. All these things Hannah performed with as much accuracy as if her heart had not been smarting with disappointment and vexation.

Mrs. Ashley was never more in her element than when she presided at a feminine tea-party.

"We won't have any of the men folks round to bother, girls," said she, as they settled like a flock of doves about the table, which

Hannah had so temptingly spread. "It's busy times on the farm now, and the Deacon likes a bit of something hearty for his tea, so I told him he and the boys might wait. Ahem, Salina, do you take sugar in your tea?" as she poured out a cup of the delicate, green flavored beverage that diffused an appetizing fragrance through the room.

"Oh, Miss Ashley," cried Nancy Duffy, "you'll tell our fortunes, won't you? There isn't a soul here to know about it, and we'll keep as whist as mice."

"Now, girls, don't make me appear simple," said Mrs. Ashley, leaning back and wiping her red and smiling face free from the steam of the tea-pot. "If Miss Whitcomb should get hold of it she'd say it didn't become a deacon's wife."

"Never mind Miss Whitcomb," broke in Susan Drake. "She thinks she's arrived at perfection, and such folks are always disagreeable. Here, do look at Salina Treadwell's cup. If I'm not mistaken there's an offer in it."

"Of course there is," said Mrs. Ashley, taking up the cup with professional interest. "Don't you see that ring almost closed, with a heart inside? And she's going to accept it. It's coming from a light-complected man. Looks like Sile Winthrop down at the Corners."

"Oh, Miss Ashley, how you do talk!" cried Salina, mincing her biscuit and blushing up on her cheek-bones.

"He ain't a-going to live long, whoever it is," the Deacon's wife went on, twirling the cup with the girls hanging over her shoulder, and her eyes dancing with fun. "Yes, Salina, you will be left a widder."

"What a sad thing it must be to lose a companion," put in sentimental Ann Davis. "I should hate to be left a relic."

"Never you mind, Salina," the Deacon's wife continued, with a wink. "If I'm not mistaken you'll console yourself with number two. Look there, girls, at the true-lovers' knot and the bow and arrers."

Miss Treadwell held up her hands in mock horror, and affirmed that she didn't believe a word of it; but it was noticeable, as Mrs. Ashley said, that she was "chipperer" all the rest of the evening.

"Come, now tell Hannah's," cried Hetty Sprague. So Hannah passed along her cup.

"Why, child, you're going to shed tears; and there's a little cloud of trouble round you; but it will clear away, and you'll get your wish in spite of every thing."

"Don't you see saddle-bags and pill-boxes there?" inquired Nancy Duffy.

"Go along with your stuff and nonsense, girls!" exclaimed the Deacon's wife, waving away the cup. "If husband should get hold of it, he'd say I was trifling."

That evening, after Doctor Bingham had fooled a good deal with Hannah—had pressed her hand at parting, and whispered he should hope to see her next evening at the singing-class—she remembered her fortune, and did let some bitter tears soak into her pillow. She was not wise enough in worldly ways to suspect that the Doctor, a town-bred man, had set Hetty Sprague's silly little heart a-fluttering while he walked home with her under the warm star-light, although, in very truth, he did not care a fip for either of them. Hannah was content to play him off against Aleck, let the consequences be what they might; and more and more as she thought the matter over, she blamed that designing girl from Hillsdale.

The next night set in with a mild drizzle; and, in spite of Mrs. Ashley's protestations, Hannah was off for the singing-class. This class had been established to improve the church music, which, as the Deacon said, sadly needed "tinkering;" and gradually it became a resort for the young people of the village, while its functions were stretched to include a good deal of mild flirtation. Hannah, on entering, looked anxiously round to discover the Doctor; but, strange to say, he was absent. Aleck, who belonged to the choir, sat in his usual place alone. Neither Jane nor her young lady visitor had accompanied him. These facts Hannah ascertained before she let her eyes drop on her note-book. She watched the door keenly all through the hour of practice; but the Doctor did not make his appearance, and her indignation grew apace. She hoped to slip away a little in advance of the crowd, before the exercises were quite over, and the cordon of young men had formed about the entrance. But just as she was stepping off into the darkness, with the warm summer rain falling steadily, a hand touched her arm.

"Let me walk home with you, Hannah. I have an umbrella, and you are unprovided." It was Aleck's voice; and Hannah was nettled to remark not even a touch of penitence in its tone.

"No, I thank you," she returned, stiffly. "I prefer to go alone."

"But you can not refuse my company for a few steps, at least," said he, pushing up his umbrella and shielding her whether or no; "for I have brought an apology from Bingham. I am going to tell you, as a great secret," Aleck went on confidentially, while Hannah kept still from sheer astonishment, "that the Doctor and that forty-'leventh cousin of ours, from Hillsdale, were engaged once. The Doctor's a capital fellow; but there's a jealous streak in him. He wanted, to keep a loose foot, and wasn't willing Mary should do the same. She's an uncommonly pretty, lively girl"—a sharp twinge in Hannah's left side—"and, of course, she wasn't going to be cooped up, and the result was, they quarreled. But they did really care for each other, and now, the thing is made up, and I guess they have found out what a sneaking, unrighteous thing jealousy is."

"There might be cause for it," returned Hannah, faintly, as she felt her spirit oozing away.

"Come now, Hannah, you mean to hit me, and I might hit back again, but I won't; for I haven't loved any body but you—just as much as you would let me—ever since I was a boy. I am one of the constant kind. Don't you know I am, Hannah?"—very softly spoken for such a big fellow. "My heart has learned one trick of loving, and it can't unlearn it."

"Why, Sir, didn't you and Jane come to my quilting party?"—spoken in a shaky voice, and showing the white feather badly—"and why did you go gallivanting off with that girl?"

"You did not ask us, in the first place, and that girl was a visitor, and I liked her."

"Don't be saucy. I sent a note to Jane, and told father to give it to Andy."

"Ha, ha!" laughed Aleck, "it is all explained now. The old gentleman sent us an advertisement of Puffer's Pills by mistake, and you will find the note quietly reposing in his pocket."

I am afraid Aleck was saucy, for when Hannah got into the house there was something very sweet and delicious tingling upon her lips. She crept into the sitting-room, where she could hear the good old Deacon calmly snoring, and slipped the little note out of the breast-pocket of his coat.

Long afterward, when she had been Aleck's wife many a year, and the colors of the pretty star-quilt had faded upon her bed, Hannah would take the little billet, grown yellow now, from an inner drawer, where she kept it long with a silky tress cut from the head of the baby she had lost, and kiss it tenderly, as if new faith and trust could emanate from its folds.

A AXIDENT

Josiah Allen's Wife, *Peterson's Magazine*, September 1872

This story is another first-person account written in typical rural dialect from the pen of "Josiah Allen's Wife" (nee Marietta Holley). After she suffered a serious accident chasing chickens in the yard, Josiah Allen's Wife spent the next two weeks in bed, where a long stream of visitors descended upon her. She was cheered and soothed by some visitors and annoyed by others. Yet none angered Josiah Allen's Wife as did Betsy Babbet. Betsy came with a huge sack of quilt scraps, a request to borrow Josiah Allen's Wife's quilt patterns, and a promise that seven more of Betsy's relatives would soon arrive to spend the day with them. One relative was Aunt Nancy, who was bringing a large basket of rags she planned to cut for rug making, The exasperated Josiah Allen's Wife exclaimed, "It was 2 much!" and brought the story to an amusing climax.

I have been real sick with a axident. I run out into the garden full sail after some chickens, and fell kerslap down over a rail that lay in the grass, and turned my ankel jint. Fever sot in, and I was laid up bed sick for 2 weeks. It makes me out of patience to think of it, for we might have a dog that is worth something if it wuzzn't for Josiah. But as it is, if he ain't to the house, I have to do all the doggin' there is done, for I might as well get the door-step started onto cattle, as to get that pup started off of it to go on to anything—and he is as big as a young elephant too—eats as much as a cow, and of all the lazy critters I ever see he is the upshot and cap sheaf.

Why when Josiah sets him on to the chickens, he has to take him by the collar and kinder draw him along all the way; I tell him he had better bark 'em out himself. And as for cows and calves, he seems to be afraid of 'em; something kinder constitutional, Josiah says. I have told Josiah Allen more than a hundred times, if I have once, that I should a great deal rather do my own doggin' than to keep that pup, especially as Josiah is a great case for barkin'. You can't tell him from a dog, when he really sets out. That very day of the axident, I says to him in the mornin', says I,

"Josiah Allen, what's the use of keepin' that pup?"

Says he, "Samanthe, he is a good feller only he wants encouragement."

"Encouragement!" says I, "I should think as much." I had jest seen him havin' a tussle with some cows.

Says he, "If I will kinder run ahead of him and keep between him and the cows, he will go on to 'em first rate. He seems to want encouragement all the time. If I will run a little ahead of him and encourage him, he will go on to things first rate."

I didn't say any more, but I didn't stop thinking, and that very day the axident happened. Josiah heard me holler, and he came runnin' from the barn, and a scairter man you never see. He took me right up and was carryin' of me in—I was in awful agony—and the first words I remember sayin' was these in a faint voice,

"I wonder if you will keep that pup now?"

Says he firmly, yet with pity onto his pale and anxious face, "Mebbe you didn't encourage him enough Samanthe."

Says I deleriously, "Did you expect I was going to carry him in my arms, and throw him at the hens? I tried every other way."

"Wall! wall!" says he kinder soothingly. "Do keep still, how do you expect I am goin' to carry you if you touse round so."

He laid me down on the lounge in the settin' room, and I never got off of it for 2 weeks. As I said, fever set in—I had been most sick for a good while but thought I wouldn't give up—but this axident seemed to be the last hump on the camel's back and I had to give in.

When the news got out that I was sick, lots of folks come to see me. If I had been a elephant layin' there on that air lounge there couldn't more have walked in and looked at me. And every one wanted me to try some particular kind of herb drink. Why my stomach would have been drounded out, a perfect wreck, if I had took half. One woman I respected. She would come in, in a calm, quiet way about 2 times a week, and say in a mild collected tone, "You have got the tizick."

Says I, "the desease is in my foot mostly."

"I can't help that," says she firmly and gently; "there is tizick with it, and I think that is what ailed Josiah when he was sick."

"Why," says I, "that was the neuraligy, the doctor said."

"Doctors are liable to mistakes," says she in the same firm and modest ackcents. "I have always thought it was the tizick. There are more folks that are tizicky than you think for in this cold and unfriendly world. I am a master hand for knowin' tizick when I see it." She would then in an affectionate manner advise me to doctor for the tizick, and then she would gently depart.

There are 2 kinds of folks that go to visit the sick. There are them low voiced still footed women that walks right in and lays their hands on your hot forehead so soothin' like that the pain gets ashamed of itself and sneaks off. I call 'em God's angels. Sposen they haint get wings? I don't care, I contend for it they are servin' the Lord jest as much as if they was standin' up in a row all feathered out, with a palm tree in one hand, and a harp in the other.

As I told a old deacon once—he is awful stingy—he has got a big wood lot, and lots of poor families freezin' round him, and says he to me one cold winter's day, "Oh, if I was only a angel—if

I only had hold of the palm tree that is waitin' for me."

Says I, "in my opinion it takes more than a palm tree to make a angel of anybody," and says I, "if it is handled right I think good body maple goes a good ways toward makin' a angel."

As I say, I have had these angels in my room, some kinder slimmish ones, some that would go nigh on to 2 hundred, I don't care if they went 3 hundred. I should call 'em angels jest the same.

Then there's them that go to have a good time of it. They get kinder sick of stayin' to home and nothin' happenin' and so they take their work and flock in to visit the afflicted, and stay to dinner and supper. I should think I had pretty near 25 a day of 'em and each one started 25 different subjects. Wild, crazy subjects most of 'em, such as fires, runaway-matches, and whirlwinds; earthquakes, neighborhood fightin' and butter that wouldn't come; great tidalwaves, railroad accidents, balky horses and over-skirts; manslaughter, politix, schism and frizzled hair. I believe it would have drawed more sweat from a able-bodied man to have laid still and heard it than to mow a five-acre lot in dog-days. And then my head was taking on as if it would come off all the time.

If I could have had one thing at a time. I could have stood it better. I shouldn't have minded a earthquake so much, if I could have give my full attention to it, but I would have conflagrations at the same time on my mind, and drunken men and crazy women and jumpin' sheep, and female sufferagin, and calico cut biasin', and the Rushan war and politix. It did seem some of the time as if my head must split open; and I guess the doctor got scairt about me, for one mornin' after he went away, when Josiah came into the room, I see he looked awful sober and gloomy, but the minute he ketched my eye he begun to snicker and laugh. I didn't say nothin' at first, and shet my eyes, but when I opened 'em agin, there he was standin' lookin' down on me with the same mournful and agonized expression onto his features; not a word did he speak, but when he see me lookin' at him, he bust out laughin' agin, and then says I, "What is the matter, Josiah Allen?"

Says he, "I am a bein' cheerful, Samanthe."

Says I, "you are bein' a natural born idiot, and do you stop it."

Says he, "I won't stop it, Samanthe, I will be cheerful." and he giggled.

Says I, "Won't you go out and let me rest a little, Josiah Allen?"

"No," says he firmly, "I will stand by you, and I will be cheerful," and he snickered out the loudest he had yet, but at the same time his countenance was so awfully gloomy and anxious lookin' that it filled me with a strange awe, as he continued: "The doctor told me that you had got to have somethin' to divert your mind, and that we had got to be cheerful before you, and while I have the spirit of a man, I will be cheerful;" and with a despondin' countenance he giggled and snickered.

I knew what a case he was to do his duty, and I groaned out to myself, "there haint no use a tryin' to stop him."

"No," says he, "there haint no use a arguein' with me, I shall do my duty," and with a despairin' countenance he bust out into a awful laugh that almost choked him.

I knew there wouldn't be no rest for me while he stood there performin' like a circus, and so says I, in a stratygim way, as it were,

"It seems as if I could eat a few oysters, if I had 'em Josiah."

Says he, "I will harness up the old mare and start for Jonesville this minute, and try to get some," and he started, but after he got out into the kitchen, and put his hat on, he stuck his head into the door, and with a mournful countenance snickered.

After he fairly sot sail for Jonesville, now thinks I to myself, I will have a good nap while I am alone, and I got settled down, and was jest thinkin' sweetly how slow the old mare was, when I heard voices in the kitchen, and Tirza came in, and says she, "Betsey Babbet is come. I told her I guessed you was goin' to sleep, and she hadn't better come in, but she acted so mad about it that I don't know what to do." Before I could find time to tell her to lock the door, Betsey came in with a bag on her arm about the size of a flour sack, and says she, "Josiah Allen's wife, how do you feel?" and she added sweetly. "You see I have come."

"I feel dreadful bad and feverish this mornin'," says I groanin' in spite of myself, for my head felt the worst it had, every thing looked big and sick to the stomach to me, kinder waverin' and floatin' round like.

"Yes I know jest how you feel," says she, "I have felt jest so, only a great deal worse. Why I have had such a fever, Josiah Allen's wife, that the sweat stood in drops all over me. But as I was sayin','," she continued sweetly, "I have come down to see you. I have come to spend the day with you. We heard you was sick and we thought we would all come and spend the day. We have got relations from a distance visitin' us, and they are all a comin'. Mother is comin' and aunt Nancy and her three children, and Betsey Jane and her baby. There is quite a lot of us, but we don't want you to put yourselves out a bit for us. Aunt Nancy is the greatest case for biled vittles you ever see, with a biled puddin', and I told her if you was well enough to oversee it, you was such a good hand at it that I shouldn't wonder a bit if you had one. We should have had one before now for her, only it scents the house up so we have been puttin' it off. I come a little ahead, for I wanted to get a pattern for a bedquilt, if you have got it. I am goin' to piece up a bedquilt out of little bits of calicoes I have been savin' for years. And I brought the whole bag of calicoes right along, for mother and Betsey Jane said they would help me piece up to day, after I got 'em cut out. You know I may want bedquilts on a sudden, there is no knowin' when I shall be snatched away. Aunt Nancy

would help me, but she is in a dreadful hurry making a rag carpet. She is goin' to bring down a basket full of yellow and orange
rags, to tear up to-day. It haint very good work to carry a visitin',
but I told her you was sick and wouldn't mind it. I guess," she
continued, "I will pour these calicoes all right out on the table,
and then I will look at your bedquilts and patterns," and she poured
out about half a bushel of crazy lookin' pieces of calico on to the
table, no two pieces of a size.

I groaned out in spite of myself, and shet my eyes. She heard
the groan, and see the agony on to my eyebrow, and says she,

"Mebby you need chirkin' up a little. I will read to you a little
before we begin to look at your patterns. I calculated to if you was
low spirited. I come prepared," and takin' a paper out of her pocket,
she says, "I will read to you one of the longest and most noble and
eloquent editorials that has ever come out in the pages of the
Gimlet, written by its noble and eloquent editor, it is concernin'
our relations with Spain.

It was 2 much, 2 much, and I sprung up on my couch and
cried wildly, "Let the editor of the Gimlet and his relations go to
Spain! And do you go to Spain with your relations!" says I, "do
you start this minute!"

Betsey was appauled and turned to flee, and I cried out again,
"Do you take your bedquilt with you!"

She gathered up her calicoes, and fled, and I sunk back and
shed one or 2 briny tears of relief, and then sunk into a sweet and
refreshin' sleep, and from that hour I gained on it. But in the next
week's Gimlet these verses came out.

BLASTED HOPES.
By B. Babbet.

I do not mind my cold rebuffs
To be turned out with bedquilt stuffs;
Filosify would ease my smart
Would say, "Oh peace sad female heart,"
But oh! this is the woe to me
She would not listen unto he.

Although no patterns could I get
Methinks I might be happy yet;
Calm reason could have held my head
As on my homeward path I fled
Did not this thought gnaw into me,
She would not listen unto he.

If it had been my soarin' muse
That she in wild scorn did refuse,
I could like marble statue rise
And face her wrath with tearless eyes,
'Twould not have been such a blow to me
As she would not listen unto he.

Was I cold females of strong mind,
I might in time become resigned;
In sufferin' sink every groan,
Alas! I'm but a clingin' one,
And still these words are hauntin' me,
She would not listen unto he.

Had I on sinkin' wreck been strung,
Or o'er a wild volcano hung,
Could I but hear his words the while,
I'd murmur with a blissful smile,
Ah, fate! sweet fate, thou'rt kind to me,
For I can listen unto he.

GRANDMOTHER'S QUILT
Annie E. S. Beard, *Pictorial War Record*, 1883

Grandmother Barkin's quilt, made from her friends' and neighbors' wedding dress scraps, had been promised to her orphaned granddaughter, Mary. The story of that special quilt's travels during the sad times of the Civil War, before it reached its final destination, is a poignant one.

Grandmother Barkin's cottage was in one of the side streets, in the outskirts of the city. A real, old-fashioned cottage it was even then, and that was more than twenty years ago. It was painted brown, and had a gabled roof and latticed windows, with a large covered porch over the doorway. The inside was divided into several small rooms, all filled with heavy, old-fashioned furniture, of which grandmother was very proud. But the most curious thing in the house, and that which the old lady valued most, was a large quilt made by her own hands, and which was really a marvelous piece of workmanship. It consisted of a heterogeneous collection of pieces of any kind and every kind of material that ever by any possibility went into the composition of a woman's dress.

But the particular feature and crowning glory of the whole, was that every single piece in it was actually a portion of somebody's wedding dress. High and low, rich and poor, alike had contributed to this wonderful quilt, with fragments of silk, satin and velvet, and sections of chintz, brocades, muslin and even calico. The centre piece was of very pale blue silk from grandmother's own wedding dress, and on it was worked in rose-colored silk the words "Love one another." Many an interesting story was connected with those once gayly colored pieces, some of them now fading from age, and time had often passed unheeded as grandmother, with an eager audience gathered around her, told of people and things suggested by the various sections. Of necessity, from the character, it had been many years in process of manufacture, and consequently most of the weddings associated with it dated some scores of years back.

Having no daughter of her own, grandmother had long ago destined this quilt for a marriage gift to the granddaughter that was first married.

Mary Barkin, who, being an orphan, lived with her grandmother, was the only prospective claimant. As there was another married son, however, still living, who might at any time become father to another female Barkin, Mary's prospects of obtaining the quilt, were liable at any day to suffer impairment. A remote contingency, certainly, but then strange things have been known to happen prior to this stage of the world's history. Knowing these facts, Mary's friends were wont sometimes to say, laughingly, "Hurry up, Polly, . . . you will lose the quilt!" Mary Barkin, however, did not seem to avail herself of the friendly suggestion. She was now five-and-twenty, and, although more than one opportunity had offered itself, yet still Mary remained unmarried and grandmother's quilt was still in its maker's possession. The truth was that she was one of those girls who are more particular as to the kind of a man they marry than about getting married. So night and morning Mary wended her way back and forth to the store where she was employed, content that both she and the quilt could wait until the rightness of things and people became manifest.

Nevertheless the monotony of the said walks was greatly relieved when, occasionally, Leonard Wynn walked in the same direction and beguiled the time with pleasant talk. And when, in the fall of 1861, he told her one night that he had enlisted and was going to start immediately for the seat of war, she suddenly realized that life was not as bright as it had seemed. Often during the lonely journeyings of that winter did she recall that last week and the farewell clasp of the hand, and then her cheeks would pale and a dread foreboding fill her heart lest, indeed, he should never come back again.

Amidst all Cleveland's busy workers during war times there was none more earnest and untiring than Mary Barkin. Like many another woman, she worked the harder for all soldiers for the sake of the one she could not aid or help.

The enthusiasm and patriotic spirit of the women of Cleveland reached through all ranks and infused themselves into the hearts of every one, both young and old. Nor was Grandmother Barkin an exception. The only son left to her had gone to fight for his country, and henceforth nothing that she could give was too good for the soldiers. Freely and abundantly did she send supplies from her stores, but the crowning sacrifice was yet to be made. Early one bright winter morning a carriage rolled up to grandmother's door, and from it stepped two eager young ladies. It did not take long to tell their mission. "What can you give us for the new hospital, Mrs. Barkin?" was the question, and to its answer grandmother gave some moments of anxious thought. Then slowly raising from her chair, the old lady left the room, and proceeded to her store closet. Out from the chest which had treasured it so long, she drew the beautiful quilt enveloped in its wrapping of white, and fragrant with the perfume of lavender. Then calling her granddaughter she said: "Mary, they need quilts at the hospital. I have no others ready made. Are you willing to give up this one?" And Mary, to whom it now brought only suggestions of possible sorrow, gave glad assent, feeling that every gift added one more chance of comfort for her absent friend. So grandmother's quilt adorned one of the cots in the hospital and gave warmth and pleasure to many a poor sufferer, while serving a purpose far other than that to which originally destined by its owner.

The weeks passed by and Christmas came at length—came, alas, to an earth not ready for its benison of peace—to a country where good will to men was, even then, buried in the flood tides of the fierce hate and rancor of civil strife. Oh Christmas! merry Christmas! your chimes rang out merrily that year, for, to many an aching heart, they woke memories like funeral bells of vacant places, never to be filled again by the old familiar faces, while the burden of anxiety that lay on other hearts shut out all realization of Christmas merriment. Nevertheless, those who missed the joy-ousness of the season for themselves did their utmost to bring to the soldiers within reach all the pleasure possible.

On Christmas morning Mary Barkin joined a group of ladies who were busily engaged in preparing comforts for the hospital inmates. If it was not within their power to restore limbs that were lost or maimed in the service of their country, or to bring back the glow of health and manly vigor to those wasted by disease, yet they could and did give unexpected pleasure by their bountiful supplies of good things. For a time, at least, the various woes were forgotten, or at most, the sense of them partly obliterated by the comfort and satisfaction of a good dinner. And in seeing the plea-sure they gave, the hearts of the givers were lightened of their own burdens, Mary Barkin even forgot for a time her anxiety as to the fate of Leonard Wynn, in watching the eager looks of the poor fellows, as she passed from cot to cot in the long rooms, distributing oranges and grapes. Then, having emptied her bas-ket, she went to assist in feeding those who were unable to help themselves. Taking a plate of jelly in her hand, she stepped to the side of one of the cots, noticing as she did so that grandmother's quilt—the treasured quilt so willingly given to the service of the country's defenders—lay upon the bed. The sight of it brought a rush of tender memories, filling her eyes with tears so that, for a moment, she did not see the face upon the pillow. Then, with a start, she recognized Leonard Wynn. Was it indeed the same who had left her more than a year ago, strong and well, in all the blooming vigor of young manhood, now stretched upon this bed of pain, with white wan face and large sunken eyes? Yes, there was no doubt about it, for the first words she heard were these:

"Ah, Mary, I have been watching and waiting for you."

"Why did you not call me or send a message for me?" she asked.

"I felt sure you would come some time," he answered; "the sight of this," touching the quilt, "made me feel sure of it."

"It is not often I get here, only sometimes on Sunday to read to the patients and write letters for them."

"Will you come next Sunday?" he asked, wistfully.

"Yes, if you wish it." He was not strong enough to talk much, and, seeing this, Mary insisted on his silence, while she fed him with the jelly she had brought, talking busily herself of all the news she thought he would care to hear. Then, promising to come again on Sunday, she went away. Once more, in the presence of this old friend, she realized that absence had done for her what, in all probability, it had failed to do for him—giving a visionary significance to the friendship of the past, and peopling the future with dreams that had no foundation in fact. For the present, the gladness of seeing him again overpowered the bitterness of this conviction. Rejoicing in the knowledge that war, with all its terrors, had not yet had power to rob her of this friend, she ignored, for the time being, all consciousness of that which might have been—a state of feeling that speedily deserted her, however, when, after a few weeks, he rejoined his regiment.

On her first visit to the hospital after his departure, Mary noticed that her grandmother's quilt had vanished from its accustomed place. Somewhat surprised, she asked one of the nurses one day what had become of it.

"That pretty quilt, ma'am, with the motto on it? That was taken away by one of the boys whose bed it covered during his stay here. He asked the ladies if he might have it, and sent another in place of it. He said it was made by an old friend of his. This is the one he sent, ma'am," and the nurse showed Mary a new quilt covered in scarlet merino, which lay on the bed. And so the Christmas of 1862 had come and gone—come, bringing to Mary Barkin a joyous surprise—a lifting of the burden of anxiety, some happy days spent in the joy of a renewed friendship, given back, as it were from the very jaws of death—gone, taking a hope dearer than life itself, and grandmother's quilt, full of tender memories.

So the days and months and even years sped on, bringing victory and defeat, joy and sorrow, into the hearts and lives of thousands. Once again Christmas dawned upon the earth, and though the wings of the dove of peace were not yet outspread over the land, and mourning hearts were yet more numerous than a year ago, yet the hope of final victory grew stronger day by day. Many hearts and homes were preparing joyful welcome for the boys in blue who were coming home on veteran furlough. The festivities held in their honor were numerous, and during their stay the city kept gala day. Mary Barkin was as busy as ever during those days, first serving on one committee of arrangements and then on another; time flew by and she had small leisure for rest or thought. Personally, she was not interested in the daily arrivals from the seat of war, for Leonard, she knew, did not belong to either of the regiments expected in Cleveland. Tired out, she

stood, at the close of the second day's proceedings, leaning, wea-
rily, against a pile of boxes in the passage-way leading from the
rooms of the Sanitary Commission. It was fast growing dark, and
for a few minutes she closed her eyes to snatch, if possible, a brief
interval of much needed repose. Was she dreaming, or was that
really Leonard Wynn's voice? How long had she been asleep, and
what was this that lay under her head? She was positive nothing
was there when she shut her eyes. The rest she was so enjoying
was so delightful that she was in no hurry to disturb it, but curios-
ity compelled her to raise her head sufficiently to examine her
novel pillow. One glance sufficed to reveal grandmother's quilt.
How did it get there? The thought roused her at once, and she
strove to rise, but before she could fully do so two strong arms
imprisoned her, and looking up into the face bent above her, her
eyes met those of Leonard Wynn.

"I've come for my Christmas gift, Mary," he said, and drawing the quilt towards him with one hand, he pointed to the inscription, 'Love One Another,' in its centre. "I wanted it a year
ago, but decided that I would not ask you to take, in return, a
maimed, sick soldier. I kept the quilt in memory of you. See, I
fixed that it should come back to you if anything happened to
me," and he showed her a label fastened securely to the quilt. "To
be sent to Miss Mary Barkin, Cleveland, Ohio." Then he told her
how, one cold Winter's day it had saved his life. While sitting
close to the fire, by which he and some comrades were trying to
warm themselves and to cook some potatoes, a stray ball, from
the enemy's batteries, came whistling through the air, taking a
straight course toward him. Being chilled through, by protracted
exposure to the inclemency of the weather, he had wrapped
around him in double folds in the old shirt with which he always
kept it covered, grandmother's quilt. The ball struck him, but in
consequence of the thickness of the quilt, got no farther than his

coat. The holes that marked its passage through the quilt remained as tokens of its protective qualities. So grandmother's quilt went back to its original owner, and Mary's right to it as a wedding gift in fair way of being established.

Another year went by and still another Christmas dawned upon a country racked by civil war. It brought no relief to the sick and wounded that filled the hospitals to overflowing.

Once again, amongst the number was found Leonard Wynn. Fighting days were over for him, for, this time, the left arm was gone. Mary, of course, was his constant attendant, and one of her first acts was to fetch grandmother's quilt and lay it over his cot. And whenever he would try to charge Mary to give him up and not sacrifice herself to a one-armed man, she would only point to the old inscription and tell him that as long as that command remained she proposed to obey its dictates as unflinchingly as he had done those of his country, adding, "you forget, Len, that I am proud to be the wife of a man who bears such convincing proof of his loyalty and self sacrifice."

THE CAREER OF A CRAZY QUILT

Dulcie Weir, *Godey's Lady's Book*, July 1884

*Two young, upper-class friends—Heloise Herbert of Roches-
ter, NY, and Marie Antoinette Cates of Albany, NY—decide
to each make a silk crazy quilt. They correspond, telling of
their progress in making their quilts. As they avidly pursue
acquiring the necessary silks for their crazy quilts, they forget
their high upbringing. They wheedle, beg, borrow, and even
cheat commercial establishments to obtain a large variety of
silk pieces. Soon the young women become objects of scorn,
hostility, anger, and derision from their friends and families.
Marie's relentless pursuit of the silk pieces causes a lover's
quarrel with her fiance. In their letters, Marie and Heloise
share their methods of working with the crazy quilts—painting on fabric, embroidering, acquiring signatures, using Kate
Greenaway figures and the "chocolate girl" figure (a design
from a popular advertisement), and using gold threads.*

It all came out of an idea that struck Heloise Herbert one day last
winter.

"You know I should never have ambition enough to begin a
crazy quilt all by myself," she said to her mother. "But if Marie
and I should undertake it together, we might finish it some time;
that is if—"

Mrs. Herbert smiled at the breadth of this unspoken hypoth-
esis, but the arrival of a letter relieved her from the responsibility
of a reply. It was a fat, fashionable-looking letter, written on terra
cotta paper, in the scrawly, scrambling hand which swell young
ladies affect.

My Darling Lois (it began, under a little Greenaway girl, holding a peacock feather,) "I am delighted with your suggestion, and shall begin at once. This very afternoon I am going out to collect samples from the stores. Grandma has given me some lovely bits of old-fashioned brocade, and mamma says there are some scraps of silk up in the attic we can have. Of course I shall divide with you, dear. Don't let us have many large pieces in the quilt; the small ones are so much more effective. Janie Roberts has a sofa cushion made of tiny little bits worked up with spangles and gold thread, and it is quite oriental looking. I will write you what success I have. Excuse this hasty scrawl.

 With love, dearest,

 Yours always,

 Marie Antoinette Craig

             Four, p.m.

I have just returned from my shopping tour, and will enclose you half of the samples I procured. I met Dory down town, and we went to Blank's and had dinner together. When I showed him my silks, and told him what we were going to do, he said: "Good heavens, Marie! you are not going to make one of those abominable things, are you?" (Did you ever hear anything so rude?) "I am going to make a crazy quilt, if that is what you mean," I said, stiffly. "I am sorry for that," he exclaimed. "But I hope you won't make yourself a bore to your friends, Marie, as some girls do. I don't want to see you plaguing men for their old neckties, and all that sort of thing." "I hope I know what is becoming to a lady," I said, with crushing emphasis. "But you won't do that, will you, Marie?" he persisted.

"Promise me you won't. You don't know how the fellows make fun of these girls that go around begging for old silk—'rag-pickers' they call them." I felt myself getting very warm, and I let him have it. "I don't intend to beg," I said, cuttingly. "Most certainly, I shall not ask you for anything; but I shall get all the old neckties I can, and be thankful for them." Then we had it! He wanted me to promise, and of course I wouldn't. The very idea! I declare, the men nowadays think that because they are engaged to a girl they can demand anything they like. Dory was furious and I don't think we'll ever make up again. He's so awfully jealous; I don't believe we could ever be happy together anyhow. Why I really believe, Lois, that he objects because he doesn't like me to have any man's neckties in my quilt except his! Isn't that ridiculous? Still I do wish he would be more reasonable. You know, I always did care more for Dory than for any other man I ever saw, and I can't be happy when we quarrel. Write me soon, dearest; I need your consolation.

Yours disconsolately,

M. Antoinette C.

Heloise answered this letter the following day, when she was down town and stopped in at her father's office to replenish her pocket-book.

"Poor Marie!" she murmured, as she took the desk which the clerk politely offered her, and laid her gloves and muff down alongside of a fat little bundle of silk samples. "I'm glad I'm not engaged, or likely to be. In nine cases out of ten it makes life a burden. Thank you! That pen will do. I don't mind writing on business paper. It makes me feel quite important."

She took up the secretary's stub and poised it over the broad commercial sheet, while the perfume of violets drifted from her gloves and kerchief, and she wrote as follows:

OFFICE OF HERBERT & JOHNSON,
BANKERS AND BROKERS,
00 SOUTH THIRD STREET,
ROCHESTER, N.Y.
Stocks and Gold Bought and Sold on Commission.
Loans Negotiated.

January 6, 1883.

Dearest Marie:—I am awfully sorry about the trouble between you and Dory, but you mustn't let it worry you too
much, for I am sure it will all come out right in the end.
You know how Dory acted up about your driving Charley
Wheeler's dog-cart, and how he came around at last. Of
course it is perfectly absurd of him, my dear; but what
can you expect of a man?

Many thanks for your lovely samples. The storekeep-
ers in Rochester are not so generous as they are in Albany. Some of them are awfully stingy; they only give you
wee little mites of samples, and they cut button-holes in
them, so that they are of no earthly use. I will send you by
this mail a few that I got this morning. You know Emory
Adams is head clerk at Hooper and White's now. Well, I
went to him and told him that I wanted some samples of
light brocade—I find the light colors are scarcer, don't
you? He gave me a lot, lovely pieces, some four inches
square, but would you believe it? They were every one
pasted on bits of cardboard, so that I couldn't use them at
all. Of course I didn't let on, but I was just too mad for
anything! When I asked him what they did that for, he
said that they were obliged to because there were some
ladies—he supposed they called themselves ladies—who
were mean enough to come there for samples when they
didn't want to buy anything at all, but just used the silks

for patchwork; that the firm had been driven to this expe-
dient in self-defense. Isn't that absurd! As though a few
little bits of silk could make any difference! "Of course, I
know, Miss Herbert, that you wouldn't do anything of that
sort," he said smiling, "but the innocent must suffer for
the guilty." Wasn't that horrid of him? I shall never speak
to Emory Adams again.

Have you done anything at your quilt yet? I have made
two patches, that are perfectly lovely. Ned says we will
never finish them, but we know better—don't we, dearest? Ned is such an absurd brother! This morning he came
in with a lot of those nasty little yellow cigar ribbons all in
a tangle, and offered them to me for my crazy quilt. But I
don't intend to mind ridicule or any difficulties. Write
soon and let me know how you are getting along; and tell
me all about Dory. With much love,

Your truest friend,

Heloise Herbert.

P. S., Tom Lee has given me a lovely silk handkerchief
he has only carried a few times. Wasn't it sweet of him?

H. H.

The answer to this came on a finely written correspondence-card
across one corner of which in embossed letters of a queer copper
color was traced in script character the word

Saturday.

"Dear Heloise," it ran. "Can't you come on and spend
a couple of weeks with me while Mamma is in New York?
I shall be horribly lonely, and we can do wonders at our
quilts. Mamma has promised to bring me stacks of samples
from New York. Aunt Annabel is going with her, for which
heaven be praised. It is dreadful to have a rich aunt to
whom you have to be agreeable whether you want to or
not.

"I have just finished doing the little girl sitting on a fence. I did her in crimson etching silk on a bit of cream-colored satin, and she looks lovely. Mamma will bring us some new patterns from New York. I have sent begging letters to my friends out of town, and have had several contributions of silk. One old maid aunt sent me a whole silk dress, all one pattern! She might have kept the ugly thing for dusters. I have been asking every lady who calls on me for a bit of her bonnet strings. Sometimes they give me several inches, and I find the pieces quite useful. No room for more. Good bye. Your own,
    Marie.

Across the card was scribbled this one line:
    Dory has not been near me.

When this missive came, Heloise was sitting in a plush-covered chair, with her toes pertly perched on a shining brass fender.

"I wish I could go," she mused, as she took a few stitches in the cap of the little chocolate girl she was working on grey damassée. "Marie has begun on the opposite side of the pattern. If we were only together we could keep up with each other. But there is no use thinking of it now. What is it, James? Always knock, please. This came this morning, did it? From Hood and Blakeley. Why didn't you tell me? I always want these business communications answered at once."

The letter in question was written in copying ink and ran as follows:

HOOD & BLAKELEY,
Dealers in Fancy and Dry Goods,
                            Rochester, Feb'y 10, 1883.
Dear Madame:—We do not furnish samples of silk except upon the deposit of five dollars as a proof of good faith on the part of the customer. If you desire samples

on these terms, the amount of the deposit will be credited on your purchase.

   We have been forced to this mode of doing business by the heavy expenses incurred in cutting up samples in compliance with the thousands of requests which we receive. Last year we cut up no less than nine thousand ($9,000) dollars worth of silks, and the salaries of sample clerks, etc., ran the annual expense up to twelve thousand ($12,000) dollars, from a large proportion of which we had no return, as in only one case out of ten have we found customers among those who have applied for samples.

   Yours very truly,
   HOOD & BLAKELEY
   per J. V. R.

"Well," exclaimed Heloise, "the very idea! Nine thousand dollars! Pshaw! I don't believe it."

   This is a woman's argument, but always suffices to strengthen her point of vantage, whatever the onslaught. If any misgiving came into Heloise's not really selfish heart, it was forgotten in the diversion created by a fashionable call.

   "Oh, you are making a crazy quilt," exclaimed Mrs. Beacham Beauchamp, a she bent over the bit of growing patch-work. "What a pretty design. Where did you get it? From Godey's, did you say? What lovely things they do have! Where do you get your silks?"

   "Oh, I don't know," Heloise replied. "A good many are given me; then I get samples, of course, and—"

   Mrs. Beauchamp burst into a rippling little falsetto laugh.

   "That reminds me," she exclaimed, pulling up her tan-colored mousquetaire gloves. "Last fall Mrs. Meredith and I—Dora Browne, you know—each made a crazy quilt, and such a time as we had getting our silks. We tried all the usual ways—old neckties, rag-bags, bonnets, and all that—and then we heard of the buyer's samples furnished by the American Silk Mills. We'd bought several lots of those cuttings they advertise, you know—you've seen them; you get so many for a dollar. But the buyer's samples are furnished free to large dry-goods firms, and Dora and I made up our minds to have some, and we got them."

"How did you manage it?" cried Heloise, eagerly.

"You mustn't tell. Well, I'll confide in you, my dear. We just organized a fictitious firm, which we called Orr, Lane & Co. You know I write a masculine hand anyway, and I conducted the correspondence. I wrote for buyer's samples, and they sent them on—lovely shades of fine silk and damassée and brocade, some of them six or eight inches square, and all bound together in a beautiful little book. Of course we had to pay the postage, but that was very little. We wrote five times, and they sent us four books. The fifth time, they made no reply. I suppose they concluded that Orr, Lane & Co. were not very good customers."

Again Mrs. Beacham Beauchamp's laugh rippled gayly through the apartment, and Heloise joined in it. It is a curious fact that when a woman undertakes a bit of crazy patchwork, all natural compunctions seem to sink out of sight and mind completely.

"That is quite an idea," Heloise said laughing; and when she wrote to Marie, telling her why she could not come to Albany just then, she suggested that they should try the same scheme.

"I have gotten to that queer little zigzag piece in the corner," she wrote, "and I do want some kind of gay-figured goods for the next block. If you say so, I will get some one to write for us to the American Silk Mills. I have done the sunflower block in filoselle. Mabel has painted me some pansies, a bit of forget-me-not, and a spray of wild roses, which I shall put in somewhere. You know she paints beautifully. I tried my hand at it, but I mixed the colors in the evening, and having produced a brick-colored cabbage in place of a rose, and a crimson violet, I am not very proud of my achievements. Did you know that there is stamped muslin sold in the stores for a foundation for crazy patchwork? And you can buy lovely little figures to appliqué on in all colors. Janie Roberts is doing me a block with her monogram on it. But I must tell you what that ridiculous brother of mine is doing. He and Fred Townsend are making what they call a crazy quilt, too. The foundation is of coffee-bagging, and the blocks are made of old flannel shirts, stockings, linen collars, striped petticoats, aprons, bandanna handkerchiefs, etc., all cut in their proper form, and stitched on with pink, yellow, and purple wrapping cord. I asked Ned what they were going to do with it, and they said it was to be raffled off for a horse blanket at the firemen's fair."

But Marie was not in a mood to enjoy her friend's letter.

Dear, Darling Heloise, (she wrote in reply,) It seems very hard that you cannot come to me just at this time, when I need you so much! All is over between Dory and me forever. I broke off my engagement with him definitely last night, for I am convinced that we cannot make each other happy. To begin at the beginning: After that quarrel we had at Blank's (I wrote you all about it), he never came near me till last night. Of course, I was not wearing the willow, and had been flying around a good deal with Charley Wheeler. Charley came to call on me last week, and he had on a lovely tie, one of those white Ottoman ones, with gold dots on it. I remarked: "What a lovely patch that would make for my quilt!" Of course, I didn't mean anything, for I never dreamed of his giving me a brand-new tie. "Would you like to have it, Miss Marie?" he said. "Yes, indeed," I answered, for I thought he was just fooling. "I would give it to you," he said, "but I can't go home without a necktie. Wait a moment—give me the scissors!" And before I knew it, Heloise, he had cut off all the portion of the tie that was hidden by his vest. I scolded dreadfully, but it was too late to stop the extravagant fellow, and all I could do was to promise to put the scarf in a prominent place. I worked it in on Saturday, and, more for fun than anything else, I embroidered on it a crimson heart pierced with a golden arrow. Last night Dory called. He came to make up, I knew, and he wanted just to ignore our quarrel entirely, but I wouldn't have it that way. My patchwork was lying on the table when he came in. "Isn't this pretty?" I said, carelessly, holding up the piece I had just finished. He recognized Charley's necktie at once, for there isn't another one in town like it. "Where did you get that?" he asked, quickly. "Charley Wheeler gave it to me," I said, sweetly; "wasn't it good of him? It's the end of his new tie." Dory strode up and down the room for a few moments, and then asked fiercely: "What do you mean by working that upon it?" (tapping the heart and arrow with his finger). "Ah!" I exclaimed. "That's a delicate question." Then he flew into a passion, matters went from bad to worse, we quarrelled and called each other names. I gave him back his ring, and told him I never wanted to see him again. So now we have separated, and I feel very, very, wretched. Dear Heloise, do write a comforting letter! You can do as you please about sending for the buyer's samples. I'm afraid I shan't be in the mood to work on the quilt for some time.

Your disconsolate,
Marie

P.S.—Papa was in a fearful rage this morning because I cut the lining out of his spring overcoat. I didn't know he wanted to wear it any more. I found it on the attic stairs and the sleeves were lined with lovely rose-colored striped satin, which I cut out. When he went for it this morning to take it to the scourer's and have it done up for spring, he found out what I had done, and we had a fearful scene. Oh, dear! I think I am the most unhappy girl alive. I wish I'd never begun this crazy quilt.

M.A.C.

Heloise wrote a prompt note of sympathy on fashionable, ragged-edged paper, but it was ten days ere she replied to Marie's letter in the following terms:

My Dearest Friend:—If your path has been strewn with thorns, mine is not much more inviting. I wrote the letter to the American Silk Mills, and signed it J. S. Osgood & Co. The book was to be sent to our box, but I received no reply till this morning, when James informed me there was a gentleman in the parlor to see me. He gave his name, and I was very much surprised to find an extremely handsome man in an elegant costume, waiting to see me. He looked at me with some surprise, and glanced from my China silk morning gown to the new ormulu cabinet. "Can I be mistaken?" he said, hesitatingly. "Is this Miss Herbert." "Yes," I replied. "Miss Herbert, who represents the firm of J. S. Osgood & Co?" he continued, and the corners of his mouth took a peculiar turn. I felt my face growing scarlet. "I—I—believe —" I stammered, and could say no more. "You wrote to the American Silk Mills for a book of buyer's samples," he went on in the most provokingly cool tones. "Excuse me! My name is Johns, and I am here in the interest of the owners of the American Silk Mills. We are constantly receiving orders for sample books, and, as we supply them at a heavy expense to ourselves, the firm deemed it advisable, at the beginning of the year, to send some one to inquire into the commercial standing of such parties as may —" "There is no such a firm as J. S. Osgood & Co." I blurted out, for I began to get dreadfully frightened. "So I have found out," he answered, quietly. "But are you aware that you have practiced a criminal deception in using such a name to obtain what does not belong to you? If the firm saw fit to prosecute —" "Oh, I didn't mean anything!" I screamed, "it was only for a crazy quilt. I did not think there was any harm in it. You won't—you can't arrest me. My father would never get over the mortification of it. Oh sir! I am very sorry! If money will do anything to—to—" Here I lost all control of myself and burst into tears. Then his whole manner changed toward me. "I was very much surprised to find that a lady in your position," he began—"I did not think you—" "No, I didn't!" I answered quickly. "I didn't mean to do anything wrong." "You have been very foolish," he said, biting his lip, and then he burst out laughing. "Pardon me, Miss Herbert," he said. "But it is too ridiculous! The idea of a young lady's stooping to such devices to get patches for a crazy quilt, when she can perfectly well afford to buy all the silk she wants." "But that isn't the same thing," I protested. "There is a great deal of excitement in collecting them." "I should think so," he said, still laughing. "But what are you going to do about it?" I urged. "Well, I don't know," he said. "Perhaps I can hush the thing up; but you must co-operate with me. I shall be in Rochester some time. You must not deem it an impertinence, if I call upon you." "No, assuredly not," I said; "you are very kind. If you can help me out of this scrape, I shall be forever indebted to you." "You want me to abet a swindle?" he said, smiling; "well, you may count on me." I gave him my hand, and he held it consciously for a moment. "And I will see what I can do for you in the way of samples," he added. "Good-morning." When he had gone, I felt dreadfully, for I seemed to realize for the first time what a mean thing we were doing in trying to cheat the shopkeepers. Besides, if it hadn't been for Mr. Johns' kindness, I might have been publicly disgraced. I feel very grateful to him, but I am ashamed to look him in the face.

Yours with discomfort,
Heloise Herbert.

A demoralized letter from Marie passed this one on the way.

> Dear Lois: (it ran,) I am not going to try for any more
> samples or bits of silk. If what I've got already won't do,
> my quilt can go unfinished. Papa said this morning that I
> was making myself a nuisance to everybody, and, if I didn't
> stop this sort of thing, he'd put my quilt in the fire. This
> sort of thing means, that while mamma and Aunt Annabel
> were in New York, I went up in the attic, and found an
> odd silk sleeve of crimson brocade. It was just what I
> wanted, and, as it didn't seem to belong to anything, I cut
> it up into patches. Then Aunt Annabel comes home and
> raises the roof because I have cut up the sleeve of a dress
> she is making over! How was I to know that the sleeve
> had been carried up to the attic by mistake? I shall never
> hear the last of it. Aunt Annabel was so mad she said she
> was going home. I wish she would go! Mamma says she
> will certainly cut me out of her will; but I'm sure I don't
> care. I haven't done a stitch at my quilt since I wrote last.
>> Hastily yours,
>> Marie Antoinette C.

> P. S. Dory Willis is away on a business trip.

Heloise wrote promptly in answer to this:

> My Dearest Marie: What you want is pleasant change.
> Pack up your things, quilt and all, and pay me a visit. We
> can work together, and it will do you good to talk over
> your troubles. I do not want to give up my quilt, because
> I said so positively I would finish it at all hazards. Mr.
> Johns has been very kind. He sent me three lovely buyer's
> books on his own account, and says he will make the other
> matter all right with the firm. But he has told me so many
> things about the sample trade, that I feel very much like a

swindler. Perhaps it will please you to know that I was properly introduced to Mr. Johns at Mrs. Vandervere's reception the other night. His first name is Archie. I would like you to meet him. Can't you come next week, or week after? Let me know at once.

Yours lovingly,
Heloise.

P. S.—I am away ahead of you with my quilt. I have just put the little boy in on a bit of sulphur satin. I worked him in black. If you come, I will help you with yours, so we can both keep together. H. H.

This was the last letter Heloise wrote about the quilt, for Marie replied that at the end of a fortnight she would visit her friend in Rochester.

It was a fair, sweet day in early spring that Heloise drove down in her phaeton to meet the 5:40 train.

Marie alighted in a pretty pongee traveling suit, richly trimmed with brown velvet.

"Oh, I am so glad to see you," said Heloise effusively, giving her a hearty squeeze. "But how pale and sad you are looking, dearie. You must get some color into your cheeks. This will never do."

"They all tell me I am working too hard over my quilt," she said, with a pathetic little smile, "and I shouldn't wonder if it would be the death of me yet."

"Oh, I guess not," said Heloise, as she drew up the linen lap-robe, and a pleased, conscious look shone in her eyes—a look that Marie did not see. "Go right up stairs, dear," she said, when they reached the Hubert mansion. "That's right, the first room to the left."

"Oh, how lovely it is here," cried Marie, sinking into a cosy chair. "And—why, Lois, is that your quilt?"

"Part of it. Isn't it lovely? Don't dare to say yours is prettier."

"It isn't. The colors are arranged somewhat differently, but the effect is no better. How cute that little dog is. I haven't finished mine yet."

"There! Don't look at it any more, Marie, I want you down stairs. You know we are our own housekeepers. Papa has gone to Syracuse to the Convention, and mamma went with him; they won't be home till day after to-morrow. Here are some roses for you. Put them on, and come down in the library when you are ready."

"How lovely!" cried Marie, as she buried her face in the dewy fragrance. "That was very sweet of you, dear."

Heloise gave her a little twinkling smile and vanished. Marie came down presently, fresh and sweet, with the roses nestling on her bosom. As she raised the portiére, she started back with a low cry.

"Dory!"

"Darling!"

He came towards her swiftly, with out-stretched arms.

"You wear my roses," he said eagerly. "Is that a sign that there is peace between us?"

"Your roses?" she faltered. "I did not know they were yours. But how came you here?"

"My friend, Archie Johns, sent me word you were coming. Marie, I have been wretchedly unhappy; there is a fault somewhere. I am not quite sure who is most to blame, but I am sorry for my side of the quarrel. Will you forgive me?"

Marie could not withstand this. She flung her arms around his neck, and sobbed out upon his breast:

"O, Dory! I have been so unhappy! I just hate that old crazy quilt, and I never want to see it again!"

Then a long silence transpired, a silence broken only by soft whispers and a gentle osculatory sound that disturbed no one. After a while—it may have been moments or it may have been hours—the portiére was swept aside, and Heloise surprised the two lovers in the midst of a fervid embrace.

"Tableau!" she cried, mischievously.

"Reflection!" cried a mellow voice at her elbow, and in the same moment she herself was imprisoned in somebody's arms.

"Archie Johns!" she said, struggling and blushing furiously, "aren't you ashamed?"

"Why, Heloise!" Marie exclaimed in confusion, "I did not know that—that—"

Then everybody laughed in a foolish way, and it was several moments before Heloise had the presence of mind to say:

"Marie, this is my affianced husband, Archie Johns. Archie, this is my dearest friend, Marie Craig, my fellow patch-worker."

This interesting scene was terminated by the ringing of the tea-bell. As Heloise and Marie went out to the dining-room, leaning on their lovers' arms, Ned, who was leaning on the banister, uttered a prolonged "Whew!"

There is little more to tell now. Archie Johns contracted to supply the young ladies with all the silk they might need to finish their patchwork, and the two crazy quilts were done in time for the double wedding that took place last fall.

For sentiment's sake, Marie gave her quilt to Heloise, and Heloise gave hers to Marie. Both quilts were finished with a beautiful rose-colored border, on which were worked the following lines:

"All precious things, discovered late,
To those that seek them, issue forth;
For love in sequel works with fate,
And draws the veil from hidden worth."

AN HONEST SOUL

Mary E. Wilkins, *Harper's New Monthly Magazine*, June to November 1884

Mary Ellen Wilkins (Freeman) was born in Randolph, Massachusetts. She lived most of her life in New England, the setting for the majority of the stories she wrote. She did not marry Dr. Charles Freeman until 1902 when she was 49 years old. As a result, many of of her earlier stories carry her maiden name as the by-line, and later stories are signed with her married name. An 1891 Ladies' Home Journal review of Mary E. Wilkins' stories stated: "They are admirably true to life and seem to pierce the rough exterior of the rustic nature and penetrate to the heart beneath. Almost every variety of character is shown in these pages, and the homely wit and pathos, the strange contrasts and incongruities that belong to the respective personages are portrayed with a firm, yet delicate touch that proves the author's entire sympathy with her subject."

Wilkins' "An Honest Soul" tells of Martha Patch, a poor seamstress who's hired to make quilts for two women. When she believes she has made a mistake in constructing the quilts, her inordinate sense of honesty results in deprivation and illness.

"Thar's Mis' Bliss's pieces in the brown kaliker bag, an' thar's Mis' Bennet's pieces in the bed-tickin' bag," said she, surveying the two bags leaning against her kitchen wall complacently.

"I'll get a dollar for both of them quilts, an' thar'll be two dollars. I've got a dollar an' sixty-three cents on hand now, an' thar's plenty of meal an' merlasses, an' some salt fish an' pertaters in the house. I'll get along middlin' well, I reckon. Thar ain't no call fer me to worry. I'll red up the house a leetle now, an' then I'll begin on Mis' Bliss's pieces."

The house was an infinitesimal affair, containing only two rooms besides the tiny lean-to which served as wood-shed. It stood far enough back from the road for a pretentious mansion, and there was one curious feature about it—not a door or window was there in front, only a blank, unbroken wall. Strangers passing by used to stare wonderingly at it sometimes, but it was explained easily enough. Old Simeon Patch, years ago, when the longing for a home of his own had grown strong in his heart, and he had only a few hundred dollars saved from his hard earnings to invest in one, had wisely done the best he could with what he had.

Not much remained to spend on the house after the spacious lot was paid for, so he resolved to build as much house as he could with his money, and complete it when better days should come.

This tidy edifice was in reality simply the L of a goodly two-story house which had existed only in the fond and faithful fancies of Simeon Patch and his wife. That blank front wall was designed to be joined to the projected main building; so of course there was no need of doors or windows. Simeon Patch came of a hard-working, honest race, whose pride it had been to keep out of debt, and he was a true child of his ancestors. Not a dollar would he spend that was not in his hand; a mortgaged house was his horror. So he paid cash for every blade of grass on his lot of land, and every nail in his bit of a house, and settled down patiently in it until he should grub together enough more to buy a few additional boards and shingles, and pay the money down.

That time never came: he died in the course of a few years, after a lingering illness, and only had enough saved to pay his doctor's bill and funeral expenses, and leave his wife and daughter entirely without debt in their little fragment of a house on the big sorry lot of land.

There they had lived, mother and daughter, earning and saving in various little petty ways, keeping their heads sturdily above-water, and holding the dreaded mortgage resolutely off the house for many years. Then the mother died, and the daughter, Martha Patch, took up the little homely struggle alone. She was over seventy now, a small, slender old woman, as straight as a rail, with sharp black eyes, and a quick toss of her head when she spoke. She did odd housewifely jobs for the neighbors, wove rag carpets, pieced bed-quilts, braided rugs, etc., and contrived to supply all her simple wants.

This evening, after she had finished putting her house to rights, she fell to investigating the contents of the bags which two of the neighbors had brought in the night before, with orders for quilts, much to her delight.

"Mis' Bliss has got proper harnsome pieces," said she — "proper harnsome; they'll make a good-lookin' quilt. Mis' Bennet's is good too, but they ain't quite ekal to Mis' Bliss's. I reckon some of 'em's old."

She began spreading some of the largest, prettiest pieces on her white-scoured table. "Thar," said she, gazing at one admiringly, "that jest takes my eye; them leetle pink roses is pretty, an' no mistake. I reckon that's French caliker. Thar's some big pieces too. Lor, what bag did I take 'em out on! It must hev been Mis' Bliss's. I mustn't git 'em mixed."

She cut out some squares, and sat down by the window in a low wooden rocking-chair to sew. This window did not have a very pleasant outlook. The house was situated so far back from the road that it commanded only a rear view of the adjoining one. It was a great cross to Martha Patch. She was one of those women who like to see everything that is going on outside, and who often have excuse enough in the fact that so little is going on with them.

"It's a great diversion," she used to say, in her snapping way, which was more nervous than ill-natured, bobbing her head violently at the same time—"a very great diversion to see Mr. Peters's cows goin' in an' out of the barn day arter day; an' that's about all I do see—never git a sight of the folks goin' to meeting' nor nothin'."

The lack of a front window was a continual source of grief to her.

"When the minister's prayin' for the widders an' orphans, he'd better make mention of one more," said she, once, "an' that's women without front winders."

She and her mother had planned to save money enough to have one some day, but they had never been able to bring it about. A window commanding a view of the street and the passers-by would have been a great source of comfort to the poor old woman, sitting and sewing as she did day in and day out. As it was, the few objects of interest which did come within her vision she seized upon eagerly, and made much of. There were some children who, on their way from school, could make a shortcut through her yard, and reach home quicker. She watched for them every day, and if they did not appear quite as soon as usual she would grow uneasy, and eye the clock, and mutter to herself, "I wonder where them Mosely children can be?" When they came she watched their progress with sharp attention, and thought them over for an hour afterward. Not a bird which passed her window escaped her notice. This innocent old gossip fed her mind upon their small domestic affairs in lieu of larger ones. To day she often paused between her stitches to gaze absorbedly at a yellow-bird vibrating nervously round the branches of a young tree opposite. It was early spring, and the branches were all of a light green foam.

"That's the same yaller-bird I saw yesterday, I do b'lieve," said she. "I recken he's goin' to build a nest in that ellum."

Lately she had been watching the progress of the grass gradually springing up all over the yard. One spot where it grew much greener than elsewhere her mind dwelt upon curiously.

"I can't make out," she said to a neighbor, "whether that 'ere spot is greener than the rest because the sun shines brightly thar, or because somethin's buried thar."

She toiled steadily on the patchwork quilts. At the end of a fortnight they were nearly completed. She hurried on the last one one forenoon thinking she would carry them both to their owners that afternoon and get her pay. She did not stop for any dinner.

Spreading them out for one last look before rolling them up in bundles she caught her breath hastily.

"What hev I done?" said she. "Massy sakes! I hevn't gone an' put Mis' Bliss's caliker with the leetle pink roses on't in Mis' Bennet's quilt! I hev, jest as sure as preachin'! What shell I do?"

The poor old soul stood staring at the quilts in pitiful dismay. "A hull fortnit's work," she muttered. "What shell I do? Them pink roses is the prettiest caliker in the hull lot. Mis' Bliss will be mad if they air in Mis' Bennet's quilt. She won't say nothin', an' she'll pay me, but she'll feel it inside, and it won't be doin' the squar' thing by her. No; if I'm goin' to airn money I'll airn it."

Martha Patch gave her head a jerk. The spirit which animated her father when he went to housekeeping in a piece of a house without any front window blazed up within her. She made herself a cup of tea, then sat deliberately down by the window to rip the quilts to pieces. It had to be done pretty thoroughly on account of her admiration for the pink calico, and the quantity of it—it figured in nearly every square. "I wish I hed a front winder to set to while I'm doin' on't," said she; but she patiently plied her scissors till dusk, only stopping for a short survey of the Mosely children. After days of steady work, the pieces were put together again, this time the pink rose calico in Mrs. Bliss's quilt. Martha Patch rolled the quilts up with a sigh of relief, and a sense of virtuous triumph.

"I'll sort over the pieces that's left in the bags," said she, "then I'll take 'em over an' git my pay. I'm gittin' pretty short of vittles."

She began pulling the pieces out of the bed-ticking bag, laying them on her lap, and smoothing them out, preparatory to doing them up in a neat tight roll to take home—she was very methodical about everything she did. Suddenly she turned pale, and stared wildly at a tiny scrap of calico which she had just fished out of the bag.

"Massy sakes!" she cried; "it ain't, is it?" She clutched Mrs. Bliss's quilt from the table, and laid the bit of calico beside the pink rose squares.

"It's jest the same thing," she groaned, "an' it came out on Mis' Bennet's bag. Dear me suz! dear me suz!"

She dropped helplessly into her chair by the window, still holding the quilt and tell-tale scrap of calico, and gazed out in a bewildered sort of way. Her poor old eyes looked dim and weak with tears.

"Thar's the Mosely children comin'," she said—"Happy little gals, laughin' n' hollerin', goin' home to their mother to git a good dinner. Me a-settin' here's a lesson they ain't larned in their books yit; hope to goodness they never will; hope they won't ever hev to piece quilts fur a livin', without any front winder to set to. Thar's a dandelion blown out on that green spot. Reckon thar is somethin' buried thar. Lordy massy! hev I go to rip them two quilts to pieces agin an' sew 'em over?"

Finally she resolved to carry a bit of the pink rose calico over to Mrs. Bennet's, and find out, without betraying the dilemma she was in, if it was really hers.

Her poor old knees fairly shook under her when she entered Mrs. Bennet's sitting-room.

"Why, yes, Miss Patch, it's mine," said Mrs. Bennet, in response to her agitated question. "Hattie had a dress like it, don't you remember? There was a lot of new pieces left, and I thought they would work into a quilt nice. But, for pity's sake, Martha, what is the matter? You look just as white as a sheet. You ain't sick, are you?"

"No," said Martha, with a feeble toss of her head, to keep up the deception; "I ain't sick, only kinder all gone with the warm weather. I reckon I'll hev to fix me up some thoroughwort tea. Thoroughwort's a great strengthener."

"I would," said Mrs. Bennet, sympathizingly; "and don't you work too hard on that quilt; I ain't in a bit of a hurry for it. I sha'n't want it before next winter anyway. I only thought I'd like to have it pieced and ready."

"I reckon I can't get it done afore another fortni't," said Martha, trembling.

"I don't care if you don't get it done for the next three months. Don't go yet, Martha; you 'ain't rested a minute, and it's a pretty long walk. Don't you want a bite of something before you go? Have a piece of cake? You look real faint."

"No, thanky," said Martha, and departed in spite of all friendly entreaties to tarry. Mrs. Bennet watched her moving slowly down the road, still holding the little pink calico rag in her brown withered fingers.

"Martha Patch is failing; she ain't near so straight as she was," remarked Mrs. Bennet. "She looks real bent over to-day."

The little wiry springiness was, indeed, gone from her gait as she crept slowly along the sweet country road, and there was a helpless droop in her thin narrow shoulders. It was a beautiful spring day; the fruit trees were all in blossom. There were more orchards than houses on the way, and more blooming trees to pass than people.

Martha looked up at the white branches as she passed under them. "I kin smell the apple-blows," said she, "but somehow the goodness is all gone out on 'em. I'd jest as soon smell cabbage. Oh, dear me suz, kin I ever do them quilts over agin?"

When she got home, however, she rallied a little. There was a nervous force about this old woman which was not easily overcome even by an accumulation of misfortunes. She might bend a good deal, but she was almost sure to spring back again. She took off her hood and shawl, and straightened herself up. "Thar's no use puttin' it off; it's got to be done. I'll hev them quilts right ef it kills me!"

She tied on a purple calico apron and sat down at the window again, with a quilt and the scissors. Out came the pink roses. There she sat through the long afternoon, cutting the stitches which she had so laboriously put in—a little, defiant old figure, its head, with a flat black lace cap on it, bobbing up and down in time with its hands. There were some purple bows on the cap, and they fluttered; quite a little wind blew in at the window.

The eight-day clock on the mantel ticked peacefully. It was a queer old time-piece, which had belonged to her grandmother Patch. A painting of a quaint female with puffed hair and a bunch of roses adorned the front of it under the dial-place. It was flanked on either side by tall green vases.

There was a dull-colored rag carpet of Martha's own manufacture on the floor of the room. Some wooden chairs stood around stiffly; an old yellow map of Massachussetts and a portrait of George Washington hung on the walls. There was not a speck of dust anywhere, nor any disorder. Neatness was one of the chiefest comforts of Martha's life. Putting and keeping things in order was one of the interests which enlivened her dullness and made the world attractive to her.

The poor soul sat at the window, bending over the quilt, till dusk, and she sat there bending over the quilt till dusk many a day after.

It is a hard question to decide whether there was any real merit in such finely strained honesty, or whether it was merely a case of morbid conscientiousness. Perhaps the old woman, inheriting very likely her father's scruples, had had them so intensified by age and childishness that they had become a little off the bias of reason.

Be that as it may, she thought it was the right course for her to make the quilts over, and thinking so, it was all that she could do.

She could never have been satisfied otherwise. It took her a considerable time longer to finish the quilts again, and this time she
began to suffer from other causes than mere fatigue. Her stock of
provisions commenced to run low, and her money was gone. At
last she had nothing but a few potatoes in the house to eat. She
contrived to dig some dandelion greens once or twice; these with
the potatoes were all her diet. There was really no necessity for
such a state of things: she was surrounded by kindly, well-to-do
people, who would have gone without themselves rather than have
let her suffer. But she had always been very reticent about her
needs, and felt great pride about accepting anything which she
did not pay for.

But she struggled along until the quilts were done, and no
one knew. She set the last stitch quite late one evening; then she
spread the quilts out and surveyed them. "Thar they air now, all
right," said she; "the pink roses is in Mis' Bennet's, an' I 'ain't
cheated nobody out on their caliker, an' I've airned my money.
I'll take 'em hum in the mornin', an' then I'll buy somethin' to
eat. I begin to feel a dreadful sinkin' at my stummuck."

She locked up the house carefully—she always felt a great
responsibility when she had people's work on hand—and went to
bed.

Next morning she woke up so faint and dizzy that she hardly
knew herself. She crawled out into the kitchen, and sank down
on the floor. She could not move another step.

"Lor sakes!" she moaned, "I reckon I'm 'bout done to!"

The quilts lay near her on the table; she stared up at them
with feeble complacency. "Ef I'm goin' to die, I'm glad I got them
quilts done right fust. Massy, how sinkin' I do feel! I wish I had a
cup of tea."

There she lay, and the beautiful spring morning wore on.
The sun shone in at the window, and moved nearer and nearer,
till finally she lay in a sunbeam, a poor, shrivelled, little old
woman, whose resolute spirit had nearly been her death, in her
scant night-gown and ruffled cap, a little shawl falling from her

shoulders. She did not feel ill, only absolutely too weak and help-less to move. Her mind was just as active as ever, and her black eyes peered sharply out of her pinched face. She kept making efforts to rise, but she could not stir.

"Lor sakes!" she snapped out at length, "how long hev I got to lay here! I'm mad!"

She saw some dust on the black paint of a chair which stood in the sun, and she eyed that distressfully.

"Jes look at that dust on the runs of that cheer!" she muttered. "What if anybody come in! I wonder if I can't reach it!"

The chair was near her, and she managed to stretch out her limp old hand and rub the dust off the rounds. Then she let it sink down, panting.

"I wonder ef I ain't goin' to die," she gasped. "I wonder ef I'm prepared. I never took nothin' that shouldn't belong to me that I knows on. Oh, dear me suz, I wish somebody would come!"

When her strained ears did catch the sound of footsteps out-side, a sudden resolve sprang up in her heart.

"I won't let on to nobody how I've made them quilts over, an' how I hevn't hed enough to eat—I won't."

When the door was tried she called out feebly, "Who is thar?"

The voice of Mrs. Peters, her next-door neighbor, came back in response: "It's me. What's the matter, Marthy?"

"I'm kinder used up; don' know how you'll git in; I can't git to the door to unlock it to save my life."

"Can't I get in at the window?"

"Mebbe you kin."

Mrs. Peters was a long-limbed, spare woman, and she got in through the window with considerable ease, it being quite low from the ground.

She turned pale when she saw Martha lying on the floor. "Why, Marthy, what is the matter? How long have you been lay-ing there?"

"Ever since I got up. I was kinder dizzy, an' hed a dreadful sinkin' feelin'. It ain't much, I reckon. Ef I could hev a cup of tea it would set me right up. Thar's a spoonful left in the pantry. Ef you jist put a few kindlin's in the stove, Mis' Peters, an' set in the kettle an' make me a cup, I could git up, I know. I've got to go an' kerry them quilts hum to Mis' Bliss an' Mis' Bennet."

"I don't believe but what you've got all tired out over the quilts. You've been working too hard."

"No, I 'ain't, Mis' Peters; it's nothin' but play piecin' quilts. All I mind is not havin' a front winder to set to while I'm doin' on't."

Mrs. Peters was a quiet, sensible woman of few words; she insisted upon carrying Martha into the bedroom and putting her comfortably to bed. It was easily done, she was muscular, and the old woman a very light weight. Then she went into the pantry. She was beginning to suspect the state of affairs, and her suspicions were strengthened when she saw the bare shelves. She started the fire, put on the tea-kettle, and then slipped across the yard to her own house for further re-enforcements.

Pretty soon Martha was drinking her cup of tea and eating her toast and a dropped egg. She had taken the food with some reluctance, half starved as she was. Finally she gave in — the sight of it was too much for her. "Well, I will borry it, Mis' Peters," said she; "an' I'll pay you jest as soon as I kin git up."

After she had eaten she felt stronger. Mrs. Peters had hard work to keep her quiet till afternoon; then she would get up and carry the quilts home. The two ladies were profuse in praises. Martha, proud and smiling. Mrs. Bennet noticed the pink roses at once. "How pretty that calico did work in," she remarked.

"Yes," assented Martha, between an inclination to chuckle and to cry.

"Ef I ain't thankful I did them quilts over," thought she, creeping slowly homeward, her hard-earned two dollars knotted into a corner of her handkerchief for security.

About sunset, Mrs. Peters came in again. "Marthy," she said, after a while, "Sam says he's out of work just now, and he'll cut through a front window for you. He's got some old sash and glass that's been laying round in the barn ever since I can remember.

It'll be a real charity for you to take it off his hands, and he'll like to do it. Sam's as uneasy as a fish out of water when he hasn't got any work."

Martha eyed her suspiciously. "Thanky; but I don't want nothin' done that I can't pay for," said she, with a stiff toss of her head.

"It would be pay enough just letting Sam do it, Marthy; but, if you really feel set about it, I've got some sheets that need turning. You can do them some time this summer, and that will pay us for all it's worth."

The black eyes looked at her sharply. "Air you sure?"

"Yes; it's fully as much as it's worth," said Mrs. Peters. "I'm most afraid it's more. There's four sheets, and putting in a window is nothing more than putting in a patch—the old stuff ain't worth anything."

When Martha fully realized that she was going to have a front window, and that her pride might suffer it to be given to her and yet receive no insult, she was as delighted as a child.

"Lor sakes!" said she, "jest to think that I shall have a front winder to set to! I wish mother could ha' lived to see it. Mebbe you kinder wonder at it, Mis' Peters—you've allers hed front winders; but you haven't any idea what a great thing it seems to me. It kinder makes me feel younger. Thar's the Mosely children; they're 'bout all I've ever seen pass this winder, Mis' Peters. Jest see that green spot out thar; it's been greener than the rest of the yard all the spring, an' now thar's lots of dandelions blowed out on it, an' some clover. I b'lieve the sun shines more on it, somehow. Lor me, to think I'm going to hev a front winder!"

"Sarah was in this afternoon," said Mrs. Peters, further (Sarah was her married daughter), "and she says she wants some braided rugs right away. She'll send the rags over by Willie to-morrow."

"You don't say so! Well I'll be glad to do it, an' thar's one thing 'bout it, Mis' Peters—mebbe you'll think it queer for me to say so, but I'm kinder thankful it's rugs she wants. I'm kinder sick of bed-quilts somehow."

A STORY OF A CRAZY QUILT

L. E. Chittenden, *Peterson's Magazine*, December 1885

Sally Fairview, the village's popular and flirtatious beauty, almost loses her true love, Ted Arfield, while making a crazy quilt.

It is sweeping-day at the Fairviews', and everything is in a 'whew!' as the old Squire says, who has prudently betaken himself downtown.

All the feminine portion of the family is busy: for Mother Fairview holds good old fashioned ideas on this point; therefore it is that her lovely daughter, Sallie, belle of all the surrounding counties, is at this moment perched high on a step-ladder, dusting the books that line the walls of the library.

This is a library where solid comfort reigns supreme; abounding, as it does, in easy-chairs, books, birds, brightness, and flowers; while an upright piano is in the bay-window, all strewn with music. Sallie works on—regardless, apparently, of everything excepting her homely task.

By and by, she hears a quick step coming up the walk, and she blushes a little; but that is all gone, and she is working away with superhuman industry, when a good-looking young fellow appears at the open window. He glances in with an expression of deep-seated anxiety upon his open countenance, which rapidly changes to satisfaction as he sees this goddess on her Olympus.

"Run right away, Ted; I'm busy," is the welcome he gets.

"That is what may truly be called a hospitable greeting," is the reply, in a deeply-injured voice. "Here I have been scouring the place for hours, hoping to catch a glimpse of you. And now, when success has at last crowned my efforts, you bid me run away. I'll do anything for you but that, Sallie. I'm here for an object, and here I shall stay; for a time, anyway."

"Well, Ted," laughs Sallie, "you have been scouring the place outside, while I have been doing the same thing inside. Gaze upon the result of my labors, in the spotless room before you, sir."

"Yes," rejoins the youth, somewhat gloomily, resting his arms on the broad window-seat, "it's lovely."

All this time, he never looks away from the pretty face above him, framed in the blue dusting-cap. Sallie dusts away with renewed vigor, and makes no reply.

"Come, Sallie, cher Sallie, let those dry-as-dust things alone. No one will be the wiser, whether they are clean or not. Come out under Old Comfort with me, and let us listen to the robins' concert. Ah! how can you stay indoors, such a perfect day? Come, Sallie."

"No, no, Ted: business before pleasure," answers Sallie, not knowing what she does say, for the youth's voice is more dangerous than his words.

"Surely the dust is in your brain, dear, if you can think of nothing more original than that. Have you forgotten," lowering his voice, "that this is our last day—that tomorrow we are gone?"

Forgotten? Not she! But she answers lightly enough: "Ah, well, you will come again."

"I don't know," replies Ted, significantly. "But aren't you coming?"

"No, Ted, I can't, at least, not now. But, this afternoon, I will bring my sewing down to Old Comfort, and you may come and read Browning to me."

So Ted is obliged to content himself with this, and walks off.

Some months before, a surveying-corps, sent out by an English company, had encamped near the Fairviews'. Very soon, every member of it—like all the other young men about—had fallen tremendously in love with pretty Sallie Fairview. But this astute young lady kept them well in hand, and enjoyed their homage very much; and danced, rode, walked, laughed—and I fear, flirted—with them all, with her whole heart.

But presently Ted Arfield joined the corps. His father was one of the English company, and the son fresh from the University of Oxford. Pining "for a lark," as his college-chums put it, he had at last obtained his father's consent to come out and join the surveyors, "to see America," as he said. It proved rather dull for Ted, though, after the novelty had worn off: very different, indeed, from London in the season, or even Oxford. But, one day, standing indolently near the camp, and meditating a push still further west, with a hunting-party, Miss Fairvew rode by, mounted on her pretty black pony. She was accompanied by young Hazleton, of the corps—a tall handsome fellow—on a tall horse, and his head held up taller still, as if in a very heaven of delight.

Sallie never looked better than mounted, and Arfield thought he had never looked upon so fair a sight. He felt a sudden accession of interest in his surroundings, and mentally postponed, for awhile, the journey "further west."

"What a lovely creature!" he cried.

"Yes; Miss Fairview is the prettiest girl within a hundred miles," answered a companion, who stood by.

"Fairview? Fairview?" said Ted, and suddenly bethought himself of certain letters of introduction in his possession, one of which he was certain was addressed to Squire Fairview.

"The very man," said his friend, on being told this.

So, later on, Ted presented himself to the hospitable Squire, who received him with great cordiality, and proved to have been a university man himself—a graduate of Harvard—and only too glad to find somebody to talk to about such things. Thus, Ted found himself adopted at once into the Squire's delightful home, Sallie treating him as a kind of brother-cousin; if you know what that is. I don't; but it was evidently highly satisfactory to Ted, who thereupon assumed great airs, and gave loads of brotherly advice to Miss Sallie. She, in response, looked so innocent and appealing, and called him "Ted" in such a musical voice, that he quite fell in love with that hitherto obnoxious monosyllable.

As this blissful state of affairs became apparent to the members of the corps, they unanimously conceived a violent hatred for lucky Ted, and took great satisfaction, as happens in all such cases, in calling him "a puppy."

But alas! poor Ted didn't remain in the safe condition of brother-cousin very long: for he straightway fell fathoms deeper in love than he had ever dreamed possible, and was correspondingly miserable, with the hot and cold symptoms we all know so well.

And now the time had come for the camp to break up: and Ted must either cut this throat, or know his fate. At times, at the lowest ebb of his feelings, he rather inclined toward the former mode of procedure: for he was sure he would cut it, if Sallie refused him, and he rather preferred dying with his fate unknown.

But, of course, this sensible course was out of the question. Everybody would laugh at him, if he did it. So, walking off, this morning, he resolves to put it to the test, in the afternoon, down under Old Comfort's branches, where he was pretty sure to find Sallie.

Old Comfort was an old gnarled apple-tree at the bottom of the garden, whose low-hung branches formed a natural arbor. Seats were arranged under its shade.

Hither comes Ted, this afternoon, where he is presently joined by Sallie, with her sewing, and looking like a live apple-blossom, in her pink foulard dress, with a ridiculously small bag, made of the same material, pendant from her arm, and supposed to contain a handkerchief. Her sewing consisted of various bits of silk, satin, etc., etc., in a basket of considerable size, which she also carried with her: the pieces being intended to make a "crazy-quilt."

She has already planned that it will be best, for both, to keep very busy: on the principle of "Satan finds some mischief still, for idle hands to do," I suppose.

The day was perfect. Old Comfort was in her holiday-attire of apple-blossoms. A robin was going to housekeeping, in the branches overhead, and was much divided between his labors and watching the idyl below. The blossoms fell like rain on Sallie's fair head, and Ted is stricken dumb. If he dies for — or of — it, he knows he can never tell his love by word of mouth.

The hours fly by; and, when Sallie finally goes to the house, on some errand, Ted writes, on a memorandum-leaf:

"I love you, my darling, so much, I cannot tell it; but, if you will come down, tomorrow morning, to Old Comfort, where I will await you, when I see you coming, I shall know, whatever befalls me after that, I can never be unhappy again, for you will be mine. Ted."

Now, if this had only been slipped into Sallie's hand, as they say good-night, or even into the basket where lay the scraps for her "crazy-quilt," all might have been so different. But Ted, seeing the bag on the chair, where Sallie had left it, slips the note in there: and there it lies, one year.

The next morning, Ted, standing beneath Old Comfort's branches—and surely there never was such a misnomer now—eats his heart up with jealous rage, as he sees young Hazleton drive off with Sallie.

"A fool, every inch of him," mutters Ted, savagely, forgetting it is no evidence of his folly to wish to spend his last hours with Sallie's bright face laughing up into his.

Ted left the camp, and Sallie heard no more of him than that he had gone back to England; and what she thought, down under Comfort's branches, no one knew but the robin, and he kept his own counsel.

But now the spring is back again, and Sallie and her dear friend, Dorothy, are out under the apple-tree; Dorothy doing nothing with consummate grace, and Sallie working on her "crazy-quilt." Somehow, this work had been laid aside for almost a year: we suspect, if Sallie would have admitted it, that it was because of its associations with Ted; she had been working on it, that last day, and for months she could not look at it without a pang at her heart. But at last she had resumed it, and now it was growing, under her nimble fingers, like unto a veritable Joseph's-coat. In thus putting apparently exactly the wrong pieces together, highly startling effects are produced; and she and her friend agree that it is "quite too lovely."

"I adore this work," says Sallie, "because it sets all rules at defiance. I do so detest anything with a pattern to be followed, and where you have to count."

"Yes," assents Dorothy, lazily, and peering up into the green shadows over her head. "Still, doing nothing is better still. This is the most romantic place. How I love the spring, with its newness! Don't you, cherie?"

"I don't know. I think it makes me rather sad," says Sallie, softly: for she is thinking of the spring a year ago; but before her friend can say "Why?" she holds up a yellow crescent, on a ground, and asks: "What do you think of that?"

"That's perfect," answers Dorothy, promptly. "But when will you have your fair?"

"As soon as the 'crazy-quilt' is finished." But for this fair, the "crazy-quilt" would never have been taken up again, perhaps. "That is our 'piece de resistance,' you know. Now, let's see. I want a bit of pink right here, and I haven't a scrap. What shall I do?"

Suddenly, while Sallie is looking over her pieces, puzzled, the robin feels his time has come to speak. So, seating himself on the bough over her head, he bursts into such a flood of melody, that the girls stop talking to listen; and this is what he seems to sing—at least, to Sallie's heart:

"Your little pink bag: get it, get it."

Sallie jumps up, eagerly.

"Oh, I know" she cries; "I believe I'll cut up my little bag like my foulard dress: it is such a small thing, it is of no earthly use. I haven't seen it for nearly a year." For it, too, was associated with Ted, and had been put out of sight, as too painful to wear.

And, before Dorothy can say "Why?" again, Sallie is half-way up to the house. Dorothy has ample time to examine the robin's housekeeping in detail: for Sallie is gone a long time: and finally, when she comes back, looks as though she had been crying.

But her friend is too discreet, or too lazy, to ask any questions, and presently takes her leave.

Now, I never knew, and never expect to know, why Ted Arfield, a year from the time when he had stood there before, found himself, later that afternoon, under Old Comfort's branches, which received him with a shower of apple-blossoms and open arms. The robin opened his throat in such a rapturous song of welcome, that Sallie wandered down there again, to find out the cause of his—happiness; and she found out: in fact, walked right into the arms of it!

The "crazy-quilt" was purchased at a most extravagant price, by Mr. Arfield, who declared there was method in its madness; for that it had brought him untold happiness. But I think the robin had quite as much to do with it. Don't you?

A NEW ENGLAND VILLAGE QUILTING PARTY IN THE OLDEN TIMES

Elias Nason, A.M., *Granite Monthly*, 1885

A vivid account of a New England village quilting party, circa 1815, describes in detail the house where the quilting was held, the apparel of the women quilters, the table setting, and the foods served for supper. The most incisive treatment is accorded to the gossiping quilters who direct their heartless deceit toward the minister, the Rev. John Baxter. Surprisingly, the story contains scant information about the calico quilt in the frame.

It was in one of those old yellow houses on Meeting House Hill just seventy years ago; and in those days a quilting party was a "great sensation" in the household. For it, the floors were scoured and sanded, and things in general brought into perfect order. Pies, cakes, preserves, and Hyson tea, with large lumps of loaf sugar, were provided liberally for the occasion. The women of the village, married and unmarried, the Rev. John Baxter, minister of the village, and Mr. Hezekiah McAdams were betimes invited. The largest room in the house was cleared of all furniture, except the flag-bottomed chairs, the old eight-day clock with the half moon upon its face, and the antique looking-glass, which had reflected faithfully the beauties and deformities of at least five generations. A calico patchwork, or sort of "crazy quilt," was extended over cotton batting on a frame of deal, and everything got in readiness for the nimble fingers of the quilters.

But hark, the knocker!

"Well," exclaims Mrs. Benson, the good-looking lady of the house, "how glad I am to see you, Molly Mansfield; why didn't your sister Katy come?"

"She sprained her ankle on her way home from meeting yesterday. What! am I the first one here?" cries Molly with surprise, on entering the quilting room.

"Yes, you are," says Mrs. Benson, "but the rest will soon be in; take off your things and make yourself at home." She does so.

But hark, again the knocker!

"Well, sure enough," exclaims Mrs. Benson, cordially, "how do you all do; Miss Hannah Blair, and my dear Angeline, and if here isn't Aunt Tabitha Pinchbeck! Walk right in; I knew you would be here; so early, too; take off your calashes."

They do so; they arrange their dresses at the aforesaid looking-glass, and then seat themselves in the flag-bottomed chairs, prepared with scissors, thimbles, thread, and needles for the work before them.

But once more the knocker strikes; the door flies open, and Mrs. Benson warmly says to those now entering: "Oh, how glad I am to see you, Mrs. Rackett and Mrs. Rugby; how well you're looking; how good in you to come!"

So group after group, in calico or gingham dresses, with hair done up pyramidally on the apex of the head and fastened with a long glistening horn or tortoise-shell comb, come posting in until the room is full. The old eight-day clock strikes two, and with tongues running fluently, they take their seats around the quilting frame and commence operations on the party-colored patchwork.

The conversation, as well might be supposed—for the public library, lyceum, railroad, telegraph and telephone had not then appeared—was not very aesthetical, literary, scientific, or instructive. The women of that period, in the rural village I am speaking of, had but little time to read, or to think of much, except domestic and church affairs, together with the faults and foibles of their friends and neighbors. Housework was the order of the day, and hence the improvement of the mind was almost of necessity neglected. Hence, too, the general tendency (for the less one knows, the more one loves to keep the tongue in motion), to indulge in idle talk and gossiping. So, as the busy needles pierce the quilt, the busy tongues, sharp as the needles, pierce the characters of the absent.

"Do you really think," say Tabitha Pinchbeck in a low undertone to Hannah Blair, "that our minister ever had that queer dream he told, about our singers and the angels?"

"No, never," replies Miss Blair in a whisper, "never! He's a droll sort of a minister, isn't he, Tabitha? I wish we had a younger man, don't you?"

"To be sure I do," returns Miss Pinchbeck, a venerable spinster with a Vandyke handkerchief and a pair of silver-bowed spectacles; "but how shall we get rid of him? He's settled for life, you know."

"But he says," interposes Molly Mansfield, who, on stopping to thread her needle, overhears the conversation, "his people will be glad enough when he's dead and gone, and I'm sure I shall."

"O, you wretch," exclaims Mrs. Rackett whose grey curls peer profusely from beneath her white muslin cap; "you wish him dead and gone, do you? What if he should hear of that, Molly? But that old beaver hat he wears is shocking, isn't it?"

"Shocking!" responded Hannah Blair, "and in that old, faded camlet cloak he looks like a scarecrow."

"What long and tedious prayers he makes!" says Mrs. Rackett.

"He never calls on anybody," adds Molly Mansfield, "and how dull his sermons are; my father says they are always personal, and that he never writes a new one."

"His hands are blistered digging his potatoes; how can he write a new one?" sarcastically chimes in Mrs. Rackett.

"I never listen to them," interposes in a high-keyed voice Aunt Tabitha Pinchbeck.

"How proud he is of his new chaise," says Mrs. Rugby, stopping to play a moment with the string of golden beads around her neck; "I wonder if I shall ever get a ride in it?"

"He said the other day," interjects Molly Mansfield, "the town had treated him worse than they did the pirate down at the castle in Boston Harbor."

"Well, he deserves it," cry out several sharp voices.

"But he is kind to the poor," modestly observes Miss Angeline Hartwell, a young lady in deep mourning, whose widowed mother had not been forgotten in the distribution of the charities of Mr. Baxter.

"What if he is?" pertly replies Miss Pinchbeck, whose father had wrung his money from the sinews of the poor; "he does it all for show; he's as tight as the bark of a tree, and his wife is tighter still."

"Yes, girls," flings in Mrs. Rubgy, shyly, "and they say he's sometimes tight another way!"

"He's a Whig too," says Mrs. Rackett, "and my husband hates him for that."

"I don't like him," cries Tabitha Pinchbeck, "for his ugly face."

"I don't like him," responds Molly Mansfield, "for his whining voice."

"I don't like him," adds Hannah Blair, "for his awkward gait."

"I don't like him," echoes Mrs. Rubgy, "for his hypocrisy."

"I don't like him," blurts out Mrs. Rackett, spitefully, "for his intermeddling with our dancing."

"So," cries Molly Mansfield, half in jest and half in earnest, "You all agree with me in wishing he were dead?"

"Yes, Molly," Hannah Blair responds, "so say we all."

"Not I, not I," objects Miss Angeline Hartwell, "we never shall find a better man."

"We never shall find," replies Miss Blair, "a worse one."

"Nor one," asserts Mrs. Rackett, taking a pinch of Macaboy snuff, "more obstinate."

"Nor one," interposes Mrs. Rubgy, "more dull and prosy."

"Nor one," ejaculates Aunt Tabitha, "more old-fashioned."

"Nor one," rejoins Miss Molly Mansfield, "more destitute of everything that makes a minister, and we wish, we wish—"

But hush; the knocker! Who comes now? It is the minister himself. It is the Rev. John Baxter in his faded camlet cloak and shocking beaver hat;—a man of sixty years, at least, of reverent, but genial face, who for more than thirty years had labored with his hand, as well as brain in this little village to keep himself and family alive on his scanty salary of $300 a year, and who had grown gray in his endeavors to upraise the minds and morals of his people.

"The minister has come," says Mrs. Benson in an audible whisper to the quilters; "the minister."

How still the tongues! How busily the fingers fly! Consciences are whispering, cheeks are reddening.

With a smiling countenance, Mr. Baxter enters the quilting room and gives the kindly salutation:

"Good afternoon, ladies, I am very glad to see you all so busily engaged in quilting here for our good friend Mrs. Benson. He passes around the frame and cordially shakes hands with every one of them and they all in turn exclaim: "We are so happy, sir (has anything such mobility as the invisible spirit?) to see you here; we feared lest something might detain you; we hope you left your family all well and that you will stay to tea with us."

"I will," says he, "with all my heart; but let me not hinder you in your quilting, ladies, nor interrupt your profitable conversation."

Here, blushes tinged some cheeks again and eyes were fixed intent upon the needle work.

Turning now to Miss Molly Mansfield, Mr. Baxter says approvingly: "I was pleased to see your self and father and mother at Church last Sabbath."

"We were glad to be there, sir," replies Miss Molly, brushing away her raven ringlets, "for you had, as you always do, an excellent sermon; my father enjoyed it very much, and so did my mother and I."

"I'm glad you think so, Molly," replies the minister, "the subject was, you well remember, Evil Speaking, from the text; 'The tongue is a fire, a world of iniquity,' and so indeed it is, when unrestrained."

"I think so, too," Miss Mansfield tremulously responds, "and I shall try to govern mine."

Mr. Baxter little dreams how close the arrow cuts; but as Sir Walter Scott has said:

"Many a shaft, at random sent,

Finds mark the archer never meant."

Turning now to Mrs. Rackett, the minister kindly enquires: "How, madam, is your husband to-day? Has he tried my wife's receipt for his rheumatism? Have the children recovered from the measles so as to attend school again?"

"They are getting better," she replies in a winsome tone, "and we all hope to be out at Church again next Sunday; we do all so miss your good sermons, Mr. Baxter, and the children are all so much interested in your fervent prayers for them. They are short and to the point. The children love you dearly, as we all do. How kind in you to enquire for them. Do come and see us; we hope you will always be our minister."

"A pastor," replies Mr. Baxter, "loves to have the good will of the lambs of his flock and to know that their parents set them good examples. I will come and see you soon. I have got a new chaise, the second one in town, and I hope now to visit my parishioners more frequently."

Then, again addressing Molly Mansfield, he kindly says: "I regret to learn that your sister Catherine has met with an accident. Here is a book by my namesake, Richard Baxter, which I have brought for her to read. I will call to see her to-morrow morning."

"And how," says he to Mrs. Rugby, "is your invalid son, Caleb? I intend that you and he, if able, shall have the first ride in my new chaise, and then to let any of my neighbors who may wish to do so, try it."

"You are, Sir, and always have been, so very kind to us; no people ever had so good a minister; we do so very much enjoy your preaching and your company. My son Caleb will be delighted to have a ride in your new chaise."

Without looking fairly at Mr. Baxter in the face, Misses Blair and Pinchbeck respond respectively to his questions, express themselves as being fortunate in having such an accomplished minister, and the latter even goes so far as to suggest that he have a donation party, especially to help to pay for his new chaise.

O, what a change the minister's face can sometimes make! Is this the group that just now wished him dead and gone?

This party was exceptional, to be sure; or I should not as an honest chronicler report its doings. It had fallen step by step into the habit of evil speaking, and when the bridle leaves the tongue the wild fire comes; the village was exceptional, and much it suffered from that wild fire.

Mr. Baxter turns the tenor of the conversation to subjects of importance, suggests improvements in the village, and encourages the mothers to bestow upon their children a good education; and then particularly invites Aunt Tabitha to go with him to visit a family near her father's house at that time struggling hard for daily bread.

But the time for supper has arrived. A line of deal tables has been arranged in the ample sitting-room, and covered with linen cloth of spotless white; it is furnished with blue-edged plates and platters, small china cups and saucers—heirlooms in the Benson family—silver tea spoons, marked with the letter B, horn-handled knives and double-tined steel forks. The board is lighted with tallow candles set into brazen candlesticks, and is liberally supplied with toasted bread, soft cakes, doughnuts, crackers, comfits, pumpkin, minced and apple pies, cup custards, cider-apple sauce, white lump sugar and butter and cheese of excellent quality.

The ladies leave the patchwork quilt completed, and surround the table, when the Rev. Mr. Baxter, standing at the head of it, invokes a blessing on the food and company.

Mr. Hezekiah McAdams, who has just come in, is seated next to Miss Molly Mansfield, and assists her and the others near him to the viands on the table. There are no napkins, and the knife instead of the fork is used in eating. The tea is taken from the china saucers. A glass of currant wine stands between the minister's and the teacher's plates, and all the tongues are glibly running.

At length, Aunt Tabitha turns her teacup over, carefully

inspects the order or disorder of the tea grounds, and then cries out:

"Who will have her fortune told?"

"I, I, I," they all vociferate; for at that period the belief was common that some mysterious link exists between the settlings in a teacup and the coming events of life. Miss Mansfield presents her cup and says:

"Now, Tabitha, be sure and tell me true!"

The prophetess, adjusting her silver-bowed spectacles and examining every particle of the black sediment, exclaims, while every tongue, except her own, is silent and every ear intent, "You, Miss Molly Mansfield, as your cup most clearly indicates, are to become a member of Mr. Baxter's Church, and one of his most earnest workers. From these grounds, also, I perceive that you are not to change your name and state and residence. I see moreover, in the distance, this crooked line of dots declares it, a smart young gentleman approaching thoughtfully. In one hand he holds a ferrule, and a spelling-book in the other. Why do you blush so, Molly? He surely comes; the children do him reverence, and you do him still more. Keep still, Molly, till I see the meaning of this other little line. O, now I have it, I can just perceive you, and I know it's you, in a white muslin dress walking arm in arm with this young gentleman towards the parsonage. I see you plainly going through a certain ceremony. I see you then ascend the Meeting House Hill together and enter a large white house; and from this cluster of grounds above the rest, I see you take the ferrule from his hand to govern him, and the spelling-book to teach the children."

"And whom," enquires McAdams, in his confusion, "does that man look like?"

"Like you, yourself," responds Aunt Tabitha.

A roar of laughter follows, and the minister laughs the loudest; for like Dr. Franklin, he believes in early marriages. The tea is finished, the party breaks up in the best of spirits, Mr. Hezekiah McAdams ventures home with Molly Mansfield; they are in due season published by the Town Clerk viva voce in the church, and married by the minister as the prophetess had predicted. For once, her tea grounds told the truth, for it was "a fixed fact" before, and with all such matters this village fortune-teller took much pains to acquaint herself.

Mr. Baxter remained a while at Mrs. Benson's after the quilters had departed, when she, good woman, wisely or unwisely, I shall not pretend to say, acquainted him with the remarks the party had made concerning him. How he took the information is not stated; but he shortly afterwards preached his memorable sermon on "Total Depravity," which almost every one of his hearers applied to his next-door neighbor instead of to himself. But I am very glad to say a few did not. Mr. Hezekiah McAdams became a noted writer of school text-books; Mrs. Rugby sent her son Caleb to college, and he attained distinction as a lawyer; Miss Pinchbeck grew more charitable as she advanced in life, and left a legacy to the Church; Mrs. Rackett learned to control her tongue and temper; Miss Hannah Blair became the daughter-in-law of Mrs. Benson.

RUTH'S CRAZY QUILT

Sydney Dayre, *Harper's Young People*, June 15, 1886

> *Ruth, who dearly loves her hard working mother, plans to become a school teacher. She will then earn money and can help her mother with the finances of the household. An accident renders Ruth an invalid unable to walk. She begins to while away time by sewing. Utilizing her considerable skills at embroidery, Ruth makes a gorgeous silk crazy quilt containing her original embroidery designs. This unique crazy quilt causes everlasting changes in Ruth's life.*

"I've passed! I've passed! Only one more year of study, and then—no more hard work for poor old mother!" Ruth flung down her books, and threw her arms around her mother's neck. "Mr. Blake has promised me a school next year with good pay. Sit down, mother; you sha'n't do another thing to-night. I'll get tea. Here, Cricket—won't Cricket have plenty of new shoes when sister's making plenty of money?" And the lively girl lifted the little one to her shoulder, and seizing a pail, danced out to the spring, singing,

"Ride a fine horse to Banbury Cross."

She was the very picture of girlish health and happiness. Happiness in spite of her life of struggle, for those who know can tell that few things in life bring more joy than the overcoming of difficulties through the strength of the blessings of a loving heart and fresh young courage and energy, all borne up by bounding health. For years Ruth had shared as far as possible all her mother's cares, always looking forward to the time when she could bring her own earnings for the general help, little dreaming how far the every-day help given by her sunny sweetness of temper and her bright hopefulness went in lightening the load.

"I'll frow oo in," said the merry youngster, as she set him down beside the spring. "Zen oo be a bid fis." He gave her a little push, but she just then stooped to the water, and he lost his balance. With a little scream he seized her arm as she quickly turned to catch hold of him, and Ruth never could tell how it came about, but the sudden weight, coming in a manner for which she was not prepared, caused her to miss her footing. With a desperate effort she managed to swing the child back upon the grass, but in doing so she fell heavily upon the edges of the stones which bordered the spring.

"No, mother, I'm not much hurt; don't be frightened," as her mother ran out at sound of Cricket's cries. But her face was white, and she could not stand up, much less walk. She was obliged to wait until some of the nearest neighbors came and carried her in.

"I'll just lie down for an hour or two," she said, trying to laugh and to hide the pain she was suffering. But hours passed into days and days into weeks of the holidays which were to have been so full of delightful recreation and of help for mother. The doctor came and went, but never looked encouraging as she would say, "To-morrow I can sit up; yes, to-morrow I surely must be up, I have so much to do before school begins in the fall."

And then summer was almost gone, when one day she looked suddenly up into his face. "Doctor, do you know that school begins the week after next?"

"I believe it does, Ruth."

"And I'm not getting strong very fast. Vacation is almost gone. I can't help that now; but—how am I going to school if I am not stronger?"

He looked pityingly at her without any answer.

"Doctor, can't I begin school when it opens?"

"No, my dear," he said, gently.

"Then when?"

He could not bear the look of appealing misery with which she gazed in his face, as if waiting a sentence of life or death.

"Oh, some time. Soon; yes, very soon, my dear," he said,

soothingly. "Be a patient, brave girl until you are well again." He went out of the room.

"Mother! mother!" she cried, in an agony of dismay, as the tender face appeared at the door. "What does he mean? When can I go to school? When can I be helping you again?"

The loving arms went around and drew her close. "Oh, my daughter! my darling! the good Lord knows when. Try to bear it for His sake and for mine."

"Mother"—her face was pressed against her shoulder—"will it be long?"

"I'm afraid so, dear."

"Will it be months?"

"Perhaps"

"Years?"

No answer came.

And then Ruth turned herself, body, mind, and soul, to the wall, and felt as if all the joy had gone out of the world. There was no brightness in the sunshine, no color in the flowers, and no music in the voice of the birds. Nothing was left in it but hopeless days of pain and weariness for her, and drag and drudgery for her mother.

"It would have been better for us all if I had been taken away at once," she said one day. "I used to think I could turn everything into gold for you, mother. But that was when I was well, and thought the world was full of gold," she added, bitterly.

"You keep all your gold away from me now, Ruthie," said her mother, shaking her head sorrowfully.

"I haven't any gold left, mother: I only give you more trouble, when my heart is aching to do something for you, and it cuts me like a knife to see you work so hard."

"You can do it yet, dear. I used to find half my courage in your cheery smile and your cheery ways. It's hard to lose them when I seem to need them most, daughter."

Ruth knew it, and began wondering if it would not be better to try to help in little things, now that the great things were gone beyond her reach. Mother's dear face and the affection of the little ones who came around her with soft cooings of, "Poor sister Ruthie!" were something to be thankful for yet.

"Give me the stockings to mend, mother." It tired her at first, but she found it pleasant to be busy again. She had her lounge brought into the family room, having fully made up her heroic little mind that she would smile for mother if she could never do anything else.

"I used to do a great deal of that sort of thing," her mother said, as Ruth finished her mending by working a rose-bud in satin stitch on the front of one of Cricket's stumpy little stockings.

"Let me have their best stockings, mother. I've read that it's the fashion for children to wear embroidered stockings, so ours shall be very stylish."

The soft, pretty work seemed just suited to her strength, and she amused herself by ornamenting the stockings with delicate flowers and traceries worthy of appearing on far finer hosiery than that of the little country children.

"Look what I have found for you!" said her mother, when these were done.

Ruth exclaimed in delight over the bundle of bright silks and velvets, and began busying herself trying how the pretty things could be wrought into things still prettier. She had seen little fancy-work, but the children brought flowers, and with patient fingers, now no longer round and firm and ruddy as formerly, but thin and delicate, she copied the daisies and pansies and lilacs until they almost seemed to stand out from the silk. With little aim but to pass away the long hours, she worked piece after piece, and her mother was fond of looking them over and declaring they were as pretty as water-color paintings, which indeed they were.

"Ess, ma'am, Oofie done 'e' posies on my tockies. S'e dess

sew 'em on wiv a needle 'n' fred. I'll so oo."

Ruth from her couch could hear Cricket chatting very freely with some one at the door, and called her mother, who presently brought in a lady, followed by Cricket with one bare foot, the stocking of which he held up for inspection, in happy disregard of its streaks and stains. The visitor sat down beside Ruth, saying:

"I have been staying for a few days in the neighborhood, and I saw on Sunday some embroidered stockings on some little tots, the prettiest I have ever seen—the embroidery, I mean, and the tots too," she laughed, as Cricket still pressed his stocking upon the general attention. "And some one told me that if I came here I could see the person who worked them. You poor child, how long have you been lying here?"

The face was so bright and kind, the pressure of her hand so warm, and the voice had such a ring of earnest interest, that Ruth felt encouraged to tell all about her great trouble, and of all the trouble growing out of it, and to show her the other stockings; and she even ventured (so little did her visitor seem like a fashionable lady, or at least like Ruth's idea of a fashionable lady) to look curiously at a wonderful bag she carried.

"Crazy patchwork, you see. Did you ever make any?"

Crazy indeed it looked. Bits of silk of all colors and shades, square, round, three-cornered, oblong—every shape or no shape at all—were pieced together in a style utterly at variance with the old-fashioned ideas of careful measurement and straight seams. And from each piece a quaint bit of needle-work peeped out—a cat's head, or a squatty teapot, or a sheaf of wheat, or an autumn-tinted leaf, or what not, all joined by stitches of various patterns, on which Ruth's eyes fastened.

"No, I never saw anything so beautiful," she said.

Mrs. Hill wanted some stockings embroidered. She came again, and came often, as she grew more and more interested in the young girl, and at last, in wishing her good-by, handed her ten dollars, and told her to work her best work on the silk pieces she should send her.

She worked through the fall and winter months, finding her fingers more skillful and her fancy more fertile as she went on. She had also begun putting together her own bits of work.

"I'll make a pincushion of crazy patchwork," she said to her mother.

But it grew fast; and she next said, "It will be big enough for a bag—a good-sized bag, too!" Then, "It will make a lovely sofa-pillow."

After that she rolled and basted it up to keep it clean as she worked at intervals upon it, grafting in piece after piece, beautified by the daintiest work her hands could do.

"There's a carriage coming up the hill. Who can it be?"

Ruth looked up from the apple blossom she was shading with infinite painstaking, and stared with the others at the unusual sight.

"It's stopping here—yes. It's Mrs. Hill!" The next moment she held Ruth's hand in a firm clasp.

"Ruth, I've come to take you home with me. Will you go?"

Ruth looked in her face in blank amazement. "I! Such as I to go anywhere!" She laughed, and then cried.

"My dear child, I've got it all arranged so that you can make the journey without pain or injury. There is to be a great exhibition of art work in the city, and I want all your work to send to it; and I want you to try a change of air, if your mother can spare you. I have found just what I want," said Mrs. Hill, looking over Ruth's beautiful embroidery with great satisfaction; "something different from every one else's work. I did not send you a single pattern, because I wanted you to work out your own ideas. Fairies might have done this."

Last of all Ruth unrolled her crazy patchwork—a bundle which had not been undone for months.

"Here, mother, I have made this for you."

It had grown into bedquilt size, and was heavy with its weight of exquisite needle-work. Into it she had wrought everything in the way of lovely model or original fancy which had come to her during these months of patient waiting. Upon it her mother could read a history which brought tears to her eyes; to any one else it was a study for more than one pleasant hour.

"This must go too," said Mrs. Hill, very decidedly. "I want to show it; it will make a sensation."

This is what mother found in a letter from Ruth about six weeks after she went away. A little bit of paper had fallen from it, which waited for notice until the letter was read:

"—So you see that is ninety dollars for the work Mrs. Hill sent me. And, oh! mother darling, I've sold your quilt—the quilt I have been eighteen months making for you, and which I though you'd keep all your life; but I know you'll forgive me. For that is the reason I am sending you a check for three hundred and ninety dollars, mother—yes, indeed! Three hundred dollars for a crazy quilt! Just think how much money these city folks must have! And they all say it is not a bit too much for the work on it.

"The way it came about: Mrs. Hill sent it to the exhibition with the other things, and one day she told me that a lady had offered three hundred dollars for it. I knew you'd be thankful enough for the money, mother, but I told them about the bits of your wedding things and grandmother's dress and the scrap of father's army coat, and the lady said I could take those out. So I'm very busy just now putting other pieces in their place, and you may be very sure I'm putting my very best work upon it, when she is paying me so much money. And show it to Jack and Polly and Cricket; they'll hardly believe it, but you try to make them understand. And, oh, darling mother, I'm helping you after all!"

Polly danced about, and Jack flung his hat up to the ceiling, and Cricket rolled over on the floor, while mother wiped her eyes, and wondered if the dear daughter would not come home very soon now.

But she did not. Spring grew into summer, and Cricket, who had begun to believe that pretty things were made for the sole purpose of copying in silk embroidery, mourned over every new leaf or bud or flower which he brought in, and Ruth not there to admire and "sew it." Summer wore away, and latterly Ruth had not said one word about coming home. How long those days seemed!

"Somebody's coming! Hooyah! hooyah!" shouted Cricket one afternoon in late August. Once more a carriage was making its way up the hill.

"It's Ruth!" screamed Jack, rushing in. "I saw her face. Give me a chair to help her out." He seized one, and tore down the path, with Cricket toddling after. Mother would have followed, but sat down with trembling limbs on the door-step. Some one else was coming too—some young person, for she was running up to the house with light-stepping feet; and then mother's eyes dimmed, and her strength seemed gone, for it was Ruth's own bright face which looked lovingly into hers, and Ruth's arms which held her up.

"Oh, mother, here I am. Look at me. I'm well again, and strong, and come home to help you at last."

"All the gold has come back to me," she said on the morning when she was going again to resume the studies she loved and to carry out her old cherished plans.

"Refined gold now, dear," answered her mother, as she looked in the sweet face, and could read there much which only the two years of patient suffering could have written.

"Ah, Ruth, if you hadn't settled yourself to stocking-mending when you could do nothing else, this might never have come about."

MAMMY HESTER'S QUILTS
Adelaide D. Rollston, *Harper's Bazar*, August 24, 1889

A mean-spirited, selfish, tyrannical old black quiltmaker, Mammy Hester, pays an uninvited and unwelcomed visit to the cabin of Aunt Lucindy and her family. Sam, Aunt Luncindy's son, has recently built a new room onto the cabin in anticipation of his marriage to Cally Hicks. To Sam's extreme dismay, Mammy Hester, with her huge stash of quilts, promptly occupies the new room and refuses to move. Mammy Hester and Aunt Lucindy are not related, but were former slaves on the same plantation, the plantation where Mammy Hester established a reputation that made everyone fear her. It was believed she had the ability to place evil spells on anyone who incurred her wrath. Mammy Hester had many beautiful quilts which she took as an entire group wherever she went. She never gave a quilt away or allowed anyone to touch her precious quilts. The story, told in Negro dialect, relates the fate of Mammy Hester and her quilts during the visit to Aunt Lucindy's cabin.

"Well, t'ank de Lawd, I's got heah at las'!" said Mammy Hester, with a sigh of relief, as she settled herself comfortably in the chimney-corner, and taking from her pocket her long-stemmed cob pipe, proceeded to fill and light it. "Wuzn't spectin' ob me, wuz you, Lucindy?" she asked, as she stooped, and with the tongs picked up a small coal.

Aunt Lucindy, a tall, gaunt woman, with a severe-looking countenance, turned from the bed on which she had just deposited a sleeping child, and gave the fire a vicious poke with her foot. "No, Mammy Hester, we *wuzn't* spectin' you, leastways befoah spring," she said, slowly, and somewhat resentfully. "You sed you wuz gwine to stay wif Cha'ty all winteh."

Mammy Hester gave her turbaned head a toss, and chuckled softly. "Now whut put dat notion into yo' head, Lucindy?" she asked. "Don't I allus' cum an' go jes as I please? An' when I gits ti'ed ob Cha'ty's grub, 'aint I got a right to cum heah an' eat *yo'* co'n-bread an' bacon? I tell you whut's de truf, honey. Cha'ty's cabin got too crowded to suit ole Hester. Dem chullen jes fight an' qua'ell frum mawnin' till night, an' I dun got ti'ed ob libin' in sich comfuzion. 'Sides, dat little shed room dey gib me to keep my t'ings in wuzn't half big 'nuff. An' when I 'plained about hit de udder day, Cha'ty she ups an' 'cuses me ob bein' ongrateful, an' me her *mammy*! I jes packed my t'ings an' lit out fur dis side ob de ribber. I tole 'em I wuzn't ' bleeged to lib ober in de black bottoms ob Eleenoy, 'long wif a pack of triflin' niggers, an' I wuzn't gwine to do it."

"How much did it cost to cum ober dis time?" inquired Aunt Lucindy, as she seated herself, with an air of resignation, by the fire, and fell to tacking carpet rags.

Mammy Hester showed her toothless gums in a broad grin. "Not a cent," she said. "I went to de cap'n, an' sez I, 'Cap'n Jim, I wanter cross ober on de ferry-boat.' 'All right!' sez he. 'Where's yo' money?' Den I jes p'inted to my baggage, an' sez I: 'Cap'n Jim, I's bin crossin' dis ferry now, off an' on, fur ten yeahs, an' I ain't gwine to pay you a cent. I's dun payin' to cross dis ferry.' An' den I tuck a seat, an' waited fur de whistle to blow. 'You's an ole humbug, Mammy Hester,' sez Cap'n Jim, when de boat landed on dis side ob de ribber. Dat wuz all de 'plaint he made, an' I sabed my money."

"You didn't bring nuffin, den, 'cept dis, did you?" asked Aunt Lucindy, touching a dilapidated valise that leaned against the chimney.

"De law! do you s'spose I'd leabe my bed dar, an' all dem fine quilts, fur Cha'ty's chullen to waller ober?" ejaculated Mammy Hester, indignantly. "No, all de t'ings is won to de ribber. Jake he's gwine to bring 'em up on his wagin d'rectly."

"I don't know whar in de world dey's gwine to be put," said Aunt Lucindy, with a groan. "Dar ain't no room to turn aroun' in now. An' dar's a leak ober yondeh in dat co'ner, so no bed kin be put *dar*. Sam sez de cabin 'll hab to hab a new roof 'foah long."

"Whut's de matteh wif de room Sam's bin a-buildin'? Jake tole me about it, an' I 'lowed you wuz havin' it built fur *me*."

"De new room? Why, dat's *Sam's* room. Didn't you heah he wuz gwine to git ma'ed Chris'mas week?"

"Sho! Now who's Sam gwine to marry? Not dat Tildy Hall, I hopes," said Mammy Hester, with a sniff.

"No, *'tain't* Tildy Hall; it's Cally Hicks, whut libs down at de Cross Roads," said Aunt Lucindy, loftily.

"What! dat stuck-up nigger? I don't wondeh Sam had to build a new room! Dat gal's got mighty high notions, if she takes arter her mudder. I knowed *her* when she 'longed to ole Squiah Hawkins. Allus t'ought she wuz bettern'n de res' ob de darkies. Let me hab a look at dat room, Lucindy."

"Sam's got de key, an' we can't git in," said Aunt Lucindy, glancing proudly at the freshly painted door that opened into the new addition to the little cabin. "He don't 'low nobody to meddle in dar. He's keppin' it shet up gin he gits reddy fur the furniture. I's makin' a rag cyapet fur it now."

"Huh!" snorted Mammy Hester, letting her pipe fall to the floor in her excitement. "Sam is gittin' high. *I'll* make him han' ober dat key—see if I don't. It's cum to a high pass, I t'ink, when a poah ole 'oman like me is shoved off into a co'ner an' dat room standin' empty. Whut's de sense in it, I say? *I* ain't gwine to hurt de room."

"We'll see whut Sam sez' about it when he cums in," said Aunt Lucindy, quaking inwardly at the thought of Sam's probable indignation at such a propsal.

"He'll say nuffin," retorted Mammy Hester. "He'll jes han' dat key ober wifout op'nin' his mouf. You knows I don't take no sass frum Sam."

And she was right. When Sam came in, a few minutes later, he was so taken aback at the sight of Mammy Hester, whom he feared and detested, and who he supposed was safely established for the winter over in the little cabin across the river, that at her command he handed over the key without a word of protest, then beat a hasty retreat into the back yard, where he gave vent to this indignation by a vigorous attack on the wood-pile. He knew by the looks of Mammy Hester's eyes that she meant to take possession of his new room. And she did.

"It's jes gwine to upset my plans, mammy," he remarked to his mother as they sat before the fire that night. There was a dejected look on his face, and something like a tear shone in his eye. "Cally's dun heerd about Mammy Hester takin' de room, fur Jake he went straight ober an' tole her."

"Well, I jes couldn't hender her frum takin' it," said his mother, with a long-drawn sigh; "dough she 'ain't got a bit ob right to it," she continued, brindling up. "Cha'ty's her own darter, why don't she stay wif *her*? Jes' kas we wus fellow-sarvants, she must be cumin' heah wheneber she feels like it, whedder we want her or not. An' she must hab de best of eberting too! I's gittin' tired ob it, I is! Hain't I got my poor dead Har'et's chullen to take keer of? An' don't Mammy Hester 'pose on dem chullen ebery time she cums heah? Course she *do*!"

"She dun tuk my hoe-cake right outen my mouf at supper-time," put in little Pete, dolefully. "My stummk's jes as holler as it kin be, 'kase it 'ain't got nuffin in it."

"An' she sopped up de las' bit ob de 'lasses," wailed Jim, who was sitting up in bed fondling a dingy-looking kitten.

"Hush, chullen, an' go to sleep!" said their grandmother, with a frown. "Fust t'ing you knows Mammy Hester 'll hear you, an' den you'll ketch it to-morrer. 'Sides, little chullen oughtn't to be puttin' in deir talk to older folks."

"If Mammy Hester stays heah ober two weeks, I's gwine to gib her a big hint to go," said Sam, in a low voice.

"Don't you say nuffin to make her mad, honey," cautioned his mother. "You don't know dat ole 'oman as well as I does, if she *has* bin cumin' heah off an' on sence you wuz a baby. Why, back on de ole plantation ebery darky, frum de ol'est to the youngest, wuz afeard ob her, 'kase she had de poweh to ha'm ennybody she pleased. Don't I 'member de time she laid dat terrifyin' spell onto M'lindy Jenkins, yeahs an' yeahs ago?"

"Tell me 'bout it, mammy," said Sam, waking up to some interest.

"Well, you see, she fell out wif M'lindy 'kase M'lindy wuz so much pearter 'bout her wuk dan *she* wuz an' made moah money offen her cotton patch dan enny udder darky on de plantation. Well, de fust t'ing we knowed M'lindy wuz tuk down wif sum strange 'plaint, an' right at de time, too, when she wuz needed in de fiel'. An' dar she laid, a-moanin' an' a-groanin' frum mawnin' till night, an' gittin' wuss all de time too, dough ole marse he had de bes' doctah in de kentry a-waitin' on her. Bimeby she got so bad dat we all 'cluded we'd sen' fur ole Uncle Beverly, de root doctah, what libed down in de swamp, fur M'lindy she tuke it into her head dat she'd bin cha'med. Suah 'nuff, de fust t'ing Uncle Beverly sed wuz, 'You's got sum enemy dat's laid dis terrifyin' spell on to you, an' de pusson is on dis plantation now.' Den he tole her to go to a sartin tree in de medder, pull off de bark close to de groun', an' she'd fin' a lock of ha'r dat her enemy had cut frum her head. When she'd fin' de ha'r de spell would be broke. M'lindy wuz powerful weak, but she managed to git to de tree; and when she peeled off de bark, suah nuff dar wuz the ha'r. I mos' forgot to say dat Uncle Beverly sed dat de fust pusson she met, when she went back to de house, would be de enemy dat laid de spell. Well, M'lindy tuk de ha'r an' started back to de house, an' when she got to de gate" (here Aunt Lucindy's voice sank to the merest whisper) "she met *Mammy Hester!*"

"Sho! I ain't afeard ob Mammy Hester layin' a bad spell onto *me*," said Sam, contemptuously. His mother's harrowing story evidently hadn't impressed him seriously, notwithstanding his natural superstition.

"But she might do Cally some harm," said Aunt Lucindy, with a meaning look.

Sam's eyes grew big with sudden fear. "Suah 'nuff she might," he said, shaking his head solemnly. "I tell you whut I *will* do, mammy," he continued, brightening up a little. "If she don't leab inside ob two weeks, I'll go ober de ribber an' git Cha'ty to sen' fur her. I knows she ain't wanted ober dar no more dan she's wanted ober heah; but Cha'ty's her gal, an' she'll do dat much to please me, I reckon."

At the end of two weeks Mammy Hester still held possession of the room, and evidently was bent on keeping it; so Sam betook himself across the river and laid his case before Charity. The result was that Mammy Hester received a pressing invitation to spend the Christmas holidays over in the "black bottoms." Greatly to Sam's chagrin, she contemptuously refused the invitation, and expressed her determination to remain in her present quarters until spring.

"If you's sot you' head on marryin', jes go ahead an' marry.

You kin lib wif yo' mudder-in-law till spring," she remarked to Sam, in a cool, off-hand way that staggered him.

For two weeks, or ever since Mammy Hester's arrival, Cally had treated him with marked coldness; and on one occasion had remarked, coquettishly, "that Jake Hall wuz buildin' a mighty nice cabin down to de Cross Roads, and she didn't know but what he meant to ask her to share it with him."

Christmas was drawing nigh, the rag carpet was finished and laid away, the furniture selected and paid for, still Mammy Hester occupied the new room, quarrelled with and scolded the children, and helped to keep Aunt Lucindy's larder empty.

"I jes can't stan' it enny longer, mammy, an' I won't!" said Sam, in a desperate tone, one night as he sat in the chimney-corner and whittled aimlessly. "I seed Cally dis mawnin a-walkin' down de big road, an' when I axed her whar she wuz gwine she jes laughed in my face, an' sed, 'I'm gwine to hab anudder look at Jake's new house.' 'You 'ain't bin ober to see *our* new house lately, Cally,' sez I. 'Wheneber you git rid ob dat ole 'oman I'll come,' she said, kinder huffish. I knows jes how it'll be"—here Sam brushed his hand hastily across his eyes—"she'll marry dat moon-eyed Jake jest to spite me if I don't git Mammy Hester outen dat room putty soon."

His mother sighed and shook her head in a sympathetic but helpless way.

"I axed Mammy Hester if she wuzn't gwine to giv you one ob dem quilts fur a weddin' gift, an you ought to hab seed her flare up! Sed I must t'ink she wuz a fool. I counted dem quilts, Sam, when she had 'em out airin' yeste'day, an' dar's ten ob 'em. She keeps 'em piled up on a box in de co'ner ob de room when dey ain't hangin' out on de line. De very nicest wo'sted quilts, too, an' neber bin used one single time. Jes t'ink ob dat, Sam, an' me an' de chullen nearly freezin' ebery night fur want ob enuff kiver!

She's bin totin' dem quilts back'ards an' for'ards twixt me an' Cha'ty's fur nigh about six yeahs, an' neber offered eiber ob us one ob 'em yit. An' she don't need 'em he'se'f."

"I wish to goodness she'd drap a coal ob fire outen her pipe onto 'em some day, an' set 'em afire so dey couldn't be put out!" said Sam, viciously.

"She counts 'em ebery day to see date none ob 'em is missin'. I believe she'd go plumb crazy if ennyt'ing wuz to happen to dem quilts."

Just then there was the sound of rain pattering against the window, and Aunt Lucindy rose and hastened to thrust an old pillow in the broken pane.

"We's gwine to hab a big sto'm, I's afeard," she muttered, as she peered out into the darkness.

Sam suddenly stopped whittling, and began to whistle softly to himself. A bright idea seemed to have come to him, for his face lost its sullen look.

"I's gwine out to see if de pigs is safe; I t'ink one's got out ob de pen," he said, jumping up from his chair and hurrying out of the cabin.

He certainly must have had a deal of trouble in getting the pigs fastened securely for the night, for when he came in, half an hour later, he was drenched to the skin, and limped a little as he crossed the room.

"I skinned my leg agin de ladder out dar," he remarked to his mother as he drew off his boots. "but de pigs is all safe," he added, with a grin.

All night the storm raged. Not for years had there been such a downfall of rain; and lying in her snug bed in the new room, Mammy Hester listened to the roar without, and congratulated herself that she was in such safe and comfortable quarters.

But early the next morning, when Aunt Lucindy rose to

prepare breakfast, she heard loud and angry mutterings in the new room and hastening in, found Mammy Hester in a towering rage.

"What's de matteh, Mammy Hester?" she asked in astonishment.

"Matteh?" shrieked the old woman. "Jes look at dem quilts!" and she pointed to a dingy heap in the corner of the room. "De las' one ob 'em ruined—de very las' one ob 'em; an' I's had 'em nigh on to eight yeahs!"

Their beauty, if not their usefulness, was certainly destroyed forever, for the bright colors had faded, and, mingling together, sent little pools of water and dye to the bare floor beneath.

"I wuz sartin dat de roof wuz good an' didn't leak," remarked Aunt Lucindy, as she gazed helplessly from the dripping quilts up to the ceiling.

"You wuzn't sartin ob nuffin!" snapped Mammy Hester. "You mought hab 'vised me to keep dem quilts under de bed, whar dey'd be safe! I's gwine straight back to Cha'ty's—dat's whar I's gwine! Whar's Sam? Tell him to hitch up de wagin an' taken me down to de ribber. I wishes him joy of his ole leaky room! I migh hab knowed *he* couldn't build a room wuf shucks. Whut you standin' dar lookin' at me fur, Lucindy? Why don't you go to wuk an' help me pack my t'ings? Fust t'ing I knows my fedder-bed 'll be wet, an' all my udder quilts ruined."

"But you must cum an' hab sum br'akfas' fust, Mammy Hester," said Aunt Lucindy, coaxingly, for the old woman's anger frightened her.

"No; I's gwine straight to de ferry! I got no time to eat bre'kfas'. I's gwine on de bery fust trip of de ferry-boat. Mebbe Cha'ty kin do sumpin wif dem quilts. Ain't you gwine to tell Sam to hitch up?"

Aunt Lucindy hurried out of the room in search of Sam. She found him at the barn, feeding the stock.

"Dem quilts is all ruined, Sam, an' she's gwine straight ober to Cha'ty's," she said, excitedly. "De roof leaked," she added, giving him a keen suspicious look.

"Is dat so?" exclaimed Sam, with a look of innocent surprise.

"Yes; an' she wants you to hitch up right away. She won't wait till bre'kfas' even. She's powe'ful mad, Sam, but I reckon she can't lay de blame onto *us*."

"Course she can't," said Sam, stoutly, as he dropped the ear of corn he had been shelling and hurried into the stable.

Half an hour later Mammy Hester, perched on the top of her bed and bedding, and with the still dripping quilts piled in the bottom of the wagon, was driven by Sam to the river. As the wagon turned into the road, Sam turned around and gave his mother a sly wink.

"Golly! she's gone! she's gone!' shouted Pete when the wagon had disappeared down the muddy river road. "An' now we'll hab de weddin', an' de punkin pies an' de roast pig, won't we, Jim?" he added, cracking his heels together, and then turning a handspring in the middle of a mud-puddle.

"Yes, an' plenty ob good 'possum gravy, wid nobody to sop it all up from us," said Jim, smacking his lips in anticipation.

"Mammy," said Sam, with a grin, when he had come back and eaten a hearty breakfast, "if you'll hunt me some nails an' de hammer, I'll go up on de house an' men' dat leak in de roof."

JOHN'S MOTHER:

THE GORGEOUS QUILT AND HOMELY SOCKS

Antonia J. Stemple, *Good Housekeeping*, March 1898

Mrs. Warner, a poor, humble, country widow, made a lovely silk patchwork quilt for her son's bride, Ethel, and knitted several pairs of woolen socks for her son, John. She planned to visit John and Ethel in the city and take her homemade presents to them. John had moved to the city and had become a successful businessman. Mrs. Warner's jealous, gossipy neighbors in the village did not believe that John and his wife wanted his poor old mother to visit them. They did not believe the "citified" Ethel would like Mrs. Warner's patchwork quilt. They doubted that John had sent his mother money to pay her train fare. Surprises awaited both the neighbors and Mrs. Warner.

See this beauty of a quilt, Mis' Andrews! I made up the pattern my own self; an' I've been collectin' the pieces nigh on ter ten years. There's five thousand of 'em, an' every stitch made by hand," and old Mrs. Warner held up a gorgeous silk patchwork quilt for the admiration of her visitor.

"Jest so. It's the prettiest one I ever seen. You'd ought ter exhibit it at the county fair. Mis' Jones' Hannah got first premium on hers at the last fair, an' it's pretty small punkins side o' that. An' my, ain't she proud of it, though! She's got it on the spare bedroom bed, an' she's always a-showin' of it off!"

"Well, nothin's too good for my John, an' I expect his wife's as good as he is. He says she's an angel. Anyhow he deserves to get the best wife livin', for they ain't many boys as good as my John. I reely believe he'd give the shirt off his back to anyone who'd ask him for it. He's doin' first rate in the city, an' he's gettin' rich. Most boys forget their folks when they're gettin' ahead in the world, but my John'll never forget me; he ain't that kind."

"John always was a likely lad. He's just like my Sam; Sam an' him us'ter be good friends. But your John has all the luck. Everything my Sam touches goes wrong; father and me have ter give him and Sary Ann many a lift, an' it comes hard on us; we hain't any too much of our own."

Mrs. Warner said nothing, but carefully folded up the quilt, and smoothed it out with great precision. Then she brought forth half a dozen pairs of good, stout, gray woolen socks, and said:

"These's for John. He always like socks o' my own knittin' better than boughten ones. He'll be right glad to get these; you can't buy this kind in New York, I'll warrant," and she regarded them with satisfaction.

"Yes, them's good ones," said Mrs. Andrews. "I most gen'lly get that gray yarn fer my man's socks,"—then—"Warn't it too bad you couldn't go to John's weddin'? Mis' Bailey said you warn't invited, an' that he didn't write an' tell you a thing about it till he'd be'n married mor'n a month," and Mrs. Andrews gave a little sarcastic smile.

Mrs. Warner gasped, but finally managed to ejaculate: "For the land's sake! Did Libby Bailey say that? They ain't a mite o'truth in it"—

"That's what I told her; that I didn't believe that o' your John," soothingly interpolated Mrs. Andrews.

"I shou'd say not! My John not invite his mother to his weddin'! The idea! It's a sin to think of it!" and the widow's little, faded face flushed quite red with anger.

"I'll tell you how 'twas, Mis' Andrews, an' you can jus' tell Libby Bailey the facts in the case. You see, my John wrote me two, or was it three months ago,—yes, 'twas three, that he was engaged, and that the weddin' date hadn't be'n set, because her aunt,—she hain't no mother, poor thing,—was sick, an' they wanted to wait till she was quite well, because, you know, weddin's make lots o' work an' fuss."

"I shou'd say they did! Don't I remember when my Lizy was married! Such work! I was all played out, an' when the weddin' day come, I could scarcely stand, and Lizy the same way. She got jest's pale an' thin!"

"Well, as I was sayin', he wrote that as soon as they set the day, he'd let me know, an' that I must be sure an' come to the weddin'. He sent me twenty-five dollars,—yes, he did,"—as Mrs. Andrews held up her hands in surprise, "an' he said he'd meet me at the depo'. About a month after that he wrote, tellin' me all about the weddin', but the letter was delayed, an' it didn't come till the day before the weddin', when I was to start. I was so disap'inted I cried, but I wou'd er gone anyway, only I had the chills and fever that time, an' the next day, my John's weddin' day, was my day to shake, an' sure as you live, next day, weddin' or no weddin', I had ter be in bed. I remember I shook wors'n ever, an' I was truly mis'rable, what with the shakin' an' the disap'intment."

"You was awful peaked that time, that's the truth. Chills an' fever is mean, so they be," and Mrs. Andrews, who was a round, rosy body, who had evidently never experienced a "shake," heaved a sigh.

"I sent a telegram by Joe Harris,—it cost seventy-five cents, and they warn't but a few words,—so's John an' Ethel, that's his wife, wou'dn't worry. I had the quilt an' socks all ready to take that time, an' it broke me all up 'cause I cou'dn't go. Pretty soon I got another letter from John, 'twas after he was married, an he said he was awful sorry I cou'dn't ha' be'n there, but that when he'd moved in ter his new house I must come an' pay them a good, long visit."

"His house!" echoed Mrs. Andrews, holding up her hands in amazement.

"Yes," returned Mrs. Warner proudly, "he wrote me all about it, an' said 'twas so handy. It's got a bathroom, an' he keeps three or four hired girls, yes, an' he's got a pianner!" she added as a climax.

"You don't say!" and Mrs. Andrews again raised her hands.

"His wife, Ethel, you know,—ain't that a sweet, pretty name, now?"—

"That's what my husband's brother's wife's cousin named her little girl,—'Ethel Clementine Jerusha Higgins,'—got the name outen a story book."

Mrs. Warner frowned, but resumed: "Well, she wrote a little note with John's letter, the beautifullest writin' you ever seen, an' she wanted me ter be sure an' come, because she wanted ter be acquainted with such a lovely woman as she was sure John's mother must be; that's jest what she said, an' John sent me another twenty-five dollars."

"I want ter know!"

"So, that's why I'm goin' termorrer. I'm goin' on the six o'clock train, an' it'll be a surprise ter him. He ain't expectin' me, because I didn't tell him I was comin'. Won't he be serprised and delighted, though?" and Mrs. Warner's face beamed in anticipation.

"Well, I must be goin'," said Mrs. Andrews, rising. "I hope you'll have a beautiful visit. I suppose you'll buy lots o'nice things down there?" and Mrs. Andrews' voice betrayed envy.

"I kalkerlate ter get me some new clothes. I was goin' ter buy 'em here, till I remembered that John 'ud like ter see me in my old gown an' bonnet, seein' as I had 'em when he was here last, though that's mor'n ten years ago. He always said they was so becomin'. You can get big barg'ins in New York, so I've heard, so I guess I'll wait till I get there, an' perhaps I can get a piece o'goods cheap."

"Good-bye, then, an' good luck ter yer," and Mrs. Andrews hastened to Mrs. Bailey with the exciting news, and told her the story in great detail.

"I don't believe half she said about her John. Why, he warn't half as smart as my Sam, an' was always down first at every spellin' match. Hired girls, pianner, an' bathroom, indeed!" and Mrs. Andrews sniffed contemptuously.

"An' the quilt she's goin' to give that stuck-up, citified Ethel! 'Taint nothin' wonderful, an' her eyesight's so poor, that if you look real close, you can see some o' the stitches in it! I rather guess she'll find out what's what when she gets to New York!"

In the meantime, Mrs. Warner went cheerily about her house, preparatory to her departure. She carried her cat over to Mrs. Miller to be cared for while she was gone, and then bustled about until bedtime. She did not sleep much, however, for fear she should miss her train. At five o'clock she was up, ate a hasty breakfast, then donned her old-fashioned gown, shawl and bonnet, and with an ancient hand-bag, containing, among other things, the precious quilt and socks, and with her umbrella and a box of lunch, she set forth.

The thin little figure in its antiquated garments, the pleasant old face with its eager, happy expression, interested her fellow passengers, and they enjoyed doing her favors, and listening to her conversation. She was happy as a child, and enjoyed the journey immensely; even when there was a delay of three or four hours, owing to an accident, she maintained her good spirits.

A tall, prosperous looking gentleman opened a conversation with her, and she soon told him of her plans.

"What is your son's name?" inquired he with a smile.

"He was named after his father, as good a man as ever lived,— John Philip Warner."

"What, is John Warner your son? He's a good friend of mine, and I'll see you safe to his house. I have often heard him say that all he is, or hoped to be, was due to his mother."

"Dear John!" exclaimed the old lady while tears sparkled in her eyes, "he always was a-tellin' me how good I was; he's such a flatterer," and Mrs. Warner looked as though she enjoyed being flattered.

When the train arrived in New York it was past nine o'clock in the evening, and Mrs. Warner, who had never been more than fifty miles from home, was completely dazed. Her new found friend soon had her in a cab, and after a brisk drive the vehicle halted in front of an elegant brick building. When her companion had helped her out he said: "This is your son's house, go right in," and bidding her good night, he hurried away.

The fine house made Mrs. Warner wink, and she stood on the sidewalk a moment gathering her senses, and gazing at the windows which were ablaze with light. She felt a little shy, but the prospect of seeing her boy impelled her to mount the steps (she did it on tiptoe) and ring.

A stern, pompous looking individual opened the door and stared in amazement at the queer figure before him. The little woman quaked, but finally stammed out: "Is John in?"

"Who?"

"John,—I mean Mr. Warner,"—faintly, as the lordly butler looked puzzled.

"Mr. Warner is in, but you can't see him. Guess your business can wait," and he gave a sarcastic grin.

The tears came to the weary woman's eyes. "Please tell John—

Mr. Warner—his mother wants ter see him. I'm come ter visit him," she added, meekly.

"A likely story! Here's company coming now, and you just clear out quick."

The face that a few moments before had been glowing with pride and joyful anticipation, now looked pale and old. Without another word, she dragged her weary limbs down the steps, and struggled along the street, she knew not whither, the tears so blinding her eyes she could hardly see. The bag containing her gifts seemd heavy as lead. Her whole figure told of grief, and she was conscious only of an overwhelming sense of disappointment and sorrow. Finally, after stumbling along for about half an hour, she encountered a friendly policeman. The pathetic, drooping form of the old lady, stirred his Irish heart, and he brought her to the home of a countrywoman who lived on his beat. There she was given a room, but the strange surroundings made no impression on her, and she was insensible to everything. As in a dream she took off her bonnet and shawl, dropped into a chair, and gave way to a flood of tears. All night she sat there, but toward morning she sank into a short, uneasy slumber, from sheer weariness. After she had eaten a light breakfast, the hostess sent her son to guide the guest to the station, and put her on the first train for home, for nothing could persuade the broken-hearted woman to stay.

Late that afternoon, as Mrs. Andrews sat in her sitting room gossiping with Mrs. Bailey, she happened to glance out of the window. She gave one startled look at the figure which trudged past; then her hands went up, and she slowly ejaculated:

"Gracious Peter! Did you ever! If here ain't Mandy Warner come back from New York, bag an' baggage! Looks as though she hain't had a good time of it, either! Guess her John, that she's always blowin' about an' that stuck-up wife o' his'n, warn't so glad ter see her as she reckoned on. Serves her right! 'Pride comes before a fall', an' so I've always said."

When her visitor had gone, Mrs. Andrews lost no time in hastening to Mrs. Warner's. When she saw the gossip coming, Mrs. Warner set her lips hard, straightened out her features and said to herself:

"Now, Mandy Warner, don't you dare give a thing away, or it'll be all over the village. You jest hold your tongue, an' don't give her any satisfaction."

"How you look, Mis' Warner!" was Mrs. Andrews' salutation, "what brought you back so quick? Be you sick?"

"Well, I don't feel very smart, Mis' Andrews. I feel kind o' tuckered out. The journey didn't agree with me I guess. I come straight back home, an' when I take some o' my herb tea, I'll prob'ly be all right again."

"How is John an' his wife?" cunningly inquired the visitor.

"Oh, you'd ought ter see their house!" exclaimed Mrs. Warner with an attempt at enthusiasm. "It's jest as big an' handsome! an' it's got stone steps! An' the stylishest man ter tend the door you ever seen. My, ain't he dressed up, though! Bettern'n the minister at a funeral."

"Did John's wife like the quilt?"

"Yes,—I don't know,—well, I didn't give it ter her, you see I was so sick I forgot all about it."

Mrs. Andrews' eyes opened to their fullest extent and her hands began to go up, but she controlled herself, and seeing that there was nothing more to find out, she uttered a few words of sympathy and went.

When she had gone, Mrs. Warner sat down to think the matter over. "I hope God'll forgive you, Mandy Warner," she said to herself, "for fibbin' like you did. But, dear Lord," and here she lifted up her eyes in supplication, "you know I cou'dn't help it. How cou'd I tell that spyin' creature about my trouble? Forgive me, dear Lord," and with a sigh she took up some work and tried to forget her misery.

The next morning, bright and early, Mrs. Andrews retailed the matter to Mrs. Bailey. "It's jest as I said," she declared. "Of course she tried to wiggle out of it, an' make out she come right home because she was sick, but I know better. The idea! An said she forgot ter give that stuck-up wife the quilt she was so proud of. Didn't want it, most likely, an told her so."

Three or four days dragged away and one afternoon as Mrs. Warner sat crying over the cherished quilt preparatory to putting it out of sight, a knock came to the front door, and wondering who it could be—the neighbors all came in at the side door—she went and opened it. There was a moment's silence and with a cry of "John!" Mrs. Warner found herself clasped in her big son's arms, while her tears were flowing on his breast. After this, the beautiful, stylish young lady was introduced as "my wife, Ethel," and the happy trio entered the neat little sitting room.

"Your heart must have been broken, dear mother, after the reception you had," said big John Warner later. "I should never have known a thing about it if Mr. Lawrence, whose acquaintance you made on the train, had not asked me yesterday how my mother was enjoying herself. In answer to my surprised inquiries he told me all, and when I questioned stupid Bates he said he had turned you away thinking you a begging impostor. Knowing how you must feel, Ethel and I left everything, and here we are to comfort you, and take you back with us to stay as long as you are contented."

"I'm quite in love with you," said Ethel, "and you will be as good a mother to me as you are to John, I know," and she imprinted a kiss upon Mrs. Warner's wrinkled forehead.

It was wonderful to see the change in old Mrs. Warner. Her New York experience seemed like a bad dream, and she asked questions, laughed, and patted her boy and her new daughter to her heart's content. When the gorgeous quilt and the homely socks were presented to the visitors, their reception of the gifts was all she could wish, and her joy was full.

"They went away this mornin'," said Mrs. Andrews to Mrs. Bailey in conclusion of a long narrative, "an' she's goin' to stay as long as she likes. She's prouder'n ever, an' won't scarcely notice her neighbors. They brought her the handsomest cape you ever seen. It's real sealskin, 't ain't plush, because I looked close on purpose to make sure, an' that stuck-up Ethel acts to Mis' Warner's though she was good's a queen. Some folks do have all the luck!"

"Some folks do," assented Mrs. Bailey.

Aunt Bina's Quilt

Mrs. O. W. Scott, *The Youth's Companion,*
September 22, 1898

In 1862 Aunt Bina Emerson made a beautiful "love quilt." It was called a love quilt because she put into the quilt only patches collected from persons she loved and admired. When the women gathered for the quilting, they did not come for their usual gossip session. Instead, they were eager to see whether their patches had been sewn into the precious "love quilt." Thus they would know how they were regarded by Aunt Bina. As the Civil War progressed, the U.S. Sanitary Commission requested from the public many cloth items, sewn and unsewn, including quilts. Would Aunt Bina donate her wonderful quilt? What happened to Aunt Bina's quilt during that tragic period is the crux of the story.

Aunt Bina Emerson had pieced the quilt from bits of calico given her by the women and girls in Eden that she liked. It was the lone woman's "love-quilt," with her shades of affection deliberately outlined in tiny triangles.

"I won't have any pieces in it that call up anybody that's stingy or stuck-up or meddlesome or cruel." she said. "I'll have it just as near like fresh air and sunshine as it can be, so when I'm sick it'll seem like a nice, bright story."

"But you needn't have counted every stitch," protested her sister, Mrs. Billings, in whose home she had her cozy room.

"Anybody would think you were an astronomer counting stars, to see how particular you've been," added pretty Hetty Barton, for whose benefit the quilt was now exhibited; and she looked at the paper, covered with cabalistic figuring which was Aunt Bina's actual record of stitches set.

"Well, stars of stitches, we like to see how many we've got, and counting is only a pastime. The minister says we can't think of two things at the same time, but somehow I can count my stitches and have most profitable thoughts right along. I like the way I've disposed of my lights and darks, don't you?" Aunt Bina shook out the great square complacently.

"It is beautiful!" Hetty exclaimed. "Why, you've got a piece of my light blue in the middle; and here is my pink, and there is my dark blue!"

"Yes; that's because I—" Aunt Bina had almost said "love you," but she was not in the habit of expressing herself in that way.

The young girl looked at her questioningly then suddenly stooped and dropped a kiss upon her forehead.

"Don't be foolish, child," said Aunt Bina.

When the last minute triangle was finally set in its corner, Mrs. Billings made a "quilting," to which every woman came who was invited, for it was well understood by this time that goodness as well as gowns—according to Aunt Bina's measurement—was represented.

"She ought to know who amongst us is angelic, after being in our sick-rooms and kitchens so many years," they said.

In those days quiltings were supposed to be enlivened by much gossip, but the women who gathered that afternoon, in the spring of 1862, wore anxious faces and had but one theme of conversation, the sacrifices that the overburdened nation seemed to be preparing to ask from them.

"They have opened a recruiting-office," said one to another.

"Captain Pillsbury's in charge. His furlough is almost up, but he means to get a company enlisted before he goes back," was the next but of news.

"I should think we were far enough out of the world to be let alone," said Mrs. Hastings, as she snapped the cord, wet in starch water, across the triangles.

"That's crooked!" interrupted her neighbor, referring to the work; then she added, coming back to the topic, "But I don't wonder you feel so, with three grown sons to worry about."

"We've no boys to spare, here in Eden," added Mrs. Thurston, "but Massachusetts hasn't failed to do her part so far, and I've expected our time would come."

"Her John'll be one of the first to enlist, now you see!" whispered two busy workers on the opposite side of the quilt.

And so it proved; for when at twilight the husbands and brothers came in to partake of Mrs. Billing's bountiful supper, bringing the Boston papers and the news of the day, they gave the names of those who had enlisted that afternoon and the first one was John Thurston's.

"And probably Harry Thurston will join that company before it's filled; but his mother needn't know about John now," they said. So it was whispered in the room where she sat; but she understood the message that passed from eye to eye. Hetty Barton understood, too, although she did not raise her eyes from the line where she was setting small, even stitches. The air waves were full of echoes in '62, and Hetty did not need even John's words, which came later in the evening, to confirm those dire prophecies.

Then how the war fever spread through Eden! Around the recruiting-office, where a large flag proudly floated, on the store steps, at the postoffice, out on the country roads and beside the fences, while horses stood still in the furrows, men gathered to talk about the boys who were going to the war. The village paper printed a long list one week, and as it was read with tear-dimmed eyes, the people said. "It seems as though all Eden is going."

Then, one bright June morning, the sun shone upon a company of eager young soldiers in new blue suits with shining brass buttons. It fell upon the fathers and mothers and friends, who stood grouped near the long wagons which were ready to take "Company I" to the nearest railroad station. The white-haired old pastor offered the last prayer, and with fluttering flags, beating drums, huzzas and waving caps, the brave soldier-boys were borne away.

A strange hush fell upon the small town. It had always been a staid and sober place; but now it almost seemed as though life had gone out of it. Hard work became a blessed necessity to old and young.

The girls learned to drive horses that were not "steady," to ride mowing-machines, to help plan the farm work, to do "everything but sing bass," which they could not learn to do. But the real life of the place depended upon news from the boys, after all; and the coming of the old yellow stage twice a day quickened heart-throbs as did nothing else.

Two years passed, and the suspense was not yet over. Some of the Eden boys had gone beyond the sound of the bugle-call, a few were in hospitals, but most of them were in action that dreadful spring of '64, when news of battle after battle flashed over the land.

Eden was at its height of anxiety as the people gathered for worship in the white church one Sunday morning the last of May. Hymns, Scripture reading and prayer were over, and the old pastor arose, but instead of beginning his sermon he said:

"Late last night word came that there is great need of everything for use on battlefields and in hospitals. The sanitary commission begs us to send cotton and flannel garments, socks, sheets, quilts, old cotton and linen—everything we can gather at once. I would be cruel to keep you women who can use needles here with hands folded over your Bibles when the need is so great. You are invited to gather immediately at the home of Mrs. Grow for work, and may God's blessing go with you."

There were children in that congregation who still remember how, with one impulse, all the women arose and reverently left the church.

The law of Sabbath observance in Eden was Puritanic, but

those who would not sew on a missing button under ordinary circumstances were soon seated, needles in hand, wearing the exalted look which meets a great emergency.

Mrs. Grow was president of the Soldiers' Aid, and her husband kept the village store. This was opened and necessary materials were taken from it. The only two sewing machines in the village were soon clicking an accompaniment to the subdued voices of the busy workers.

A delegation, one of whom was Aunt Bina, was sent out to gather whatever could be found ready for use.

"I'm glad to get out in the open air." said she. "It stifles me to sit there like a funeral in Mrs. Grow's parlor. Seems's if it would kill me to see the look in Mis' Hastings's eyes since Harry was shot."

"They knew you could tell just where to go for supplies," replied Mrs. Kent. "We must get sheets and quilts and old linen. Have you any quilts to spare at your house, Aunt Bina?"

"I'm sure sister has some, and—yes, I've got an extra blanket or two. Come in."

While Mrs. Billings was collecting her contribution, Aunt Bina was in her room upon her knees. When she entered the parlor again a few minutes later, she bore in her arms a pair of soft, white blankets—and her love-quilt.

"Bina Emerson!" exclaimed her sister. "You don't mean that you're going to send that quilt?"

"Yes, I am!" cried Aunt Bina, her face quivering. "Nothing's too good for our boys. I won't send 'em old things I don't want; they shall have this."

It was useless to argue, nor in that hour of supreme devotion did any one care to do so; but when it was known that Aunt Bina had sacrificed her treasure, it aroused a splendid rivalry which brought together just such stores as were needed.

All day the good work went on, and at night the men, weary of their enforced idleness, packed barrels and boxes ready to ship in the early morning.

Aunt Bina reached her room again at twilight, taking with her Hetty Barton. "You know I've sent my quilt to the soldiers?" she asked, hesitatingly.

"Yes, they told me so. I think it was so generous of you." Hetty replied, in an absent-minded way, as she twisted the plain gold ring on her finger.

"I had planned to give it to you, Hetty. There's nobody I like so well as you and John; but now—"

Hetty's eyes were full of dumb agony. Suddenly slipping from the chair to her knees, she buried her face in Aunt Bina's lap. "Oh! oh!" she sobbed, "you needn't think about that. It has been two long weeks since I heard from him. John wouldn't neglect me so, Aunt Bina, unless—" and then the girl could say no more.

Aunt Bina's tears fell upon the brown braids. "There, there! don't give way. I guess John is all right."

"Oh, but he always wrote! He wasn't careless like some of the boys. Do you know his father and mother are almost sick. They think he—is —"

"There, there!" comforted Aunt Bina. "I believe John will live to come home; that's my faith. Why, we've got to believe it, Hetty! If we didn't, how could we live through it!"

Even while they wept and talked, John was lying in one of the Washington hospitals. He had been terribly wounded, and after many delays was brought there with one leg amputated and his right arm disabled. His nurse, a bright little woman from Maine, tried in every way to arouse him.

"I believe he wants to die," she said to the surgeon. "I can hardly persuade him to eat."

"Probably he does," replied the weary-eyed man. "He had a magnificent physique, and such a fellow feels that he cannot face life maimed in this fashion. I've often had such cases. If you can only get him past this first shock—"

The busy man hurried away without finishing his sentence, but the nurse understood.

A few nights later a lot of boxes arrived in response to the urgent call for hospital supplies, and John's nurse eagerly claimed some of their precious contents. "I need blankets in my ward," she said, "and oh, here is a beautiful quilt! This will cheer my poor boys like a bouquet of flowers."

The nurse from Maine was one of the best in the hospital, and no one objected when she carried away the quilt and placed it gently over her favorite patient.

"Perhaps it will keep his eyes off the blank wall," she said to herself, with a sigh.

When the first morning light shone in through the long narrow windows, the young soldier opened his eyes, almost resenting the knowledge that he had slept better than usual. As he looked languidly to see if his nurse had given him an extra blanket, he saw the new quilt, and at the same moment was conscious of a faint perfume of rose-leaves, perceptible even in that sickening atmosphere.

He closed his eyes and saw the bushes under the parlor windows at home, laden with great red roses, as they had been the morning he left Eden. He had started out that morning with a bud in his buttonhole, and another between his lips, "decked for the sacrifice," he thought, with a spasm of bitterness.

With his left hand he pulled the quilt nearer. It was made of many, many small triangles! "Mother's dress," he murmured, placing his finger upon a brown bit with a tiny white spray in it. "Hetty!" and a wave of color rose to his pale face, as he caressed a triangle of pink.

For the first time since he was placed upon that cot, great tears rolled down his cheeks. The spell of despair was broken. Life was sweet, after all.

"Mother and Hetty won't mind if I am a poor one-legged fellow," he sobbed.

All the bitterness and rebellion melted out of his heart as he lay there quietly crying; and when his nurse came in he greeted her with a smile that transfigured his face.

"This is Aunt Bina's quilt!" said he. "I don't know how it got here, but it is. Now, nurse, bring on your broth, for I'm going to get well."

"It's been better than medicine," the delighted woman declared to the doctor. "He's given me his address, and I've already written to his mother.

"And I've shown that quilt to all my boys, and told them about the dear old maid who counted all the stitches and thought so much of her 'love-quilt,' and how hard it must have been to give it up. They're all brighter and better for it. 'Why,' they say, 'do the folks at home think so much of us as that?' "

Years have passed since that day, and John and Hetty are elderly people now, with boys and girls growing up around them. John found that his brains could do better service for him than even physical energy, and has become a successful and conscientious lawyer. In their busy, happy lives they have never forgotten the woman whose sacrifice meant so much to them, and when Memorial Day comes round and the veterans gather to decorate their comrades' graves, John and Hetty reserve the choicest flowers of their garden for Aunt Bina's humble resting-place.

And the quilt? Through the thoughtfulness of the nurse from Maine, it was returned to the generous donor, who bestowed it, as she had intended, upon her young friends. If you had the privilege of examining the contents of a certain chest in the Thurston homestead, you would find a soldier's cap and suit of faded blue, and very near it, carefully wrapped in tissue-paper, Aunt Bina's quilt.

THE BEST HOUSEKEEPER IN BANBURY

Edith Robinson, *Ladies' Home Journal*, June 1905

What a stern taskmaster Aunt Mitty was! She did not allow little Abby Jane to participate in any of the pleasurable fads the other little school girls enjoyed. Abby longed to have an autograph album in which her school friends would write a verse of poetry or a sentiment. But Aunt Mitty would not permit that. Abby wanted to collect 999 buttons (a charm string). Although Aunt Mitty had a bag of buttons accumulated by three generations of her family, little Abby was not given even one button.

Aunt Mitty believed that duty came before pleasure, so every day after school, Abby could not go out to play until she had completed her "stent" (stint) — her duty. Her "stent" was to make a patchwork quilt, block by block. How little Abby hated that interminable, hideous patchwork of the most drab, dark ugly colors imaginable! Every stitch must be perfect or Abby would have to sew the block again.

Perfection was important to Aunt Mitty, as she prided herself on being the best housekeeper in Banbury. A fly or a moth or dust was considered mortal enemies by Aunt Mitty and would not be tolerated. So confident was Aunt Mitty in her housekeeping perfection that she sneered at neighboring women whose housekeeping standards did not meet hers. When the new minister and his wife came to Banbury, Aunt Mitty learned the folly of having overweening pride.

"Please Aunt Mitty!"

"Not till you have finished piecing that quilt," returned Miss Mitty sternly. "Why, when I was your age I had pieced a whole bedspread and made a shirt for my father—all by hand—and you couldn't have told any two of them stitches apart, either. I guess machine-work wouldn't have been thought much of those days!"

"Just a little piece!" pleaded Abby, with unusual pertinacity. "No bigger than—" she spread out the palms of both hands by way of illustration. "And only a tiny bit of worsted. All the girls are working cardboard mottoes. Most of them say 'God Bless Our Home,' and they're real pretty. The girls take them to school and work recess and show them to each other. I'm the only little girl who isn't working a motto." Her voice trembled and her eyes filled at the thought of those lonely recesses and homeward walks. "I wish, just once, I might have something like other little girls. I'd get up early every day to work on the patchwork," she added tremulously.

"Abby Jane, when I've said a thing you know 'tain't a mite of use saying another word about it. Have you done your stent to-day?"

"No'm," faltered Abby.

"Then you can just sit down and 'tend to it. When it's done you may go into the spare-room and take the pins out of the bedspread," returned Aunt Mitty. "If you can't remember that duty comes before pleasure it's my duty to learn you," she added solemnly.

Abby did indeed know that when Aunt Mitty "put her foot down" words or tears were unavailing. In some vague way, however, she felt that if pleasure only came after duty—or in any other order of precedence—duty would not be so intolerable. Duty, to Abby, always seemed typified in that hideous patchwork. She had been at work upon it ever since she had taken a needle in hand. The task seemed to her like the problem in Colburn's Mental Arithmetic of the snail at the bottom of the well, who for every five feet that he crawled up fell back four. Every stitch in those horrid calico squares that was not an absolute mate with its fellows was sure to be detected by Aunt Mitty's sharp eyes, when the pieces must be ripped apart and done over. In the years ahead, when she should be as old as Aunt Mitty, Abby saw herself still bending over that interminable patchwork! If the squares had only been pink, or blue, or yellow, she thought she might not have minded the daily "stent" so much. But they were drab, or black, or dingy purple, remnants, for the most part, of Aunt Mitty's gowns, which were bought chiefly for their durable qualities—of which properties there could be no doubt, for after a long season in Aunt Mitty's service they were made over for Abby, a size too large, to allow for growth. She had never had a frock that did not fairly shriek out, "I've been made over!"

Her "tires" were of the same disheartening blacks and drabs and purples when all the other little girls at school wore white dimity tires, daintily ruffled. But worse than not being dressed like other children was the fact of always being left out in those "crazes" that one after another prevailed at school. When every one else was making a worsted rope by means of four pins stuck in a spool Abby had to pretend that she did not care about such silly things. Then everybody—except her—had an autograph album, in which her friends wrote a verse of poetry, or a sentiment— "Be good and you'll be happy," being a favorite; or inscribed in the corners, "Remember the picnic," or a mysterious allusion such as "Sunflowers" or "February 17." After autograph albums came the craze for collecting nine hundred and ninety-nine buttons, and, with a bag in which the buttons of three generations had accumulated, Aunt Mitty refused to part with one! Then there was the mania for advertising cards. Mr. Jessup, who kept the village store, gave her a lovely picture of somebody's "Food," and Abby hung it in her own little room. Aunt Mitty found it the next day and tore it into fragments. She couldn't have the house littered up with such truck, she said. "Flightiness"—in any form— Aunt Mitty regarded as a weakness that should be promptly crushed.

Only once had the child's repressed longing to have things like other little girls found vent. That was a long while ago, when she was a very little girl, and Aunt Mitty's cousin by marriage was on a brief visit to Banbury. Lizzie Pearson, who was distinctly "flighty," wore a bonnet with pink roses and long blue strings; it was the most beautiful thing Abby had ever seen. A dreadful temptation assailed her to own a little piece of that wonderful blue ribbon. The voice of the tempter whispered insidiously that if she took only a tiny bit each day Cousin Lizzie would never miss it and no harm would be done. On the last day of Miss Pearson's visit, as she was tying her bonnet strings, she said in a puzzled tone:

"I can't think what has happened to this ribbon. I never knew anything to shrink so! There's hardly enough to tie in a half bow."

Detection and punishment came swift upon the guest's departure.

"Abby Jane, what does this mean?" demanded Aunt Mitty sternly, producing a little box filled with snippings of blue ribbon, discovered beneath Abby's bureau.

Then and there Abby received her first and only whipping. Yet despite the vivid recollection of the smart of the rod—ever after associated with blue ribbon—she had never been truly sorry for those moments of rapture when she took out that little box of precious snippings and fingered them as a miser does his gold.

There was, indeed, little need of punishment. Except for that solitary instance of revolt the idea of rebelling against Aunt Mitty's rule never entered Abby's humble little soul. Her very appearance indicated a crushed personality—the pale blue eyes, habitually downcast; the sensitive little mouth; the "shingled" hair, when all the other little girls wore flowing locks, and the sad-colored frocks hanging loosely on the slender figure.

* * *

Abby was well fed and warmly clad, and was being brought up to be a good housekeeper—a term that, in Banbury, held all of woman's duty and achievement. As a good housekeeper it was generally conceded that Miss Mitty had no superior in the village. She was known never to be behind in her spring cleaning or fall preserving. She was always asked to contribute her sweet pickles and cream sponge-cake to the church suppers. As for a fly or a moth one would never have dared show itself within her house, and Miss Mitty did not hesitate to express a scathing opinion of those folks who from lack of "calcerlation," or that thorough going cleanliness that took due heed to the corners, allowed dust, with all its attendant evils, its wicked way. Most of these strictures were openly directed against Mrs. Tebbits—who, being the wife of the senior deacon, felt herself ill used that Mehitable Parsons should have too much of her say about church matters. For Miss Mitty's "faculty" was notable in other directions as well as housekeeping. It was she who cut the work for the Sewing Circle and planned the Harvest Home supper and the minister's donation parties. With a family of five children Mrs. Tebbits actually had time to crochet a mantel lambrequin for her best room and was not ashamed to let it be known that she used "compress yeast," instead of home-brewed, in her bread-making. What more could be expected of such a person—though a deacon's wife—than a houseful of flies, when every window stood wide open in the summertime? There were awful rumors, too, afloat in Banbury, to the effect that moths had been seen fluttering about Mrs. Tebbits's best room, and that in the attic—a deacon's attic—were stores of rags unlooked-over for years, known to be the breeding places of those pestilential insects.

"Lord knows what keeps us from the plague!" Miss Mitty had more than once ejaculated, with a significant look in the direction of the senior deacon's wife.

"There's them that thinks life is just made up of soap and water," observed Mrs. Tebbits with dignity. "If folks who have only one child to look after had five young ones traipsing round they'd have something else to do besides hunting moths!"

If a moth had been "a dragon of the slime," or the mysterious Beast of the Apocalypse, it could not have been held in dire horror by Miss Mitty, nor its invasion of a Christian household a deeper disgrace.

If possible, Miss Mitty's spring cleaning was being done this year with extra thoroughness. The new minister and his wife were to spend the first Sunday of their arrival with her, instead of taking possession at once of their own home. The last minister was unmarried and had taken his meals at Mrs. Tebbits's across the street from the parsonage. It was Miss Mitty who had been largely instrumental in having the call extended to a married minister. Not but that an unmarried incumbent might fill the duties of his sacred office with equal satisfaction, but—what was of far more importance—the parsonage under bachelor rule was in a constant state of "sixes and sevens" that was an ill example to the community. By heedful inquiries Miss Mitty had ascertained that Mrs. Liscom was a good housekeeper before she bent her energies to having the call extended to the Reverend Caleb Liscom. It was Miss Mitty, again, who did the spring cleaning at the parsonage, preparatory to the reception of the new minister and his wife.

"I guess even Mis' Liscom can't say but what the house is clean," declared Miss Mitty. "Cousin Lizzie Pearson says folks used to say that a moth didn't dare turn down the street where Mis' Liscom lived. And the minister don't need to be going back and forth into other folks' houses, tracking in dear knows what!"

"Mitty Parsons will be dealt with for her sinful pride one of these days," said Mrs. Tebbits to her husband. "I don't know as I ought to say it, being a church member, but I should kind of like to see retribution overtaking her. Sure as Lot's wife, she never calls here that she don't have a big piece of camphor in her pocket. 'Tother day it dropped out, and there was all of a pound!"

Mrs. Tebbits did not take it kindly to be deprived of both the honor of the minister's daily presence at her table and of the stipend for his board.

Abby finished her "stent," but never had the somber squares been so hateful; one or two tiny stitches that did not keep rank with the rest were instantly detected by Aunt Mitty, and the patchwork had to be ripped apart and done over. Most of her playtime was taken up in this occupation. A ripple of rebellion was stirring in Abby's soul that needed only opportunity to rise to a tidal wave.

With aching hands and knees she crept about the floor of the spare-room, taking out the pins with which the Marseilles spread had been stretched to dry. A thought came into her mind that for the moment made her fairly tremble with joy.

Opportunity was come. The tidal wave arose, sweeping in its course all thought of consequences, all trace of conscience!

Without giving an instant to reflection she crept beneath the bed, and there, concealed, in her own fancy, from the Eye that watches wrong-doing, the minutes flew as they fly in Paradise.

"Lan' sakes, Abby, ben't you most through?" called Aunt Mitty's voice from the foot of the stairs.

The little girl crept from beneath the folds of the spread, flushed and trembling, not with contrition or apprehension, but with triumph. In both hands, clasped tightly to her heart, was something for which joy had no name!

Giving a final twitch to the Marseilles quilt that hung almost to the floor—for Aunt Mitty would be sure to detect the fraction of an inch from the horizontal—Abby answered meekly:

"Yes'm, I'm coming."

* * *

For the next few days Abby arose before it was fairly light, and still in her nightdress, bent over something by the window with a fearsome eagerness that kept one ear on the alert for Aunt Mitty's footfall without. But guilty though she was those stolen minutes were the sweetest the little girl had ever known since she snipped Cousin Lizzie's bonnet string! It did not detract from her enjoyment that she did not take her work to school. It was sweeter to hug the stolen pleasure to herself, occasionally outspreading her work on her knees and giving it little pats of rapturous approval.

"It's as pretty as Lena Chapman's," she thought, as she paused to admire the effect of the red against the green. "The red's most gone—and so is the blue. Guess there'll be time to get some more before Aunt Mitty wakes up!"

In her bare feet she stole to the spare-room and noiselessly crept under the bed.

The house was spic and span from attic to cellar as Miss Mitty, arrayed in her black merino, sat in the best room awaiting the arrival of the new minister and his wife. With two rigorous spring cleanings accomplished, what mattered it that she was "clean tuckered out," and that weary flesh and overstrained nerves seemed incapable of bearing the added burden of a feather's weight!

"Dear knows what the heart can suffer and not break!" Miss Mitty said solemnly afterwards.

The minister's wife was a tall, angular woman, quite unlike the gentle, yielding little personage whom Miss Mitty had pictured as the fitting character for a minister's helpmeet. Instinctively she braced herself against future conflicts in the Sewing Circle and "Ladies' Aid." The minister himself was a soft-voiced little man, somewhat over-liberal in the matter of smiles. Abiel Boyd, who ran the local express, and who had brought the reverend guests' trunk from the station, took the occasion to say to Miss Mitty, on his departure:

"Guess you'll find it's her who wears the trousers. I took my orders from her—had to p'int out all the houses of everybody in town as we came up along. Tell ye what, 'tain't going to take her long to manage the reins."

"There's them that's been wanting to hold 'em long enough!" returned Miss Mitty majestically. "I ain't one to speak ill of my neighbors, but I do say that folks who can't manage to keep their own house and home decent ain't fit to run the parish!'

The following morning, before Banbury was fairly awake—for, being the Sabbath, it treated itself to an extra nap—Abiel Boyd was surprised to receive an imperative summons to Miss Mitty's house. To his amazement there was the trunk he had brought from the station over night, and there stood the minister's wife, with her bonnet on, grimly resolute.

"Je-ru-salem!" ejaculated Abiel. "What's happened? You ain't leaving before breakfast?" he queried, with the freedom of a privileged character.

"Take it to the parsonage," was the brief order.

"There ain't no fire kindled, and I dunno as the walls and floors have had time to dry proper," remonstrated Abiel. "I dunno how I'm going to get into the house, either." "I don't wish the trunk taken into the house at present. Leave it on the piazza. Mr. Liscom has gone to Deacon Tebbits's for the key," the minister's wife condescended to explain.

Abiel yielded with unwonted meekness. Mrs. Liscom was at the parsonage almost as soon as he. Mrs. Tebbits, at the window opposite, was watching proceedings with open-mouthed interest. She beckoned to Abiel, who readily complied.

"What under the canopy has happened?" he exclaimed.

"It's really too dreadful to tell," returned Mrs. Tebbits, sinking her voice to a tragic whisper. "I wouldn't breathe a word to mortal soul, only I think folks ought to be warned before such a calamity comes upon Banbury!"

"Can't ye tell a fellow what's struck 'em?" queried Abiel, a note of pathos in his voice. "Miss Mitty didn't turn 'em out for not wiping their shoes?"

"The minister himself told me. He said his wife wouldn't remain a moment longer in that house. It seems hard, but when one comes to know the truth it ain't to be wondered at! Dear knows what the minister's wife must be thinking of us. I'd like to run over this blessed minute and let her know we ain't all like that," meditated the deacon's wife. "I'll send some beans and brown bread over right away!"

After one of the children had been dispatched on this hospitable errand Mrs. Tebbits turned again to the impatient Abiel, adjusting her bonnet before the kitchen looking-glass as she spoke.

"The minister's wife looked under the bed last night to see if there was anybody there. What she did see was"—this prolonging of suspense was so pleasing that the deacon's wife took a full half-minute to pull out her bonnet strings before she went on—"was the carpet completely riddled from top to bottom! Abiel Boyd, that carpet hadn't been down a week!" continued Mrs. Tebbits solemnly. "I know it for gospel truth, because Mehitable Parsons wouldn't put her carpets out while mine were being beaten, and kept all her windows closed on my side of her house. There was only one thing that could have done the work—worse than flies— moths ain't in it!"

"St. Joseph's goat?" gasped Abiel.

"Abiel Boyd, it was buffalo-bugs!"

"What's them?"

"They're a fearful pest. Nobody in Banbury, nor even in all Camberwell, was ever afflicted with 'em before. Dear knows how they ever come into this country. Some folks do think they were sent, like the locusts, because of our unrighteous dealings with the heathen!" concluded Mrs. Tebbits solemnly.

"Maybe they were brought in like the gypsy-moth, that they do say some fool wanted to learn about, and it got upset and has gone on working dissolution and havoc ever since," returned Abiel, anxious to justify his entomological knowledge.

"Mr. Tebbits's sister's cousin told me a tur'ble sight about them buffalo-bugs. They'll eat you out of house and home in twenty-four hours, and there's no getting rid of them. They thrive on borax and get fat on Paris green. If you were to shut them up in a bottle they'd live on air for a hundred years, and come out only a little mite hungrier than common. I'm going straight over to Mitty Parsons and see if I can't do something. She ain't always spoken of me just right, but at such a time as this one should let bygones be bygones and remember only that we are brothers and sisters in the Lord. I wish I had some camphor," she added anxiously, "but the price of camphor has gone up so this year that I bought something Mr. Jessup said was real good for moths—only one doesn't exactly know whether buffalo-bugs would mind it a grain being, as you might say, a little peculiar in their habits."

"My mother used to think an awful sight of raw onions—just cut 'em in halves and put 'em on the windows-sills; and I've heard that a piece of red flannel was kind of good, too. I know it helped me a lot when I was down with rheumatism," advised Abiel.

Miss Mitty was in the kitchen washing the breakfast dishes, though from her clouded brow and compressed lips one might have inferred that she was making arrangements for her own funeral.

"I've come just to see if here wa'n't something I could do," began Mrs. Tebbits, seating herself ostentatiously near the door. She was redolent of raw onions, and about her neck was a strip of red flannel. "Maybe if you shut all the windows and burnt sulphur in every room—to be sure it does take the color out of everything—"

"If you'd give me a notion what you're talking about I'd be beholden!" snapped Miss Mitty.

"Dear me, then you don't know why 'twas the minister and his wife left in such a mortal hurry?" queried the deacon's wife mildly.

"I'm not knowing nor caring," answered Miss Mitty shortly. "I shall go to meeting all the same, for all the insult that's been put upon me. I hope I know my duty—and what ain't my duty— which is, poking my nose into other folks's affairs!"

"It's a real trial, I know, and I don't wonder you're sort of up-set," returned Mrs. Tebbits soothingly. "I'm not saying but what such an affliction might have come upon any one, but it does seem a kind of pity that the new minister and his wife should have got such an idea of Banbury the first thing. I've heard tell about buffalo-bugs, but ain't never had a chance to see one. I'd like to see one of the creatures, real well," observed the deacon's wife tentatively.

"It's getting near meeting-time," remarked Miss Mitty, look-ing significantly at the clock.

Mrs. Tebbits shook her skirts as she arose.

"I hope the house will be standing when you get back," she observed by way of a parting shot.

Miss Mitty wiped her hands from the suds and hastened to the spare-room. It seemed as incredible that a buffalo-bug—of whose ravages she had heard as one hears of the plague in far-off lands—should have penetrated the sacred portals of her house as that a buffalo should have done so! Beneath the bed she beheld the awful work of the heathen insect! Scarcely a thread, red or blue or green, was left to show what color had once glowed in those tapestry breadths!

As she made ready for meeting she noted that several small boys were hanging on the front fence. She saw that every one, on his way to church, looked curiously at her house.

"Abiel Boyd ain't lost much time in spreading the news,"

thought Miss Mitty grimly. "I might as well hang out a red flag!"

But even in her sore perturbation she recalled that today was the date when the winter bonnet of velvet was replaced by the summer one of rice straw, carefully put away in the spare-room closet.

"I s'pose every one in town knows about it by this time," she thought, as, with mind far away, she adjusted her bonnet before the spare-room looking-glass.

With Abby by her side she walked along the village street to the meeting-house; her pew was just beneath the choir seats. She was conscious of a faint stir and rustle above, followed by an ill-suppressed snicker. Presently Mrs. Tebbits sailed down the aisle, followed by her brood. She looked in astonishment at Miss Mitty, then put her handkerchief to her face in some sudden uncontrollable emotion. Leaning over her neighbor's pew she whispered:

"Put your hand to the crown of your bonnet!"

Mechanically Miss Mitty did as she was bidden. There was no crown there!

"It's just awful what them creatures will do!" gurgled the deacon's wife.

Miss Mitty felt, rather than heard, an ill-suppressed giggle in the choir seats, followed by a hasty movement. Summoning all her courage she settled resolutely into her seat and sat erect, with eyes fixed upon the pulpit. It was but little, however, that she heard of the new minister's sermon, nor did she linger, after the Doxology, to exchange greetings and comments with friends and neighbors. Looking neither to right nor left, she walked home, Abby by her side, the child in frightened silence, with an occasional sidelong look at her aunt's face. Though she did not know the exact cause of Aunt Mitty's evident disturbance, a more miserable, guilty little soul was not to be found in the entire township.

It was a terrible temptation that assailed Miss Mitty to begin without delay the warfare against the buffalo-bug. Almost, indeed, did it seem a sacred duty, as though the "heathen bug" typified the "Devil and all his works." But conscience and habit prevailed, and she spent the afternoon, as usual, in the best room with the Bible open on her knees.

Abby had long ago crept to bed, but still Miss Mitty sat there, her eyes fastened upon the clock that she had brought in from the kitchen. She was chilled to the bone, for the stove, of course, had been taken down the first of April.

As she watched the minutes creep on till the hand should point at twelve o'clock her thoughts went drearily back over the past weeks and their grinding toil. All the striving of her life, too, to outdo others as a notable housekeeper arose before her. All was come to naught, and she sat there alone and shamed, and everybody in Banbury was rejoicing at her downfall! Napoleon at St. Helena, Zenobia in the conqueror's train, might have understood the abject misery of the best housekeeper in Banbury, deposed from that proud eminence!

"The Lord sanctify unto me this affliction!" breathed Miss Mitty, looking alternately from the Bible to the clock.

By-and-by her thoughts took another train. She might have answered Abby less harshly when the child pleaded for a white dimity tire with ruffles! Perhaps it may have been harder for a little girl than she had ever paused—in her ceaseless toil of broom and soapsuds—to take thought. And the other matters—what were they?—oh, yes, a handful of buttons, some bright worsted. They were trifles, after all. She wished—almost—that she had let Abby rummage in the button-bag. It was odd, now that her thoughts were turned in that direction, how the look upon the child's face, as she refused the trifling boons, returned again and again. It was not a pleasant thing to be shamed before one's mates.

The clock began to strike the midnight hour; Miss Mitty waited till the last stroke had ceased vibrating on the air. The workday week was begun. She went to her own room, and, taking off the best merino, put on her calico gown. With broom and dustpan, scrubbing-brush and pail of hot soapsuds, she toiled up the attic stairs and began spring cleaning—for the third time that year. Though she perished in the struggle, the buffalo-bug, like his namesake of the Western plains, was doomed.

Abby dared speak no word at breakfast and set out for school with an innocent face, but sorely disquieted in spirit. In the course of the morning Miss Mitty reached Abby's room (in the house-cleaning process). As the first step she removed the feather bed from the mattress. There lay the crown of her best summer bonnet, the starch removed from the interstices of the fine straw by careful pin thrusts, worked with gay threads that close inspection revealed as thrums of the spare-room carpet!

Miss Mitty sank on her knees, partly overcome by such un-paralleled audacity, partly in genuine thanksgiving that the obloquy that had fallen upon her was removed. She was still the best housekeeper in Banbury!

There was scarce room in her heart for anger against Abby's misdeed. Instead, the softer feelings of last night's vigil returned with redoubled force as she examined the painstaking little cross-stitches in the straggling blue and red and green letters:

"God Bless—"

A clean home it had been, unquestionably. But had she ever tried to make it a blessed one to the child committed to her care? Could she, a church member, expect God to bless that in which she took no hand? It was a long time since she was young. Perhaps she had forgotten what trifles make up the sum of a child's happiness or unhappiness.

***

It was washing day all over Banbury, but the occasion, thought Miss Mitty, was sufficient justification to have "called Queen Victory from the tub." The first house at which she paused was the parsonage. It had been too serious a matter for Miss Mitty to see anything absurd in the situation when she solemnly displayed the evidence of her innocence to the minister's wife. Mrs. Liscom was polite and regretful, and asked Miss Mitty for the recipe for her cream sponge-cake, the fame of which had reached her; and this incident went far toward soothing Miss Mitty's injured feelings. Besides, she had the satisfaction, at least, of recognizing in the new minister's wife a foe worthy of her steel.

Abiel Boyd was in the store when Miss Mitty entered to make a purchase of white dimity and some other trifles. She explained the mishap to Lulu Jessup, too, who waited on her.

"I'll just drop in on my way home and set Mrs. Tebbits right," she added. "If some folks were in as much of a hurry to stop talk as they are to set it a-going there'd be less mischief done in the world!"

When Abby came home from school she found Aunt Mitty at work cutting out some dimity 'tires.'

"You can hem those ruffles if you want to," she said curtly. "Never mind about your stent to-day. There's something for your fol-de-rol," nodding to a piece of cardboard, stamped with a motto, and a generous roll of bright worsted. "And, Abby," she added, in a softer tone, as the little girl gave a gasp of astonishment and delight, "I guess you'd better let be my best bonnet and the spare-room carpet!"

THE BEDQUILT

Dorothy Canfield, *Harper's Monthly Magazine*, June to November 1906

A research of American quilt fiction disclosed a number of notable authors who have contributed to this genre of literature. In the nineteenth century authors who achieved considerable fame, such as Harriet Beecher Stowe, Louisa May Alcott, Marietta Holley, and Mary E. Wilkins wrote quilt stories. Twentieth century authors of renown, such as Dorothy Canfield (Fisher), L. Frank Baum, Kate Douglas Wiggin, Eliza Calvert Hall, Pulitzer Prize winners Willa Cather, Julia Peterkin, MacKinlay Kantor, Susan Glaspell, Alice Walker, and other award-winning writers such as Eudora Welty and John Updike either wrote quilt stories or featured quilts prominently in some of their works. A story "The Yellow Quilt" by H. E. Fraenkel was awarded the O. Henry Award in 1921. "The Bedquilt" by Dorothy Canfield (Fisher), published when she was twenty-seven years old, is one of the better examples of a carefully crafted, well-written piece of quilt fiction.

A maiden lady of sixty-eight years, Aunt Mehetabel Elwell, lived with her brother's family. Shy and retiring, Aunt Mehetabel earned her keep by doing much work, always the most tedious chores in the home. Her brother's family did not treat her unkindly; they were just indifferent to the old woman. Mehetabel's one passion was quiltmaking. She made many quilts and accumulated a large collection of quilting patterns. An idea came to her to make a completely different quilt, an original design. Mehetabel was so timid, so unassuming, that she would not begin to make this special quilt until she first asked permission of her sister-in-law. The bed quilt is a triumph for Aunt Mehetabel, in ways she never dreamed possible.

Of all the Elwell family Aunt Mehetabel was certainly the most unimportant member. It was in the New England days, when an unmarried woman was an old maid at twenty, at forty every one's servant, and at sixty had gone through so much discipline that she could need no more in the next world. Aunt Mehetabel was sixty-eight.

She had never for a moment known the pleasure of being important to any one. Not that she was useless in her brother's family; she was expected, as a matter of course, to take upon herself the most tedious and uninteresting part of the household labors. On Mondays she accepted as her share the washing of the men's shirts, heavy with sweat and stiff with dirt from the fields and from their own hard-working bodies. Tuesday she never dreamed of being allowed to iron anything pretty or even interesting, like the baby's white dresses, or the fancy aprons of her young lady nieces. She stood all day pressing out a tiresome, monotonous succession of dish-cloths and towels and sheets.

In preserving-time she was allowed to have none of the pleasant responsibility of deciding when the fruit had cooked long enough, nor did she share in the little excitement of pouring the sweet-smelling stuff into the stone jars. She sat in a corner with the children and stoned cherries incessantly, or hulled strawberries until her fingers were dyed red to the bone.

The Elwells were not consciously unkind to their aunt, they were even in a vague way fond of her; but she was so utterly insignificant a figure in their lives that they bestowed no thought whatever on her. Aunt Mehetabel did not resent this treatment; she took it quite as unconsciously as they gave it. It was to be expected when one was an old-maid dependent in a busy family. She gathered what crumbs of comfort she could from their occasional careless kindnesses and tried to hide the hurt which even yet pierced her at her brother's rough joking. In the winter when they all sat before the big hearth, roasted apples, drank mulled cider, and teased the girls about their beaux and the boys about their sweethearts, she shrank into a dusky corner with her knitting, happy if the evening passed without her brother saying, with a crude sarcasm, "Ask your aunt Mehetabel about the beaux that used to come a-sparkin' her!" or, "Mehetabel, how was't when you was in love with Abel Cummings." As a matter of fact she had been the same at twenty as at sixty, a quiet, mouselike little crea-ture, too timid and shy for any one to notice, or to raise her eyes for a moment and wish for a life of her own.

Her sister-in-law, a big hearty housewife, who ruled indoors with as autocratic a sway as did her husband on the farm, was rather kind in an absent, off-hand way to the shrunken little old woman, and it was through her that Mehetabel was able to enjoy the one pleasure of her life. Even as a girl she had been clever with her needle in the way of patching bedquilts. More than that she could never learn to do. The garments which she made for herself were the most lamentable affairs, and she was humbly grateful for any help in the bewildering business of putting them together. But in patchwork she enjoyed a mild, tepid importance. She could really do that as well as any one else. During years of devotion to this one art she had accumulated a considerable store of quilting patterns. Sometimes the neighbors would send over and ask "Miss Mehetabel" for such and such a design. It was with an agreeable flutter at being able to help some one that she went to the dresser, in her bare little room under the eaves, and ex-tracted from her crowded portfolio the pattern desired.

She never knew how her great idea came to her. Sometimes she thought she must have dreamed it, sometimes she even won-dered reverently, in the phraseology of the weekly prayer-meet-ing, if it had not been "sent" to her. She never admitted to herself that she could have thought of it without other help; it was too great, too ambitious, too lofty a project for her humble mind to have conceived. Even when she finished drawing the design with her own fingers, she gazed at it incredulously, not daring to be-lieve that it could indeed be her handiwork. At first it seemed to her only like a lovely but quite unreal dream. She did not think of putting it into execution—so elaborate, so complicated, so beau-tifully difficult a pattern could be only for the angels in heaven to quilt. But so curiously does familiarity accustom us even to very wonderful things, that as she lived with this astonishing creation of her mind, the longing grew stronger and stronger to give it material life with her nimble old fingers.

She gasped at her daring when this idea first swept over her and put it away as one does a sinfully selfish notion, but she kept coming back to it again and again. Finally she said compromisingly to herself that she would make one "square," just one part of her design, to see how it would look. Accustomed to the most complete dependence on her brother and his wife, she dared not do even this without asking Sophia's permission. With a heart full of hope and fear thumping furiously against her old ribs, she approached the mistress of the house on churning-day, knowing with the innocent guile of a child that the country woman was apt to be in a good temper while working over the fragrant butter in the cool cellar.

Sophia listened absently to her sister-in-law's halting, hesitating petition. "Why yes, Mehetabel," she said, leaning far down into the huge churn for the last golden morsels—"why yes, start another quilt if you want to. I've got a lot of pieces from the spring sewing that will work in real good." Mehetabel tried honestly to make her see that this would be no common quilt, but her limited vocabulary and her emotion stood between her and expression. At last Sophia said, with a kindly impatience: "Oh, there! Don't bother me. I never could keep track of your quiltin' patterns anyhow. I don't care what pattern you go by."

With this overwhelmingly, although unconsciously, generous permission Mehetabel rushed back up the steep attic stairs to her room, and in a joyful agitation began preparations for the work of her life. It was even better than she hoped. By some heaven-sent inspiration she had invented a pattern beyond which no patchwork quilt could go.

She had but little time from her incessant round of household drudgery for this new and absorbing occupation, and she did not dare sit up late at night lest she burn too much candle. It was weeks before the little square began to take on a finished look, to show the pattern. Then Mehetabel was in a fever of impatience to bring it to completion. She was too conscientious to shirk even the smallest part of her share of the work of the house, but she rushed through it with a speed which left her panting as she climbed to the little room. This seemed like a radiant spot to her as she bent over the innumerable scraps of cloth which already in her imagination ranged themselves in the infinitely diverse pattern of her masterpiece. Finally she could wait no longer and one evening ventured to bring her work down beside the fire where the family sat, hoping that some good fortune would give her a place near the tallow candles on the mantelpiece. She was on the last corner of the square, and her needle flew in and out with inconceivable rapidity. No one noticed her, a fact which filled her with relief, and by bedtime she had but a few more stitches to add.

As she stood up with the others, the square fluttered out of her trembling old hands and fell on the table. Sophia glanced at it carelessly. "Is that the new quilt you're beginning on?" she asked with a yawn. Up to that moment Mehetabel had labored in the purest spirit of disinterested devotion to an ideal, but as Sophia held her work towards the candle to examine it, and exclaimed in amazement and admiration, she felt an astonished joy to know that her creation would stand the test of publicity.

"Land sake!" ejaculated her sister-in-law, looking at the many-colored square. "Why, Mehetabel Elwell, where'd you git that pattern?

"I made it up," said Mehetabel, quietly, but with unutterable pride.

"No!" exclaimed Sophia, incredulously. "*Did you*! Why, I never see such a pattern in my life. Girls, come here and see what your aunt Mehetabel is doing."

The three tall daughters turned back reluctantly from the stairs. "I don't seem to take much interest in patchwork," said one, listlessly.

"No, nor I neither!" answered Sophia; "but a stone image would take an interest in this pattern. Honest, Mehetabel, did you think of it yourself? And how under the sun and stars did you ever git your courage up to start in a-making it? Land! Look at all those tiny squinchy little seams! Why, the wrong side ain't a thing *but* seams!"

The girls echoed their mother's exclamations, and Mr. Elwell himself came over to see what they were discussing. "Well, I de-clare!" he said, looking at his sister with eyes more approving than she could ever remember. "That beats old Mis' Wightman's quilt that got the blue ribbon so many times at the county fair."

Mehetabel's heart swelled within her, and tears of joy moistened her old eyes as she lay that night in her narrow, hard bed, too proud and excited to sleep. The next day her sister-in-law amazed her by taking the huge pan of potatoes out of her lap and setting one of the younger children to peeling them. "Don't you want to go on with that quiltin' pattern?" she said; "I'd kind o'like to see how you're goin' to make the grape-vine design come out on the corner."

At the end of the summer the family interest had risen so high that Mehetabel was given a little stand in the sitting-room where she could keep her pieces, and work in odd minutes. She almost wept over such kindness, and resolved firmly not to take advantage of it by neglecting her work, which she performed with a fierce thoroughness. But the whole atmosphere of her world was changed. Things had a meaning now. Through the longest task of washing milk-pans there rose the rainbow of promise of her variegated work. She took her place by the little table and put the thimble on her knotted, hard finger with the solemnity of a priestess performing a sacred rite.

She was even able to bear with some degree of dignity the extreme honor of having the minister and the minister's wife comment admiringly on her great project. The family felt quite proud of Aunt Mehetabel as Minister Bowman had said it was work as fine as any he had ever seen, "and he didn't know but finer!" The remark was repeated verbatim to the neighbors in the following weeks when they dropped in and examined in a perverse silence some astonishingly difficult *tour de force* which Mehetabel had just finished.

The family especially plumed themselves on the slow progress of the quilt. "Mehetabel has been to work on that corner for six weeks, come Tuesday, and she ain't half done yet," they explained to visitors. They fell out of the way of always expecting her to be the one to run on errands, even for the children. "Don't bother your aunt Mehetabel," Sophia would call. "Can't you see she's got to a ticklish place on the quilt?"

The old woman sat up straighter and looked the world in the face. She was a part of it at last. She joined in the conversation and her remarks were listened to. The children were even told to mind her when she asked them to do some service for her, although this she did but seldom, the habit of self-effacement being too strong.

One day some strangers from the next town drove up and asked if they could inspect the wonderful quilt which they had heard of, even down in their end of the valley. After that such visitations were not uncommon, making the Elwells' house a notable object. Mehetabel's quilt came to be one of the town sights and no one was allowed to leave the town without having paid tribute to its worth. The Elwells saw to it that their aunt was better dressed than she had ever been before, and one of the girls made her a pretty little cap to wear on her thin white hair.

A year went by and a quarter of the quilt was finished; a second year passed and half was done. The third year Mehetabel had pneumonia and lay ill for weeks and weeks, overcome with terror lest she die before her work was completed. A fourth year and one could really see the grandeur of the whole design; and in September of the fifth year, the entire family watching her with eager and admiring eyes, Mehetabel quilted the last stitches in her creation. The girls held it up by the four corners, and they all looked at it in a solemn silence. Then Mr. Elwell smote one horny hand within the other and exclaimed: "By ginger! That's goin' to the county fair!"

Mehetabel blushed a deep red at this. It was a thought which had occurred to her in a bold moment, but she had not dared to entertain it. The family acclaimed the idea, and one of the boys was forthwith dispatched to the house of the neighbor who was chairman of the committee for their village. He returned with radiant face. "Of course he'll take it. Like's not it may git a prize, so he says; but he's got to have it right off because all the things are going' to-morrow morning."

Even in her swelling pride Mehetabel felt a pang of separation as the bulky package was carried out of the house. As the days went on she felt absolutely lost without her work. For years it had been her one preoccupation, and she could not bear even to look at the little stand, now quite bare of the litter of scraps which had lain on it so long. One of the neighbors, who took the long journey to the fair, reported that the quilt was hung in a place of honor in a glass case in "Agricultural Hall." But that meant little to Mehetabel's utter ignorance of all that lay outside of her brother's home. The family noticed the old woman's depression, and one day Sophia said kindly, "You feel sort o' lost without the quilt, don't you, Mehetabel?"

"They took it away so quick!" she said, wistfully; "I hadn't hardly had one real good look at it myself."

Mr. Elwell made no comment, but a day or two later he asked his sister how early she could get up in the morning.

"I dun'no'. Why?" she asked.

"Well, Thomas Ralston has got to drive clear to West Oldton to see a lawyer there, and that is four miles beyond the fair. He says if you can git up so's to leave here at four in the morning he'll drive you over to the fair, leave you there for the day, and bring you back again at night."

Mehetabel looked at him with incredulity. It was as though some one had offered her a ride in a golden chariot up to the gates of Heaven. "Why, you can't *mean* it!" she cried, paling with the intensity of her emotion. Her brother laughed a little uneasily. Even to his careless indifference this joy was a revelation of the narrowness of her life in his home. "Oh, 'tain't so much to go to the fair. Yes, I mean it. Go git your things ready, for he wants to start to-morrow morning."

All that night a trembling, excited old woman lay and stared at the rafters. She, who had never been more than six miles from home in her life, was going to drive thirty miles away—it was like going to another world. She who had never seen anything more exciting than a church supper was to see the county fair. To Mehetabel it was like making the tour of the world. She had never dreamed of doing it. She could not at all imagine what it would be like.

Nor did the exhortations of the family, as they bade good-by to her, throw any light on her confusion. They had all been at least once to the scene of gayety she was to visit, and as she tried to eat her breakfast they called out conflicting advice to her till her head whirled. Sophia told her to be sure and see the display of preserves. Her brother said not to miss inspecting the stock, her nieces said the fancy work was the only thing worth looking at, and her nephews said she must bring them home an account of the races. The buggy drove up to the door, she was helped in, and her wraps tucked about her. They all stood together and waved good-by to her as she drove out of the yard. She waved back, but she scarcely saw them. On her return home that evening she was very pale, and so tired and stiff that her brother had to lift her out bodily, but her lips were set in a blissful smile. They crowded around her with thronging questions, until Sophia pushed them all aside, telling them Aunt Mehetabel was too tired to speak until she had had her supper. This was eaten in an enforced silence on the part of the children, and then the old woman was helped into an easy chair before the fire. They gathered about her, eager for news of the great world, and Sophia said, "Now come, Mehetabel, tell us all about it!"

Mehetabel drew a long breath. "It was just perfect!" she said, "finer even than I thought. They've got it hanging up in the very middle of a sort o' closet made of glass, and one of the lower corners is ripped and turned back so's to show the seams on the wrong side."

"What?" asked Sophia, a little blankly.

"Why, the quilt!" said Mehetabel in surprise. "There are a whole lot of other ones in that room, but not one that can hold a candle to it, if I do say it who shouldn't. I heard lots of people say the same thing. You ought to have heard what the women said about that corner, Sophia. They said—well, I'd be ashamed to *tell* you what they said. I declare if I wouldn't!"

Mr. Elwell asked, "What did you think of that big ox we've heard so much about?"

"I didn't look at the stock," returned his sister, indifferently. "That set of pieces you give me, Maria, from your red waist, come out just lovely!" she assured one of her nieces. "I heard one woman say you could 'most smell the red silk roses."

"Did any of the horses in our town race?" asked young Thomas.

"I didn't see the races."

"How about the preserves?" asked Sophia.

"I didn't see the preserves," said Mehetabel, calmly. "You see, I went right to the room where the quilt was, and then I didn't want to leave it. It had been so long since I'd seen it, I had to look at it first real good myself, and then I looked at the others to see if there was any that could come up to it. And then the people be-gun comin' in and I got so interested in hearin' what they had to say I couldn't think of goin' anywheres else. I ate my lunch right there too, and I'm as glad as can be I did, too; for what do you think?"—she gazed about her with kindling eyes—"while I stood there with a sandwich in one hand didn't the head of the hull concern come in and open the glass door and pin 'First Prize' right in the middle of the quilt!"

There was a stir of congratulation and proud exclamation. Then Sophia returned again to the attack. "Didn't you go to see anything else" she queried.

"Why, no," said Mehetabel. "Only the quilt. Why should I?"

She fell into a reverie where she saw again the glorious cre-ation of her hand and brain hanging before all the world with the mark of highest approval on it. She longed to make her listeners see the splendid vision with her. She struggled for words; she reached blindly after unknown superlatives. "I tell you it looked like—" she said, and paused, hesitating. Vague recollections of hymn-book phraseology came into her mind, the only form of literary expression she knew; but they were dismissed as being sacrilegious, and also not sufficiently forcible. Finally, "I tell you it looked real *well*!" she assured them, and sat staring into the fire, on her tired old face the supreme content of an artist who has realized his ideal.

MRS. HANNAH

F. Roney Weir, *The Youth's Companion*, June 13, 1912

Mary Fales' childhood memories were filled with her mother's stories of Mrs. Hannah. Mrs. Hannah and Mary's mother, Harriet, were close friends, and although they lived far apart they wrote long letters to each other consistently. Their letters contained family news, and they exchanged recipes and quilt patterns. After Mary grew up, married Mather Fales, and moved to the big city, she continually looked for a Mrs. Hannah. Although Mrs. Hannah had died, the story makes it clear what Mrs. Hannah epitomizes for Mary. One day, quite by chance at a quilting among strangers, Mary, at last, finds "a Mrs. Hannah."

"How I wish I might find her!" Mrs. Fales surreptitiously dabbed her eyes with the sleeve of her morning wrapper while she watched her husband hurriedly packing his traveling-bag.

"Who?" he asked, abstractedly, as he closed the bag with a final, satisfied snap.

"Mrs. Hannah."

They both laughed. "I thought you had found her, as Sairy Gamp found Mrs. Harris—made her up."

He put on his coat, still in a hurry. "You won't be likely to find any Mrs. Hannah in a big city, I'm afraid, dear. But you have your flat to look after, and your music; and then you must get out as much as you can. Go down-town shopping once in a while and to the parks; and don't forget to write to your old hubby every day. Why, the weeks will fly before you know it, and this is to be a short trip, anyhow."

"Oh, I shall get on splendidly. I always have, haven't I? Only— as long as you are away so much of the time, it would be lovely if I could find her. I had an idea I should find her when I was married, but I have about given that up."

"Won't Abbie Norton be your Mrs. Hannah, dear?"

"Mercy, no! Abbie Norton lives in an apartment house, plays Grieg, and—"

"How would Howard Lang's wife do?"

"Alice Lang? Why, Mather, you know she flirts, and tells gossipy stories about her friends. Imagine confiding your heart's inner-most secrets to Alice Lang!"

Mather looked at his watch. "Fifteen minutes before I need to start. Tell me all about Mrs. Hannah."

"Mother got acquainted with her just after she was married and went to live in Rosendale. She was a trifle older than mother, not much. She was dear and old-fashioned and sweet as a June rose, mother used to say. They told each other everything. They were Harriet and Hannah to each other always, and during all the time that mother lived in Rosendale were never-failing friends. After mother moved away they corresponded for years. In my childhood days the event of the month was the letter from Hannah. If only I had kept those letters!

"After mother was gone, and the home broken up, I went to Aunt Lucy, and when I awoke to an interest in my mother's friend, it was too late; the letters had been destroyed, and I don't even know her name. Mother called her Hannah, and I always called her Mrs. Hannah. Mother used to read me the letters sometimes, and show me the enclosed samples of Hannah's dresses—blue gingham, black Henrietta, and once, a striped green percale, which mother said she knew would become Hannah. They would tell each other how many chickens they had, and how their berry-bushes thrived, and they exchanged pickle recipes and quilt patterns, and in sudden family emergencies mother would say, 'If only Hannah were here, she would know what to do.'

"I never knew how I hungered for a Mrs. Hannah until I came to live in this big city and was left so much alone. So when you go, I just pretend. I tidy up the house because Mrs. Hannah is coming; and sunny afternoons I walk out, and make believe I'm going to see her.

"Now it's time you were going. Don't worry about me, dear; I shall keep busy and happy. Good-by, and come back as soon as you can."

For two weeks after her husband's departure Mary Fales kept her promise to be busy and happy. During that time it rained almost every day; Mary did not care to face the weather often. She did not even go to the library, but, with a childishness that she would have hesitated to admit even to Mather, she sometimes laid a plate opposite her own for "Mrs. Hannah." She cut out pieces for a bedquilt, and consulted her imaginary friend about the combination of colors. This was the work that she tucked hastily away under a sofa-pillow the day Alice Lang came to call, and that she immediately returned to when that lady had departed.

Mather had been gone three weeks, and there seemed every prospect that he would be kept away another week.

"I need not lay a plate for Mrs. Hannah to-day," Mary Fales said to herself. "It's such a fine morning that she won't have time for visiting. The hens will be clucking all about her back door; she will be taking the covering off the 'pineys,' and putting in her sweet-pea seed."

Then suddenly Mary decided that it was time for her to return some of Mrs. Hannah's many calls. She was tired of her practising, and her quilt was finished. She would get ready and go to Mrs. Hannah's.

For an hour or two she wandered through unfamiliar streets— unfamiliar because her feet had never trodden them before, but tiresomely familiar because they were all like the one she lived on. She crossed a number of tracks before she was moved to take a trolley-car.

The car took her to the lake, and the accommodating conductor warned her as she leisurely descended that she would have to hurry to make the boat. She thanked him, and more to gratify his kindly desire to be of service than from any thought of embarking, hurried forward in the direction of the wharf where the little lake steamer was waiting.

From the wharf the lower stern deck looked so lonely and inviting that Mary stepped aboard. She found a placid pleasure in her make-believe again; in imagining that the level reaches of the lake were the fields that surrounded the farmhouse back East, where she had passed her childhood; that the foam-capped waves were little drifts of wind-driven snow.

The steamer puffed and snorted and sidled up to long-drawn-out wharves, where it gathered or discharged a few passengers, and then went on to others, and so to the very end of its run, which, as Mary learned from a real estate sign at the landing, was Kirkmere.

Kirkmere would have been the loneliest dock of all but for a group of women who came down the short hill together to take the boat. There were a dozen of them, some tall and angular, others short and fat. One, despite the crispness of the early spring day, wore a green-striped percale dress. Like the others, she was bareheaded. Her dark hair rippled away from a neat part above her low, brown forehead, and her comfortable double chin rolled above a collar clasped by a cameo pin.

This woman fascinated Mary. To her hungry imagination, she was like Rosendale—like Mrs. Hannah. Perhaps the green-striped percale dress offered the suggestion; perhaps the sentence, half-heard, describing a "star basket quilt" that she was making in blue and white.

The boat swung out into the lake, puffed away a few min-utes,—a very few, it seemed to Mary Fales,—then blew its whistle. The women rose, shook out their skirts, and prepared to land.

Mary was disappointed. She knew that they had not taken the boat for the city, but she had hoped for a longer opportunity to watch people who so reminded her of her mother's long-gone youth.

But there they were, all crowding along the little gangplank; soon she would see them march up the hill path that led away among the trees, "Mrs. Hannah" among the rest, on the way to their jolly, homely meeting, and then the boat would take her back to town, to paved streets and apartment houses.

Actuated by a sudden impulse, Mary rose and passed over the gangplank with the others. She edged her way to the side of Mrs. Hannah, who, as the party began to climb the hill, looked up at her and smiled.

Although the exigencies of hill-climbing stilled the chatter somewhat, it flowed forth again when the party reached the top. Somewhere in a near-by field a meadow-lark was singing, and the robins everywhere were fussily busy with their spring work. A cottage appeared from behind a group of trees, and in the door stood a smiling woman in a white waist and apron, evidently ready and waiting for her guests.

There was an outburst of greetings, and one of the women called, "Don't stand there, Hetty Smith, and let the muffins burn, for I can smell 'em clear out here!"

Mary Fales knew that there was only one thing for her to do—to wander on out of sight over the hill for a reasonable length of time, and then to return to the dock and await the next boat for the city.

The woman in the green percale was gazing at her curiously. Mary blushed.

"Excuse me," she stammered, "but—are you Mrs. Hannah?"

She put the futile question merely to prolong for a moment her pleasure in the woman's kindly presence. Mary knew that the Mrs. Hannah of whom she thought would have been old and withered and gray had she been alive. She knew, also, that Hannah had long been sleeping peacefully under the sod. She remembered her mother's bitter tears at the news of her friend's death.

"No, I am Mrs. Clark."

"Oh!" It was such a fluttering, disappointed ejaculation that it was almost a sob.

Mrs. Clark gazed compassionately into Mary's face. "And you thought I was somebody else, and now you have lost your boat?"

"Yes," Mary murmured, "but it's no matter; I'll take the next one."

"The next one doesn't come till five o'clock. Maybe you'd like to come in and help us this afternoon; it's our Ladies' Aid. We're going to make aprons for the church fair."

"Oh, I should love to! Oh, you don't know how I long to go in with you! My name is Mrs. Fales."

"All right. You just come right along in with me." Mrs. Clark tucked a plump hand under Mary's elbow, and they walked into the cottage together.

There was a delicious odor of coffee in the little rooms, and there was much talk and laughter.

Mrs. Clark, who had misunderstood the hurriedly whispered name, introduced her as Mrs. Hale, and Mary let it go.

She passed a delightful afternoon. As luck would have it, it was the afternoon for collecting the dues of the members, and Mary insisted upon dropping into the collection basket the price of the various small amusements that she had not had. She did her best upon the apron that fell to her. All the afternoon she sat beside her Mrs. Hannah, and while they sipped their coffee and ate their muffins together Mary told her new friend why she had followed her party.

They went down to the landing together, and Mary, after getting aboard the boat, watched the green percale dress as long as she could see it. All the way back to town her mother and Mrs. Hannah and her own childhood and youth seemed very, very near and sweet.

It was dark when she reached home, and there was a light in the windows of her flat. That meant another joy. What a happy day it had been! And, sure enough, there was Mather, with an anxious expression that at sight of her changed to a relieved grin.

"I was just about to call the police and get out the militia," he said. "Where have you been?"

"Oh Mather," she sighed happily, "I've been having such a dear, old-fashioned, happy day with Mrs. Hannah!"

THE "ROSE AND LILY" QUILT

Elsie Singmaster, *The Youth's Companion,*
October 2, 1913

> *Grandmother Miller, a seventy-year-old Pennsylvania Ger-*
> *man woman, ages beautifully, yet staunchly retains her inde-*
> *pendence. She becomes vexed with her well-meaning but mis-*
> *guided children and grandchildren who want to subject her*
> *to unnecessary kindnesses. Much to Grandmother Miller's*
> *annoyance, her family proceeds to do things for her that she*
> *is capable of doing for herself. Unasked, they make her clothes;*
> *they bake her pies and cakes; they sweep her house, gather*
> *her eggs, and inform her she is no longer to cook Christmas*
> *dinners. When Grandmother Miller makes a "Rose and Lily"*
> *quilt, and the family again interferes with unwanted help—it*
> *is the final indignity for the old woman.*

Grandmother Miller sat before the fire in her wide kitchen, with
her hands clasped in her lap. The kitchen was warm, sunny, and
with its plain walls, its rag carpet, and its beautifully carved mahogany dresser, even handsome. A Pennsylvania German kitchen
is usually dining-room and sitting-room both. In this house there
were many other rooms, but they were closed, and, since it was
November, as cold as Greenland. There were other great pieces
of furniture, carved like the dresser, and worth a large price from
a dealer in antiques, if he had known of them, or if Grandmother
Miller could have dreamed for an instant of parting with them.

Grandmother Miller was a picture of beautiful old age. She
wore a black dress, and had a little black-and-white checked breakfast shawl folded about her shoulders. Upon the table and upon
the chairs lay spread three new dresses, and many colored and
white aprons—evidence of the loving care in which she was held.

If a stranger had looked in at her through any of the four windows,—two on the side toward the pike and the church, and two on the side toward the village,—he might easily have grown sentimental about gracious and placid old age.

But Grandmother Miller was at least not placid. Her black eyes snapped, her hands clasped each other tightly, and occasionally her foot struck the floor a sharp tap.

"They have made my clothes for me!" said grandmother, angrily. She repeated it as if she were not only angry, but frightened: "They have made my clothes for me!"

She rose and paced the floor.

"I am no child! I am no baby! They want to make out that I am old enough to die! I will not have it! But"—Grandmother Miller sat down once more in her chair before the fire—"I cannot help myself!"

In her misery she began to rock back and forth.

"My own children that I brought up have respect for me," she thought.

"But these others have no respect for me. They are not like their pops and moms. I say yet to-day to my children, 'Do so and so,' and they do it. But these others are different. I was kind to them always. I learned English for them. I let them cut whole pies in the cupboard. When their pops and moms were little, they did not dare to take pie except what was cut. I let them sleep here, three, four at a time. I let them fight with pillows, my good feather pillows. I let them walk over me. This is what I get. Ach, in a year I will be in my grave with trouble!" Grandmother Miller lifted one clenched hand into the air. "If they do not make it different, I will—I will—yes, what will I do? I am old, they walk over me. They have made clothes for me!"

Six months ago Grandmother Miller's subjection had begun. Hester, her namesake and her darling, pretty Hester, with whose bringing up she had concerned herself as much as Hester's father or mother, was the first aggressor. Hester had almost finished her schooling in Millerstown; after another year she and her Cousin Ellen would go away to a normal school. She came into her grandmother's kitchen one bright June morning with a basket in her hand.

"Here are doughnuts, gran'mom, and here are 'schwingfelders' and here is bread."

Grandmother Miller looked with delight upon the viands. She had taught Hester to bake, and she had reason to be proud of her pupil. She patted Hester on the shoulder, praised the bread and cake, and planned to carry some of her own baked things to the Weimers, in whose home were five small children. Hester had on a pink calico dress with a tight waist and a full skirt, such as the girls in Millerstown wore in the seventies, and her curly hair lay damp about her forehead.

Hester had no sooner gone than her Cousin Ellen ran in. She was much darker than Hester, but she and Hester dressed alike, because their grandmother wished them to do so, and presented them constantly with pieces from the same bolt of cloth.

"I have some pie for you, gran'mom," said she, "and some fine cake."

Grandmother patted Ellen on the shoulder as she had patted Hester. Now she could carry all her baking to the Weimers.

To Grandmother Miller's astonishment Hester and Ellen appeared the next week on baking morning, and each carried a basket.

"Here is pie and fine cake, gran'mom," explained Hester.

"And here is bread and doughnuts and schwingfelders," said Ellen.

"We changed round once," they said together.

Their grandmother looked at the two girls proudly. They wore pink sunbonnets this morning, and they were even more engaging than usual.

"They are fine," said she. "But don't bring me any more. I get all the time so many things on hand. I will bake myself to-day. But the things are fine. I have a new dress for each of you. You are good girls."

"But mom baked the bread and the doughnuts and the schwingfelders," explained Ellen.

"And my mom baked the pies and the fine cake," said Hester.

"Then why do you bring them? I thought you wanted me to see how good you could bake."

"Ach, no!" said Hester, laughing. "It is because you are not to bake any more, ever."

"Not to bake any more!"

"You are not to have it so hard," explained Ellen. "We have it all planned."

Grandmother Miller laughed until she could hardly see. When the girls had gone, she chuckled, "The dear children!" She got out her baking-board and heated the old-fashioned oven, and decided that she would bake rhubarb pie and cherry pie. "Then I will send one to each of these girls for a present," she thought.

One morning early in July young John Adam appeared on his way to school. He and Hester were the children of Adam, Grandmother Miller's oldest son. John was short and sturdy and blue-eyed, and he went about work or play with equal vim.

He now took the broom from his grandmother's hands. "You are not to sweep the porch any more, gran'mom," he said. "I am the sweeper. And John Edwin is coming to hunt the eggs in the evening always and feed the chickens."

Grandmother Miller did not laugh. She had laughed at Hester and Ellen, but they continued their unwelcome gifts of pie and cake. She stammered out a Pennsylvania German equivalent for "Nonsense!" and made up her mind grimly that she would sweep the porch and the pavement in the morning and gather the eggs in the evening long before John Adam and John Edwin should appear.

In August, grandmother protested angrily to her son Adam.

"What ails these young ones? Why are they all the time after me?"

Adam looked down at his mother uneasily. Although he was forty years old and six feet tall, and she hardly came above his elbow, he was still a little afraid of her.

"Come to us to live, mom. You oughtn't to live here alone any more."

Grandmother laughed. Adam was her child; she had borne him, nursed him, spanked him. She knew how to deal with Adam.

"Pooh!" said she.

As August changed to September, and the days grew shorter, Grandmother Miller began gradually to be aware that she was never alone. Accustomed to visits from her grandchildren, she was slow to notice that before Ellen, who had slept with her, departed, Hester came in to do the breakfast dishes, and that Edwin's children stopped on their way from school at noon, and Henry's children on their way back to school.

When in September grandmother wondered idly whether she should have turkeys or geese for the Christmas feast, Hester told her that she was not to have the Christmas feast.

"We will have it at our house, gran'mom. You are not to have Christmas dinners any more. It is too hard work."

At that, when she had a few moments to herself, grandmother wept. She was hurt and angry, but, worse than that, she began to feel old.

"I didn't know it would ever be like this," she said to herself, bitterly. "I did not think the day would ever come when I would wish to die. But now I wish to die."

Grandmother Miller always did her winter sewing in November. At that time she made herself three warm dresses and many white and colored aprons.

But in September Ellen and Hester, sewing after school hours and in the evenings, made grandmother's aprons and dresses, and a new silk sunbonnet. Ellen and Hester sewed with lightning speed; it was the one art in which they had not obeyed their grandmother's instructions. Grandmother did not like their sewing; their stitches were too long, and an occasional pucker showed where all should have been smooth.

When they presented their grandmother with her wardrobe, she was at once too polite and too confused to express the amazement and disappointment that she felt.

She laid down the apron that she had begun, and looked at them stupidly.

"But how will I fill in my time?" she asked, with a mighty effort to keep her voice steady. "What will I do from morning till night?" "You will rest," said Hester, affectionately. "You are to rest, so that you will be with us for many years."

"Your hand trembles, gran'mom," said Ellen. "Let me thread your needle."

Speechless, grandmother let Ellen take the needle from her hand. When the girls had gone, she sat for a long time, and looked at her gifts spread out on the chairs and the table.

"They have made my clothes for me!" she said again.

Then her gaze wandered. She looked down the street toward the village and up the road toward the church. Opposite the church was the cemetery; from where she sat, grandmother could see a tall monument.

Suddenly, as if some firm foundation were slipping from beneath her feet, or as if she were being dragged down by some powerful force, Grandmother Miller clutched the arms of her chair. Then she rose, and without stopping to put on her shawl, ran down the street to the village store.

"I want muslin," she said. "Muslin and cotton batting and tailor's chalk."

Still moving as if she were pursued, Grandmother Miller

returned to her kitchen, climbed thence to her garret, brought down her quilting-frame, and set it up in the kitchen.

"I must have work!" she cried. "Cannot sew! Cannot thread a needle! I will show them! I must have work!"

Overseaming neatly and beautifully, she sewed the breadths of muslin together, laid the cotton batting between them, and fastened them into the frame. Upon them, by means of an intricate pattern in which tiny rose was set close to tiny rose, and tiny lily close to tiny lily, she printed a design for her quilting. Then, although night had come, and Grandmother Miller was seventy years old and owned no spectacles, she began her work. After her thimble had clicked against her needle for about fifteen minutes, she breathed a loud "Ah!" of complete satisfaction.

"Cannot sew!" said she again. "Cannot thread a needle!" Her eyes sparkled. "Whichever leaves me the most alone, Hester or Ellen, will get this quilt."

"But, grandmother, you cannot see!" protested Ellen, when she came to spend the night.

"Perhaps she could if I threaded a lot of needles." Hester spoke a little absent-mindedly; perhaps she was already planning the great surprise for grandmother.

In the morning, after Hester and Ellen had gone, grandmother unthreaded their needles.

Every fall grandmother visited the farm that she had inherited from her father. Thither her son Adam took her in the high buggy, and for her arrival her tenants made great preparations. It was not, as a matter of fact, necessary for grandmother to make the eight-mile journey; the Dieners could easily bring in the fat goose and the red ear of corn and the panhas and the sausage that they annually presented to her. It would even be easier for them to bring in the new baby than for grandmother to go to see it.

But to grandmother's amazement, she was allowed to go this year without protest. Adam's wife and Ellen and Hester and a few other women of the family were on hand to wrap her up, and to charge Adam to keep her wrapped up; but beyond that they did not interfere.

Grandmother was unspeakably happy. The thought of her rose-and-lily quilt, growing slowly under her exquisite stitches, gave her great satisfaction; her mind had now something to rest upon when she sat before the fire or lay wakeful at night. Never was quilt so carefully made. With its beautiful close pattern, followed in fine white stitches upon the white background, it would be handsomer than any Marseilles spread. Moreover, grandmother loved to visit, to go armed, as she was now, with gifts—a gold piece for her tenant's Christmas present, a shawl for the mother, a coat and cap for the newest baby, and nuts and candy and oranges for the other children.

Having made her visit, having eaten her dinner with the Dieners, having listened to Mr. Diener's report, and having even inspected the corn-crib and the barn and the spring-house, she let herself be lifted into the buggy, and she and her son started homeward. They stopped at the store for a fresh supply of tailor's chalk to make a new section of the rose-and-lily quilt. Adam did not call for the store-keeper to come out, as Ellen or Hester would have done. He said, "There, mother, hold the lines," and went in himself.

Sitting there in the dark street, grandmother was for an instant disturbed in her contentment. Two women, hooded and shawled against the cold, came down the street, talking busily.

"Ach, she is too old!" said one, and the other answered with a hearty, "You have right!"

"They are talking about some poor soul," said grandmother to herself. "But I am not old."

To grandmother's surprise, Ellen and Hester and the others were not at hand to help her down when she got home. She was delighted. Now she would work a little upon her quilt. Adam held the horse while his mother clambered out; then he handed her the basket, and she trotted happily up the brick walk. The girls, her daughters-in-law and granddaughters, were fine girls; they would have the fire burning brightly and the lamp lighted. After supper—seventy-year-old grandmother meant to have a little of the fresh sausage!—she would stamp the new section of her quilt, and work one rose and one lily. She dreaded the moment when her dear task would be accomplished.

She opened the door of her kitchen. Then she put her basket down and supported herself with her hand against the frame of the door. The fire was burning, the lamp was lighted, on the table was spread the cloth for her supper, and on it were the precious silver spoons and the sugar-bowl and the cream-pitcher that Ellen and Hester insisted she must use—"While you live, gran'mom."

But the quilting-frame was gone, and on grandmother's arm-chair lay the finished quilt!

Presently, when she could gather strength enough, grandmother walked across the room, picked up the quilt, examined it, and laid it down. Then she climbed into the garret and brought the frame down once more, set it up, and into it sewed the finished quilt. It was not only quilted, it was hemmed. The girls must have worked with incredible speed. Grandmother lighted two other lamps, flung wide the closed shutters, and began to work at the quilt. But she worked with a long pin, instead of a needle. It was pathetic to see her bending close over her eager strokes.

It does not take long for news to travel in Millerstown. Within five minutes, some one coming down the road saw grandmother's brilliant light, went to find out what in the world she was doing, and then flew, saddened and horrified, to announce that grandmother had gone mad. Hester and Ellen were all ready to start to her house to spend the night; the others ran with them, and all came, panting and breathless, to grandmother's door.

"O gran'mom! gran'mom!" wailed Hester, as she flew. "Oh, dear gran'mom!"

"We should 'a' stayed every minute by her," said Ellen.

Then, with their fathers and mothers and sisters and brothers behind them, to say nothing of other uncounted Millerstonians, they burst into grandmother's kitchen, where grandmother stood by the quilting-frame with the long pin in her hand. The rush of their coming would have been enough to drive a sane person into insanity.

"Oh, what are you doing, dear gran'mom?" said Hester.

Grandmother straightened her shoulders and flung back her head.

"I am ripping," said she, in the steady tones of one who, after unendurable provocation, rejoices to give battle. "I am ripping, and I will keep on ripping till every long, crooked stitch is out of my quilt. I thank myself,"—grandmother's tone was firm, her eye was bright and steady,—"I thank myself for all the trouble, but from now on I will do my own quilting.

"And"—grandmother did not know that at this moment she was adding just twenty happy, independent, useful years to the seventy that she had already enjoyed—"from now on I do my own sewing and sweeping and cooking and baking and egg-hunting and chicken-feeding. And on Christmas, one month from to-day,"—grandmother's voice became excited, jubilant, laughing, and she waved her long implement for ripping in the air,—"on Christmas I will roast here in this oven, for whoever will come, a turkey and a goose!"

QUILT SCRAPS
Louise Platt Hauck, *Argosy*, April 10, 1920

Although they had been married fifty years, Ma and Pa
Cameron only recently cleared their consciences by confess-
ing which traits each had that annoyed the other. Pa was
shocked at Ma's comments. He retaliated by complaining vig-
orously about Ma's quiltmaking, and her frequent travels over
the countryside to collect minute quilt scraps from her women
friends. He forbade Ma to make another quilt to place in the
annual county fair. Ma replied that she would agree only if
Pa did not enter his colt, Blue Streak, in the county fair races.
For Pa, such an ultimatum was not only unreasonable but
unthinkable. A surprising turn of events ends the impasse.

"Morning, grandad!"

Dr. Geoffry Karnes paused at the door of the barn and sent
his voice ahead of him through the vast, dusty spaces. At the far
end the big sliding doors were open, and seated in a decrepit
chair which was propped against the casing was Pa Cameron. His
hands were in his pockets, his eyes on the fields of blossoming
alfalfa. Myriads of tiny white butterflies hovered over the flowers
and the hot sunshine drew from them a honey-sweet perfume. It
was a day to make the blood in old veins sing, but Pa's arterial
system showed no symptoms of vocal expression. The dejected
droop of his head, the resigned slouch of his shoulders indicated
that the goddess of June was spreading her loveliness before him
in vain. He turned his head at Dr. Geoffry's hail, but made no
reply.

"Dozing, sir?" The young physician covered the space between them. "Glorious morning, isn't it? How'd you like to take a
spin with me out to Ridgeville? I've got a couple of calls to make
there."

Pa glanced backward over the other's shoulder.

"Been in the house yet?" he inquired.

"Yes, I left some patterns Cynthia sent grandma."

"What was she doing—Ma, I mean?"

"Why, let me see"—Dr. Karnes reflected. "I believe—yes, she was over-hauling some scrap-bags—cutting quilt blocks, it looked to me. Why?"

Pa groaned and brought the front legs of his chair to the floor.

"Ridgeville, did ye say? Yes, I'll go. Run in and bring my hat and duster out of the sitting-room closet, will you, doc? And tell your grandma where we're bound. I'll wait in the car."

Wondering a little at Pa's unusual mood, Dr. Karnes obeyed, and in a few minutes the gray runabout was rolling up the long country road. Pa cleared his throat.

"Did ye tell ma? What did she say?"

"I don't believe she spoke," Dr. Geoffry smiled. "I think she merely sniffed and went on with her work. What's the matter, grandad? Something gone wrong with the domestic machinery?"

"I sh'd say so," was the mournful answer. "Home's a good place to get away from these days."

There was a short silence during which the doctor looked keenly at Pa and Pa looked steadily ahead.

"Want to tell me about it?" Dr. Karnes asked at last with just the right shade of sympathy, just the correct lack of impressiveness.

"It was a death-bed confession," Pa announced, and appeared to think this statement adequate, for he said no more. Dr. Karnes rapidly reviewed the mortality list for the last few weeks. There was old Pete Timmons at the county infirmary, and Katie Flannagan's still-born baby–

"Whose death-bed?" Pa's grandson-in-law employed direct methods.

"Ma's—your grandma's."

"But grandma hasn't died—"

"No, but she nearly did; at least she thought she was going to. It was that canned lobster," he explained patiently as he saw Dr. Geoffry's bewilderment was verging on to apprehension for the old man's sanity. "It was the first time ma ever was that sick, and she was pretty scared. After you got her easy and went home that night, she called me over to the bed and sort of freed her mind of what was troublin' her. It was to all intents and purposes a dying statement, the only difference bein' that she didn't die, but lived to drink hot milk for breakfast. She disposed of all her earthly possessions like she wanted 'em, and then she began on the confession part." He drew a long breath and went on with a visible effort. "Seems for one reason and another she's been cherishin' some hard feelings toward me, and it was weighin' heavy on her conscience. So she told me about it, and asked me to forgive her for feelin' so."

"Well?" Dr. Karnes reminded him, for Pa had come to another full stop. "What had you done to cause her hard feelings?"

"Oh, one thing and another," Pa said evasively. "Nothing I didn't know about before, except a couple of trifles. Seems I've got a habit—maybe you've noticed it—of kind o'hummin' a certain song when I'm thinking."

Dr. Karnes nodded, a sudden twinkling in his brown eyes.

"'Tell me one thing, tell me truly, tell me why you scorn me so,'" he sang.

Pa's expression was one of surprise tempered with sorrow.

"I guess it's true, then," he admitted. "Ma insisted on it, and I couldn't out and out contradict her, for I wa'n't just sure myself."

"But what's that got to do with canned lobster and grandma's hard feelings toward you?"

"Seems it gets on her nerves. Seems my wife thinks I'm a pretty fine man, but she can't bear to hear me sing. Seems I don't know the right key when I hear it, and I hum out of time and through my nose. And ma's borne the cross of it for fifty years and never complained till now." His manner was aggrieved, his voice bitter. The doctor's roar of mirth checked itself suddenly.

"I fancy we all have some such grievances if the truth were known. Perhaps grandma herself —"

"Yes, I told her so," Pa assented. "She didn't have a monopoly on the conscience cleanin' that went on that night. She pulls her eyelashes when she's bothered, and I told her I often 'd wanted to speak to her about it. It was a cute enough trick when she was a girl, but a woman of her age had better be saving of all her natural adornments, and so I pointed out to her when she come at me about my singin'."

"And she—how did she take it?" Geoffry questioned cautiously.

"'Bout as well as you'd expect," was the grim reply. "First she didn't believe she did it; then she couldn't see for the life of her why that should bother any human being; and after all they were *her* lashes, and she reckoned she'd a right to pull 'em if she pleased. That wasn't a thing that could reasonably be complained of like my singin' off key and the same old thing year in and year out."

"What did you say to that?"

Pa's sidelong glance was so full of meaning that that doctor smiled involuntarily.

"I give her another of those quietin' powders you left, and before long she went to sleep."

The car breasted a gentle slope from the summit of which could be seen the spires of two villages. It was a pretty sight—the low white buildings huddling among the trees—but far from cheering Pa it seemed to increase his depression.

"Ridgeville and Parkinson," he groaned. "And over to the left is Gentry."

"Nice little towns," the doctor responded heartily. "What have you against them?"

"Mis' Polk lives at Gentry, and so does Sallie Williams," Pa informed him in gloomy accents. "Tulie Portor's in Ridgeville, and there's half a dozen of ma's friends scattered between them."

"Grandad, you're too cryptic for me this morning," Dr. Karnes said after a brief mental wrestle with these statements. "Why should the fact that grandma has friends all over the county disturb you? I should suppose you'd enjoy her popularity."

"Oh, I do." Deep and subtle sarcasm pervaded Pa's usual kindly voice. "I enjoy most more than anything I know drivin' round exchangin' quilt scraps with old ladies. Next to bringin' up a family of gold-fish I don't know anything more exciting."

"I begin to understand," Geoffry nodded comprehendingly. "Grandma's getting ready to exhibit another quilt at the fall fair, and it's up to you to collect the material. But I thought—didn't grandma say last year—"

Pa broke shortly across his meditative sentences. "Your grandma promised me she wouldn't piece another of them darned quilts. She's been at it for twenty years or more, and she's had the blue ribbon for sixteen of them years. That ought to satisfy any woman. I near ruined my best mare last spring travelin' up hill and down dale changin' scraps and waiting while Molly Jones sorted her pinks and Mattie Sallee collected her purples. I told ma then it 'd be the last time I'd ever do it, and she agreed to quit. Now—"

"Now?"

"It's that death-bed confession. She's takin' it out on me, you see, for rememberin' what she never meant to tell; also on account of that eyelash business I mentioned a while back."

The car had reached the outskirts of Ridgeville and was slowing before a large, white pillared house.

"I'll wait here in the car for ye, doc. This is one of the places ma swaps scraps, and I ain't a goin' to let it be known I'm here. Mis' Melton sick?" he asked hopefully.

"No. Sorry to disappoint you, grandad, but it's her husband, and it's only a boil at that. I'll be out as soon as I lance it."

Pa, watching stealthily from the far side of the runabout, saw the front door close upon him, and settled back in the seat to wait. In a few minutes the door opened again and the doctor came out, followed by a pleasant-faced, elderly woman, who exclaimed:

"Well, Henry Cameron, it's a wonder you wouldn't come in and see your friends. Did you know Will's got a boil? Right on the back of his neck. Too much pork sausage, I tell him; but he lays it to the sulfur and molasses I give him last month. How's Mar'gret these days? Why didn't she come over with ye?"

Pa answered vaguely, hoping to escape what seemed inevitable. And it was.

"Mar'gret figurin' on piecin' a quilt this year? Tell her I got a lot of blue gingham Jim's wife sent me from Moundhurst. I'll trade for some of them pink scraps she saved from Cynthia's troosew."

Pa straightened determinedly.

"Mis' Cameron," he began; "Mis' Cameron, ain't—" The words died on his lips as a vision of his wife's face rose before him. Its expression was what Pa described briefly to himself as "sot." "Mis' Cameron ain't with us to-day," he finished somewhat unnecessarily. "I'll tell her what you said. Better get on, hadn't we, doc?"

The drive home was broken only once, and that by Pa, who announced in a tone compounded equally of resolution, nervousness, and apprehension:

"If she's counting on me to collect her scraps, your grandma ain't going to piece another quilt."

"Stick to it, grandad," Dr. Geoffry advised. "Manly determination and assertiveness, that's all you need. I'll lay you ten to one grandma will respect you all the more if you don't give in to her on this."

It was close on the dinner hour when Pa went slowly up the flagged walk to his door. He sniffed the enticing odor of baked ham and fresh gingerbread, and insensibly his irritation diminished. His wife was sitting where Dr. Karnes had found her, sorting and smoothing the rainbow heaps of pieces. She glanced over her spectacles at her husband, but left it to him to make the first remark, a strategic advantage which Pa resented. A new weekly paper lay upon the table, and he seized it and buried himself in its pages.

Ma rocked and sorted. Pa read. Occasionally he cleared his throat. Presently from behind the rustling sheets came another sound, a subdued humming which developed half articulate words.

" 'Tell me one thing, tell me truly– ' "

Ma cocked her head like a hound on the scent. At the end of the long "truly" which rose and fell and rose again in a riot of notes of which the composer of that touching song had never dreamed, she stuffed her scraps into the big striped bag and sailed from the room.

"Tell me why– " Pa's mouth remained open on the question. The slam of the sitting-room door quenched his desire for information. He flushed a dull red and sang no more.

A month of the summer drifted by. The piece sorting had given place to stitching, now. Pa came up from the stables one afternoon to find his wife bending over the infinitesimal bits of gingham and calico, a flush of combined heat and exertion in her thin cheeks. The sight goaded Pa to speech.

"Now, see here, ma, I'm going to put a stop to this blamed foolishness. Here you sit hour after hour wearin' yourself to a frazzle, sewing bits of cloth together. I want you should put that mess of rags back into the bag and hang it in the attic."

"All right, I will, Pa," his wife said unexpectedly. "I'll agree not to enter a quilt this fall if you'll promise not to enter Blue Streak."

Pa's jaw dropped.

"What you talkin' about, ma? Not enter the colt, the likeliest two-year-old I ever raised! Shucks, ma, you're fooling."

"Not so you'd notice it," ma retorted, whose recent association with a company of movie actors had done strange things to her speech.

"There's been a Cameron colt in every West County fair for twenty-two years, Margaret, and my collection of blue ribbons ain't equaled by none," Pa said with great dignity.

"And there's been a *Mrs.* Cameron quilt in every West County fair for twenty-three years, Henry, and *my* collection of blue ribbons has got four more in it than yours," ma made answer with equal dignity.

Pa tacked.

"I see what you mean, but the principle's not the same, not at all the same. Quilts take work, colts don't."

"Oh, they *don't!*" The pungent sarcasm of ma's tones fairly seared the air. "What about the trainin' and the exercisin' and the hours you spent on diet lists, and the teachin' of jockeys? Work! Piecin' a quilt's an invalid's job compared to gettin' a colt ready for the fair races. Besides, when the quilt is done I wrap it up and lay it away, off my mind until opening day, whilest the nearer that day gets the more het you grow."

Ma smoothed the block on her knee and eyed it complacently.

"Might as well give up, Pa. You're talkin' foolishness. I'm willing to give up if you are. I think, myself, we're getting some old to be wearin' ourselves out with this competition business, and I'll withdraw my quilt if you'll withdraw your colt. Not unless." Her little mouth took an obstinate curve with which Pa was sadly familiar, and he shrugged his shoulders resignedly.

"Have it your way, then," he said. "Stitch, and stitch, and stitch the doggoned summer if you want to. Race all over the country to trade a half-inch triangle of pink cheese-cloth for a scrap of red bunting big enough to cover a postage stamp. If that's your idea of enjoyin' yourself, go to it! But I want you to distinctly understand that *I* ain't figurin' on playin' errand-boy for you. I– "

Ma's voice came cool and sweet across his irritated tones.

"I wouldn't lose my temper, Henry, if I was you. You haven't any call to get excited as I know of. I'm perfectly willing to do my own collecting and trading. All I ask is that you tell Milt to harness the mare whenever I want her."

The Camerons were nearer to serious disagreement than they themselves realized. Perhaps the intense heat of July and August told upon them. Certainly the long drives which ma took with the mare attached to the light buggy left her fagged and worn to an unusual degree. Dr. Geoffry spoke to Pa about it more than once; even remonstrated, or it is perhaps more accurate to say that he attempted to remonstrate with ma herself.

The crisp opinion of young doctors in general, and of this young doctor in particular, which was delivered in ma's best style, sent him away amused and convinced of the uselessness of further words. Cynthia brought up baby Geoff for many a morning gossip on the shady porch and ventured a few warning words on her own behalf. Ma brushed them aside with the same irritation she had shown at every attempt to dissuade her.

The quilt grew daily, and Pa stole a glance now and then at its splendors. The day when it was mounted on its frame for the quilting, he drew a long breath of relief. Ma's pale face and encircled eyes had worried him more than he cared to admit.

With September and the cooler days he devoted himself steadily to developing Blue Streak's speed. Four or five miles from the farmhouse was a level meadow which had long been dedicated to the training of the Cameron colts. Here day after day went Pa, the colt, and a diminutive stable-boy. That the progress of Blue Streak was satisfactory was attested by her owner's growing good nature. Once or twice he attempted to interest ma in the colt's possibilities, but not the most optimistic could read encouragement into her attitude.

The county fair was barely a week off when the morning mail

brought a letter whose contents visibly disquieted Pa Cameron.

"Ma," he burst forth, "here's a letter from Cal Thurston. He's sending Ragged Ann up from Sturgis."

"Ragged Ann?" ma said interrogatively.

"Yes, you know. Out of Pollux by Cynthia. She ought to be the best colt Thurston's stables have sent out since—Rex II."

Ma's eyes met his own in sympathetic comprehension. Back in the days when the Cameron stable had been among the finest in Missouri, she had shared her husband's pride in his equine treasures. The memory of that black day when the bay colt from Kentucky, looking every inch his name, had come in home an easy winner over the Cameron entrant, was with them yet. With the advent of the automobile the races at the county fair had lost much of their importance, and except for a colt or two maintained for his own enjoyment, Pa had allowed his stables to fall into disuse. The old sparkle now shone in his eye, the old excitement set him pacing up and down the room.

"I declare it takes me back twenty years to hear from Cal. I wrote him I had a colt could put it all over anything he ever bred in Sturgis, but I'm blamed if I ever thought he'd take me up on it. Well, well! West County Fair 'll see some races as is races next week."

He paused in his restless walk and stood by his wife's chair.

"Don't you care, Margaret? Ain't you a bit interested?" he asked wistfully.

For a moment the impulse to yield him the warm sympathy he had known all his life possessed her, then she set her lips.

"Was you intersted when I showed you my quilt? Did you care a bit that it's the handsomest piece of work I ever got ready for the fair? No, just because you didn't want me to enter this time I couldn't strike a spark out of ye. And now you want I should be all a-tiptoe about *your* entry. It's not fair—it's not fair, and so I say to ye, Pa!"

Unwonted tears dimmed her eyes, unwonted emotion quivered in her voice. Pa stared aghast, not knowing that the fatigue of the long, hot summer was manifesting itself in her lack of control. His hand stole to his chin and caressed it while his mind dealt perplexedly with the problem.

"Tell me one thing, tell me truly—"

The psychology of hysteria is an interesting study. The earnest student might well ponder the reason why the tuneless sounds which issued from Pa's lips sent his wife's face down into her hands, while sobs and gasping laughter shook her from head to foot. Dr. Geoffry Karnes, in answer to his grandfather-in-law's agonized summons, came racing to the farm in defiance of the speed laws. Ma was dosed with veronal and put to bed, and the physician endeavored to unravel the string of the old man's confused account of the episode.

"It's that darned quilt," Pa ended miserably. "She's stewed herself into a mother over some new pattern she's worked out. Why, one night she sat up in bed in her sleep, working out how many three-cornered bits it'd take to make the wing feathers of an eagle."

"You bet it's that darned quilt," Dr. Geoff acquiesced. "Haven't I seen her bending her poor little old back and straining her poor old eyes over it when she should have been resting, or working in her garden or visiting with Cynthia? Can't you—"

"I can't do a thing—not one dad-blamed thing," his grandfather-in-law assured him. "When ma's head is sot, it's sot, and that's all there is to it."

If he had cherished a hope that his helpmate would be softened by her attack he was speedily undeceived. Ma's chin was a little firmer, her lips more tightly set the next morning than ever. Pa watched her uneasily as he announced that business would take him into the next township for the day.

"I suppose you know that your quilt must be in the hands of

the committee by tomorrow," he said with what he tried to make a kindly tone. "If you'll have it ready for me when I get back, I'll drive in with it the first thing in the morning."

In an instant ma's little figure became primly erect. "I can see to it myself, thank you."

"Mar-ga-ret, you must promise me you will not leave this house to-day." Pa's voice took on a sonorous note which moved his wife to secret mirth. "Do you hear me?"

"I do. Henry, I thought I heard Blue Streak cough last night. Is he getting a cold?"

Her spouse eyed her with suspicion. He realized that he was being diverted from the subject in hand, but the bait was too alluring to resist.

"Blue Streak," he began enthusiastically. "Blue Streak never was in better condition. He did his mile in two minutes and a quarter yesterday. I'd like to see old Cal's colt beat that!"

"Henry," ma said quietly, "I'll make you that proposition I made you early in the summer. I'll withdraw my quilt if you'll withdraw your colt. We're both of us too old to be workin' ourselves up like this."

"It ain't the same thing at all," he protested hotly. "Your quilt's kept your nose to the grindstone all summer—used you up for nothing. The colt's training has done me good. It ain't right and fitten that a woman of your age—"

"Quilt piecin's supposed to be a grandmotherly occupation," she interpolated neatly. "I don't remember that I ever heard that colt racin' was a grandfatherly one."

Pa flung himself out of the house in exasperation, and ma smiled grimly as she heard the wheels of the sulky drive over the gravel into the road. Late that afternoon she had the small buggy brought around, and with her quilt in a carefully wrapped parcel, set out for the fair grounds. A sudden cold wind had sprung up, and she drew the lap-robe about her knees.

"Must have had rain near by," she mused. "I believe I'll turn off into the pasture and see if Blue Streak is all right. I did hear him cough, and that fool Jim wouldn't know enough to blanket him if he got too hot."

She always declared afterward that it was her woman's intuition of disaster which made her turn the buggy wheels into the lane which led to the pasture. Whatever the motive, the need for some helpful presence was instantly apparent. Jim, the young stableman, leaned heavily against the fence, while the colt, foam on his glossy neck, blood showing in his nostrils, stood quivering at a little distance.

"It's my foot," the boy groaned in reply to her questions. "Blue Streak's been nervous all day, and when I come up sudden like behind him just now he plunged and stepped on my foot. Smashed all the bones, it feels like," he complained.

"Nothin's broken—it's bruised bad, that's all," Mrs. Cameron assured him after a hasty examination. "What's the matter with the colt? What's makin' him sweat like this?" she demanded.

"He—he's been runnin'," Jim answered sullenly. "He set out like a blue streak of lightning and got all het up, that's all."

"Yes, but what made him run?" she dema'nded inexorably. "Jim Sterns, listen to me: did you hit him?"

"I—I—" His eyes fell before the anger in hers. "I just give him one crack—I was so mad like with the pain."

Ma wasted no time in recrimination. Henry could attend to the boy later. The thing now to do was to get Blue Streak in his stall before a chill developed. Her practised eye noted the tremors which already agitated the thoroughbred.

"Jim," she ordered swiftly, "you climb into the buggy and drive in after the vet. Bring him straight to the stable. I'll be walking the colt toward home. Wait—give me that bundle out of the buggy."

Only a wife, and one who knows herself unjustly judged, can appreciate the actual pleasure which the strapping of the pre-

cious quilt about Blue Streak's lathered body brought to Ma
Cameron.

"This colt's not going to take cold if *I* can help it," she said as
she set out, a valiant little figure, leading the queerly caparisoned
Blue Streak toward home.

The five miles seemed stretched into fifty before she came in
sight of the white buildings. Her dress was spotted and dusty, a
brier had torn a long rent in her skirt, and her face was haggard
with fatigue. Pa, just stepping from the sulky at the stable door,
looked in amazement at the strange procession.

"It's Blue Streak," ma said superfluously. "He—was havin' a
chill. I led him—home—from the pasture. Hurry and get him to
his stall. I think he'll be all—right—now."

Her husband's glance traveled from the drooping figure of
his wife to the colt; noted the improvised blanket, now soiled
with dust and lather. Pa may not have been gifted with feminine
intuition, but he possessed a masculine power of deduction. The
sum of the two and two he saw before him brought a great lump
into his throat.

"Ma—Margaret—" he began huskily.

"You sound like a goat," his wife assured him with tartness.
"Ain't you going to put the colt in?"

Something in his glance flushed her cheeks with rosy color.
Unconsciously her fingers stole to her lashes and she began to
pull them violently. Then she remembered and withdrew her
hand with an angry start. Pa took the withered little fingers and
kissed them gently.

"I always did think that was the prettiest trick," he whispered.

Blue Streak, finding himself free, sagaciously picked his way
into the stable. Dr. Geoff and Cynthia, with the veterinary on the
back seat of the car, beheld the unusual sight of their grandparents clasped in each other's arms, oblivious alike of colt or quilt,
human or equine spectators.

THE ASHLEY STAR

Marjorie Hill Allee, *The Youth's Companion,*
April 7, 1921

> *Ellen, an impressionable girl, had visited her friend, Amy*
> *Winston, last Christmas. Ellen had been enraptured with the*
> *beautiful, stylish furnishings she saw in the Southern home*
> *of the wealthy Winston family. In her thoughts, Ellen con-*
> *trasted the Winston home with her own home. Now Mme.*
> *Lucy Winston and Amy were coming to town, and Ellen*
> *wanted to have a tea party for them. As much as Ellen dis-*
> *liked and was offended by the overcrowded, fussy Victorian*
> *room of her Aunt Susan, it was the nicest room in her home.*
> *And so, Ellen was compelled to ask her stern, rather forbid-*
> *ding great-aunt if the proposed tea party could be held in*
> *Aunt Susan's room. Aunt Susan surprisingly agreed. She ca-*
> *sually asked Ellen the names of the other invited guests, what*
> *"entertainment" was planned, and continued to work on the*
> *pink and white "Ashley Star" quilt. Aunt Susan, an inveter-*
> *ate quiltmaker, made many quilts for the family. In Ellen's*
> *opinion quilts were old-fashioned, and she had little appre-*
> *ciation for them. After much preparation, the day of the tea*
> *party came, and all of the guests arrived punctually. No one*
> *was more surprised than Ellen when she learned the "enter-*
> *tainment' Aunt Ellen provided for the guests. She was even*
> *more astounded at Mme. Lucy and Amy Winston's reaction*
> *to the "entertainment."*

Ellen rapped cautiously at the door of Aunt Susan's room. If you
knocked too softly, Aunt Susan did not hear; but if you knocked
much harder, she greeted you with the tart announcement that
she was not so deaf as that yet!

A brisk "Come in" sounded over the transom, and with relief
Ellen turned the knob; she had particular reasons for hoping to

find her great-aunt in an unruffled humor. Aunt Susan sat in a high-backed rocking-chair, sewing patchwork squares. The rocker, which was placed on a braided rug to save the Brussels carpet, was the only chair she ever used; but the big room was crowded with other furniture, and pictures and gift books and little china figures elbowed one another on the mantel, on the walls and on the tables. The whole room offended Ellen's taste. She liked plenty of space, plain colors and simple lines; and ever since she had visited Amy Winston at Christmas time had longed for the Southern mahogany she had seen in Amy's home.

"If this were only colonial!" she thought. "But it isn't; it's just old-fashioned enough to be queer."

Aunt Susan's needle twinkled down to the end of her seam before she raised her head, and Ellen stood waiting like a little girl told to be seen, not heard. However much she might try to assume the dignity of a young lady, the room and Aunt Susan nearly always made her feel uncomfortably young and unimportant. She rebelled against the feeling even more than against the Victorian parlor set; but her rebellion was of no avail.

"Well?" inquired Aunt Susan. "What is it?"

Ellen braced herself and pitched her voice as tactfully as possible. "Mother said I might ask you, Aunt Susan, if you would mind a tea party in your room Thursday afternoon for Mme. Winston and Amy. You know they were so very good to me last Christmas." She paused and watched Aunt Susan's unchanging face. It was a constant wonder to her that Aunt Susan could make her feel so uncomfortable without losing her own composure and without noticing that she was disturbed.

"Who's invited?" Aunt Susan asked at last.

"I haven't spoken to anyone yet. I thought we might ask Cousin Charity and Cousin Mattie; then with Mme. Winston and Amy that would be all."

"Ask Mary Henley, too," directed Aunt Susan. "She was a great friend of Lucy Winston's when they were girls together."

Ellen felt encouraged. "I can make the tea and the cakes and the sandwiches, and I'll dust and bring in flowers Thursday morning."

"Any entertainment?"

"Why, no," answered Ellen, astonished. "They never have anything except music at teas. I don't believe you'd care for that."

"No. I guess we can do better," agreed the old lady dryly. She selected a pink-and-green triangle from the basket beside her and ran down the seam with one swift motion of her needle.

Ellen understood that the interview was over; she left the room much cheered. Aunt Susan had not objected to a single essential point. Ellen searched her memory for details of an at home at which Mme. Winston had poured tea. She assured herself that she could make even Aunt Susan's room attractive. To Ellen's polite invitations all of the guests replied that they would be glad to come. It was indeed an event for them to see Lucy Winston, who rarely came back to her girlhood home. They loved her for the same gracious and friendly qualities that had made them love her fifty years ago; they held in delighted remembrance her beautiful dresses, which were not quite like any of the pictures in the fashion books, and for the stories she told of people and of places she had seen on her travels.

Aunt Susan seemed not to be taking the event seriously. She sewed long hours on the pink-and-green patchwork. She told Ellen that the pattern was called the Ashley star, and Ellen promptly forgot it. On Thursday morning, when she came in with her dust cloth, a great expanse of white squares alternating with blocks of Ashley star lay over Aunt Susan's knees; the quilt top was nearly done.

"Do you want me to help you dress this afternoon, Aunt Susan?" she asked uncertainly. She hoped to get a chance to suggest that Aunt Susan wear her best lace collar.

"Come in about one o'clock," replied Aunt Susan, speaking through a mouthful of pins with the skill of long practice.

After dusting Ellen started to make sandwiches. Luncheon time still found her cutting rounds of bread, and she begged off from eating with the family on the ground that she had tasted too much sandwich filling to be hungry. When the sandwiches were stacked in the refrigerator she returned to the scene of the party, wondering just why Aunt Susan wished to dress so early and cherishing the hope of unobtrusively slipping some unnecessary furniture out of the room, though she did not quite know how she should manage it.

She had difficulty in believing what she saw. With the exception of four ladder-backed chairs that stood out in a fine open space in the centre of the room, Aunt Susan's multitudinous furniture was pushed back hard against the sides of the room, tea table and all. The chairs supported four stout wooden pieces laid in a square, with their ends crossing; Aunt Susan had brought out her quilting frame.

"I'd ask Sarah, but I know she's busy," said Aunt Susan in the most matter-of-fact tone. "You can help me tack this in well enough." Ellen opened her mouth to protest, but no words came; she did not know how to begin. Aunt Susan could not have forgotten the tea party. What earthly reason could she have for deliberately setting up a quilt?

Mechanically, Ellen began smoothing the unbleached muslin laid down for the back of the quilt; she worked patiently, spreading the cotton batting in a thin even layer, and when the gay top was pinned down she helped sew it into the quilting frame with stout cord.

"We ought to get it well toward three fourths done this afternoon, if everybody works," said the old lady, surveying it with a professional eye.

Then the horrid truth dawned on Ellen: this was Aunt Susan's idea of entertainment for their guests. She expected Mme. Winston and Amy to quilt!

"Did they quilt at tea parties when you were a girl?" Ellen ventured to say in a trembling voice.

"What?" asked Aunt Susan sharply:

Ellen repeated her question. The tears were very near.

"No, no; they didn't have sense to, any more than they seem to have now. It takes a lot of living to find out you're happier when you're busy." That bit of philosophy was of no comfort to Ellen; she fled to her own room, and there her tears dried in a fever of indignation. She thought about Aunt Susan, about her deafness, her queerness, her disregard of plans. It seemed to her impossible to go on living in the same house with Aunt Susan.

At three o'clock Ellen dressed carefully and then went downstairs. Her party had been completely spoiled, but she should have to go through with it just the same. She did not tell her mother; the party had been given into her hands at her own request, and she was too proud to ask for help, even if she had had any hope that the quilting frame could be bundled out at the last minute.

Village guests are painstakingly punctual. All arrived at the same time, and they were too much absorbed in Mme. Winston to pay attention to Ellen's hot, unhappy face. She and Amy followed her mother and the four old ladies down the dim hall to Aunt Susan's open door. A little cry of surprise and interest rose as they came in full view of Aunt Susan, who was busily making circles on the quilt top with a teacup for a pattern.

"What is it?" asked Amy. Ellen's embarrassed answer stuck in her throat, and she turned her head.

"My dear granddaughter, I'm ashamed of you," said Mme. Winston. "Ellen, she hasn't had your liberal education; she doesn't know a quilting when she sees one."

"Oh–h!" breathed Amy respectfully. She came closer to the frame and touched the quilt with one finger. "Grandmother, do you remember when we were in the mountains two years ago we tried to get back to that settlement where they still made quilts? You said then that quilting was almost a lost art. What is the name of this? Those mountain quilts had the quaintest names. One was Philadelphia pavement, and one was the rose basket."

Aunt Susan beamed on Amy in a manner that astonished Ellen.

"This is the Ashley star," she said proudly. "My mother, Ellen's great-grandmother, named it herself for the little Virginia town she came from, where she learned to piece the pattern. She was about twenty when she married and came West in a covered wagon. I guess she was young enough to get lonesome many a time for that little town. She always pieced the pattern in pink and green just like this, and when I was a little girl I used to think that all the stars over Ashley were pink and green."

"I suspect," said Mme. Winston, "that there would be stories for a great many of these things you have, Susan."

Aunt Susan's eyes swept the chairs that were pushed back into the corners and the knickknacks that were piled on the shelves. "Plenty of stories," she said. "Yes, plenty of stories. Most of this great lot I wouldn't keep at all if they weren't almost as much company to me as the people they belonged to used to be. Mother was so proud when she could buy that little table and set it in her log cabin. 'Twas built by an old cabinetmaker out of a walnut tree on father's farm. This tea set Sister Emmeline bought with her first money from school-teaching to put into the parlor of the new house. I seldom look at it but I think of the time she had with the big boys that winter. She wasn't large enough to whip them, and they knew it; but she wouldn't give up, and she succeeded." Aunt Susan broke off abruptly. "Mary, can you quilt with an open-end thimble? This was Emmeline's too."

Ellen stood back, wondering. She looked at the little tea table with eyes as puzzled as if she had expected to find its story tied to it. Aunt Susan had never told her the tale. The guests rustled happily round the quilting frame, admiring the quilt, trying on thimbles and exchanging reminiscences of other quilting times. Ellen moved over and threaded needles for them.

"May I try?" asked Amy.

"Do!" said Aunt Susan, and Amy was soon stitching laboriously round a penciled circle. On a sudden decision, Ellen took a needle and went to work. She had not tried to quilt for several years; she had forgotten the effort and the exactness required to sew with tiny even stitches through the two layers of cloth and the filling of cotton. When she straightened up to rest a wry neck she watched with admiration and envy the ease with which Aunt Susan's needles traveled in and out.

The guests soon recovered their expertness at an accomplishment they had learned well years ago. They rolled the quilt from the sides again and again as they traced the intricate pattern toward the middle.

After a while Ellen and Amy were glad to relieve their cramped muscles; but the old ladies were much surprised when the two girls appeared with a kettle of hot water and the tray of cakes and sandwiches.

"I don't know when I've had so good a time!" exclaimed flushed little Cousin Mattie. "Why, I declare, it took me right back again to the days when we were girls together!"

"I feel so, too," announced Cousin Charity. "I declare, I'll take a cup of tea, Ellen. I'd just as soon stay awake tonight to think over this party!"

Mary Henley ate her specially prepared toast and followed it with three cakes and a marmalade sandwich. A group of small girls could hardly have disposed more effectively of the food. Doubting Ellen herself could see that everyone was enjoying the afternoon, and none more than the Winstons.

"I wish we could stay to finish it," said Amy, wistfully regarding the narrow unquilted strip that was left, "I wish we could."

"It won't take long," Aunt Susan assured her. "I aim to have it quilted and bound when you go back home, so you can take it with you. Mother always said a girl ought to have the first quilt she quilted."

"Oh–oh!" exclaimed the enraptured Amy. "Grandmother, did you hear that?"

Guiltily Ellen remembered a quilt upstairs on her closet shelf. Aunt Susan had given it to her two or three years ago because it was the first quilt on which she had ever worked; and she had not valued it at all. They had so many quilts in their family!

After the last reluctant departure Ellen conscientiously swept up the crumbs and washed the plates and the cups. It was twilight when on tired feet she went to the hammock to rest and to arrange her confused impressions of the day.

Presently she knew that her mother had gone into Aunt Susan's room to help her off to bed. Aunt Susan's voice—the high voice of a deaf person—came faintly through the window, "Sit down till I get this finished, Sarah."

Soon it rose again. "Lucy Winston was speaking to me about Ellen. Did she say anything to you? Yes? Well, I thought she would. The trip would be a good thing for Ellen. I want you to let me pay for her clothes. She's done plenty of things for me that I know well she never wanted to do, and she never complained."

Ellen gave a joyful little bounce in the hammock. Aunt Susan must be referring to the Hawaiian trip that the Winstons had spoken of. For six whole months she might exchange the commonplace of her home for the romance of the far-away islands.

Her mother's firm voice brought her down to earth again. "She said that a girl often appreciated her own home more for having seen a thorough contrast. I think it may prove true. Ellen seems perfectly indifferent to the good things we have; she wants whatever other people like, whether it's clothes or family history."

"Oh, well," responded Aunt Susan, "that's natural enough. So did I at her age; but now I cling to family things almost more than I should, whether they're good or not. It's the way of life. Ellen's a good girl, and Lucy Winston will enjoy her."

The lamplight and their voices died away together as they left the room.

Over the tops of the trees a star shone suddenly in the deepening night. "Why, it's the Ashley star," said Ellen happily, "green and pink! And how bright it is! I wonder if it looked like that to great-grandmother!"

THE HOROSCOPE

Eliza Calvert Hall, *Woman's Home Companion*, January 1922

One scorching June day, an old farm couple, Ezra and Amanda McDavid, sat dejected; he, on the front porch; she, on the back porch. A drought that had come to the area soon after planting proved to be disastrous to their farm crops and garden. An air of gloom overlaid their run-down home place, which needed painting and repair. Amanda, who as a young woman was considered a fine housekeeper, was now depressed, and so the interior of their home was woefully neglected. That evening as she readied herself for bed, Amanda saw a newspaper advertisement from an astrologer, Leo Alcazar, who promised to send readers "a full horoscope of your life" for one dollar. From her Scotch-Irish ancestry, Amanda had inherited a broad vein of superstition, and a belief in the occult. So the next day she surreptitiously sent for the horoscope but never mentioned the advertisement to Ezra. When the horoscope arrived in the mail, Amanda was amazed at the good things it predicted would happen to her. The horoscope even stated she would receive a legacy from a relative— she, who had no rich relatives. A beautiful old floral quilt, originally made in Scotland, plays a significant role in the series of predictions

How each prediction came true and radically changed the lives of Amanda and Ezra makes a fascinating story. What more pragamatically inclined persons would attribute to simple cause and effect, Amanda attributed to the "magic" of the horoscope.

Amanda McDavid sat on the back porch doorstep in the breathless twilight that was closing a scorching June day. The front porch would have been a more comfortable resting place, for the house faced the south and whatever ghost of a breeze might chance to wander by, the occupant of the porch would feel its presence. but while her husband sat there at ease, smoking his pipe and meditating placidly on the weather and the crops, Amanda huddled forlornly on the bottom step of the kitchen porch, her knees almost touching her chin and her tired eyes looking no higher and no farther than the white-washed fence that separated the back yard from the vegetable garden. She knew what lay beyond the whiteness of that paling fence—wilted vegetables, half-grown corn whose leaves were twisted by the sun's heat, and ground cracked and seamed like a piece of badly fired pottery.

A drought that comes in the latter part of summer or in the fall may be borne philosophically, but when it follows close on the time of planting it is a calamity that only the stoutest heart can meet without repining, and Amanda was past the time when she could bear troubles hopefully and cheerfully. She had reached the sad, gray years of middle age.

"Nothin' but the same old thing, day in and day out," she thought; "get up and cook breakfast, and wash the dishes, and clean up the house, cook dinner and wash dishes again, cook supper and wash the dishes, go to bed, get up again, and there's everything to be done over. What's the use of it, anyhow? If the children had only lived it might have been different, but nobody but me and Ezra—it's not worth while; it's not worth while."

She heaved a deep sigh and leaned her aching head against the railing of the porch.

"Mandy!"

It was Ezra's friendly voice calling through the darkness, and she knew that he wanted her to come and sit with him on the front porch. But her mood best suited the back porch. So she sat still without replying, and gave herself without reserve to the sway of bitter thoughts and memories.

Ezra was too well acquainted with his wife's gloomy humors to insist on her coming to him. He smoked another pipe, searched the heavens for a sign of rain, then went up-stairs to bed, yawning loudly. A half-hour passed and the harsh stroke of the old kitchen clock warned Amanda that the hours of rest were passing. She rose heavily, groped her way to the front room and lighted a lamp. As she lifted the lamp from the table her glance fell on the farm journal that had come in the morning's mail. An advertisement on the outside page arrested her attention.

> Would you know yourself? Your Past, Present and Future?
> All is written in the stars and may be read for you. If you care to have this knowledge, that will make life a glorious success, send one dollar and the date of your birth to Leo Alcazar and receive in return a full horoscope of your life.

From her Scotch-Irish ancestors Amanda had inherited a broad vein of superstition. Her great-grandmother, Elsie McHarg, had seen the fairies dance on the moor, her great-great-grandmother had had the gift of second sight. These worthy dames had bequeathed to their posterity a valuable store of signs and omens relating to such things as cats, tea leaves, the new moon, the days of the week, and Amanda had made these superstitions the guide of her life.

Awe and wonder were in her eyes as she read the astrologer's advertisement a second time, and its words fell into her mind as good seed falls on good ground. She was tired of past and present. Oh, for glimpse of the future! And if one dollar could purchase this glimpse, it should be hers, though one dollar was just half of her present bank account, the bank being a small pasteboard box with a slit in the top and the deposits depending on the uncertain conduct of her hens, geese, and turkeys. She folded the paper and hid it in the table drawer lest Ezra should use it the next morning to kindle the fire, then crept up-stairs and lay for an hour, open-eyed and excited as a child on Christmas Eve, composing the letter to the astrologer and wishing impatiently for the sunrise.

As soon as breakfast was over she wrote the letter, and was lucky enough to find a stamp for it.

In six days, or perhaps five, she would know the future. Wonderful thought! It sustained her through another blazing week of hateful toil, and when she opened the mail box the following Friday she was surprised to find the mystic letter, because Friday was an unlucky day, and she had expected it either Thursday or Saturday. But there it lay, "Leo Alcazar" printed in the upper left-hand corner, and a blazing star on the flap of the envelope. Her fingers, moist with dishwater, stuck to the paper, and she tore the envelope in her haste to release its precious contents. Her knees were trembling and her heart beating violently, as was natural for one standing before the veil that separates the present from the past. She unfolded the thin paper and ready the badly printed words:

I greet you as one highly favored by the stars! If the hand of fate seems to lie heavily upon you just now, know that these troubles that beset you are but the prelude to greater prosperity and happiness than you have ever know.

You were born under the planet Uranus, which is the star of sorrow and of hope. Your life will be one of many changes, but the good will always overbalance the evil, and you will never have a trouble that you are not able to bear, for you are born to be not the slave, but the master of circumstances. You have in you great possibilities that have never yet been unfolded; but the time is at hand when your latent talents will be drawn out and developed, making you stronger, more successful, and more influential than you now are. You are naturally refined; you love beauty, order, cleanliness and elegance in all your surroundings. Your health is generally good, and if you are sick, your best remedies will be rest and outdoor exercise.

You are a faithful wife, mother, and friend, and the older you grow the wider will be your circle of friends and the greater your influence over them.

There are indications that some family trouble seems to threaten you in the near future, a quarrel with one of your near relatives, perhaps; but this may be averted by good judgment and forbearance on your part.

Your lucky days are Tuesday and Friday, but in reality there are no unlucky days. The occurrences that we call "bad luck" are only occasions for showing our own power and bringing good out of seeming evil.

Much money will pass through your hands and you are likely to have a legacy left you by an aunt or some other near relative. During the months of August, September, and October of this year you will be under the influence of friendly planets, and all your affairs are likely to take a turn for the better. You will make influential friends, and through them you will attain something for which you have long been striving. Keep this in mind. Expect good, and good will come to you. Be of good courage! Keep a stout heart and all will be well. Your last days will be your best days.

Slowly and solemnly she read again the words of the horoscope, while the look of awe on her face melted into something like a smile. A hissing sound from the kitchen warned her that something was about to burn. She hurried in to rescue her dinner from the fate that had overtaken everything out of doors. Ten minutes ago she would have groaned fretfully over the slightly scorched potatoes, but the words of the oracle sounded in her ears —

The occurrences we call "bad luck" are only occasions for showing our own power —

and she resumed the work of cooking dinner, while the closing words of the horoscope rang through her brain like a strain of music:

Keep a stout heart, and all will be well. Your last days will be your best days.

It was a meager meal that she placed on the table an hour later, and Ezra looked quizzically at the fried chicken, the corn bread, and last year's potatoes.

"Curious sort of a dinner for a hard-working farmer to be sittin' down to in the month of June," he observed. "There ought to be six kinds of vegetables on this table. Paul planted, but Apollos forgot to water, and where's the increase?" He smiled cheerfully and passed Amanda her favorite part of the chicken.

"It's pretty bad," said Amanda; "but it might be worse."

The optimistic words seemed to have some difficulty in passing her lips, and Ezra looked at her in quick surprise.

"Right you are, old lady," he said approvingly; "and I'm going to replant that garden. I look for rain when the moon changes, and before it changes I'll get my seed in, and we'll have a fat year after all. I'll have to get some more seed when I go to town Friday. I reckon there's no use askin' you to go with me?"

If Amanda hesitated before answering, the hesitation was not perceptible.

"I've got some tradin' to do," she said sedately.

"Friday or no Friday, I reckon I'll go." To herself she said, "Tuesday and Friday are your lucky days!"

What was going to happen? Amanda looking on the bright side and going to town on Friday! In all the years of their married life Ezra had never known his wife to make a journey or undertake anything on that day, but he wisely kept his amazement to himself.

Amanda hurried through her after-dinner work and stole again up-stairs to consult the oracle. Over one passage she fell into a reverie:

"You love beauty, order, and cleanliness," said the oracle. She looked around at the neglected bedroom. The curtains hung limp and torn over windows dim with dirt. A ragged carpet long unswept covered the middle of the floor. The chairs were rickety, the bed quilt was faded and dingy.

"Looks like I loved pretty things and clean things and orderliness, don't it?" she muttered.

And yet the horoscope was a true one. Glancing back to the first years of her married life, Amanda saw a bedroom, a kitchen, a parlor as they had been in the good days when her hand was strong and her heart was light, and she and Ezra had just joined hands. But now—what did it matter, if things were not up to the notch? She and Ezra were both old; a few more years, and they would both be at rest under the cedars where the baby lay. The current of her thoughts was running in the old channels that care and sorrow had worn in her brain; but instantly she turned it back. Her face grew radiant again as she pored over the horoscope, and only one doubt marred her joyful acceptance of its prophecies. A legacy from an aunt? Amanda had an unusual number of aunts, for her father and mother belonged to old-fashioned families in which children were counted by the dozen; but the aunts, with one exception, were married and had sons and daughters to inherit all their worldly goods. The exception was Great-aunt Ailsie, who had neither land, house nor money, and who lived on the bounty of a great-nephew in an adjoining county. However, when one wants to believe a thing, belief is easy, and the small matter of a missing aunt need not be allowed to invalidate the genuineness of the horoscope. And if the words of the oracle were true, they were not merely a prophecy but a call to action, If good fortune was on its way to her, she must prepare to meet it.

Making plans is one of the delightful occupations of forward-looking youth, and Amanda had long since ceased to look beyond the narrow horizon of each day; but now a voice was proclaiming that the last days of her life were to be better than the first. Oh, it was glorious to have a future once more, something to live for, something to work for, something to hope for! New wants, new desires were springing up in her mind, and on Friday when they started homeward from town Ezra was surprised at the number of bundles that Amanda stowed away under the seat of the buggy, and surprised again at the patience and cheerfulness with which she bore the heat, dust, and other discomforts.

"I don't know what's come over Mandy McDavid," said Anne Crawford to Ma Harris. It was three weeks after the horoscope had begun its beneficent work, and she and Mrs. Harris were having a comfortable gossip in the latter's shady sitting-room. "You know, Mandy's been lettin' things go for a good many years, and everything's been sort o' run down at the heel, inside the house and out."

"Yes," sighed Ma Harris; "it's a way we all have as we grow old. Anybody can stand on my front doorstep and tell, by jest lookin' in the front hall, that I ain't the housekeeper I once was."

"But now," resumed Anne, "it looks as if she had turned back twenty years and was just startin' out in life. I was over there Wednesday, and such a change I never saw. The house looked like a new pin: white ruffled curtains at the windows; furniture all polished up, and everything was clean as soap and water can make it, and Mandy had on a blue and white gingham and a white apron with lace on the bottom of it. You'd have thought she was a young woman just settin' up housekeepin'.'"

Ma Harris shook her head in sober disapproval. "Mandy must be in her second childhood," she sighed.

And to Amanda herself the change noted by Anne seemed, indeed, a second childhood. The tasks she had so long hated and performed with a grudging hand became once more sweet to her, and she smiled and sang over the drudgery of the farm in a way that made Ezra think of their honeymoon and the first years of their married life. As her work of regeneration went on indoors, he did a similar work outdoors, till the run-down farm began to take on an air of neatness and beauty. The replanted garden was making up for lost time. Soft showers fell exactly when they were needed, and summer, with gentle haste, was doing her own work and also the work of spring.

The horoscope lay between the pages of Amanda's Bible in the top drawer of her bureau. Within that Bible were promises of a happy heaven after life's toil and pain; but—children of Earth that we are—we need some nearer, sweeter lure than heaven to keep our steps from flagging on the long march from cradle to grave. So Amanda seldom opened her Bible except to take out of it the pagan horoscope, and at every reading its witchery seemed to grow stronger and its promises sweeter.

One day about the middle of July a letter came to Amanda bringing the tiding of Great-aunt Ailsie's death. The letter was from Cousin Cynthia McDavid, and the writer announced her intentions of journeying soon to Greenwood to visit her brother

Daniel, and staying over one day with Amanda. "There's something coming to you from Aunt Ailsie," ran the letter, "and she made me promise to deliver it with my own hands."

A legacy from an aunt! Here was the first fulfillment of the horoscope's forecasts, and a kind of awe-struck anticipation filled Amanda's mind as she prepared for Cousin Cynthia's coming.

Ezra drove into town to meet her and bring her out to the farm. In silent, unsmiling dignity she entered the house, and deposited on the sofa a huge bundle securely wrapped and tied. "Well," she said, turning to Amanda, and speaking with solemn emphasis, "we've all been surmisin' these many years as to who was Aunt Ailsie's favorite niece, and now we know. She's left you the Ailsie Ferguson quilt and the Ailsie Ferguson cookbook." Cousin Cynthia paused. She had created a dramatic climax whose completion required some utterance from Amanda, but none came.

Amanda untied the bundle and unfolded the quilt. There was an absent-minded look in her eyes and a deep disappointment in her heart. The quilt and the cookbook had the venerableness of great age and the aura of legend that clings to every heirloom, but—a legacy should be houses or lands, or silver or gold; could this time-stained quilt and old cookbook be called a legacy? And if they were not a legacy then the horoscope was a false prophet.

"Well," said Cousin Cynthia coldly, "I thought I was bringin' you somethin' you'd appreciate; but it looks like Aunt Ailsie's left things to the wrong person."

The words of the horoscope flashed into Amanda's brain: "Some family trouble—a quarrel with a near relative." It was no easy matter to avoid offending Cousin Cynthia, and once offended her favor was hard to regain. Amanda summoned all her tact to avert the threatened trouble.

"Maybe I am the wrong person, Cousin Cynthia," she said gently. "But sometimes a person appreciates a thing so much that she can't tell her appreciation. I never expected to own the Ailsie Ferguson quilt and the Ailsie Ferguson cookbook, and it'll take time for me to get use to the idea that they're mine."

Cousin Cynthia's face softened. "That's so," she assented. "I remember the Christmas James gave me the silver water pitcher, I was so set back I never did thank him properly."

Amanda unfolded the quilt and Ezra lifted a corner and looked wonderingly at the work of a woman's hand. "Sakes alive!" he exclaimed, "how many million stitches do you reckon there are in this thing?"

Its ample folds of hand-spun, hand-woven linen billowed over the floor, and the morning sunshine was like a magnifying glass, bringing out the delicacy of the stitches and the beauty of the design, tiny sprays of heather as accurately outlined as if an artist had drawn them with a pencil. It was not merely a quilt, it was a Scottish moor in full bloom and pictured by needle and thread instead of brush and paint.

The Ailsie Ferguson who had just died was the third to bear that name: the quilt and cookbook had come to her from the second Ailsie, who had inherited them from Ailsie the First, maker of the quilt.

"How long do you suppose it took her to make it," asked Ezra.

"She worked on it, off and on, for fifty years" said Cousin Cynthia. She was engaged to be married and she was makin' this quilt for her bed; but the man died, and she put the quilt away—she couldn't bear the sight of it—and it was years before she could work on it again. She was a young girl when she started it, and when she finished it she was an old woman."

The three were silent for a moment, thinking of the long-dead woman. Then Cousin Cynthia straightened herself up with a jerk. "Here's the cookbook," she said abruptly, drawing a small package from the black silk bag that hung on her arm. "No, don't open it," she exclaimed, as Amanda started to untie the string that bound it. "I wish to goodness you could, for I've always wanted to see the inside of that old book; but it was Aunt Ailsie's request that as long as you lived no one but you could read the book or use the recipes, and when you die you're to will it on the same conditions."

Amanda turned the book over and looked at it, with a growing sense of the honor conferred on her by Great-aunt Ailsie.

"There's a pickle recipe in that book," declared Cousin Cynthia, "and if you once eat pickle made by it you'll never to able to relish any other. Some day, if you happen to make a batch of that pickle, I'd be glad to have a small jar of it. But I don't know whether you'll ever be able to get all the ingredients it calls for. The last time Great-aunt Ailsie made it she come to a dead stop for lack of somethin' or other, and the pickle wasn't what it ought to be."

It was mid-autumn before Amanda found time to try Aunt Ailsie's pickle recipe. It had been an unusual cucumber year, and the large crop had been stored away in brine, and all the mysterious ingredients were assembled in the pantry. To Amanda the making of the pickle took on the aspect of a sacred rite, and when she laid the book on the kitchen table where the afternoon sun could illuminate its pages, she wondered if the wraiths of its former owners were not hovering around to see that she did her work well.

Slowly she deciphered the faded writing, studied the minute directions, and measured out the ingredients with cup and spoon. By three o'clock the house was filled with the breath of many spices and herbs, and the pungent odor of boiling vinegar floated even to the front gate. Amanda was scalding the jars when the heavy roll of an automobile reached her ear. It seemed to stop in front of her gate, and in a flutter of pleasurable excitement she hurried to the front of the house and peered through the shutters. There stood a shining car and in it two strange ladies. The chauffeur was working on a front wheel, and one of the ladies in the car was speaking to him in a clear, musical voice. Amanda saw at a glance that they were beings from another world than hers, but this could not deter her from offering them the customary hospitality of the country. She filled two goblets with cool water, placed them on a tray, and walked courageously up to the elegant strangers.

"I thought you might be thirsty," she said simply.

"Oh, thank you, Mrs. McDavid," said the elder lady. "You are Mrs. McDavid, aren't you? We saw the name on the mail box."

"I am Mrs. McDavid," said Amanda. "Won't you come in and rest a while?"

"Indeed, we will," said both ladies. They got out of the car with swift, graceful movements. Inside the yard they paused and looked around, then looked at each other and laughed an understanding sort of laugh.

"Looks natural, doesn't it?" said the younger lady. "See that row of altheas and the beehives. We use to live on a farm when we were young girls," she explained, turning to Amanda, "and— Oh, we haven't introduced ourselves! I am Emily McFarland, and my sister is Mrs. Meriwether."

They used to live on a farm, these elegant city people! Amanda's heart warmed to her stranger guests.

"Perhaps you'd like to go up-stairs and wash your hands and faces?" Amanda suggested; "it's dusty traveling on the old pike."

On the threshold of the spare room, the guests paused. The painted floor was dotted with gay rag rugs, the white-curtained dormer windows opened on a network of tree tops, and the old-fashioned cherry four-poster was spread with Great-aunt Ailsie's quilt.

"Wouldn't it be heavenly to lie in that bed and look out into the branches of these elms?" said Miss Emily. "One would feel like a bird in a tree top."

Her sister did not answer; she had crossed the room and was lifting a corner of the venerable quilt.

"Emily!" she exclaimed, in the tone of one who has suddenly found a long-desired treasure. "Come here! Did you ever see such a piece of needlework? Look at those stitches, and those flowers are as perfect as if an artist had sketched them."

Sister Emily crossed the room and bent a keen gaze on the bedcover.

"It's the very thing for Mildred Maynard's Colonial room," she said decisively. "What exquisite needlework! Where, where did you get this quilt, Mrs. McDavid?"

Amanda's heart was beating high with the pride of possession. While her guests washed their hands and faces, she told them the history of the Ailsie Ferguson quilt.

"What is that delicious odor?" asked Mrs. Meriwether as they went down the narrow little stairway.

"Why, that's Aunt Ailsie's pickle," she said; "the same one that made the quilt." And when she had finished the story of the second half of the legacy, she offered her guests a saucer of the pickle that was simmering on the back of the stove.

Sister Emily tasted it first critically, then approvingly, and laid the spoon down with a dramatic gesture. "I've tasted the pickle before," she exclaimed, "but where?" She closed her eyes in an effort to remember, and took another taste of the pickle. "I have it! Don't you remember the time we motored through Scotland stopped at that queer little inn on the way to Glasgow? We had pickle exactly like this for dinner. I'm sure it was made by Great-aunt Ailsie's recipe. Historic quilts, historic pickles. Oh! but this is the House of a Thousand Romances!"

"It's the best pickle I ever tasted," said her sister; "better than Mintz's best. Have you ever thought of making it for sale, Mrs. McDavid?"

No, Amanda had never thought of selling any, and far be it from her to sell to a guest.

"It's precious little pickle we eat," she said, "and if it won't be too much trouble to carry it with you I'd be glad to give you a jar of it."

"Trouble!" echoed Miss Emily. "Why, I'd carry it in my hands all the way to Indianapolis, if it were necessary."

Amanda had filled a jar and was fastening the top when the voice of the chauffeur was heard:

"The car is ready, madam."

The ladies started up, hastily donning their wraps and veils. Amanda followed them to the car.

"I hope you'll never have another break-down," she said gravely; "but if you do, I hope it'll happen right in front of my house."

"So do we," said the departing guests speaking in unison, and then Miss Emily added:

"We're not going to depend on a breakdown to bring us together again. We're coming this way next October, and you must be sure to have a kettle of Great-aunt Ailsie's pickle on the stove."

"And you'll hear from us as soon as we get home," said Mrs. Meriwether. "Good-by! Good-by!"

The car started, and the afternoon sun made a golden nimbus of the dust cloud in its wake. Amanda gazed after it till it disappeared, and then hurried back to the kitchen. Suddenly the words of the oracle came into her mind:

"During the months of August, September, and October you will be under the influence of friendly planets, and you are likely to make influential friends, and through them attain something for which you have long been striving."

Here was the second fulfillment of the oracle's words, and all her half-formed doubts as to the horoscope's truth were swept away by a wave of faith in some great and ultimate good that was fast coming into her life.

Two weeks later Ezra came in with two important-looking letters, both addressed to Amanda. The envelope of one was gray and it was sealed with blue wax. Amanda broke the seal.

"Read it out loud," urged Ezra. Slowly Amanda read:

"My dear Mrs. McDavid: Mrs. Meriwether has told me about the Ailsie Ferguson quilt. I am afraid you will not care to sell such an interesting heirloom but I would like very much to buy it. Would you consider two hundred dollars a sufficient price for it?"

The letter dropped from Amanda's hand.

"Two hundred dollars?" ejaculated Ezra. "Why, that's pretty near as much as my tobacco crop brought me last year!"

"If I had two hundred dollars," said Amanda solemnly, "I believe I could buy everything in the world I want; but—" She paused thoughtfully. Family pride and loyalty rose up against the mercenary spirit that for one moment had possessed her. "I don't believe it would be right to sell anything that's been handed down from generation to generation like this old quilt. Aunt Ailsie willed it to me, but it really is not mine; it belongs to the family, and when I die I am expected to pass it on to some of the kin. No, I can't sell it, not if the lady offered me ten times what she has."

Ezra's face expressed intense approval of his wife's words. "I knew you'd do the right thing," he said; "besides, it gives you a sort of set-up feelin' to know you've got somethin' worth as much as that old quilt."

"It certainly does," said Amanda emphatically.

"Let's read the other letter," urged Ezra. Amanda opened it with clumsy fingers. Her face brightened as she spelled out the signature.

"I knew she'd keep her promise," exulted Amanda. But Mrs. Meriwether's hand-writing had so many queer angles, curves, and flourishes that much study was necessary to get at the meaning of the letter, which was that the pickle was all eaten, that everyone who had tasted it wanted more, and would it be possible for Mrs. McDavid to send at least a dozen jars at once, and would two dollars a quart be a satisfactory price?

Amanda and Ezra looked at each other, and for some seconds neither spoke. Amanda's brain was trying to calculate the number of quarts that could be made from a barrel of cucumbers, and Ezra was busy with the problems of packing and transportation. And it seemed to Amanda that she was about to set foot on a new, strange road. It was overarched by a rainbow and at the end of that rainbow there was a pot of gold.

Winter was an early comer that year. Snow fell the first week in November and the north wind wailed and moaned around the old farmhouse. Amanda's customary winter mood was one of despair and feverish longing for spring; but this winter there was something in her life that made her forget the discomforts of the season. Her kitchen was nearly always fragrant with spices and herbs; letters came to her, and the postman wondered and jested about their frequency. Ezra seldom went to town without a barrel or a box to be shipped by freight or express, and Amanda no longer kept her money in a pasteboard box.

It was another June night a year later. Amanda was sitting on the front porch enjoying the breeze that blew across the meadow gathering up fragrance and scattering it like incense at the shrine of the night.

This year's June had been a pleasant month of frequent rains and not too ardent suns, and in field, garden, and pasture all was well. The porch glistened with a new coat of paint and Amanda's dress and apron were crisp and clean. She had the look of one in possession of some happy secret, and Ezra's face expressed something more than the temperamental content of the man who takes things easy.

"That's a wet moon up yonder," he remarked, with his eyes on the slender crescent that hung horns upward in the evening sky. "This is a mighty different June from last June. This time a year ago we were prayin' for rain, and mighty little hope of our prayers bein' answered."

Amanda made no reply. To-morrow on Friday, her lucky day, and she was wondering what good fortune fate had on hand for her. It was part of the horoscope's witchery that, whereas she had formerly anticipated ill fortune, she now looked only for good.

"And it's not only the weather, pursued Ezra, as he puffed contentedly at his corn-cob pipe. "Everything's different and better than it was a year ago. We'd been kind o' goin' down-hill, you and me, for a long time. I knew it, and I reckon you did, too, but I didn't know exactly how to stop it; and, all at once, without any tryin' on anybody's part, things took a turn for the better, and it looks as if we'd both wheeled around, and gone about ten or fifteen years back, to the time when we were young and spry and had plenty of ambition. It's right curious, and I'd like to know what did it."

Magic work, indeed! But a work done by magic may be undone if the magic is explained away, and Amanda was wise enough to know this.

"I reckon," she said thoughtfully, "that we used to think we had to go down-hill, and so we went down-hill. But now—there was a prophetic note in her voice—"we're goin' up, and we'll keep on goin' up, and our last days will be better than our first."

The Quilt-of-the-Cloth-of-Gold

Annie McQueen, *The Youth's Companion*,
December 11, 1924

Grandfather Streeter, who was the captain of a ship that sailed to foreign lands, promised his young wife that on his next voyage to China he would bring to her Chinese silk for a dress. Forty years later, he brought a whole bolt of gorgeous golden yellow Chinese silk. Although yellow had formerly been her favorite color, now an old woman, Grandmother Streeter believed a yellow silk dress was inappropriate for a woman of her age. She cut enough of the fabric for a dress, dyed the material black, and made a black silk dress for herself. A large amount of the golden yellow Chinese silk remained. Grandmother Streeter decided to make a whole-cloth silk quilt from it. What a quilt it turned out to be! People came from far and near to see The Quilt-of-the-Cloth-of-Gold. A huge wreath of roses was centered on the quilt top; its flowers and leaves stood in exquisite bas-relief, and a graceful festoon of wines formed the border. Only Grandmother Streeter and one or two of her most capable quilting friends had worked on this quilt, which was beautiful beyond description. The Quilt-of-the-Cloth-of-Gold was never used and was only taken from the cedar chest, where it was stored, to display to admiring friends who came to the home to see it.

After Grandmother Streeter's death, the precious quilt was handed down in the family until many years later it came into the possession of a great-niece, Cynthia Streeter, an unmarried lady. Cynthia's nieces, Lucy and Cynthia (named for her aunt) each wanted the Quilt-of-the-Cloth-of Gold, and believed she should be the recipient of the quilt after Aunt Cynthia's death. Lucy and Cynthia quarreled bitterly about the quilt, much to Aunt Cynthia's dismay. The eventual fate of The Quilt-of-the-Cloth-of-Gold brought surprise, yet satisfaction to Aunt Cynthia, and solved her dilemma.

Grandfather Streeter, who was captain of a ship that sailed to foreign lands bringing cargoes of all sorts of precious stuff, once promised Grandmother Streeter that the next voyage he made to China he would fetch her some Chinese silk for a dress. He kept his promise, but he saw in his mind the rosey-cheeked brunette lass that grandmother had been forty years before, and he bought silk the color she had liked best when a girl, golden yellow, and a whole bolt of it.

Grandmother Streeter like the old woman in the family tale who thought everything the old man did was right, gasped at first in astonishment; but when she looked at her husband's beaming face she kissed him warmly and thanked him as much as if he had brought what her heart desired—black brocade.

When grandfather sailed again grandmother dyed enough of the glittering stuff black to make her a dress, and it served for best for a long time; it was quite good when she gave it away to old Mrs. Elder, who lived in the Hollow and who had never before had a silk dress, and who never would have one again. Then grandmother looked at the rest of the goods and considered.

"It would make the prettiest quilt in all the world, Drusilla," she confided to one of her neighbors, "and—I do believe I'll make one and call it 'cloth-of-gold' like one Aunt Nancy had—only hers was yellow calico. I'm minded to do it, Drusilla, seeing as

I've not a chick or child to care about it, or fuss about it rather."

Drusilla's eyes sparkled. "Do it, Mis' Streeter," she urged, "and we'll have the whole winter long to quilt it. I wouldn't have any-body but the best quilters to stick a needle in it. And I'd get Rosetta Powell to draw off the patterns to quilt by. Rosetta can draw flow-ers natural as the blooms on the bush."

There was enough of the lovely golden stuff for top and lin-ing both. Grandmother carded the finest and whitest cotton into long, fleecy rolls for wadding. The lining was basted in the quilt-ing frame, the wadding laid smooth, the top basted on, and the quilt was ready for the designs to be traced for the quilters to fol-low.

With a sharp-pointed stick of chalk Rosetta Powell drew wreaths of roses and graceful festoons of vines with tiny leaves and buds an even thorns. Then the expert quilters were invited, and the ones who could do their best work in the kitchen pre-pared a great dinner for them all. It was a quilting party long to be remembered.

But of course Grandmother Streeter could not have a party every day, and it took many days to complete the quilt. The quilters came over whenever they had time, and grandmother and one or two of her best friends quilted between whiles, so that by the time winter was over the quilt was ready to come out of its frame.

Never was seen such a quilt! The neighbors came for miles to get a sight of it. Rosetta had drawn an enormous wreath of roses in the center, and each rose petal was quilted in outline, so that the wadding puffed out under it and formed a raised design on the smooth surface. Every leaf, bud and stem was quilted that way, so that the completed design stood out in beauty. Graceful festoons of vines formed a border, and there were single flowers, roses and buds, scattered over the whole as if by a prodigal hand. The whole surface of the quilt between the raised designs was quilted in tiny diamonds, making the flowers and vines stand out more prominently. It was stiff with quilting, and the finest quilting that had ever been done in all the village. Every stitch was made with yellow silk thread that cost a good deal of grandmother's egg-and-butter money, for they couldn't use cotton on such a quilt!

Of course it was never used; it was never intended for use. It must be kept clean and shining, for it could not be washed. When she was not displaying it to admiring visitors Grandmother Streeter kept it wrapped first in oiled silk, then in brown linen and placed in a box sprinkled thickly with cedar chips to keep away moths. Then it was laid carefully in the big cedar chest among other less precious and more useful bed covers.

At Grandmother Streeter's death the quilt went to her sole descendant, little Enoch Streeter, who grew up, married and had two boys and a girl. The girl, Cynthia, naturally inherited the quilt.

Miss Cynthia Streeter was now fifty years old and was living in a pleasant little house with one maid, Sibilla, a girl for whom you had to make allowances.

"She's a good child and willing, and after a while I think I'll make good help out of Sibilla," Miss Cynthia confided to her sister-in-law, Mrs. Jim Streeter, who had run over with her knitting. "But she's very literal. Sometimes it doesn't matter; other times it does."

"That dinner when the minister came, for instance," mused Mrs. Jim, "and Sibilla cooked the fowl literally whole."

Miss Cynthia chuckled; she had a fine sense of humor. "Sibilla said afterwards that a fowl couldn't be whole with a hollow big as your fist through it. So she obeyed orders. Said she knew folks had different ways of cooking, and that maybe I didn't draw fowls. But she never repeats the mistake; I will say that for Sibilla."

Lucy Streeter, Mrs. Jim's daughter, and Cynthia Streeter, Mrs. Tom's daughter and Miss Cynthia's namesake, came in just then, bringing a new girl, Sally Spate, whose folks had just moved to town and who was a schoolmate and friend of the Streeter girls.

"Hello, auntie," they greeted Miss Cynthia, "we've brought Sally over to look at the Quilt-of-the-Cloth-of-Gold. She was just telling us of a cheesecloth spread with sateen flowers appliqued on. So we brought her over to see ours."

"You see, I can't rightly call it mine," Miss Cynthia said and laughed, "the family must keep it for posterity, and so it keeps going-or staying rather, for it's of no earthly use that I can see. We just keep it wrapped up for moths and hope if the house catches fire somebody'll save the quilt!"

She went out into the kitchen where Sibilla was making cocoa. At first when Miss Cynthia had told her "a spoonful to a cup" she had measured the entire contents of the can. She hadn't been told how many cups! The trouble with Sibilla, unfortunately, was that she didn't ask full directions—until the next time!

"I'll attend to that, Sibilla; you take my keys and look in the cedar chest in the attic—the chest that has the quilts and blankets in it, you know. Bring me down that box on top—the one that has the Cloth-of-Gold in it, you know."

Sibilla knew. She had beheld it when Miss Cynthia was housecleaning and the precious heirloom had been aired. Privately she wondered why the beautiful cover hadn't been placed on the bed in the spare room. If it were hers, thought Sibilla, she'd use it all the time.

"Lawsy me, 'twould have been spang wore out, had it been mine," she decided as she tiptoed downstairs bearing the treasure in her arms.

Sally Spate marveled enough to please the Streeter girls. "Oh, what in the world are you going to do with it, Miss Streeter?" she asked, fingering the golden folds with careful fingers. "It is so beautiful!! I didn't know people ever did such work!"

"They don't any more; they've learned better sense," said Miss Cynthia dryly. "And as for what I'm going to do with it, I'm sure I don't know. Never did anything at all with it since it's been a quilt. It is so precious that my folks wouldn't risk displaying it at fairs, or it might have taken some premiums for labor or sewing or quilting or such. It just stays in the cedar chest."

Sally Spate kept on talking about the Quilt-of-the-Cloth-of Gold; she thought the name so beautiful and fitting. And she was curious to know which Streeter girl would inherit the quilt.

Miss Cynthia overheard a conversation among the three one day in summer when they were all in the hammock on her front porch. She had been taking a nap in her room just over the porch, and their talk had roused her. She lay blinking a bit, uncertain whether to get up or try to resume her interrupted nap when the subject of conversation came to her ears. The girls were discussing the quilt, and Sally Spate wanted to know whether Cynthia, as Miss Cynthia's name-sake, wasn't the proper person to get it.

"I don't know about that," put in Lucy Streeter warmly. "I'm the eldest girl in the family, and mother says Aunt Cynthia'll probably give it to me—maybe when I graduate from high school next year."

"College comes after high school," said Cynthia, "and I am going to college. That's settled! And you are going to take a business course and get you a job. I've heard you say so."

"Maybe she'll give it to the one who marries first," suggested Sally diplomatically. "That is usually the way heirlooms are disposed of in stories."

"She'll more likely give it to the one who stays unmarried," declared Cynthia, "or at least to the one of us who marries latest in life. Aunt Cynthia is an old maid, you see."

"I wish she'd let us know anyway; I'm tired wondering," observed Lucy fretfully, "for of course she's not going to let it stay in that cedar chest for moths to eat until she. . . ."

"Now I wouldn't talk about Aunt Cynthia's dying if I were you, Lucy," remarked the other niece tartly. "I'd hate to think about the death of our only aunt, no matter if she left me a fortune."

"Why not let you draw straws for it; I wonder if she wouldn't do that?" suggested Sally, who was bent on peacemaking.

But both girls declared that there would be no justice in such a chance procedure, that it ought to go to Aunt Cynthia's niece who—

"Is named for her," asserted Cynthia.

"Is the elder," delcared Lucy.

"Or goes to college—"

And so on till the young voices grew bitter.

"Poor things, so it's come to this," Miss Cynthia said and sighed. She rose from her bed and went to the mirror to arrange her disordered hair, for sleep was now impossible. "Actually quarreling and before a stranger about that quilt! And which shall have it—which ought to have it, I wonder? Tom is the elder, and his girl the younger. Jim is the younger, and his Lucy the elder girl. I'm sure I don't care for one more than the other, though I had thought of Cynthia, but now—well, I'm at my wits' end!"

Then Miss Cynthia sighed again and remarked to her mirror that she wished to goodness Great-Aunt Streeter had had children of her own to leave the quilt to.

The next morning, having the subject still on her mind, Miss Cynthia was a little impatient in answering one of her maid's numerous questions. A most important question it was, and, if she hadn't been thinking about her Quilt-of-the-Cloth-of-Gold and the dissension it was causing between her nieces, she would have considered before replying. As it was, she said rather impatiently:" "Indeed I meant just what I said—the very oldest, and quite good enough!"

"I should think so, ma'am; yes, indeedy, Miss Cynthia." Sibilla nodded with a beaming face that showed plainly that she quite understood.

"And after you've done that errand just get yourself a lunch of anything you like," said Miss Cynthia with a softening voice. It was impossible to stay vexed with Sibilla—she was so good-natured and tried so hard to please. "I'm spending the day with Mrs. Tom and Mrs. Jim, and I won't be home till tea time."

She wished to ask the advice of the mothers of Cynthia and Lucy on the vexed question of the quilt. But somehow she could not bring herself to mention the subject. It would be hard for a mother to decide that the lovely quilt should be given to any other than her own daughter.

After a long and rather fatiguing day Miss Cynthia came home with the burden of the quilt still on her mind and was greeted by a radiant Sibilla, who had made cup cakes for tea without a mistake. Her little sister had come to say that their brother from the city had come home on a visit, bringing them all presents, and Sibilla was to go back with the little sister to see her brother and her own present if Miss Cynthia could spare her.

"Surely, Sibilla," said Miss Cynthia kindly, "I don't mind at all staying alone one night; and you needn't hurry back in the morning, for I can make myself a cup of coffee and some toast without any trouble."

The two had departed in a little whirl of delightful excitement and Miss Cynthia had washed up the tea things and was seated in her sitting room with a new book when a visitor rapped at her front door. It was Mrs. Jones, a newcomer in town, a member of Miss Cynthia's church and a leader in all good works; she had conducted the rummage sale that day for the benefit of their state church orphanage; this time it was beds for the new baby cottage that had just been built.

"Come in: I'm lonesome and mighty glad to have company," said Miss Cynthia heartily. "Tell me how much money you made from the sale."

"My dear," said Mrs. Jones, beaming, "we did wonderfully! And all owing to you! I don't see how we are to thank you for that wonderful donation."

"Why, it was very old, but whole and clean," said Miss Cynthia, a bit confused.

"I should think so!" exlcaimed Mrs. Jones. "Your maid told us it was very, very old. I thought at first there was some mistake and talked about calling you up, but the girl assured me you had told her that you wanted the orphanage to have it. Said maybe you wanted it to do some good in the world at last for it had lain wrapped up for nearly a hundred years. A lady who has been staying at the hotel came in at that moment. She wanted it at sight for a room in the woman's club, a room dedicated to the pioneer women of our state and filled with their handiwork. She was a rich lady, and I asked her a good price—not exorbitant, however. She paid it without batting an eye!"

"How much?" asked Miss Cynthia weakly. Distinctly she remembered Sibilla's questions of the morning: "Did you mean the very oldest, Miss Cynthia? I must take the oldest quilt in the attic to the rummage sale at the fire station?" And her answer: "The very oldest, Sibilla, and quite good enough!"

"One hundred dollars!" breathed Mrs. Jones. "I sent the money from the sale off this evening. Just think how many comforts and blankets it will buy for those baby beds! And the lady wrote out her address—she went away today—in case, she said, it was a mistake, and if you refunded the money you could get it. But she hoped you wouldn't for it will look lovely in that Pioneer Women's Room along with the samplers and embroideries. She said they would hang it on the wall like a beautiful pciture, and that they'd fix it so it would be preserved from dust and decay. Here's her address."

Mrs. Jones rose and took her departure. Miss Cynthia sat by the fire and mused. Covers to keep many babies warm and a place besides in a memorial room, where it would outshine all other works of the pioneer women! Grandmother Streeter had wrought wiser than she knew; the women who quilted the golden cloth would still live in their needlework.

Miss Cynthia leaned over and dropped the paper with the buyer's address onto the flames. "That," she said, "disposes of the Quilt-of-the-Cloth-of-Gold!"

WHAT LETTY'S QUILT TOLD

Bessie M. Barker, *The Home Circle*, June 1938

When his wife died, Mr. Howarth reared his three children alone. The children—Jim, the eldest, Margaret, and the youngest, dear little retarded Letty—loved each other dearly. Letty spent her time making quilts that the family admired greatly. Later Jim married Ruby but unfortunately he soon died with pneumonia. After his death Ruby moved in with the Howarth family. Mr. Howarth became gravely ill and required much care from Margaret and Ruby. After a time Ruby insisted that Margaret take a six-week holiday. Ruby promised to care for Mr. Howarth and Letty while Margaret was away.

During Margaret's absence Mr. Howarth died. When Margaret returned, Ruby presented her with a new will that Mr. Howarth had made. The new will left Margaret and Letty practically penniless and even dependent on Ruby for a home. In the will the family home was left to Ruby. Margaret was puzzled because long before Mr. Howarth had stated his two daughters would be amply taken care of after his death.

Soon Ruby was exerting her authority and even suggested that Letty be sent to an institution. Dejection overcame Margaret as it now seemed she would never marry Walter Gregory, to whom she had been engaged for two years. Most bewildering were the reasons why her father had written the new will. Had his memory failed during his last illness? Could Mr. Howarth been out of his mind? The role of Letty's quilt in answering Margaret's questions makes for a fascinating story.

Margaret Howarth laid her knitting in her lap and leaned forward to look out over the lawn, yet she did not see it, with its brilliant flowerbeds, and she did not hear the hum of the bees in the borage bed close to the house. Her eyes dimmed with tears as she gazed, her hands playing with a fold of the thin black dress she wore. How she loved this home—and yet it was not hers now, as her father had promised it should be, nor did she have a share in it, she and Letty. That cruel will, that she could scarcely believe her father had made, had cut it away from both of them.

She turned and looked at Letty, her fair-curled head bent over her sewing. Letty was making another quilt. Letty would never know—she could not realize that anything was wrong, for her mind had never passed childhood. She asked only for love and care and for the gaily-colored bits of print to make up into quilts, a task of which she never tired. These things her sister had given her faithfully ever since they had been left motherless, when Margaret was sixteen and Letty fourteen, and Jim, their only brother, nineteen. Their father had been kindness itself to all three—it was terrible to think that he was gone, and that Ruby, Jim's wife, was in possession of practically everything. Things would all be right if Jim were alive, but he had passed away from pneumonia during the previous winter, just a few months before his father, and now Margaret and Letty, by the terms of the will, were dependent upon Ruby for a home. Ruby had already taken charge, and lost no time in emphasizing her new authority.

Margaret could still recall every intonation of the words as she had heard Mr. Moore reading them, giving to her and Letty each a thousand dollars, and to Ruby the property, their home, on terms that she allow Margaret and Letty to live in it with her. How could he have left them under those conditions. Ruby already had said that Letty would be better off in an institution, but she was to Margaret a sacred charge, and Letty would be unhappy to be away from the sister she trusted.

There was Walter Gregory too. She and Walter would have been married two years ago, had it not been for her father's need of her in the years of poor health which had preceded his death. Her father had known what she had given up—Walter had known that she could not part with Letty, and there was no thought of anything other than that the girl should come to them in their new home, but Margaret could not look to Walter to take the financial burden. No, their wedding would have to wait, as it had waited before—but for how long?

Margaret pressed her hands over her eyes and tried to think. Surely her father could not have been in his right mind, or he would not have failed as he had done to fulfill his promise to her. She tried to review all the things that had taken place in the last year. Ruby had come home to live with them after Jim's death— she had been very friendly and had insisted on Margaret's having a six-weeks' holiday, while she cared for Mr. Howarth, bed-ridden now, and Letty. She had gone away not without qualms, and returned to learn to her dismay that her father had suffered an acute illness, from which he had, however, rallied success-fully. Letty was overwrought and tearful. "She missed you, of course, Margaret," Ruby explained easily, "and with Father's sick-ness things were upset."

"Father made his will when you were away," she informed Margaret in the same easy tone, a few days later.

"Made his will!"

"Yes, he became alarmed about his condition, and thought it best to get his business cleared up."

"Did Mr. Moore draw it up for him?"

"Well, no. A friend of mine, Mr. Cassell, a lawyer from my home town, was here, and he did it. He saw that everything was done properly, and I put the papers in the vault at the bank."

Margaret had said nothing further. There had been many things to do for her father, and she had to be much away from home, leaving him with Ruby and Letty, and there was much responsibility, for his memory was failing. Letty presented no prob-lem. She sat quietly by her father's bed, sewing on her gay quilts. Margaret was often called upon to admire her newest pattern, little hexagons arranged symmetrically, the patches first basted over paper cut to shape, then sewed together by the feeble-minded girl's fingers, which were so clever.

It was three weeks ago that Mr. Howarth had passed quietly. Margaret remembered his words. "Don't worry about yourself and Letty, Margaret. I've left you well provided for. You've been a good daughter to me, and a good sister to Letty, and there's nothing to stand in the way of your having a life of your own now."

But then the will had been read, and Margaret had heard with bewilderment the terms of it. She and Letty were almost penniless, and dependent upon Ruby for a home. She had thought endlessly about the question, but there seemed no way of escape. Surely her father could not have been in his right mind when he distributed the property so. Mr. Moore had come to her after the reading of the will, genuine distress on his kindly face.

"Margaret, there has been a terrible mistake made somehow. The will I've just read was made early last summer, and by Mr. Cassell. Only a few weeks ago your father asked me to witness his signature to a self-written will. I read it through and the bequests were altogether different, as I remember it, but I cannot swear to the exact sum left to each party. Where is that will now? We must look for it, for it would take precedence over this one."

They had searched for it, Margaret and Mr. Moore, in every nook and corner of Mr. Howarth's desk and trunk, and everywhere it could have been concealed, but could find no trace. Ruby found them searching, and joined in, yet all to no avail. Mr. Moore shook his head sadly as Margaret went to the door with him to say goodbye.

"I'm heart-sorry about this, Margaret. I know your father intended that things should be otherwise—he said as much to me. The later will must have been destroyed by accident."

"If only I had been here—I understood things so much better than Ruby—I shouldn't have gone away."

"It would have made a difference, perhaps. That will is legal—he stated a definite amount to both of you, so it can't be broken on that score. You would all have to agree on the question of having it broken—and maybe your sister-in-law would not be willing."

"I know she would not."

"I wonder—was your father's mind clear when he made it?"

"I wasn't here. Ruby was the only one with him—and Mr. Cassell."

It had not seemed possible to do anything further in the matter, and today Margaret gazed out with a heavy heart over the garden, Letty, happily sewing, at her side. Ruby was becoming more domineering. Only that morning she had told Margaret that Letty must be confined more closely to her room; she must be kept there, away from the living room and veranda.

"But Letty has always gone there, Ruby, and it will make her very unhappy. This is her home, and she doesn't understand."

"Yes, but you must understand that it is my home too. I want to begin entertaining friends, and you know I can't do that with an idiot always present."

"Letty isn't an idiot, Ruby, and she has never bothered or annoyed you in any way."

Ruby's lips met in an ugly line.

"Please remember that I am mistress here now. Do you not realize that it is hard on me to have two people depending on me for their living, without their interfering with my few pleasures."

Margaret did not answer. It was useless to try to talk things over with Ruby, for she invariably took refuge in taunts and sneers. If only—but she could not marry Walter, when it would mean burdening him so heavily.

They were upstairs now, in Letty's room, listening to the voices below them, where Ruby was entertaining. She had asked Margaret to come down, but she had refused. She knew it would be merely to serve the lunch for the guests, and she would not go without Letty. Letty had always loved having visitors. She never spoke to them without their first speaking to her, but she would sit in the corner for hours, gazing at them with her wide blue eyes, a shy smile on her face. Nobody enjoyed company more than Letty, but now she was denied company of her own, and banished. Margaret's eyes filled with tears as she leaned forward to gaze down at the line of shining automobiles which stood outside the gate. Letty tugged at her sleeve.

"Margaret, don't cry—what makes you cry? Come and see my pretty quilt."

Margaret turned toward the quilt where Letty had spread it over the bed, and once more admired the little hexagonal patches. The paper inside the blocks crackled as she passed her hand over it.

"Don't cry, Margaret," Letty coaxed. "See—isn't it funny, all nice and pretty on the outside and all raggy on the inside."

She tossed the quilt over to reveal the back, and Margaret fingered it absently. Suddenly she stiffened. Through the uneven opening at the back of one of the blocks she caught a gleam of yellow paper. That was paper from their father's desk. How had Letty got hold of it? She pressed the edges of the cloth aside, and saw her own name written on the scrap, in her father's careful hand.

"—Margaret, I bequest—" the rest was cut away.

"I bequeath—," trembling from head to foot, Margaret snatched up the scissors, then controlled herself.

"Suppose you let me help you, Letty. These blocks are all sewed in now, aren't they? Couldn't I take out the papers for you, and then you'll be ready all the sooner to start another new quilt."

"Oh yes, you take the papers out, Margaret."

Eagerly Margaret searched and snipped. Letty objected:

"You're not taking them out neat, Margaret—you're going all over the quilt."

"Yes. but I'm taking out all these yellow papers first—that's a nice neat way of doing it."

Letty became interested and left her sewing, while she searched for the yellow papers, piling them on the pillow. She had cut her foundation papers from brightly-colored advertising circulars, and fostering her passion for neatness, Margaret had made a pattern and showed her how to cut the pieces without wasting any paper. The yellow sheets had been cut with the same pattern. The little pile of scraps grew, and Margaret began piecing them together.

She had found it—the will that Mr. Moore was so sure had been written. By some strange chance it had fallen into and had been cut up by Letty's innocent hands. Feverishly Margaret scanned the part she had reconstructed. This was more in keeping with what her father had promised. The home and all that was in it for herself and in trust for Letty—two thousand dollars to Ruby, a bequest to the church, and other smaller sums here and there. She turned to Letty, striving to keep her voice calm:

"Letty, where did you get this paper? Think hard and try to tell me."

Letty's blue eyes became intense in an effort to concentrate her wandering thoughts. Margaret waited tremblingly.

"She threw it out—Ruby threw it out, Margaret. You were away and she took everything out of the desk and threw it on the floor and then the telephone rang and she went and I took the paper. It was too pretty to throw away and she thought it was pretty too for she left it on the desk and some other papers and I took it and she didn't know I saw it and—"

"What did she do with the rest of the stuff?"

"I saw some more pretty papers there and some more pretty yellow ones and I wanted them too but she came back and she picked them all up quick and burnt them in the kitchen stove and then you came in right away. I thought she'd burn mine too so I hid it and I used it all up quick so she wouldn't see it and I was afraid she might hear me telling you about it so I didn't tell."

That explained everything. Ruby had taken advantage of her father-in-law's illness—had managed to have him make his will out in her favor, then, finding this document, which swept away the ground from beneath her feet, she had tried to destroy it, only to be outwitted by the innocent desires of the girl she despised as an idiot. Margaret stood up.

"Would you like to go for a walk, Letty? It's lovely outside."

In a few minutes they were away, Letty carrying her precious quilt carefully wrapped in brown paper, and Margaret with the pieces of yellow paper secure in her purse. Ruby called to them as they reached the gate.

"Where are you going?"

"For a walk. We want to show Letty's quilt to a friend."

Ruby turned to her friends with a contemptuous smile.

"She treats that girl as if she were something worth having around," she sneered.

In Mr. Moore's office Margaret poured out her story, and showed the evidence she had gathered, while Letty again told her story. Mr. Moore's face was stern as he listened, but he smiled as he examined the will.

"This is the document I remember, Margaret—look, there is my signature, where I witnessed your father's signature. It looks as if the house is yours again, and Ruby will have to go elsewhere with her money. Well, you run over and stay with my wife till the party is over, and then I'll go home with you—we'll spare her the embarrassment of a scene before her friends."

Ruby's face paled and then crimsoned as she was confronted with the fragments of the will she had believed destroyed, now carefully pasted to a sheet of legal paper. She opened her lips to utter a denial, but closed them again. Mr. Moore nodded with satisfaction as he examined Mr. Howarth's bankbook.

"There is enough to pay you your bequest as soon as this will is probated," he said. "Do you intend to remain here, or go elsewhere till this is attended to?"

That evening Margaret sat on the veranda, listening to the tapping of hard heels upstairs as Ruby hurried through the packing of her belongings. Letty sat beside her sister, whispering happily to herself over a magazine that Mrs. Moore had given her, with some new, and to Letty, exquisitely beautiful quilt patterns. She would remain so, perfectly content, as long as there was light for her to see. Margaret's eyes frequently turned to the street, watching for Walter Gregory. She had telephoned him—asked him to take her for a walk, told him that she had news for him.

"Is it good news?" he had asked.

"What do you call good news?" she had parried laughingly.

"You know there's only one thing that I would call good news, where you are concerned."

"Then in that case—I have it for you."

"Well—under the circumstances.—"

Missouri Rose
Martha Cheavens, *Good Housekeeping*, July 1939

During the time of the Civil War, Martin Boyd, a wounded Confederate soldier, escaped from bushwhackers and fled to the rural Missouri home of Zarelda Jennings. Bushwhackers were not Union or Confederate soldiers. They were mercenaries who captured people for money. Although Martin was a stranger, Zarelda hid him from the bushwackers who came looking for him and searched her home.

After the bushwhackers left, Zarelda cleaned and bandaged Martin's wound. She made a bed for him and covered the soldier with her best quilt, the Missouri Rose. Zarelda lived alone and supported herself by quiltmaking and weaving. She considered her Missouri Rose her masterpiece quilt, as it was so carefully constructed and was made from new store-bought cloth. Martin stayed in Zarelda's home to recuperate and to continue to hide from the bushwhackers, who were certain to return. Martin and Zarelda fell in love. Nevertheless, the course of their love did not run smoothly and even tragedy occurred.

Zarelda Jennings blew the light out quickly and set the little grease-lamp back on the mantel. She was sure she had heard shots and the sound of running feet out in the yard. She went to the door and looked out. Everything was silent again. The stars hung still and large in the quiet sky. The moon had set. It seemed that the very breath of the summer night had been cut off.

Zarelda stepped out noiselessly on the stone doorstep, put her feet down with caution on the grass. She walked around the house with long easy strides, the full skirts of her home-spun dress making no sound.

The house was a double log one, an unfloored passageway between the two rooms. This passageway served as storeroom for a variety of objects, chicken coops, firewood, sacks of carpet rags hanging on pegs, a grindstone, an axe, a hoe, a basket of chips, a churn. All of the coops were empty except one, and Zarelda paused here and thrust her hand within; she withdrew it at once with a sharp intake of breath.

"You old Dominecker, you!" she exclaimed. "I do believe you have teeth!"

The old hen in the coop scratched around trying to get settled again, and Zarelda, stooping low, turned her head to one side and listened. She thought she had heard a sound, like a man chuckling to himself not far away. But again there was nothing but silence, an eerie hush.

She straightened up and went on with her tour of inspection. She went as far as the cellar house. It was not a house, exactly. It was a small cave dug back into the side of the hill that rose abruptly behind the farmhouse. It was very cool and moist in the dugout; she had kept her milk pans there once, her cream and her butter-milk and her cheese. But that was before the war, when she was well off and kept two cows, old Brindle and old Bess. The Yanks had got one of the cows, and the Rebs the other. The low door to the cellar house was grown over now with wild-rose brambles and blackberries and morning-glory vines. The lock was rusted fast. She hadn't opened it for two years.

Zarelda paused again, listened. The August air was sweet with the smell of wild roses, but everything was too still. It was so still that, even though the door made no definite sound, she knew that someone had opened it and gone into the house. She felt it rather than heard it, and she knew that somebody was in the kitchen waiting in the darkness. Some stranger.

The thought of somebody walking into her house like that, without invitation, had the effect of changing her first feeling of terror to that of anger.

She picked up her skirt in one hand and ran to the house, opened the door, and slammed into the kitchen without thought of danger.

"Whoever you are," she called out sharply in the dark kitchen, "you ain't got the right to be here. Get out!"

Anger and sobs choked her, and she stopped for breath. Then came a strange response—the sound of somebody whistling a tune, softly, pleadingly. It was a rollicking tune, a gay one, and yet there was a desperate note beneath its bravado. It was the last thing in the world Zarelda expected to hear, and she could think of no reply. She walked uncertainly toward the mantel, took down the grease-lamp, and started to light it with a twisted paper which she had held against the coals in the stove. The whistling stopped abruptly.

"Don't light no light yet, ma'am. Please!"

It was a man's voice—peremptory, arrogant. But it had that same urge of desperation in it. She put the lamp back. She was beginning to get accustomed to the darkness now; she could make out a man's form crouched in one corner by the loom.

"What are you here for?" she asked.

"A little kindness, ma'am. If you've got any to spare."

There seemed to be no answer to that, either. She went up closer to him, saw that his clothes were half torn off, that there was something wild and hunted about him as he hid there in the shadows. He spoke to her in rapid but not incoherent sentences. He was a Confederate soldier, he said. Martin Boyd was his name. He had been sent by his captain on a personal mission to Jackson County, and on his return trip had been captured by a gang of bushwhackers. They thought he was a spy, were taking him to St. Louis to claim their reward. But tonight he had escaped.

"I would have got clean away," he said, "but one of their bullets snagged me in the leg and it slowed me down. Then when I seen your light, I come in."

"Oh, you're wounded!" Zarelda did not know why, but it did not occur to her now to do anything but try to help him. Over the kitchen, she told him, was an attic without windows or visible opening.

"A couple of boards are loose in the ceiling," she explained, "and you can crawl through there."

As soon as he was in the attic, he looked down through the opening before he replaced the board. It was too dark for her to see his features plainly, but she fancied there was a roguish twist to his mouth as he whispered to her:

"How did you like that tune I was whistling? It's a play-party tune. The name of it is 'Oh, Sister Phoebe.' I'll sing you the words when —"

"Put that there board back and keep quiet. This ain't no time for tunes. I hear horses' hoofs crossing the ford."

"Yessum."

He replaced the board, and she lighted the lamp, sat down in a low slat-bottomed rocking-chair, and took some sewing from a basket and went composedly to work.

The soldier in the attic applied his eyes to a crack in the floor and observed with disappointment that his benefactress was not, as he had judged by her voice and the grace of her movements, especially beautiful. Her straight hair was parted in the middle, looped upon her ears, and fastened in an abundant knot at the back. Her dress was severe and without adornment. Her whole bearing was grave, detached, self-contained. Her eyelids, however, as she looked down at her sewing, were white and firm; her black eyelashes lay richly upon her cheeks.

They swept upward at the sound of horses, of men dismounting and yelling at one another. Still holding her sewing in one hand, she got up and went to the door when they knocked. They brushed past her—three of them. Bushwhackers. Neither Confederates nor Federals, but out for themselves in a private warfare of loot and pillage and murder.

Without any sign of fear Zarelda took a tin lantern from a peg, lighted it, and handed it to them and invited them to look around.

While they were looking, she waited at the door. She fastened her thread, bit it off, flattened the seam with her thumb and forefinger, looked at the quilt patch a moment, then dropped it in her pocket. And Martin Boyd, watching her, thought he had never seen such courage.

When the bushwhackers finished the search, they were

ill-humored and dissatisfied, but there seemed nothing for them to do but go. As they were leaving, there came from the yard the sound of a hen's angry but triumphant squawking, followed by a spot of profanity from one of the men. A small stiff smile appeared briefly on Zarelda's face, and Martin Boyd wanted to laugh aloud. It seemed a long time before she raised her eyes and said quietly:

"I reckon they've gone. But you better stay up there. I'll take a look at that place where their bullet snagged you." She handed the lantern up to him, also a jug of water, a tin wash basin, some rags, a pillow, and a quilt. Then she followed. She made a pallet with the quilt, washed and dressed his wound. It was not deep— the bullet had just grazed the flesh. When she had finished, she took a small bottle from her dress pocket, held it to his lips.

"It's elderberry wine," she said, "It'll give you back your strength."

"Thankee, ma'am. I never expected such kindness as this."

"I never expected to give it to you."

She observed the man's dark face in the lantern's uncertainty, the wild enchantment of his eyes, his unruly hair. There was, indeed, something of the knave about him, picaresque, disturbing; but there was another quality, too—a wistfulness, painstakingly hidden. She was unaccountably touched.

"I'd better get you a cover," she said.

She came back presently with another quilt. She carried it with a sort of radiance, spread it over him with pride.

"This pattern," she said, "is called The Missouri Rose."

Her eyes glowed as she talked. They were blue eyes, he could see now, extravagant eyes for so plain a face. "I rid all the way to Jeff City, mule back, to buy the goods for this quilt. All my other quilts is pieced of whatever I had on hand. But this one was boughten special."

"I'm right proud to sleep under it, ma'am," he said, "but it's too fine for me."

"I've been saving it for company," she replied. "It's my best."

She blew out the lantern. "This is the first time anybody has slept under my roof but me," she added.

He laughed softly in the darkness. "I'm sure obliged to you for it tonight," he said "but to be plumb honest with you, ma'am, I don't like roofs. Nor walls. Nor fences."

"What do you like, then?" Her question was like a sting.

"The road, ma'am," he answered at once. "I'm a horse trader. Born and raised on the road. Son of Passion Boyd—maybe you've heard of him?"

"Yes," she interrupted flatly, "I've heard of the Boyds."

There was an uncomfortable pause. The south wind blew in softly through the chinks in the logs; fragments of starlight sprinkled though the roof.

"I'd admire to know *your* name, ma'am?" suggested Martin Boyd.

She told him.

"Zarelda," he repeated, "Zarelda."

"Some folks call it Rildy."

"Sure is a sweet-sounding name, either way you say it, Miss Rildy."

When she had gone, Martin stretched out comfortably on the pallet she had made for him. The pillowcase under his cheek was smooth and cool—like a woman's hand. Damme! What was he thinking about, anyways? Her a farm woman, rooted to the place same as if she'd growed there. He pulled the quilt up under his chin, traced with his finger the design of its flowers and leaves. The Missouri Rose! Prettiest name of a quilt he'd ever heard tell of. "It's my best," she had said. Never before had a woman given him that.

Downstairs Zarelda turned down the covers on the spooled cot. Maybe, she thought, stern with herself for a moment, she oughtn't to have gave him one of her best pillow-slips and her Missouri Rose quilt. My, he was dirty and ragged! But his eyes had a careless fling to them. And his face was plumb scarred with smiling, like he'd done a lot of it in his life.

Smiling . . . Zarelda thought grimly that she had never smiled much. There had not been much gaiety for her, nor any tenderness. "Miss Rildy," he'd said. It *was* a pleasurable name, the way he said it . . .

She raised herself on her elbow and looked out the window, looked long at the shadowed hills, the woods, the road.

The road, she thought bitterly! It had been her home too. How she hated it even in her remembrance! Her father had been a peddler of patent medicine. They'd go down the road in a wagon, her and her pap, stopping at the farmhouses along the way and selling things. She didn't remember her mother; she had died when Zarelda was so small.

The road. God in Heaven! What a home for a lonesome little girl when she wanted a real one so bad!

Later on, when she got bigger, her pa let her stay and work for her keep and schoolin'; first with one family and then with another. But that wasn't home either.

Someday, she would sob to herself, she would have a home of her own! And she began planning for it then—planning and getting ready.

She was seventeen when her pap died. She sold out the stock he had left, added the money to the few dollars he had saved, and bought three acres of land. It was rich, creek-bottom land, heavily wooded. Her house was built from her own timber. She bought a loom and a quilting frame at a sale and let it be known around that she was handy at weaving and sewing. So she built her house little by little, and there was singing in her heart.

But she had few friends. The neighbors praised her skill and courage, they admired her snug little home, they brought her work to do and paid her well. But that was all. She was too grave, too self-sufficient, too close-mouthed.

Her loneliness began to press down on her. She would think wistfully how nice it would be to have company come for dinner. And to spend the night. She wanted somebody to feel how soft her featherbed was, how silk-smooth her sheets. She wanted people to know the Jenny Lind bed in the parlor was as comfortable as it was pretty, the wood rubbed with beeswax till it shone like linn honey. But she had come here a stranger and was a stranger still.

Until tonight. She had company, now—but she didn't dare give him the Jenny Lind bed. The bushwhackers might come back. So he had to sleep in the attic.

"And if he offers to sing me the words of that song tomorrow," she thought shyly, "I'll give him leave."

But he didn't offer to sing the words the next day. He whistled and sang other tunes—"Old Brass Wagon" and "Weev'ly Wheat" and others she'd never heard of before—tunes that went in at her ears and tried to come out at her feet. La', she had a hard time keeping her face straight, the words tickled her so!

His wound started getting well right off and he was able to hobble down from the attic and get in her way while she was doing her work, joking and singing and telling her about all the places he'd been to. Indian Territory, Texas, Californy even. . . . He made life on the road seem almost nice, the way he talked about it. He was trying to make it seem nice, looked like. But she firmed her heart and battened down her mouth to keep it from smiling. You couldn't pull out and leave your troubles behind you forever, she told him. His face hardened. The road was not for a woman, she maintained. Not when there were children. Children . . . Zarelda's face flamed, and she lowered the whiteness of her lids over the magnificent embarrassment in her eyes.

But all he said was he reckoned one of these days soon he'd better hit the road again and try to find his outfit. His leg wouldn't bother him much, he thought. But though he said it, several days passed and still he didn't go. And she didn't ask him to. But all along she was uneasy. The bushwhackers would come back; she had seen it in their eyes that night . . . Martin laughed at her fears.

But Zarelda had a plan of her own. In fact, the very next day after he had come she had slipped out to the cellar house, pulled the vines and brambles away carefully without breaking them, then replaced them. The door was well hidden. She greased the key and worked with the rusty lock until she got it open.

"I'll entice him in *somehow*," she assured herself, "if they show up again. I'll tell him there's a snake in there, or something . . . They wouldn't find him in there in a month of Sundays.

And then one day, when he had been there almost a week, a butterfly flew in the house when she opened the kitchen door. That, she knew, was a sign of somebody coming. A sure sign. She didn't say anything to Martin, but she kept one ear cocked, and she kept an eye on the road.

It was a lush afternoon, corntasselers seesawing their cadences through the air, grapes over the garden gate hanging ripe in the sun. Zarelda went into the parlor, opened her round-topped tin trunk and took out her Sunday dress and looked at it. She'd looked at it every day since he'd come, wanting to put it on, but afraid he'd think she'd put it on for him. She'd bought the goods in Jeff City when she bought the goods for the Missouri Rose quilt. It was a dimity dress, fine as a starched cobweb, sprinkled over with little rosebuds. She'd made it stylish, too, like the ones she saw in the city; she had even run a willow branch through a tuck, to make a hoop. My it was pretty!

"Why don't you put it on?" He was standing in the door, laughing at her, his hat on one side of his head the way he wore it. "It looks like a cooler dress than the one you have on."

Her eyes flooded with relief and gratitude. "Why, it is hot today, ain't it?" she exclaimed. "I believe maybe I will."

So she put the dress on and dusted her face over with cornstarch and then came outdoors and sat down beside him on the bench by the kitchen door. She picked up her sewing and set to work.

"This here quilt pattern," she explained, "is called 'The Chips and Whetstones.' Each block has sixty-nine pieces."

He observed the quilt block absently. "I like the Missouri Rose best of all," he said. But he was looking at her dress.

The dress gave her courage. "I've been waiting for you to sing me the rest of that song," she said. "I reckon you forgot to."

It frightened her, the way he waited so long to answer.

"I didn't forget. You see, ma'am, it's a play-party song. You just sing the first serve, the second verse you choose your gal, and the third—you kiss her. I was aiming to play it with you, at first. Before I knowed you. But I can't now. I couldn't kiss you like that, ma'am, casual—"

She felt her fingers grow cold against the needle. Gone was all the mockery from him now, all the banter.

"I couldn't kiss you without making a proposal of marriage first, Miss Rildy," he said. "So I have."

Tears of happiness and unbelief stabbed her eyes; she couldn't see her sewing.

"I ain't got much to offer, ma'am. I'm just a trifling good-for-nothing horse trader, but I can make a living. When the war's over, I thought I'd take up again where I left off—"

The song of the corntasselers rasped. The summer air was heavy like a weight. Zarelda leaned away from him, pressed her head against the logs of her house.

"No!" she cried, "No! I hate the road. I couldn't go back to it." She told him about her father, about her childhood, about this house she had built. "Don't you see?" she finished at last, "this place is home."

He was, for the first time since had come, inarticulate. "I thought—" he began, stumbling for words—"I thought when a man and woman loves each other—well, that's what I figured home was. No matter where."

"It ain't enough. Home is love, but it's more, too. It's building something you can hold on to, planting things and seeing them grow. Home is having children and giving them something solid to stand on. Home is a roof."

"I don't expect to live under no roof I can't fold up and put away," he said.

They quarreled bitterly. Hot words flew between them like sparks from a grindstone, sharpening the edge of their anger. But when she got up to go, he caught her hand, held her back.

"Oh, Rildy! I wish it hadn't of turned out like this. Can't you see it my way?"

She shook her head.

"Do you remember that first night," he continued gently, "up there in the attic in the dark? You spread that quilt over me and said, 'It's my best,' and I reckon I must have started loving you right then. I didn't want to, but I did. And after you'd gone, I could still feel your hands on my shoulder, smoothening the quilt out—"

Zarelda didn't answer. She couldn't. As she stood there mutely, there came to her ear the sound she had been afraid to hear. Her hand tightened in Martin's grasp . . .

"Please," she whispered, "please come with me—"

She could scarcely have told afterward what ruse she employed to get him into the cellar house and lock the door. It didn't matter. He was safe, and she was able to face the bushwhackers again, and tell them to look. Even when they ripped the covers from the Jenny Lind bed, tore up the kitchen ceiling, and slashed her Missouri Rose quilt into shreds with their bayonets, she faced them with calm defiance. The twilight was deepening. Soon the door to the dugout would recede even farther into the purple shadows.

But the men were frenzied, inhuman with frustration. "If you don't tell us where he's hiding, we'll burn your house and everything in it," they shouted. "We know he's here. Tell us where he's at, or we'll burn—"

"Go ahead. Burn it."

But she turned from them and covered her face with her hands; sobs shook her body; she could not look. She heard the crackling of the flames, heard the men shouting, heard them run from the log cabin to the outhouses. They would burn everything, they had said, everything.

The flames leapt against the sky, scorched the evening stars, burned holes in the soft, fleecy clouds. But Zarelda saw none of it. It seemed to her that she was in the midst of the fire, too.

It did not take long to burn. There was a good breeze, and it had not rained in several weeks. Everything was dry. It did not take long. One moment there was the neat log house with the honeysuckle over the door, and the next there was nothing. A stone chimney. A three-legged iron cooking pot standing in the smoking ashes.

Zarelda could not look at it. She did not look up when the men left at last, shouting thickly, swearing at her and at one another. It seemed to her that she had burned, too—she did not feel alive. But Martin was safe. They would never come back now. Martin was safe.

But when she opened the door of the dugout and let him out, and when he saw the desolation of the ruined house, his mouth twisted convulsively. "I tried to get out," he said. "I beat my fists on the door and yelled. I would have gave myself up."

"I know you would."

He looked again at the smoldering grave of Zarelda's house. "It was all you had, wasn't it?" he asked.

She nodded.

"Oh, Rildy, I wasn't worth it! A dozen of me wasn't worth it. Why did you do it?"

"You know why."

She didn't know that arms as strong and hard as his could be so gentle, that lips like his could be so soft. She had never before had any tenderness such as that and it was like to break her heart now, it was so sweet.

"From the very first," he murmured, "you've gave me your best. Missouri Rose . . ."

He led her to the stile and spread his jacket on the step and helped her to sit down. Then he went away and came back after a while with something in his hand. A stick of wood and all that was left of her axe. Most of the handle had burned. He sat down on the grass and began whittling the wood with his pocket-knife.

"What are you making?"

The old look of devilment had come into his eyes again—the boldness, the laughter—but somewhere beneath all of that there was pride, too, and responsibility. He didn't answer her question at once. He even teased her a little, whistling a few bars of "Oh, Sister Phoebe," like he'd done that first night. But when he left off, he was serious.

"I'm making an axe handle, honey," he said "and when that's done I'm going to try to make us a roof."

THE BLAZING STAR

MacKinlay Kantor, *Good Housekeeping,*
September 1940

*Old Judge Sheffield was out hunting squirrels one day when
someone untied his horse, Old Dick, from the fence gate. Old
Dick, once untied, would always go back home to his barn.
And so he did this day, leaving Judge Sheffield stranded in
the country. It meant the judge had to walk. On the way he
stopped at the country home of Widow James and her three
sons. She kindly invited Judge Sheffield to stay for supper,
and as it was late, to stay overnight.*

*The family was quite proud of their mother's quilts —
she had made so many. Her sons eagerly recited the quilts'
names — Log Cabin, The Bluebird, Jacob's Ladder, Rose of
Sharon, Wedding Ring, Lock and Key, Morning Glory, Fish
Tail — that one the first quilt their mother made. Widow James'
son Jim-Jim wanted Judge Sheffield to sleep under his favorite
quilt, the Blazing Star. The judge was awed by the quilt and
declared it was the most beautiful quilt he had ever seen. Some-
time later Jim-Jim committed a crime and it befell Judge
Sheffield's reluctant task to be the judge at Jim-Jim's trial. In
connection with his case, Jim-Jim manages to rescue Widow
James' quilts from being sold. And the Blazing Star quilt's
fate is to be appreciated and loved until the end.*

This happened out in our county a long time ago. Maybe
Judge Sheffield wasn't so old in those days; but they called him
"Old Judge Sheffield" on account of the ponderous way he walked
and the ministerial voice he had. But many people swore that
Nathan Sheffield was a boy at heart. I guess a man wouldn't go
hunting squirrels unless there was some boyishness in his nature,
and that's what Judge Sheffield did on the day that he first saw the
quilts and felt their beauty with his hands.

Up into the Glencoe neighborhood was where he traveled, a
good ten miles northwest of Minnehaha and considerable dis-

tance to drive behind a sedentary horse like Old Dick.

He tied Dick against a timber fence near the Chicken River. He took his rifle and walked amid the walnut trees. Thin and yellow the leaves shone against the autumn sky, and you could hear crows bickering all through the fragrant bottomland. There was a taste of frost in the air and the taste of red haws in Judge Sheffield's mouth. Now and then his nostrils sucked in the wild, cool, smoky smell of prairies that burned in the afternoon sunlight, north and west for a hundred miles.

This was Judge Sheffield's way of worshiping God, and he didn't really care whether he shot a squirrel or not. He used to be quite a commanding figure in church, and he even taught the Junior Baraca class; but plenty of autumn mornings his soul was up and gone among the walnut trees.

Well, he had the pleasantest afternoon possible; but when he came whistling back through the first blue dusk, he was treated to a surprise. He had expected to find Old Dick tied and contented, and the buggy waiting. Neither the buggy nor Dick was to be seen.

Judge Sheffield pondered, and was annoyed, because he had looked forward to an easy drive, and now it looked like a tramp of three hours. Buggy marks led across the colored, fallen leaves into the road. Old Dick had gone to his barn in Minnehaha, just as he always did if he were untied, for he was a kind of independent horse.

Just then, as the Judge always told it, he heard turkeys over across the river—not wild turkeys, but the barnyard kind. So there was a house not far away, and maybe he could get a bite to eat before he took out for home.

As he turned to walk toward the bridge, a big man came out of the woods and crawled between the fence rails.

The face of the man was familiar to the Judge—not this particular face, but one like it. He could see it plainly—a big, vacant face, redder than the hillside oaks and a good deal more surly.

"Hello," said Judge Sheffield. "Did you happen to see a white horse hitched to a single buggy with the top down? He was tied up to the fence."

The young man was fleshy. He was about twenty-five. He stood and grinned down at Judge Sheffield, though the Judge was no little man. "Who had the top down, Mister? The buggy or the horse?"

The Judge shot fire out of his eyes. "Young man," he said, "you look like a Heffelman to me."

"That's right, Judge," the fellow smirked. "I'm Anson Heffelman."

Judge Sheffield said gravely: "You know me then. Maybe you know my old horse Dick. I left him tied this afternoon; but he seems to have strayed away. I'm afraid that he's gone home without me."

"That's too bad," said young Anse Heffelman, and he went away up the road, swinging the bucket he was carrying.

Well, the Judge looked after him and shook his head. He had a good notion who had untied Old Dick from the fence post, and it seemed a mean trick to play, especially if the prankster knew, as most of the county did know, that Dick would march for home the moment he was given a chance.

The Heffelmans were like that. The old man was coarse and mean; doubtless his offspring were meaner. Judge Sheffield kept walking. His feet resounded on the log bridge across the Chicken River.

There was a house beyond the stream. It wasn't much of a house; but blue smoke came from the chimney, and as the kitchen door swung open, the red eye of a wood range beamed out. The Judge wiggled his nose and thought how steak and gravy might smell if they were preparing themselves upon that stove. He turned in at the gate, where a friendly shepherd dog rubbed against him. And he hallooed, and the Widow James came at his call.

She was a little woman, the widow. Sheffield didn't remember about her; but later, he recalled that a fellow named J. O. James had fallen through the ice up there on the Chicken River a couple of seasons before and got himself drowned. This was the widow he had left, and with her appeared two young sons.

The widow had started having sons pretty late in life, or else maybe she was worn down and aged by work and worry. She was short and round-shouldered, and her tanned face was a mass of lines. The same acts of God and Fortune that put those lines in her face had thinned her hair and bleached it white. She had bright brown eyes that looked quizzically out from under wide, curving black brows. She wore a ragged coat—a man's coat—for she was busy with her poultry when Judge Sheffield came.

He made known his situation, and he didn't even have to hint about supper.

"Land alive!" she said. "I don't know whether we can set a very presentable table for you, Judge Sheffield; but we'd be tickled to death to try. It isn't every day you get to sit down with a distinguished judge."

The two young boys stood aloof and maybe a little frightened, but pleased withal.

"George and John, these are." She introduced them. "George is fifteen, and John's thirteen and a half. My eldest ain't home yet. He's off a-hunting, as usual; but he'll soon be with us. Jim-Jim, he is."

Judge Sheffield repeated "Jim-Jim," and wondered at the name.

"I guess it's on account of we're Welsh," said Mrs. James. "We called our eldest James, for his first name, and that's a fashion amongst Welsh people. My own grandfather's name was Lewis Lewis; but we've always just called our eldest Jim-Jim. Now you come in and sit yourself down."

Judge Sheffield wouldn't have anyone make company out of him if he didn't want to be made into company. Despite anything the widow might say, he chopped wood for her kitchen fire while the boys finished their chores. There weren't many chores to do. They didn't do much farming in the James family, although they had a good piece of arable land attached to the place. A couple of cornfields and a kitchen garden, hogs and chickens and two cows—that was the extent of their husbandry.

In the sitting room, they had a lynx and a grouse and a woodpecker, all stuffed at home. And Mrs. James said with pride that Jim-Jim had done the stuffing. He had his own ideas about taxidermy, and they were original. The lynx in particular struck Judge

Sheffield's fancy. It looked as if it were lying down on one elbow, stroking its chin, trying to decide whether or not to eat you up. But Judge Sheffield praised it and the spread-winged wood-pecker, too.

Supper was sizzling all over the stove before Jim-Jim put in an appearance. They heard the baying of a couple of hounds far up the Chicken River, and later the rickety porch trembled under Jim-Jim's boots. The Judge had expected him to be big—maybe as big as Anson Heffelman—but he was nowhere near that size. He was skinny and wiry, and he had that same fierce Welsh face his mother had, with the brows and all.

The widow introduced Jim-Jim to Judge Sheffield. Jim-Jim wasn't one to make great speeches. He simply said that they were honored, and his little old mother beamed fondly upon him.

Fried chicken, pork, gravy, biscuits, hominy and potatoes, cabbage salad, layer cake, and two leftover pies. That was what they ate, together with liberal coffee and more kinds of pickle than ever hung upon a vine. Judge Sheffield began to be almost glad that Old Dick had become untied that afternoon.

"But won't your folks be worrying, Judge?" said Mrs. James, passing him his third helping of chicken.

"No, they won't," said the Judge. "There's just my sister, and she's used to having Dick traipse in. He comes home frequently that way. She'll just think I stopped at my nephew's place out on the Diamond Hill Road, and she'll never worry a whit."

"I wonder," said the youngest boy, "who could have untied him?"

Jim-Jim put down his fork and stared across the table with his queer, shining eyes. "Untied?"

"Certainly," said Sheffield. "I had him tied with a halter-hitch and an extra half-hitch beside. If Dick untied himself, he's more adept with his hoofs than I think he is. Human hands did that."

"Where was he tied?"

"Just across the river."

Jim-Jim said, kind of pondering, "That's the road toward the

Heffelman place," and Judge Sheffield jumped, for as we know he had his suspicions.

The two younger boys said in chorus, "Anson Heffelman!" It rather sounded as if they were saying "Tweed Ring" or "Yellow Fever" or something like that.

"Of course," Old Judge Sheffield soothed them, "we don't really know that Anson Heffelman did it."

"I do," said Jim-Jim, breaking the silence in which he usually sat. "If a trap is sprung with a stick, it's Anse Heffelman that did it. If our Shep comes home weeping with a dose of pepper and salt in his hide—and he has done that—you can bank on Anse Heffelman. There are other things that have happened here, and I only hope they don't keep on happening, or I'm going to sample Anse Heffelman with a piece of 25-20 lead."

His mother shook her head. She looked grave and frightened. "Now, Jim-Jim."

"Just a weentsie sample," said Jim-Jim.

And the next boy muttered something about plugging a watermelon.

"Sure," agreed Jim-Jim. "A 25-20 doesn't make a big hole."

Judge Sheffield looked at them all severely. "I don't like such talk, my boys."

After that rebuke they were silent for a while. Mrs. James looked at the Judge with appreciation. You could see that she was thankful to have this admonishment spoken. It was hard for any woman, even a middle-aged one, to raise three wild-tempered boys, whose father was gone.

Woodsmen they were, and woodsmen they always had been—not farmers. Judge Sheffield got the story while Mrs. James washed the dishes and the youngest helped her kindly and Jim-Jim sat cleaning his rifle. Three years earlier they had come from Indiana—southern Indiana, what they called the "Knobs"—and no one of the Jameses was ever any fancy hand at farming. The boys liked to pretend among themselves that they were relatives of Jesse James; but there was no just cause for such claim.

It was growing late. The widow had to speak to Jim-Jim about hitching up the horse and wagon and driving Judge Sheffield into town.

"Not just yet, Ma," Jim-Jim pleaded. "Judge Sheffield doesn't want to go yet, do you, Judge?"

Sheffield sat back and smiled. "Well, guess I did say my sister wouldn't worry."

The widow declared: "It's as good as settled. You can sleep in the little back bedroom, and heaven knows when we've been honored with a guest. I guess," she added a bit bashfully, "that you'll have to lay slantwise, the bed's so short. But you'll be warm as toast, for I'll give you the Log Cabin."

Jim-Jim and the boys began to dance. "Not the Log Cabin. No, no," said young George. "The Bluebird, Ma!"

"Give him Jacob's Ladder," said little John. "I guess that's the warmest."

But Jim-Jim just smiled as if he knew best, and shook his head. "The Blazing Star," he said, and his mother nodded.

"Of course," she murmured, "there's the Rose of Sharon."

"Of course," agreed Jim-Jim haughtily "and there's the Wedding Ring and the Lock-and-Key and the Morning-Glory too. But I think he'll like the Blazing Star!"

Well, you might believe that Judge Sheffield's jaw was hanging down, but what they intended to offer him he didn't exactly know. Log cabins, ladders, rings, locks and keys, and such rubbish didn't sound as if he were going to be in entire comfort.

The boys raced into the tiny front parlor, and then ensued a tremendous banging and bumping and clatter. Out they came, the three of them, each dragging a round-topped trunk. And Mrs. James stood and looked proud and rolled her crooked hands in her apron. The straps were unbuckled, the lids thrown back. Then Judge Sheffield understood.

Those three trunks were filled with quilts. And he said they were the loveliest quilts human eyes ever rested upon. Pink, cream, snow blue, yellow—they were every kind of quilt that great makers could devise and many that the Judge had never seen before. He began to think that Mrs. James was running a quilt factory, and he marveled when he heard that she had worked all of them by her very own self.

"I never saw so many handsome quilts in my life," exclaimed the Judge, and then he persuaded her to tell him about them.

Meanwhile, the boys unfolded one after another, and their brown faces were excited. They acted as a bunch of young girls might have acted over an equal treasure.

The Judge blinked. This was a race of hunters and woodsmen. These boys, he knew, spent their winters trapping and wading the cold snows, and their ancestors had before them. But they took a fervent pride in the soft and delicate stitching of the calico folds.

"It was my grandmother started me," said Mrs. James in her mild and humble voice. "She was a great one for seaming and quilting, and even when her eyes went bad on her, she could still do it, because of the sense that lay in her fingers. I used to sit by her when I was very small and thread the needles that her old eyes couldn't see to thread. That Fish-Tail—the one John's holding up—that brown-and-white Fish-Tail was the first I ever pieced, my own self. I've kept on making them through all my life. We've got everyday ones—crazy quilts—that we use on our beds now. But the boys won't let me use these except for special occasions, and their father never would before them."

"I don't wonder," gasped Judge Sheffield, and he stroked the Blazing Star, which Jim-Jim had spread across his gaunt knee. It started with flame and pink in the center of every huge exploding pattern. The little diamond-shaped pieces turned on through orange into yellow and then green and lilac, and finally they blazed again all around the edges. And the lines of quilting themselves, the painstaking stitches, the millions and millions of little thread dots in the whole rainbow expanse—they were a miracle to see.

"You did all this yourself?"

The widow nodded, as if she were a trifle ashamed of having spent so much time. "Oh, I did it when the boys were little. When one of them had the croup, maybe, and I had to more or less sit up with him. And before that—well, I was a maiden lady for some time previous to my marriage to Mr. James. Though I worked hard daytimes, I had to do something with my hands in the evening, too. So I made a lot of quilts, to cover my family when finally I had one."

She picked up a quilt in her awkward, calloused hands, touching it as lightly as one might caress the petals of a flower. "Kerosene lamp and candlelight, too," she said, and she seemed to be speaking to herself then. "But my eyes are good; they always were. I can sew easy enough. Sometimes when conditions were hard— when hard times have come upon us, I have been tempted to sell my quilts."

Judge Sheffield nodded. "I don't wonder. I calculate that they would bring ten dollars apiece from any storekeeper in Minnehaha."

Mrs. James fairly glowed with pleasure. "Oh, not that much, Judge Sheffield!"

"Yes, madam," he insisted. "Ten dollars is a good week's wages to many people, and certainly one of these is worth a week's wages."

The widow arose suddenly. Her face was still shining. "Come, boys. Put those back in the trunks now."

Judge Sheffield thought that she had indulged her pride beyond its common limits and dared do so no longer.

"Fold them careful and put them back in the trunk."

"But not the Blazing Star, Ma," said Jim-Jim.

And that night Judge Sheffield slept beneath it.

You might have thought that Judge Sheffield would have pursued his new friendship with the James family more closely. And indeed he would have, had it not been for law business and court business, which kept him occupied through the last weeks of autumn and on through the first snowfalls. Often he planned to visit the Jameses; but he never seemed to find a free afternoon to allow Old Dick to take him out that way.

His next acquaintance with any member of the family came unexpectedly and with tragic surprise, on a cold day of early December, when the Judge heard a rush of snow-covered boots along the wooden platform outside his office.

He saw two bobsleds drawn up near the hitch rail. From the

first sled men dragged out the weight of Anson Heffelman, pale-faced, wound in blankets, but still able to swear between his blue lips. And a few moments afterward, from the second sled, two deputy sheriffs escorted Jim-Jim James, with his hands tied in front of him.

Old man Heffelman, Anson's father, was beside himself—waving a shotgun and calling the whole county to witness what he should do to Jim-Jim, who, he said, had shot down young Anse in cold blood and with malice aforethought.

That big bully of an Anse Heffelman was not nearly dead yet. They lugged him into Doc Ottway's office, and the mighty fellow fainted, in all his weakness, when he was brought near the warm stove. Doc Ottway probed for the bullet. It was a 25-20, all right, and lodged under Heffelman's shoulder blade. A few inches farther down, and they wouldn't have needed a doctor to do any probing.

Meanwhile, Jim-Jim was being blamed and badgered and threatened in the courthouse. His mother and the two young boys came driving into town soon afterward; but they weren't allowed to do more than speak a kind word to Jim-Jim. He was a felon now, charged with Assault with Intent to Kill. Preparations were made to bind him over to the Grand Jury.

Anse Heffelman's story went one way, when he was able to talk, and the James boy's story went another. Heffelman said that Jim-Jim had threatened him at various times, and on this day he was walking through the brush near his father's farm, not harming a soul or thinking any but the kindest thoughts, when Jim-Jim, carrying some furs, stepped from behind a tree and fired at him.

Jim-Jim, on the other hand, swore that he had been missing fur out of his traps. Trap after trap had been sprung, especially along the river next to the Heffelman farm—deadfalls and steel traps alike. There were signs of blood and fuzz, the marks of animals that had been caught.

Previously, the James boys had built up a respectable fur trade. That was how they made most of their living. They caught muskrats, mink, weasels, foxes, and other creatures and shipped the fur to a well-known trading house, the Lefty Larsen Company of Minneapolis. Thus the missing fur represented a loss of income for the Jameses, and it was a serious situation with them.

This day the man tracks near the plundered traps were fresh in new-fallen snow. James James set out to follow them. He came out of the timber into the Heffelmans' western cornfield, and there he saw young Anse striding through the stubble with a dead mink and a coon and a fox, all swung over his shoulder.

Jim-Jim yelled, "You put down my fur!"

Anson told him to get the hell off the Heffelman land.

Jim-Jim couldn't remember aiming or firing. When he came to himself, the sound of his rifle was echoing across the field and big Anse was howling in the snow.

The Heffelman tribe came running at the shot; but they called a lot of neighbors before they essayed to take Jim-Jim into custody. The Heffelmans were a numerous, but not a courageous clan.

The thing that made Judge Sheffield feel most sorrowful was the thought that James James had certainly committed the deed in cold blood and with malice aforethought. The Judge himself had overheard a threat made by Jim-Jim, though naturally the Judge wasn't planning to mention it unless he were called upon to do so.

There were some political wires dangling in Minnehaha—trailing out of the county's political machinery, so to speak. Judge Sheffield couldn't refrain from pulling a few of them. One thing— and that was good, since matters would soon get down to Jim-Jim's word against Anse Heffelman's—they reduced the charge of Assault with Intent to Kill. It was changed to Assault with Intent to Commit Great Bodily Harm. The authorities were persuaded that no one could ever prove that Jim-Jim really wanted to do any killing.

Bail was placed at a thousand dollars. When the legal machinery had ceased its preliminary creaking, Jim-Jim found himself in the county jail, with nothing but brick walls and an unhappy, broken-legged stove for company. His mother left the younger boys in their old homemade sled and came and lamented in the snow outside the jail window.

Judge Sheffield swore that the whole thing gave him a terrible turn. He might have been able to scrape up the bail himself—although he was far from being a rich man—but he knew that public opinion wouldn't stand for that. The Heffelmans were politically active and politically venomous; they would have managed to have Judge Sheffield removed from the bench if he won their disfavor. The Judge reasoned correctly that he might better serve the needs of people like the Jameses if he remained in office.

"Jim-Jim," said Mrs. James, standing in the snow in her worn-out shoes, "you have to bear up for the next seven weeks. They say your trial won't come up till late in January. It would take a thousand dollars to release you."

Jim-Jim couldn't reply. His face was set and greenish pale; his hands twitched at the bars as if he hoped to tear them apart. Deadfalls were kinder than this to a trapper like Jim-Jim, although certainly steel traps were not. It seemed to Judge Sheffield that this was rather a judgment of Nature—a steel trap catching and holding a wild creature, who primitive and single-minded as any bobcat, had captured and held so many other things scarcely wilder than he.

That was on Friday, when it happened. On Monday, town talk recited how Mrs. James was trying to mortgage her farm to win bail money for Jim-Jim. But her place wasn't worth much, and times were extremely hard that year. There was little livestock on the farm; the buildings and improvements were of the crudest sort. Eight hundred dollars was the most that any money-lender would offer her, and even then she had to beg and persuade, which doubtless pleased the Heffelmans no end.

Late that evening, Judge Sheffield walked slowly homeward. He looked into the dark hulk of the little jail, and he shook his head. It was cold in there, and lonely; the jail fare wasn't of the best, though privately and secretly the Judge had done what he could to improve Jim-Jim's condition.

But when he reached his house, he was surprised to see a

little box sled and an old thin horse before the door. The horse was blanketed against the frost.

In the sitting room waited the Judge's old-maid sister and — he looked again — Mrs. Widow James. She sat stiff and straight on the platform rocker, still holding her shawls and knitted tippets around her, for she claimed she was too distraught to remove them.

Heaped over the carpet, hanging on chairs, bulking large across the table were her treasures: the quilts that Judge Sheffield had seen drawn proudly out of their trunks the autumn before. Blazing Star, pink-and-tan Log Cabin, bold, bright Bluebird, the green-and-cream-colored Lock-and-Key — they were all there.

The widow shivered her hands and worked her shrunken little jaw. It was some time before she could speak.

"They're all here, Judge," she said. "All I have, except the crazy quilts, and I'm sure those wouldn't fetch much. But here are twenty. I recall you said that they ought to bring ten dollars apiece. I don't mind seeing them go, if they'll help to get Jim-Jim out of jail until his trial time. I've mortgaged the farm and raised eight hundred dollars that way.

The Judge could only stand there and gaze at the smooth, quilted beauties.

"Ten dollars apiece," said Mrs. James. "Maybe they ain't really worth it. But I recall you estimated that. Oh, it was just needle and thread and more needles and thread, and old pieces of left-over dress goods, and a few ends of bolts that I bought special. A lot of these quilts are pretty old, so maybe they're not worth that much." She stood up and swallowed bravely. "That would add up to make the thousand dollars," she said. "The thousand dollars for Jim-Jim. If you know just where the two hundred dollars for the quilts could be had."

Judge Sheffield said afterward that he had more trouble managing his voice than the Widow James had managing hers.

"I'll find the two hundred dollars," he said. "It will be simple as skat. Don't you worry any longer about Jim-Jim's bail. We'll have him out of there tomorrow morning." Mrs. James dug down in her reticule and brought out her roll of greenbacks, squeezed from mortgaging the farm, and before ten o'clock the next forenoon Jim-Jim was temporarily freed from jail and hurrying through the white countryside to join his mother and brothers.

That was on December eleventh, when Jim-Jim left the discomfort of the jail behind him. I don't know what kind of Christmas and New Year's season the Jameses enjoyed, for Judge Sheffield's story used to skip over the time that elapsed until January nineteenth. That was the day word reached town that Jim-Jim had disappeared.

The trial was due to begin on January twenty-sixth, and Judge Sheffield was terribly concerned about it. He hadn't wanted to try Jim-Jim himself. He thought he had things managed nicely regarding the bar docket, and Jim-Jim would be tried during the time when old Judge Pettingill was sitting. Judge Sheffield couldn't trust himself. He had always administered justice fairly and wished to continue doing so. But he knew that his instincts would lead him to contrive an unconditional acquittal for Jim-Jim if it were a possible thing.

And that would not have been justice in its righteous and legal sense. After all, the shooting was a violation of the law. Judge Sheffield scratched his thin gray hair and thanked the Lord for old Judge Pettingill. He needn't have bothered, really. It appeared that the Lord loved Judge Pettingill so well that He gathered him unto Himself some three weeks after Christmas, with the aid of apple brandy, pork pie, overindulgence, and an outraged stomach. It happened that Judge Sheffield was the only judge available to try the cases coming up at that term of court. He scratched his hair even harder.

Then came the news of Jim-Jim's vanishment. The sheriff went out to talk to Mrs. James and the other boys.

"They don't know, or at least they claim they don't know, anything about Jim-Jim," said the sheriff on his return. "And you ought to hear the Heffelmans howl about how the bail was placed too low! The Jameses just insist that Jim-Jim started before dawn, day before yesterday, to look at his trap line, and that he didn't come back. The younger boys found some furs and the rifle hanging in a tree on Glencoe Creek; but Jim-Jim's snowshoes had made tracks for the prairie." Judge Sheffield chewed his penholder. "Do they seem worried?"

"Not precisely. I can't hardly tell. They seem to think the boy's able to take care of himself in the woods or on the prairie, though the mother swears she didn't advise him to run away and that he never mentioned planning to do so."

It wasn't his two hundred dollars that Judge Sheffield minded so much—that was about all the ready cash he had in the world, too. The important thing was that Jim-Jim had elected to become a fugitive from justice. Important, and sad.

"Seven days to go," murmured Sheffield, and he prayed that Jim-Jim would return.

The Judge said that when he was at home he used to go in and look at the neat, folded quilts piled high on the spare bed downstairs. He'd finger them admiringly and touch them as if he expected foolishly to work mysterious magic and compel Jim-Jim to rise before him as the genie rose when Aladdin stroked the lamp. But the genie was a lot more accommodating than Jim-Jim.

No, the Judge couldn't sleep much, the night of January twenty-fifth. When he appeared at the courthouse next morning, there was a terrible rumpus going on. People were gossiping and quarreling and saying bitter things about Jim-Jim. Old Man Heffelman appeared, squalling about how he had been cheated out of justice and telling lugubriously that poor young Anse was still suffering so grievously that he wouldn't be able to appear until he was called as a witness.

Then came Mrs. James, with young George and John pale-faced beside her. She whispered, when she could get Judge Sheffield's ear, that she would be willing to stand trial in Jim-Jim's stead. The Judge smiled sadly and patted her seamed hand.

"That can't be, Mrs. James," he declared. "But I do feel that Jim-Jim has done a cowardly thing in his failure to face the music."

Court had not been convened officially yet, for the county

attorney and the lawyers and bailiffs and everybody else wrangled loudly about whether there was any use in picking a jury when the prisoner couldn't be produced. Judge Sheffield sat aloof behind his desk, trying not to look at Mrs. James and her two thin-faced sons, as they stared from a far corner of the courtroom.

There was a thunder of boots on the stairs. Men bellowed: "He's here! Here he comes! We've got the prisoner!"

James James it was; but he had a growth of beard on his face, and one of his boots was broken open and tied with filthy, frozen rags. A deputy sheriff hauled him up to the bar. After Judge Sheffield had split his gavel and threatened everybody with contempt of court, he managed to achieve silence—a silence broken only by the queer little sound that Mrs. James made now and then when she gazed at Jim-Jim.

"I figured to get back by last night," Jim-Jim muttered in explanation. "I'm terribly sorry to have been delayed by a snowstorm up the line and hope I haven't committed any extra crime. But it's a dreadful long way to Minneapolis and—"

Judge Sheffield exploded. "Minneapolis? How on earth did you ever reach Minneapolis?"

"I walked, sir."

"But why did—"

"It was the quilts, Judge. Ma's quilts, I couldn't bear that she should lose them. They might not seem like much to some people, but to us Jameses—And then, when I went out on my trap line that early morning and there it was—dead under the deadfall—it seemed like it was a heavenly gift. I couldn't wait. I just had to light out and go, Judge. I had to!"

"Go?" the Judge demanded. "Go where, and with what?"

Jim-Jim said: "To Minneapolis. With that silver-tipped fox. I knew all along that there was one in the region, for I had seen him twice. And the Lefty Larson Company had promised me two hundred dollars if the fur was prime. I was afraid to trust to shipment. My brothers were too young to send."

Well, that was it. He had caught a silver fox underneath one of his deadfall traps and he had lugged that fox through days of tramping in the snow all the way to Minneapolis. Now he had the two hundred dollars, all folded up in a little dirty envelope, and he shoved it up on the desk into Judge Sheffield's hands.

"But, boy alive!" the Judge gasped. "This wasn't necessary. You were out on bail. It had all been arranged."

"It was Ma's quilts," said Jim-Jim. "If we'd had anything else fit to sell, I wouldn't have cared. But can't she have them back now—the quilts—as long as the silver fox brought two hundred dollars? I'm eager to have you start with my trial, though men told me on the stairs that Anse Heffelman isn't here to testify against me."

Old Man Heffelman brayed out: "He'll be here, all right! Just as soon as it's time for him to talk."

And from his seat on the clerk's desk near by, big fat Doctor Ottway rolled his eyes. "I doubt it," he said distinctly.

Everybody looked at him astonished.

"What do you mean?" demanded Mr. Heffelman. "You doubt it?"

Ottway smiled and looked mysteriously wise, as doctors do sometimes. "Just doubt it. That's all. I've got a little paper in my pocket that doubts it, too."

Judge Sheffield knit his brows and dashed some fire from his eyes, for his nerves had had about all they could stand. If you've anything to disclose, Ahab Ottway, disclose it right now. We'll see if we can save the state some money."

Thus enjoined, Doctor Ottway reluctantly produced his paper, though he had been planning to have himself called as a witness and create a sensation during the trial. It seems that young Heffelman got scared and feverish and thought he was going to die, that first night after he was shot. He worried about meeting the Lord's judgement, and he babbled and talked, and finally he made a full confession about stealing the fur and doing other annoyances to the Jameses. Doctor Ottway made him sign the confession. That's the reason young Anse pretended to be too sick to come to court on this day, though he didn't have the nerve to explain to his father.

Judge Sheffield said that it was all as plain as the nose on your face. He went into hurried consultation with the State. Then they produced the intelligence that such a shooting was a justifiable act, for any citizen had a right to defend his own personal property against robbers, and they quoted the State vs. Monahan, 1866, and the State vs. Schultz, 1871, as proof.

There were many things about the situation that couldn't occur now, when there are silver-fox farms here and there, and when two hundred dollars aren't running loose in the woods on four legs any more. Courts and legal machinery are streamlined and formalized. Doubtless in this day and age a man like our good Doctor Ottway would be prosecuted for withholding such information in the hope of making his courtroom sensation and maybe winning new patients thereby.

And people nowadays would know more about the processes of law and bail, for it was explained honestly by those Jameses that they believed the bail money was all gone up Salt Creek. They thought they would never see it again—mortgaged farm, twenty quilts, and all. They thought, in simple words, that they had to pay a thousand dollars to get Jim-Jim out of jail until the time of his trial, and poor Jim-Jim believed it, too.

They were primitive people and knew more about turkeys and mink than they knew about courtrooms. Still, I hope that there are many of that breed left in America today.

So at last Judge Sheffield went home, to find the mound of quilts disappeared from his spare bedroom, carried happily away by Mrs. James and her boys in their sled. All but one—and that was the best and brightest quilt, the Blazing Star. They had left it as a sign of their love for Judge Sheffield. He used it always. It was over him when he died.

THE ORANGE QUILT

Della T. Lutes, *Woman's Home Companion,*
October 1940

*In upstate New York Sofia Damion Zalenski, a poor widowed
Polish immigrant, worked hard to support her large family of
six children and her aged mother, Anna Damion. One day,
Sofia's wealthy employer, Mrs. Jerome Collins, gave Sofia an
orange and white patchwork memory quilt. Mrs. Collins had
acquired the quilt as a church raffle prize during a visit to a
small town, Falina, Illinois. Mrs. Collins did not like the bright
orange and white quilt and believed it clashed with the color
scheme of her beautiful home.*

*Sofia treasured the bedcover and spent many hours read-
ing the names inscribed on the memory quilt. When she found
a name on the quilt, "Dabroski," she was reminded of her
childhood in Poland. Karol Dabroski and Sofia had been
friends since the earliest memory. They were budding sweethearts when their parents decided to immigrate to America.
The Damion family settled in New York state, and the
Dabroskis moved farther west to Illinois. The two families lost
touch with each other during the more than twenty intervening years. A strange series of events followed Sofia's discovery
of the Dabroski name on the orange and white memory quilt.*

"Sofia!"

"Yes, Mrs. Collins?" A tall finely built woman with pleasant
Slavic features joined Mrs. Jerome Collins in her bedroom where
she was unpacking bags. Mrs. Collins pointed to a patchwork quilt
of orange and white lying on her bed and harshly dominating the
room. The quilt was a combination of white and orange triangles

forming a square. On each white half a woman's name was traced and outlined in orange-colored thread. It was a memory quilt.

The woman called Sofia (born Polish but raised on a farm near this little town of Richfield Springs in New York State) bent over the quilt. "It is beautiful," she said warmly. "Such fine work."

"The work's all right." Mrs. Collins touched the quilt negligently. "But it does not fit in my home."

Sofia Zalenski lifted her head with its coil of light brown hair and looked questioningly at the woman for whom she worked by the day. "No?" she said doubtfully. "I thought it was beautiful." Her hand moved over it caressingly.

"I got it," Mrs. Collins explained, "on our way home, in a small town in Illinois—Falina—where I've an old friend. I bought five dollars' worth of tickets at a church fair and drew it."

"Five dollars!" To the Polish woman, a widow with six children and who because of them was on relief, five dollars represented wealth. "That," she said, "is a lot of money."

" 'Tisn't the money," said Mrs. Collins, "it's the *color*. Sofia," she looked at the serious handsome face of the other woman speculatively, "will you take it?"

"Oh," Sofia said with quick breath, "I should love it, but—I couldn't afford it."

Mrs. Collins thrust the folded bulk upon her. "Take it," she said eagerly. "I want you to have it." Sofia Zalenski, burning with desire to exhibit her treasure, hugged the bundle close and sped on her strong urgent legs down the main street, past the rambling summer hotel, past the village stores and traffic light she went, to the side street on which stood her own modest and greatly overcrowded home.

"Look!" she cried to her old mother and Francesca, the eighteen-year-old daughter, and together they pored over the names etched with orange thread on the white blocks. Art meant little to them. Color and the unusual meant a lot. But these names—strange people, strange homes—thrilled them.

Evenings Sofia pored over the quilt. Sometimes, when her high-school lessons were done, Francesca read the names with her. They cleared the dining table, spread the quilt upon it and made stories about them.

"Francesca!" Sofia's voice cried out, sudden and sharp. Her head was bent intently upon a yellow thread, her index finger held it down lest it escape into that mysterious west whence it had come.

Francesca lifted her yellow head, startled. "Mother!" she exclaimed. "What is it?" For Sofia's healthily colored cheeks had actually paled.

"Look! Look at this name." "What name, Mother? Whose?"

"Dabroski!" She traced the letters slowly with a rigid index finger. "Lucy-Dabroski."

The old grandmother started up from her half sleep. "What!" she cried sharply. "What name did you say?"

"The name," Sofia's voice was hushed, "of our friends who came to America with us—from Poland—Dabroski."

"Where?" cried the grandmother sharply, peering. "Where is he? Who said the name?"

"It is on the quilt." Sofia pointed. "It is the name—but—where did they go, Matka, when they left here?" "Henryk Dabroski? He went west. It was far away. We also left the place. Yadviga cried when they went. And the boy, Karol, he wanted to stay—"

"How old would that boy be, Matka? He was older than I."

"He was twelve when you were eight. His mother and I thought that you two would marry—as you would have done if we had not had to leave our home. You should remember."

"I do remember. We rolled hoops together before our cottages in Poland. And on the boat he wrapped me in his cloak."

"It was March and it was very cold. You were," her old mother nodded slyly, "his sweetheart."

"Mother!" Sofia protested consciously. "That is foolish. We were children."

The old woman smiled. "Polish men," she insisted serenely, "choose their women early." Henryk Dabroski was that boyhood friend and neighbor of her own long-dead husband, Wincenty Damion, who had fled the land of oppression with him when the taxes became so heavy that they could not pay—and live. "Have you found Henryk?"

"Matka, you go too fast. We have not found Henryk. We have not found anyone. Only a name—Lucy Dabroski."

The grandmother shook her head. "She does not belong to Henryk," she said sadly. "But you should write."

"I do not even know where this place—Illinois—is," said Sofia. "Francesca, get the geography."

Francesca, Jakob and Anna all ran for the geography. They fought to find this Illinois. The younger two thrust tousled heads over the shoulders of their elders. They found the state of Illinois. They could not find the little town, Falina.

"It is a very long way off, Illinois," said Sofia wistfully and she sighed.

"You must write," urged the grandmother impatiently. "Ask about Yadviga. I should like to hear from Yadviga. Tell them Wincenty is dead. And ask about little Karol—"

"Why, Matka," tolerantly Sofia laughed at her mother, "little Karol is now a man," she said, "older than I, and I am thirty-six."

The old woman tsck'd her tongue against her teeth. She could hardly believe. "Still," she persisted, "you should write."

Sofia was against the venture. If she wrote at all, she assured herself, it would be to please her mother. As for the "little boy Karol"—of him she found herself thinking. How had he grown?

He had been a handsome lad, fair, of great prowess and stubborn. He would have his way. And he sang. She remembered how on board the slow ship he had stood up before the sailormen and sung.

Sophia caught herself a dozen times a day thinking not so much of Karol as of this Lucy whom she had convinced herself was Karol's wife. Not a Polish Lucy-a, but an American Lucy with brown eyes, maybe, plump and small. Polish women were not likely to be plump or small. They were big and strong. Karol's wife would be frail and sweet and Karol would lift and carry her. No man had ever lifted and carried Sofia.

They wrote the letter. Sofia told Mrs. Collins of finding the name, of her mother's insistence (laying it all on her mother's old shawl-covered shoulders). Mrs. Collins advised that they send the letter in care of her friend at Falina and said that she herself would write and ask if they knew a family of that name.

It was by now the first of June and Sofia was working at the big hotel washing dishes, in order that the demands upon a patri-archal treasury might be lessened and her own self-respect corre-spondingly retained. And as she sprinkled powdered soap into the steaming water and whirled it to a foamy suds, she read the letter over and over in her mind. She was proud of the way Francesca had done it; these Dabroskis would know that the Zalenskis were at least educating their children.

The letter was addressed to Mrs. Lucy Dabroski and it told how the quilt was acquired, the reason for their interest; if it should be that she was of the Dabroskis who had come to America with Wincenty and Anna Damion, would she write and tell them of Uncle Henryk and Aunt Yadviga? It was her grandmother, now nearly eighty, who was eager to know.

Unbelievably there was a reply. The grandmother, who from

the very hour that Francesca's letter went, had sat out on the porch trustfully waiting for its reply, rose to her rheumatic feet.

"Zosia!" she cried. "The letter! The letter!"

Sofia came running and took the letter from the postman's hand. She stood transfixed, studying the legend on the envelope: "Dabroski Dairy Farm."

"Read it!" screamed the grandmother.

Sofia looked at her mother, focusing slowly. The unbelievable had come true. Her eyes went back to the envelope.

"It is for Frances, Matka," she said slowly.

Exasperated, the old woman went to her chair. Sofia, with the letter in her hand, watched the street. When Francesca came in sight Sofia ran to meet her.

The letter was opened at last:

" 'My dear Francesca:

Your letter has arrived. My wife began the quilt of which you speak years ago. Then it was laid aside and but recently given to the church. And to think that it should restore me to my father's friends . . .' "

"Henryk!" broke in the grandmother impatiently.

"Wait, Matka," said Sofia.

Francesca read: " 'I am sorry to say that my father and mother are both dead–' "

"Ach!" broke in the grandmother.

"Hush, Matka. Let Frances read."

" 'As for me, I am that little boy Karol whom your *staruszka* must remember, and your mother, Zosia, should.' "

" 'Zosia'!" Sofia repeated the word, whispering.

" 'Zosia'!" The old grandmother repeated the word, shouting. "See? The little name. The pet name—Zosia! Go on quickly."

" 'We are leaving tomorrow for New York City. We are driving our car and we had already planned to see if on our way back we could find our old friends. It will be toward the middle of June, I should think. Tell Zosia I am glad she has a daughter as I have a son. I shall bring him with me.

Karol.' "

Sofia laughed. "A daughter," she said. "He will be surprised to find me with three daughters and three sons. Karol. I cannot believe this, Francesca."

He must have done well—this little Karol who had brushed her knees when she fell over coiled ropes lying on the steerage decks of the boat in which they crossed, and who, until his father took them away, had played with her in and around the barns and stables of that farm where they had first found refuge. Even then Karol had loved the cows and the little calves.

And how she had wept and suffered when Henryk Dabroski had taken his family to that far country where, he said, money was, and how Karol had kissed and comforted her and told her that he would come back for her as soon as he had grown to be a man. But—he had never come. After they had moved to Richfield Springs, no letter, if one were written, had ever reached them.

But now—Karol was coming! And Karol—of "Dabroski Dairy Farm"—would find she had been on relief! She, Sofia Zalenski, who while her husband, though ill, was still alive and could stay with the children, had walked three miles in coldest weather to her daily job by which she kept them reasonably warm, reasonably fed and clad by the grace of God through kindly hearts. But with Antoni gone she could not carry the load, and suitable nourishment for her children with hurt pride was better than pride saved and children hurt.

Perhaps, however, Karol need not know—nor Karol's wife, this Lucy whose name on a quilt had led to Karol's coming. She looked around her poor little house with dread. Karol might not notice the patched linoleum or mended curtains, but Lucy would.

Francesca went back to school and forgot the letter with its imposing legend, even the impending visit of the mythical Karol.

The old grandmother thought only of the past into which Karol's letter had flung her, for the future was not hers. She thought of that hurried flight of the two men—Wincenty Damion, her own husband, and Henryk Dabroski, his neighbor, when they had been caught red-handed hauling a sled full of fagots from the near-by wood to warm their poor hearths, and fined. Rebelling at this climax to a long tale of injustices they had sold off every available piece of property, borrowed the needed remainder, taken train from Danzig to Hamburg and sailed across a strange and hostile sea to a stranger but, so they had heard, friendlier land, where a man could pick up a crooked stick without being fined or jailed and where his children might speak the tongue of his fathers without fear of punishment. That these children might in due time prefer the language of their adopted country was beside the question. It was the fact of denial and compulsion that irked, and freedom of speech and deed seemed a vast and precious benison for which to barter one's birthright.

The letter had said about the middle of June. For a week Sofia had been cleaning the house. This had already been scrupulously done in March, but now from the rafters in the attic to the beams in the cellar went Sofia's broom and a surf of suds.

Before the middle of June her small meagerly furnished house was immaculate.

A room had been especially prepared for Karol and Lucy. Jakob and Ludwig were banished to a mattress and blanket on the attic floor, with another for Karol's son, while their room was turned into a guest room such as Sofia's limited furnishings would allow. The grandmother had crocheted a small rug of white and orange rags, and Sofia had dyed some cheesecloth the same orange hue for curtains. Francesca had brought black-eyed Susans for the bureau and the orange quilt, spread handsomely over the wide bed, found nothing in its surroundings to roil its golden mood. Even Lucy should be pleased.

On the morning of the fifteenth Sofia was up before dawn and routed all the family out so she could make the beds and dust underneath them; even the little ones had clean blue coveralls (washed and ironed during the night) and went forth with shining faces and the admonition to keep in that condition. Francesca had slept with her hair in irons, so to speak, and Sofia herself had shampooed her own fine head and set a little wave.

But the fifteenth went by and no car drew up before the little house on the short side street. The sixteenth passed and by the seventeenth Sofia's heart ceased to halt its rhythm as she came in sight of her own door and the little old withered figure waiting on the porch. But every night she washed the children's faded blue coveralls and ironed them.

On the night of the seventeenth of June they all sat late on the little porch for it was very hot.

Francesca's beau came and they walked away. The grandmother got up silently and retired. The smaller boys went to bed and Sofia lifted little Marya and carried her in. When she returned to the porch Jakob had got home from the garage and taken off his shoes and his shirt. He sat on the bottom step with his feet on the grass.

"Gee, Ma," he said comfortably, "this feels good. It's been fierce today."

Sofia drew her chair to the edge of the stoop and was about to sit when her eye was caught by the glint and flash of a car turning the corner, its great lights flooding the street. It was a huge and shining car and it crept slowly, nosing its way. Neither Sofia nor Jakob spoke but Jakob hastily slipped into his shoes and shirt. The car slowed and stopped. A door opened, a youth got out. The street lamp shone fully upon him. He came up the path.

"Can you tell me," he spoke diffidently, "where Mrs. Sofia Zalenski lives?"

Jakob spoke. "She lives here," he said and the boy turned to the car. "Okay, Dad," he said.

A man got out and walked to them. Sofia stepped down off the porch.

"Is this," a large warm hand grasped hers, a deep warm voice spoke as the big man bent to her, "Zosia?"

Sofia was a tall woman with square shoulders but as he stood before her he blocked out the light.

She found her voice.

"Are you—Karol?" At that it was not much of a voice.

"Yes," he said, and put his arm about her shoulders, "I am Karol. And this is my boy, Stefan." The boy was tall like his father, but thin.

"And this is mine," said Sofia, equaling him pridefully, "Jakob."

"Well!" Karol stepped back to sweep her with his eyes. "So you are Zosia! Stefan," turning to his son, "go with Jakob to put our car in the hotel garage, and register for us."

Sofia spoke. "We have a room," she said hesitantly. "We arranged it—specially—for you—and Lucy. Where is Lucy?"

Karol glanced at the little house. "Lucy," he said gently, "is dead. Stefan is all I have."

"Oh," said Sofia softly, "I—am sorry. But—there is the room."

Karol could not think of it—all the bother. "But I must know a hundred things," he said seating himself at the top of the steps near Sofia's chair, "and at once. Your husband—"

"He is dead too. Five years. He died soon after Marya was born. Marya is the baby."

"You have two children?"

Sofia laughed. "I have six, Karol. Francesca is eighteen. Jakob is next. He works Saturdays and summers at the garage. Francesca is now with her beau. The others are asleep—and Grandmother—"

"*Staruszka*," he corrected her, laughing. "I like the Polish words."

"I speak it to Mother," she told him. "But the children will not. They are all American."

"As they should be. I speak it because there are a good many Poles where I live. We still do some of the Polish things, as at Christmas and Easter. I like to keep the old customs that were good. If this country is really a melting pot we ought to bring the best from our old countries to the new. Especially," he added sadly, "as there grows such danger to the old countries as has happened to ours."

The boys came back.

"It is late," Karol said. "but in the morning we will talk. We will talk all day."

Sofia stood, hesitating. "I shall not be able," she said slowly, "to—talk tomorrow. I work—during the day."

Karol looked up into her face in the dim light. It was very tired—a little pale. Paler than a sturdy Polish woman's should be.

"Work?" he repeated after her.

"You mean—away from home?"

Now he will know, thought Sofia miserably; now he will find it out.

"Yes," she said defiantly, "I work at the hotel. I like to. It is very gay—people always coming and going—"

"What do you do?"

"I—wash dishes."

He was so long silent that Sofia wished she had not told. Her thoughts fled to that big house of his in Falina, Illinois, so far away. To that Lucy who had lived there but had never washed his dishes.

"Zosia," he said finally, "you must not work tomorrow. I have come a long way and I have been a long time coming. And a long time wanting to come. I can stay only one day and I want to visit."

Sofia was troubled. She could not afford to lose her job. But—

"You need not worry," he said gently, reading her thoughts. "I will tell them tonight that you will not be there." She was still troubled, but she smiled a little remembering how stubborn he had been as a little boy. How stubborn were all Polish men.

In the morning the old grandmother berated her daughter for letting her sleep through Karol's coming. How dared Zosia, when she knew how her mother had been waiting to see this boy. ("Boy!" Sofia's thoughts shyly smiled.)

Sofia hurried the children into their clothes, clean and fresh. They were all going in Uncle Karol's beautiful new car on a pic-nic—all but Francesca and Jakob who would go with Stefan in a car from the garage which he had hired. They were going over to Cooperstown, to Otsego Lake where they would all have dinner together. Even the grandmother was excited and changed her apron three times, finally choosing in honor of the occasion the black silk (cracked a little at the folds) with lace and rich embroi-dery which she had worn as a bride and which she kept folded away against her burial.

Sofia packed the lunch. She had got up very early to bake the poppy seed cakes that Karol once had loved.

Karol sat facing the lake. "I have read about it," he said. "I read all the Cooper books. Stefan is reading them now." Then, as they ate, he told them how he had dreamed of this eastern country where his emigrant father had first set foot. How he had longed to come; how he had thought of them—Aunt Anna, Uncle

Wincenty—and of his little sweetheart Zosia. Always he had meant to come, but there had been the long struggle to live and get ahead; his education, for that, like the good Poles they were, his father and mother had attained at great cost to themselves. Then his early marriage, the desire to found a family—an American family—by marrying an American wife. Her illness and death. But now he was here and they must make the most of it.

They cleared the table and packed the baskets. The little ones played in the water, skipping stones. Karol skipped stones with them. "Here," he said, "you should sing. Polish children always sing while they play. This is a song about the lake." He sang in Polish and his fine strong baritone sent the strange notes out toward the hills from whence they returned, echoing.

The grandmother nodded, clapped her hands, patted the ground with her foot. Sofia stood entranced, the speech of her infancy echoing faintly from the long past. The children shouted and begged for more.

Then they again got into the big car—Sofia, at Karol's insistence, sitting beside him—and drove away from the lake over the hill to the old farm where they had lived as children.

The house—a plain frame building—was unoccupied now and in great disrepair. It stood high on the land and their eyes swept the lush fields where hay that very day had been cut, to the far valley of the Mohawk and the misty ridges of the Adirondacks far beyond.

"Ach," breathed Karol happily, "it feasts the eye. Not much like my flat smooth fields, Zosia. It is a fair state, my Illinois, but I love these hills."

"It's not like home," muttered the grandmother, "where the cottages were close and moss grew in the thatch."

"No," said Karol, "it is not like that. Nor is there the hunger—nor the fear. It is safe here—in this America, and I love it. I love these mountains, but I love best my own fields of corn, my cattle, my filled barns—because it is my home."

The grandmother went to bed. Jakob went with Stefan to see that the car was ready for the early morning trip. Francesca's beau called and they walked away. Sofia came down from putting the children to bed, with a folded bundle in her arms. Karol rose.

"It is the quilt," she told him softly, spreading it. "The orange quilt, where I found her name. I want you to have it—to take it—to your home. It belongs there."

Karol followed her finger tracing the name—Lucy Dabroski. Then he folded the quilt and laid it on a chair.

"Yes," he said, "I think it belongs in my home. But, Zosia—so do you."

She drew away from him a little, staring.

"You," repeated Karol gravely. "So do you. And always did. But—you married. I—did not know—anything more. At last I thought about it, and you, so much that I had to come. Now I shall come back for you. You, and the *staruszka*, for my mother's sake. And the children for Stefan's sake. And you—for me."

"And you," said Sofia softly, "for me. And home—for us."

"An American home," said Karol with his strong farmer's arms around her wide warm shoulders and his lips against her warm high cheeks.

TIME LINE

This time line is an illustrated chronological listing of American quilt fiction, quilt plays and quilt poems published from 1844 to 1945. In addition, it informally inventories non-fiction essays, quilt catalogs and quilt patterns whose pertinence to historical events can be established. Correlating historical occurrences, aesthetic trends and other notable works of selected authors are cited on the time line to provide a complete frame of reference for the period in which the quilt stories were written.

Before women could vote or were expected to have political opinions they found ways to express political ideas by the making of special quilt designs. In the nineteenth century, quilt patterns appeared both as unrecorded folk patterns and later in the century, as published patterns. For documentation purposes, quilt patterns on this time line are from published sources. It should also be noted that frequently a quilt pattern was designed and published to celebrate an occasion many years after the event's actual occurrence. Therefore, it should not be assumed that placing a quilt pattern name next to an event means the quilt pattern's origins necessarily coincided with the date of the event. Quilts and quilt patterns devised to commemorate historical episodes have been placed parenthetically after those listings. Inscribed dates and circa dates, when known, of full-sized celebratory quilts are given.

1844

"The Patchwork Quilt" by Ann S. Stephens, *Graham's Magazine*, January. (fiction)

Prolific period lasting until the end of the decade for the making of increasingly elaborate Baltimore Album quilts in that city. (Baltimore Album quilt, 1849, made for Miss Elizabeth Sliver, Baltimore Museum of Art collection)

James K. Polk elected President, defeating Henry Clay. ("Star of the West" pattern, Ladies Art Co.; "Clay's Choice" pattern, Finley; "Polk in the White House" pattern, *McCall's* magazine)

Morse sent first telegraph message, "What hath God wrought!" from Washington, DC to Baltimore.

1845

"The Patchwork Quilt" by Harriet Farley or Rebecca Thompson, *The Lowell Offering, v. 5.* (fiction)

"Annual Fair of the American Institute of Niblo's Garden" by Benjamin J. Harrison, Collection of the Museum of the City of New York. (painting)

Woman in the Nineteenth Century by Margaret Fuller, early feminist work. (non-fiction)

Texas accepted annexation and became the 28th state. Mexico attempted to stop the annexation. ("Texas Tears" pattern, "Crossroads to Texas" pattern, Ladies Art Co.)

1846

"The Patch-work Quilt" by Miss C. M. Sedgwick, *The Columbian Lady's and Gentleman's Magazine*, March. (fiction)

Elias Howe patented a lock stitch sewing machine. ("Song of the Sewing Machine" by George W. Bungay, *Demorest's Magazine*, May 1882, poem)

Smithsonian Institution established by Congress.

US-Mexican War began.

A group of American settlers raised the Bear Flag at Sonoma, CA and proclaimed the free and independent republic of California. The flag included a piece of red flannel torn from a woman's petticoat.

Irish famine, potato crop failure. Signaled influx of Irish immigrants to America.

1847

Liberia became a free and independent republic. Repatriated African-American former slaves practiced American style quiltmaking in their new homes in Africa. (Former Virginia slave Martha Ann Ricks of Liberia presented a quilt to Queen Victoria of England, ca. 1892.)

("Nautilus" pattern, Stone—name of ship that carried repatriated slaves to Liberia in 1828)

1848

Zachary Taylor, nicknamed "Old Rough and Ready," elected President; Millard Fillmore elected Vice President. (Album quilt with inscription ". . . from one of the Rough & Ready," 1848, St. Louis Art Museum collection)

John Humphrey Noyes established the Perfectionist Community at Oneida, N.Y. (Album quilt, made in 1874 for the wife of John Humphrey Noyes as a testimonial by the women of the Oneida community, *House and Garden Magazine*)

Women's Rights Convention held at Seneca Falls, NY, led by Lucretia Mott and Elizabeth Cady Stanton.

Treaty of Guadalupe ended the Mexican War, ceded to US were California, Arizona, Nevada and parts of New Mexico, Colorado and Wyoming.

Gold discovered at Sutter's Mill, CA, resulting in the "gold rush," as many gold seekers traveled west. ("Rocky Road to California" pattern, Ladies Art Co.)

1849

"The Quilting Party" by T. S. Arthur, *Godey's Lady's Book and Magazine*, September. (fiction)

"Aunt Maguire's Visit to Slabtown" *Godey's Lady's Book and Magazine*, December. (fiction)

Sarah Josepha Hale became the editor of *Godey's Lady's Book and Magazine*.

Amelia Bloomer began American women's dress reform movement.

Lydia Marie Child published a children's magazine, and became one of the editors of the *Antislavery Standard*.

Walter Hunt, NY, formed the first modern safety pin.

1850

Godey's Lady's Book published a number of patchwork patterns in 1850–1851 issues. However, the patchwork designs looked strangely unlike the patchworks of American women of the mid-nineteenth century. Recent research by quilt historian Virginia Gunn has disclosed the reason why the Godey's patterns were different.[1]

President Z. Taylor died. Millard Fillmore became President.

Fugitive Slave Act required citizens of free states to turn in run away slaves. ("The Underground Railroad" pattern, Finley)

Slave trade abolished in the District of Columbia.

Census population—23.1 million including 3.2 million slaves and 1.7 million immigrants.

1851

Isaac Singer, NY, patented a continuous stitch sewing machine.

1852

Franklin Pierce elected President.

Uncle Tom's Cabin by Harriet Beecher Stowe published. Book was suppressed in most slave states. 500,000 copies sold in five years. (Quilt made by Harriet Beecher Stowe while attending anti-slavery meetings in Cincinnati, OH) (fiction)

1853

"A Stray Patch from Aunt Hannah's Quilt" by Frances D. Gage, *The Saturday Evening Post*, July. (fiction)

America's first World's Fair at the Crystal Palace, New York, NY (World's Fair Block pattern, "World's Fair Puzzle," Ladies Art Co.)

1854

"The Quilting Party," *Gleason's Pictorial Magazine*, October. A painting in Colonial Williamsburg is based on this magazine illustration. Painting in Abby Aldrich Rockefeller Folk Art Center. (Quilt made by Bertha Stenge, Chicago, replicated the painting, ca. 1940s. Private collection.)

Marie Daugherty (Webster) born in Wabash, IN.

Kansas-Nebraska Act established that all territories could decide whether to permit or prohibit slavery.

A new political party formed as a reaction to the Kansas-Nebraska Act—the Republican party.

Arrival of 13,000 Chinese immigrants, most employed in building the transcontinental railroad. ("Railroad" pattern, Ladies Art Co.)

1855

Frank Leslie's Illustrated Newspaper (later *Leslie's Weekly*) began publication in New York City.

Settlement of Kansas under Douglas doctrine of popular sovereignty led to bloody war between pro- and anti-slavery groups, "Bloody Kansas." ("Kansas Troubles" pattern, Ladies Art Co.)

1856

James Buchanan elected President. (*Broderie perse* quilt in "Wheatland," President Buchanan's home, now a museum, is believed to be an original furnishing dating from the time he lived there.)

1857

Godey's Lady's Book resumed the publication of patchwork patterns and produced them at intermittent intervals. Responsible for popularizing the autograph quilt later.

Frank Leslie's New Family Magazine began publication.

The Atlantic Monthly was founded.

1858

The Lady's Manual of Fancy Work: A Complete instruction in Every Variety of Ornamental Needle-work by Mrs. Pullan, NY: Dick and Fitzgerald was published. (instruction book)

Abraham Lincoln–Stephen Douglas debates. ("Lincoln's Platform" pattern, Bergen; "Little Giant" pattern, Finley)

1859

The Minister's Wooing by Harriet Beecher Stowe was published. Chapter XXX "Quilting" widely quoted in many sources. (fiction)

The Ladies Complete Guide to Needlework and Embroidery by Miss Lambert, Philadelphia: T. B. Peterson & Bros. published. (instruction book)

Ladies Handbook of Fancy and Ornamental Work by Florence T. Hartley, Philadelphia: G. G. Evans. (instruction book)

Daniel Emmett composed song "Dixie," that became very popular in the southern states. ("Rose of Dixie" pattern, Webster)

1860

Abraham Lincoln elected President.

South Carolina seceded from the Union. (Secession Quilt made by Mrs. P. D. Cook, Fairfield, SC, 1860. Private collection.)

Pony Express began overland mail service from St. Joseph, MO to Sacramento, CA.

Anna Mary Robertson (Moses) aka "Grandma Moses" born in Washington County, NY.

1861

"Stars and Stripes," A Patriotic Quilt, *Peterson's Magazine*, July. (Quilt of this design now in the collection of the Smithsonian Institution.)

Civil War began.

Numerous fund-raising fairs established, to be held under the auspices of the US Sanitary Commission. (A "Streak of Lightning" silk quilt made for General Sherman was donated by him to a US Sanitary Commission bazaar held in St. Louis, MO. Quilt in collection of Jefferson Memorial, Missouri Historical Society, St. Louis.)

West Virginia broke away from Virginia and became the 35th state in the Union. Some of the people of West Virginia were called "Radicals." ("Radical Rose" pattern, *House Beautiful*; also called "Abolition Rose," *McCall's*)

The Country Gentleman magazine founded.

Vassar College established in Poughkeepsie, NY.

1862

"Battle Hymn of the Republic" written by Julia Ward Howe became the Union force's rallying song.

1863

Emancipation Proclamation issued by President Abraham Lincoln, freeing slaves in areas in rebellion against the Union.

Gettysburg Address delivered by President Lincoln at the dedication of the national cemetery.

Ebenezer Butterick, Sterling, MA, invented the first paper dress pattern sold in the US.

"Prudie's Patchwork" by Sophie May, *Little Prudy*, Boston: Lothrop, Lee & Shepard Co. (juvenile fiction)

1864

President Abraham Lincoln re-elected.

General William Tecumseh Sherman captured and burned Atlanta. Sherman's army marched through Georgia to the sea. ("Sherman's March" pattern, Cappers)

The "Pullman Car," the first railroad sleeping car, was built by George Pullman. ("Pullman Puzzle" pattern, Ladies Art Co.)

1865

Civil War ended.

President Abraham Lincoln assassinated at Ford's Theatre, Washington, DC. (The Abraham Lincoln spread, third quarter of the 19th century. In collection of the Shelburne Museum, VT)

Thirteenth Amendment to the Constitution abolished slavery in the US (Silk quilt with center inscription "Liberty" made by former slave, Elizabeth Keckley, ca. 1870. Quilt in collection of Ross Trump. Numerous pejorative depictions of two dancing black figures with inscriptions "We's Free" made by white needleworkers on various textile items; quilt blocks, rugs, mats, samplers)

1866

Cultivator Magazine and *The Country Gentleman* merged.

Carrie A. Hall born in Caledonia, WI.

Metropolitan Museum of Art founded in New York.

1867

"Mrs. Yardley's Quilting" from *Sut Livingood's Yarns* by George Washington Harris. (fiction)

Harper's Bazar, New York, began publication.

US bought Alaska from Russia. ("Klondike Star" pattern, Stone)

Congress set up reservations in Indian Territory (now Oklahoma) for the Five Civilized Tribes: Cherokees, Chickasaws, Choctaws, Creeks and Seminoles.

1868

"Quilting at Miss Jones's" by Josiah Allen's wife (Marietta Holley), *Godey's Lady's Book*, July. (fiction)

Hearth and Home For the Farm, Garden and Fireside Magazine, Pettingill, Bates & Co., NY began publication.

William Rush Dunton born in Chestnut Hill, Philadelphia, PA.

President Andrew Johnson impeached, tried and acquitted by the US Senate.

General U. S. Grant elected President. (Quilt made by General Grant's mother in collection of Jefferson Memorial, Missouri Historical Society, St. Louis.)

1869

"Quiltings" in *The Pennsylvania Dutch* by Phebe Earle Gibbons, *The Atlantic Monthly*, October. (non-fiction essay)

"How a Giant Managed Matters" by Frank R. Stockton. *Hearth and Home* (Pettingill), January. (fiction)

Wyoming granted women's suffrage.

Little Women by Louisa May Alcott published. ("Little Women" quilt pattern by Marion Cheever Whiteside, *Ladies' Home Journal*)

1870

"Hannah's Quilting" *Harper's Bazar*, March. (fiction)

"The Shadow of Moloch Mountain" Chapter 27, Busy Bees; Chapter 28, Stinging Bees; Chapter 29, Feeding the Bees by Mrs. Jane G. Austin, *Hearth and Home*, (Pettingill). (fiction)

"Making Log Cabin Quilts" by Lou Lightheart, Scioto County, OH, *The Cultivator and Country Gentleman Magazine*, March. (instructions)

Great Atlantic and Pacific Tea Co. (A&P) organized; largest single chain of grocery stores.

Cartoon using the donkey as a symbol of the Democratic Party printed first time in *Harper's Weekly*. ("Giddap, A Very Democratic Donkey" pattern, *K.C.S.*)

1872

"A Axident" by Josiah Allen's wife (Marietta Holley), *Peterson's Magazine*, September. (fiction)

"Blasted Hopes" by B. Babbet, *Peterson's Magazine*, September. (poem)

"Patty's Patchwork" by Louisa May Alcott, *Aunt Jo's Scrapbook*. (juvenile fiction)

Montgomery Ward mail order store opened in Chicago.

1873

"The Parlin Patchwork" by Sophie May, *Miss Thistledown*, Boston: Lee and Shepard. (juvenile fiction)

1874

"Hints about Silk Quilts" by J. S. M., *Hearth and Home* (Pettingill), April. (instructions)

Women's Christian Temperance Union (W.C.T.U.) organized in Cleveland. ("W.C.T.U." pattern, Ladies Art Co.)

Thomas Nast, cartoonist, established the elephant as a symbol for the Republican Party in a cartoon that appeared in *Harper's Weekly*. ("Arrarat," a pattern named for a Kansas City zoo elephant became symbol for the Republican Party, *K.S.C.*)

1875

"Trials" by Farmer's Wife, *The Cultivator and Country Gentleman*, November. (fiction)

Household Elegancies: Suggestions in Household Art and Tasteful Home Decorations by Mrs. C. S. Jones and Henry T. Williams, NY: Henry T. Williams. (instruction book)

Anne Champe (Orr) born in Nashville, TN.

1876

"Doings of the Polly's Christmas Society" by Olive Thorne, *Ballou's Monthly*. (fiction)

"Patchwork" by Farmer's Wife, *The Cultivator and Country Gentleman*, March. Mentions the making of charm quilts and the collecting of 999 prints. (instructional)

Ladies Fancy Work, Hints and Helps to Home Taste and Recreations by Mrs. C. S. Jones and Henry T. Williams, NY: Henry T. Williams. (instruction book)

Centennial Exposition to celebrate the 100th anniversary of the Declaration of Independence, Philadelphia, PA. Elizabeth Duane Gillespie, great granddaughter of Benjamin Franklin, originated the Women's Pavilion at the Centennial Exhibition. ("Centennial" pattern, Ladies Art Co.; "Centennial" pattern, "Centennial Tree" patterns, Stone)

Many early women journalists concealed their true identities behind pseudonyms. Grace Greenwood was the pen name of Kate Field who was published in the *New Orleans Picayune* at age eight. Reader-contributors to magazines also engaged in this practice.

Rutherford B. Hayes and Samuel Tilden, opponents for President in a disputed election.

Alexander Graham Bell invented the telephone.

Thomas Alva Edison invented the phonograph.

General George Armstrong Custer's Last Stand; overwhelmed by Sioux Indians at the Battle of the Little Big Horn.

1877

Ladies Guide to Needlework by S. Annie Frost. NY: Adams & Bishop. (instruction book)

Congress declared Rutherford B. Hayes President.

Lucy Hayes, wife of the President, was a strong temperance advocate. She was referred to as "Lemonade Lucy" by those who attended social functions at the "dry White House."[2]

Reconstruction era ends.

1878

"Crazy Cushion" by S. B. Sawyer, *The Cultivator and Country Gentleman*, March. (instructions)

Crazy quilt phenomenon gathering momentum, soon to become a national fad and the late nineteenth century's quintessential quilt. Crazy quilts were made full sized and as smaller sofa or parlor throws. (Silk and satin crazy quilt throw with braid trim and tassels instead of usual border, circa 1873–1885. Collection of Jefferson Memorial, Missouri Historical Society, St. Louis, MO.)

Other popular quilts made during the late Victorian period were pieced silk or velvet quilts in Fan, Log Cabin, Baby Blocks, Zigzag and Roman Stripe patterns. Pieced block quilts in silk or plain cotton overlaid with a very heavy ornate embroidery were much admired, as were the simple outline embroidery quilt designs. Charm quilts, pieced from a multitude of cotton prints, no two alike, were also made.

Women's Exchange founded by Candace Wheeler and Mrs. William Choate in New York.

1880

James A. Garfield and Chester A. Arthur elected President and Vice President.

Joel Chandler Harris used American Negro dialect in his work *Uncle Remus: His Songs and His Sayings.* Later research disclosed the stories were adaptations of African folk tales.

1881

"Grandma's Patchwork Quilt," *Household Magazine*, October. (fiction)

Woman's Handiwork in Modern Homes by Constance Car Harrison, NY: Charles Scribner's Sons. (instruction book)

President Garfield shot in a railroad station in Washington, D.C. Died eleven weeks later. ("Garfield's Monument" pattern, Ladies' Art Co.)

Chester Arthur became President. ("Gay Nineties" quilt showing countenances of President Garfield and President Arthur, Peto)

Clara Barton established National Society of the Red Cross. ("Clara Barton Rose" pattern, Mary McElwain, 1930)

Booker T. Washington, former slave, organized Normal and Industrial Institute for Negroes (later Tuskegee Institute).

1882

"Bessie's Silk Patchwork" by J. E. M., *The Cultivator and Country Gentleman*, August. (fiction)

"Patchwork," *Harper's Bazar*, September. (instructions)

The Dictionary of Needlework: An Encyclopedia of Artistic, Plain and Fancy Needlework, by Sophia Caulfeild and Blanche Saward. London: A. W. Cowan, publisher. (instructions)

Oscar Wilde came to America for a literary tour. In England he was a leading contributor to the popularization of the sunflower as a decorative motif. American quiltmakers began stitching an "Oscar Crazy Quilt" containing appliquéd and embroidered sunflowers.

Schuyler S. Wheeler, NY, invented the electric fan. ("Electric Fan" pattern; "Electric Fan No. 2" pattern, Stone)

First Labor Day celebration in New York City.

Market Report: "Cotton—Good white goods are doing well and leading makers of Marseilles and crochet quilts are still sold ahead."

1883

"Around the Quilting Frames" by J. E. McConaughy, *The Cultivator and Country Gentleman*, August. (fiction)

"Viney's Conversion and Courtship" by Sophie Shepard, *Harper's Weekly*, April. (fiction)

"The Patchwork School" by Mary E. Wilkins, *Wide-Awake Magazine*, December. (juvenile fiction)

"Grandmother's Quilt" by Annie E. S. Beard, *Soldier's Bulletin*, reprinted in Pictorial War Record. (fiction)

Ladies' Fancy Work, edited by Jennie June, NY: A. L. Burt Co., publisher. (instruction book)

Ladies' Home Journal began publication.

Brooklyn Bridge completed.

"Quilts and Quiltmaking" by G. A. O., *The Cultivator and Country Gentleman*, July. (instructions)

1884
"The Quiltin' at Old Mrs. Robertson's" by Betsy Hamilton, *Harper's Weekly*, February. (fiction)

"The Career of a Crazy Quilt" by Dulcie Weir, *Godey's Lady's Book*, July. (fiction)

"An Honest Soul" by Mary E. Wilkins, *Harper's New Monthly*. (fiction)

"The Crazy Quilt" by Margaret E. Sangster, *Harper's Bazar*, January. (poem)

Florence Gawden (Peto) born in New York.

Household Conveniences, NY: Orange Judd Farmer Co. (instruction book)

Crazy Patchwork : All the New Stitches Illustrated; And Plain Instructions for Making the Patchwork. Philadelphia: Strawbridge & Clothier. (instruction pamphlet)

Instructions For Patchwork: A New Book of Patterns and Instructions for Making Fancy Patchwork. NY: J.F. Ingalls (instruction pamphlet)

"Appliques for Crazy Quilt," *Peterson's Magazine*, October. (instruction pamphlet)

Ruth Ebright (Finley) was born in Akron, OH.

Mrs. Julia Ward Howe reported as satisfactory the progress of the Women's Department of the New Orleans Exposition (which was expected to eclipse that of the 1876 Philadelphia Centennial Exposition). "Women will exhibit work there as artists, authors, photographers, publishers, wood-carvers, designers of interior decoration in stained glass, metals and textile fabrics, in scientific work, in the production of silk and in domestic and practical ways."

Washington Monument dedicated.

Grover Cleveland elected President. ("Cleveland Lilies" pattern, Ladies Art Co.)

1885
"The Crazy Quilt" by Madge Carroll, *Arthur's Home Magazine*, October. (fiction)

"A New England Village Quilting Party in the Olden Times" by Elias Nason, *Granite Monthly*. (fiction)

"A Story of a Crazy Quilt" by L. E. Chittenden, *Peterson's Magazine*, December. (fiction)

Fancy Work: Recreations by Eva Marie Niles, Minneapolis: Buckeye Publishing Co. "Patchwork." (instruction book)

Beautiful Homes: How To Make Them by Mrs. C. S. Jones and Henry Williams, New York: Henry S. Allen. (instruction book)

Good Housekeeping began publication.

1886
"Ruth's Crazy Quilt" Sydney Dare, *Harper's Young People*, June. (fiction)

Needlework as Art by Lady Marion Alford, London: Sampson, Low, Marston, Searles and Rivington. (instruction book)

Rose Good (Kretsinger) born in Hope, Kansas.

The Progressive Farmer magazine established.

Electric motors were installed on sewing machines.

Former slave, Harriet Powers, Athens, GA, made an appliqued pictorial Bible quilt that has become world renowned. In the collection of the Smithsonian Institution's National Museum of American History.

President Grover Cleveland married Frances Folsom in a White House ceremony—the first marriage of a President in the Executive Mansion. ("Mrs. Cleveland's Choice" pattern, Ladies' Art Co.)

Statue of Liberty installed in New York Harbor. (One hundred years later, to celebrate the centennial, a national Statue of Liberty quilt contest was held in New York, sponsored by the Museum of American Folk Art.)

American Federation of Labor (A.F.L.) was founded in Columbus, OH.

1887
First issue of *The Priscilla Magazine* published at Lynn, MA by T. E. Parker. In 1893 it became *The Modern Priscilla Magazine* and was moved to Boston by the new owner, W. N. Hartshorn. The first editor of this women's needlework magazine was a man, Isaiah R. Parrott, who used the pseudonym Mrs. Beulah Kellogg until 1918.

1888
"Mrs. Paxton's Quilting Story" by J. L. Harbour, *The Youth's Companion*, September. (fiction)

"Bed Quilts for Invalids" by Aunt Addie, *The Cultivator and Country Gentleman*, March. (instructions)

Benjamin Harrison elected President. ("Harrison Rose" pattern, Webster)

1889
"Ann Lizzy's Patchwork" by Mary E. Wilkins, *St. Nicholas Magazine*, November. (fiction)

"Mammy Hester's Quilts" by Adelaide R. Rollston, *Harper's Bazar*, August. (fiction)

Chapter IX, "Artistic Designs for Patchwork Quilts and Sofa Pillows," *Needle and Brush: Useful and Decorative Metropolitan Art Series*, NY: Butterick Co. (instruction book)

Ladies' Art Company, St. Louis, MO established. It was the first company to offer hundreds of quilt patterns in a mail order catalog. Had an extraordinary influence on American quilt nomenclature.

"Nursery Rug or Cot-Counterpane-Applique," *The Young Ladies Journal*, December. (instructions)

Oklahoma (Indian Territory) was opened to white settlers on a specific day. People who tried to go in illegally ahead of the others were termed "Sooners." Today Oklahoma is called the Sooner State. ("Oklahoma Boomer" pattern, Ladies Art Co.)

1889, "Cake Walk" cushion, Campbell, Metzler, Jacobson Co.

1890

Former slave Harriet Powers, Athens, GA was commissioned to make a second Bible quilt by the faculty wives of Atlanta University. Today that quilt shares equal acclaim with the first Powers' quilt. In collection of Museum of Fine Arts, Boston.

1891

Bertha Sheramsky (Stenge) born in Alameda, CA.

"Prudy's Patchwork" in *Little Prudy* by Sophie May, Rebecca S. Clarke, Norwood, MA: Norwood Press. (juvenile fiction)

1892

Ladies Fancy Work, Avon Edition, NY: F. M. Lupton. (instruction book)

1893

World's Columbian Exposition, the Chicago World's Fair. ("Columbia Puzzle" pattern, "Columbia Star" pattern, Ladies Art Co.)

The Ladies' Model Fancy Work Manual, The People's Handbook Series, NY: F. M. Lupton, 106–108 Reade Street. (instructional book)

"Easter Fancy Work" by Alice Chittenden, *The Cultivator and Country Gentleman*, March. (instructions)

1894

Art and Handicraft: Illustrated Designs for the Needle Brush and Pen, edited by Maude Howe Elliot. Chicago: Rand, McNally & Co. Published as a report of women's activities at the World's Columbian Exposition,

Chicago. ("Columbian Puzzle" pattern, Stone)

Dainty Work for Pleasure and Profit by editor of "Home Art," Addie Heron, Chicago: Home Manual Co. (instructions)

"The Tapestry of the New World" by Fanny D. Bergen, *Scribner's Magazine*, September. A lengthy essay and one of the first attempts to write an historical report of American quilts. (essay)

"Bowlders and Bed-Quilts," *The Cultivator and Country Gentleman*, September. (essay)

"A City Quilting Party" by Ilka, *The Ohio Farmer*, August. (essay)

"Revival of the Patchwork Quilt" by Sybil Lanigan, *Ladies' Home Journal*, October. (instructional)

Jacob S. Coxey, Ohio, led a large band of unemployed dissidents in a "March on Washington" to petition the U.S. government for reforms. ("Coxey's Camp" pattern, Ladies Art Co.)

"Patchwork Quilt" by Margaret Bottome, *Ladies' Home Journal*, January. (sermon)

1895
Sears, Roebuck & Company opened a mail order business.

John Pierpont Morgan and his syndicate helped to stabilize entire US economy by floating a bond issue to increase the gold reserve. ("Mrs. Morgan's Choice" pattern, Stone)

"Patchwork," *The Housekeeper Magazine*. (instructions)

1896
"Patchwork," read by Mrs. J. H. Haskell at the Euclid, OH Independent Institute, held January 29 and 30, *The Ohio Farmer*, February. (lecture, sermonette)

"With Cigar Ribbons: A Sofa Cushion" by Honorine, *The Cultivator and Country Gentleman*, January. (instructions)

House Beautiful published.

Society of Blue and White Needlework of Deerfield, MA, established by Margaret Whiting and Ellen Miller. It was a needlework cottage industry and a forerunner of later quilt cottage industries of the twentieth century.

William Jennings Bryant delivered his famous "Cross of Gold" speech at the Democratic National Convention. ("Mrs. Bryan's Choice" pattern, Stone)

William McKinley elected President.

1897
"A Quilting Bee in Our Village" by Mary E. Wilkins, *Ladies' Home Journal*, February. (fiction)

"A Pieced Quilt Story" F. H. P., *Orange Judd Farmer*, March. (non-fiction story)

"Katzenjammer Kids" the first US comic strip. ("Katzenjammer Kids" quilt pattern, many years later in the 1930s, by Laura Wheeler, a needlework pattern syndicate)

Tennessee Centennial Exposition at Nashville; The Women's Building was an idealized enlargement of the Hermitage, the Tennessee home of President Andrew Jackson. "Each branch of the decorative and applied art will be represented," the promotional materials read.

1898

"John's Mother: the Gorgeous Quilt and Homely Socks" by Antonia J. Stemple, *Good Housekeeping*, March. (fiction)

"Aunt Bina's Quilt" by Mrs. O. W. Scott, *The Youth's Companion*, September. (fiction)

"Quilts Versus Blankets" by A. B. M., *Orange Judd Farmer*, July. (essay)

"A Plea for Patchwork" by Marie Sias, *The Housekeeper*, September. (illustrated article)

Spanish-American War began.

US Fleet under Admiral George Dewey destroyed the Spanish fleet at the Battle of Manila Bay in the Philippines. ("Dewey's Victory" pattern, "The Dewey Block" pattern, Stone; "The Philippines" pattern, Ladies Art Co.)

Treaty of Paris ended Spanish-American War. ("Victory" pattern, "Victory Star" pattern, Stone)

1899

The Silver Buckle: A Story of Revolutionary Days, Philadelphia: Henry Altemus Co. (juvenile fiction)

1900

"An Old Quilt" by Bishop John Heyl Vincent, *The Outlook*, April. (fiction)

Carry Nation, ardent temperance advocate, denounced saloons and liquor. ("Carrie Nation" pattern, *K.C.S.*)

Cake Walk most fashionable dance. Cushion covers showing black people engaged in "Cake Walk" contests were popular and advertised in *Home Needlework Magazine*. (A ca. 1890 quilt made of Cake Walk cushion covers depicting black people was found in the Arizona Quilt Project).

Quilt Pattern "Twentieth Century Star," Stone, signaled the new century.

President William McKinley re-elected.

1901

House and Garden magazine first published.

President William McKinley shot and died later. Theodore Roosevelt became 26th President.

"Some Old Bed Coverings" by Margaret Chura, *House Beautiful*, November. (photo-essay)

1903

Mandy's Quilting Party and Other Stories, the Saafield Publishing Co., New York. (fiction)

"Patchwork" by M. E. Francis, *Littel's Living Age*, January. (essay unrelated to quiltmaking)

Orville and Wilbur Wright successfully fly a powered airplane.

1904

The Quilt That Jack Built by Anne Fellows Johnson, L. C. Page Co., Boston. (juvenile fiction)

Louisiana Purchase Exposition, celebrating the centennial of the Louisiana Purchase, St. Louis, MO World's Fair. Quilt contest held. ("Princess Feather" quilt, 2nd prize winner, Finley; "Crazy Quilt," 3rd prize winner, McMorris). Sold at the fair were hot iron transfers for embroidery of buildings on the fairgrounds. (Outline embroidered quilt made from the transfer designs, ca.1905, collection of Carol Hastings). The fair is credited as place where the ice cream cone originated. Previously, ice cream had always been served in a dish. ("Ice Cream Cone" pattern, *K.C.S.*)

"Dower Chest Treasures" by Helen Blair, *House Beautiful*, February. (essay)

"A Thing of Shreds and Patches" by Helen Blair, *Ladies' Home Journal*, April. (photo-essay)

The Revival of Handicraft in America published by US Bureau of Labor.

1905

"The Best Housekeeper in Banbury" by Edith Robinson, *Ladies' Home Journal*, June. (fiction)

Quilt designs by famous illustrators published in *Ladies' Home Journal*:
January—"Wild Animal Bedquilt" by Ernest T. Seton
March—"Circus Bedquilt" by Maxfield Parrish
May—"Dragon Bedquilt" by Gazo Foudj
August—"Alice in Wonderland Bedquilt" by Peter Newell
November—"Child's Goodnight Bedquilt" by Jessie Wilcox Smith.

"Of Shreds and Patches" by Mary Harriett Large, *House Beautiful*, November. (interview)

1906

"The Bedquilt" by Dorothy Canfield, *Harper's Monthly*, November. (fiction)

San Francisco earthquake, most devastating quake in recorded US history.

1907

Aunt Jane of Kentucky by Eliza Calvert Hall, Boston: Little, Brown & Co. Chapter 3, "Aunt Jane's Album" about quiltmaking, has been widely quoted in literature. (fiction)

Hearth and Home, a Vickery-Hill publication, Augusta, ME, had needlework pages, "Useful and Fancy Work" edited by Mary E. Bradford. The editor urged readers to submit quilt block patterns named for each state. The patterns could be original designs or renamed favorites. Reader-contributors responded and submitted patterns named for states. The contest ended in 1912. Subsequently, a contest was begun for blocks of outlying possessions, such as Alaska, Hawaii, Guam, Samoa and the Philippines. (A collection of these state patterns is in the book *The United States Patchwork Pattern Book* by Barbara Bannister and Edna Paris Ford, New York: Dover, 1976.)

"Some New Designs for Patchwork" by Mrs. Wilson, *Ladies' Home Journal*, October. (photo-essay)

"The Mother of the Sunbonnet Babies" by Julia Darrow Cowles, *The Housekeeper*, September. Article about Bertha L. Corbett, originator of Sunbonnet Babies. ("Sunbonnet Girl" pattern, Rainbow Co.)

Practical Needlework: Quilt Patterns, Vol. III, No. 2 by Clara A. Stone, Boston: C. W. Calkins Co., a mail order quilt block pattern catalog containing 186 patterns. The Stone catalog reflected an East Coast orientation just as the Ladies Art Co. catalog reflected a midwest one. The majority of the patterns in the Stone catalog had previously appeared in *Hearth and Home* and in other Vickery-Hill periodicals. Clara A. Stone was a prolific contributor of block patterns to *Hearth and Home* from the 1890s. Apparently she was an accomplished needlewoman, as articles on other needle arts, such as lacemaking, appeared in different publications with her byline.

Mother's Day observed first time through efforts of Anna Jarvis.

1908
"Anne's Christmas Idea" by Alice Louise Lee, *The Youth's Companion*, November. (fiction)

"When Patchwork Becomes An Art" by Mrs. Leopold Simon, *Ladies' Home Journal*, August. (photo-feature)

"Patchwork Quilts and Philosophy" by Elizabeth Daingerfield, *The Craftsman Magazine*, August. (photo essay)

William Howard Taft elected President. ("Mrs. Taft's Choice" pattern, *Happy Hours Magazine*)

1909
"The Christmas Blessing" by Rosa Kellen Hallet, *The Youth's Companion*, December. (fiction)

Needlecraft Magazine, Augusta, ME, began publication. This magazine and *The Modern Priscilla Magazine*, Boston, were the two most influential needlework periodicals during the first four decades of the twentieth century. They introduced new concepts, fostered trends, and shaped the tastes of American needlewomen. Over the years, *Needlecraft* was subject to title changes, such as *Needlecraft, The Magazine of Home Arts* (1929), *Needlecraft, The Home Arts Magazine* (1932) and finally *Home Arts–Needlecraft* (1935). It ceased publication in January-February, 1941.

"Kentucky Mountain Patchwork Quilts" by Elizabeth Daingerfield, *Ladies' Home Journal*, July. (photo-essay)

Admiral Robert Peary, his Negro aide Matthew Henson and four Eskimos were the first to reach the North Pole. ("Peary's Expedition" pattern, Nancy Cabot)

Newark Museum (NJ) founded under director John Cotton Dana.

1910
Halley's Comet passed the sun without incident, although many people anticipated tragedy. ("Halley's Comet" pattern, Nancy Cabot)

Boy Scouts of America and the Campfire Girls were established. (Several years later, *Ladies' Home Journal* published a full color layout of "A Boy Scout's Room" by Helen Pettes; "Boy Scout" quilt pattern, *Woman's Day*, 1945.)

"Old Fashioned Patch Quilt Designs" by Charlotte F. Boldtman, *Farm and Fireside Magazine*, October. (photo-essay)

1911
"The Quilting Bee" by Mrs. C. J. Alloway, *Pictorial Review Magazine*, New York. The ten dollar first prize winner was Mrs. J. B. Pearce, IL, for her "The Rocky Mountain" quilt (today often called "New York Beauty"). (photo-feature)

The Patchworker's Companion, Hoboken, NJ: Joseph Doyle Co.

"Ornamental Stitches for Embroidery," *Comfort Magazine*, Augusta, ME, a reprint pamphlet of an 1898 booklet published by Vickery that gave instructions for making crazy patchwork. (instructional pamphlet)

"The New Patchwork Quilt" by Marie D. Webster, *Ladies' Home Journal*, January. (photo-feature)

"The New Patchwork Cushion" by Marie D. Webster, *Ladies' Home Journal*, August. (photo-feature)

"A Light Red Coverlet" by Marion Ware, *Ladies' Home Journal*, February. (photo-essay)

"Patchwork Quilts of a Hundred Years Ago" by Charlotte F. Boldtmann, *Woman's Home Companion*, January. (photo-essay)

1912
"A Compromise" by Mary Barrett Howard, *The Youth's Companion*. (fiction)

"Mrs. Hannah" by F. Roney Weir, *The Youth's Companion*. (fiction)

"The New Flower Patchwork Quilt" by Marie D. Webster, *Ladies' Home Journal*, January. (photo-feature)

"The Kentucky Mountain Quilt" by Elizabeth Daingerfield, *Ladies' Home Journal*, February. (photo-feature)

"The Baby's Patchwork Quilt" by Marie D. Webster, *Ladies' Home Journal*, August. (photo-feature)

Woodrow Wilson elected President. ("Mrs. Wilson's Favorite" pattern, *Farm and Fireside Magazine*)

New Mexico became 47th state; Arizona became 48th state.

1913
"The 'Rose and Lily' Quilt" by Elsie Singmaster, *The Youth's Companion*, October. (fiction)

"Jimmy Scarecrow's Christmas" by Mary E. Wilkins Freeman, *Christmas Stories Every Child Should Know*, New York: Doubleday Doran & Co. for the Parents' Institute. (juvenile fiction)

The Patchwork Girl of OZ by L. Frank Baum, Chicago: Reilly & Lee Co. (fiction)

Patchwork Quilt Contest, *The Family's Magazine*, Simmons Publishing Co., Springfield, OH. (quilt block contest)

"Quilts and Quilting Bees, *Orange Judd Farmer*, February. (photo-essay)

The Quilting Bee, Rye, NY, an early cottage industry, was established.

Hollywood became the center of the motion picture industry, replacing New York City. ("Hollywood" pattern, Stearns and Foster, Inc.)

150,000 garment workers in New York went out on strike and won wage concessions, reduced working hours and gained recognition for their union.

O Pioneers! a novel about Nebraska settlers by Willa Cather, was published.

Sixty-story Woolworth building, designed by Cass Gilbert, was completed.

1914

Newark Museum (NJ) held its first quilt exhibition.

Picture of two women in colonial-type dresses looking at a quilt, signed by George W. Colby, *The Modern Priscilla*, May. (magazine cover)

Quilt Block Contest sponsored by *Peoples Popular Monthly Magazine*, Des Moines, IA. (quilt block contest)

Aunt Jane's Prize-Winning Quilt Designs, *Household Journal Magazine*, Springfield, OH. (contest winners and mail order catalog)

World War I began in Europe.

President Woodrow Wilson issued proclamation of United States neutrality between warring nations in Europe.

Popular dances were the waltz and the two-step.

1914, *The Modern Priscilla* magazine cover, showing two women in Colonial-type dress looking at quilt. By George W. Colby.

1915

Quilts, Their Story and How to Make Them by Marie D. Webster, NY: Doubleday and Page Co., the first full length quilt history book published in the United States.

"How the Hodja Lost His Quilt" in *Quilts, Their Story and How to Make Them* by Marie D. Webster. (fable)

"The Quilt That Built a Battleship" by Katherine Hopkins Chapman, *Southern Woman Magazine*, February. (historical fiction)

"A New Kind of Patchwork" by Marie D. Webster, *Ladies' Home Journal*, October. (photo-feature)

"Patchwork Quilts You Cannot Buy" by Frances Garside, *The Mother's Magazine*, March. (photo-essay)

"A Nine-Patch" by Mary Elizabeth Gloeckner, *The Modem Priscilla*, February. (instructional)

"Old-Fashioned Patchwork Quilts" by Sarah McConnell and Lillian Sutherland, *Pictorial Review*, January. (photo-feature)

Sinking of the Lusitania.

Margaret Sanger jailed for publishing *Family Limitations* and supporting birth control.

1916
Martha Washington Patchwork Book, St. Louis Fancy Work Co. (pattern catalog)

Colonial Patchwork Book, Bentley-Franklin, New York. (pattern catalog)

Picture of girl sewing a tulip quilt in patriotic colors, unsigned, in *The Embroidery Catalog Illustrating Pictorial Review*. (magazine cover)

Home Needlework Magazine was bought by *The Modern Priscilla*, Boston.

"A Set of Patchwork for the Bedroom Not Like Grandmother Used to Make" by Marian Kirkland, *Plain and Fancy Needlework Magazine*, September. (instructional)

"New Patchwork and Crochet," *Ladies' Home Journal*, August. (photo-feature)

Ruby Short collaborated with author Thornton Burgess to design an early twentieth century series quilt pattern, "Quaddy Quiltie." The series pattern, a twentieth century innovation, was published one block each week in newspapers.

Norman Rockwell began to create cover for *The Saturday Evening Post* and continued until 1963. ("The Spooners Quilt" from a Norman Rockwell magazine cover, made by Chris Wolf Edmonds, 1977)

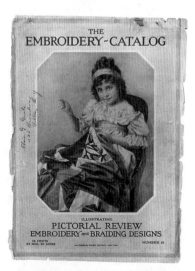

1916, *The Embroidery Catalog* cover, girl sewing quilt in patriotic colors. Unsigned.

Electric clocks introduced.

Woodrow Wilson re-elected President.

1917
"A Jury of Her Peers" by Susan Glaspell in *Bedside Book of Famous American Stories*, New York: Random House. (quilt-themed play)

"The Quilt of Happiness" by Kate Douglas Wiggin, *Ladies' Home Journal*, December. (fiction)

United States declared war on Germany and entered World War I.

"War Time Activities of Significance to Women: One Thousand Dollars for the Red Cross Can Be Raised on a Memorial Quilt" by Clara Washburn Angell, *The Modern Priscilla*, December. (instructional)

Picture of a grandmotherly type figure making a patchwork quilt, signed Harold Cue, *The Modern Priscilla*, May. (magazine cover)

"An ABC Crib Quilt" by Ethel Gates, *The Modern Priscilla*, March. (instructional)

"A Modern Patchwork Quilt," *Plain and Fancy Needlework Magazine*, October. (instructional)

Congress adopted the 14th Amendment (Prohibition Law).

George M. Cohan wrote World War I song "Over There."

As a safety measure, women in factories cut their hair; "bobbed hair" fad swept Britain and the US.

1917, *The Modern Priscilla* magazine cover, grandmother making a patchwork quilt. By Harold Cue.

1918
Embroidered Patch-Work Applique by Mary E. Fitch, Series No. 14. (instructional manual)

"Patchwork Quilts for Devastated France" by Elinor Gardner, *Needlecraft Magazine*. September. (instructional)

"Calling Quilts Into the Service of Our Country," *The Modern Priscilla*, September. (instructional)

"The Coverlet and the Cushion," *Ladies' Home Journal*, December. (photo-feature)

Stars and Stripes, the official newspaper of the US armed forces, established.

Popular song was "Oh, How I Hate to Get Up in the Morning."

Armistice signed, ending World War I.

Influenza epidemic swept the nation.

1919
Collector's Luck by Alice Van Leer Carrick. Boston: The Atlantic Monthly Press. (book on antiques, including quilts)

"Patchwork Romance" by Frances Garside, *House Beautiful*, January. (interview)

Anne Orr began writing needlework pages for *Good Housekeeping*; wrote continuously until 1941.

President Woodrow Wilson suffered a stroke.

Geneva, Switzerland chosen as seat of the League of Nations.

1920
"Quilt Scraps" by Louise Platt Hauck, *Argosy*, April. (fiction)

This decade saw the advent of quilt entrepreneurs, women who gained national reputations as researchers and commercial sellers of quilt patterns and quilt kits.

The Practical Patchwork Co., a quilt cottage industry led by Marie D. Webster and Evangeline Beshore, was established at Marion, IN.

Rosemont Industries, a quiltmaking and coverlet weaving cottage industry organized by Laura Copenhaver at Marion, VA.

"Dollar Signs in Quilting" by Maud Bass Brown, *The Modern Priscilla*, October, chronicle of the Wilkinson sisters' quilt cottage industry in Ligonier, IN.

"Patchwork Up To-Date" by Rita Newbold, *Ladies' Home Journal*, January.

"Old Patchwork Revived" by E. Seal, *Ladies' Home Journal*, August. (essay)

Home Art Studio, Des Moines, IA founded by H. Ver Mehren, a mail order pattern service, later syndicated nationwide.

Nineteenth Amendment to the Constitution ratified, giving suffrage (right to vote) to women.

President Woodrow Wilson awarded Nobel Peace Prize.

Warren G. Harding and Calvin Coolidge elected President and Vice-President.

1921
"The Ashley Star" by Marjorie Hill Allee, *The Youth's Companion*, April. (fiction)

"The Yellow Quilt" by H. E. Fraenkel, *Liberator*, December. Story won O. Henry Award. (fiction)

"A Quilt Block and Patchwork Contest" sponsored by *Comfort Magazine*, Augusta, ME. (quilt block contest)

"Patchwork" by S. M. Avery, *The Century* magazine, July. (not related to quiltmaking)

Winifred Clark Transfer Designs for Applique and Embroidery Book No. 15, St. Louis: W. L. M. Clark Co. (instruction book)

American Samplers by Ethel Bolton and Eva Coe, Massachusetts: Society of the Colonial Dames of America. (historical text)

Knee length skirts for women became the fashion, causing much comment in the press.

First burial at the Tomb of the Unknown Soldier.

The Reader's Digest founded by DeWitt Wallace.

Former President Howard Taft appointed Chief Justice.

1922
"The Wishing Quilt" by Helen Waite Munro, *Metropolitan Magazine*. (fiction)

"The Horoscope" by Eliza Calvert Hall, *Woman's Home Companion*, January. (fiction)

"The Bible Quilt: Plantation Chronicles" by Eleanor Gibbs, *The Atlantic Monthly*, July. (essay)

"Patchwork" by Ruby T. Weyburn, *Needlecraft Magazine*, June. (poem)

Quaint Quilts by Carlie Sexton, Des Moines, IA: Register and Tribune Co. (pattern catalog)

Added Attractiveness in Your Bedroom by the Wilkinson sisters, Ligonier, IN: Art Quilts. (sales catalog)

"Applique and Patchwork: Revival of Old Time Patchwork & Applique," edited by Mrs. Wheeler Wilkinson, Augusta, ME: *Comfort Magazine*. (quilt contest catalog)

Book of Applique Patchwork by Deaconess, St. Louis, MO: Ladies Art Co. supplementary catalog. (pattern catalog)

Art Institute of Chicago held first quilt exhibition.

Magazine Antiques began publication.

Tomb of Tutankhamen (King Tut) was discovered in Egypt. ("King Tut" pattern, Carlie Sexton)

Arthur Wing, English playwright, published *The Enchanted Cottage*. ("Enchanted Cottage" pattern)

Fruit, Garden and Home began. Later became *Better Homes and Gardens*.

1923
"Designs in Patchwork Applique," *Comfort Magazine*, September. (photo-feature)

"Colorful Embroideries for the Home" by Bennie Hall, *Better Homes and Gardens*, October. (instructional)

"The Covered Wagon" voted one of the ten best movies of the year. It set the style and popularity of western films. ("The Covered Wagon States" pattern, *Omaha World-Herald*, 1939)

"Ancient Art of Quilting" by Helen Bowen, *Magazine Antiques*, November. (photo-essay)

"Old-Time Patchwork Quilts" by Carlie Sexton, *Successful Farming*, January. (instructional)

President Harding died suddenly in San Francisco. Calvin Coolidge was sworn in as President by his father in Vermont. ("Tumbling Block" quilt that Calvin Coolidge helped make when 13 years of age is in his home, now a museum).

1924
"The Quilt-of-the-Cloth-of-Gold" by Ann McQueen, *The Youth's Companion*, December. (fiction)

"A Block for Friendship" Part 1, 2, 3 by Gertrud West, *The Farmer's Wife* magazine, June, July, August. (fiction)

"Grandmother's Quilt" by Dorothea Ellen Young, *Needlecraft Magazine*, August. (poem)

"The Patchwork Quilt" by Eve Eggleston Hoyt, *Farm and Home*, March. (poem)

"A Hollyhock Bedroom," edited by Caroline B. King, *The Country Gentleman*, January. (instructional)

"A Fascinating Crib Quilt: Just the Thing for Baby's Crib," *American Needlewoman Magazine*, November. (instructional)

Old Fashioned Quilts by Carlie Sexton, Des Moines, IA: *Register and Tribune*. (pattern catalog)

American Wing of the Metropolitan Museum of Art, New York, established.

Toledo Museum of Art (Ohio) held exhibit "Early American Quilts," featuring the collection of George H. Ketcham.

Calvin Coolidge elected President.

1925
"The Quilting Party" by Helen Coale Crew, *Stone's Silent Reading*. (juvenile fiction)

"Calico Print" by Edith Bernard Delano, *The Country Gentleman*. (fiction)

"The Patchwork Quilt" by Dora Sigerson Shorter, *Home Book of Modern Verse*, NY: Henry Holt Inc. (magazine cover)

Picture of a child's quilt with a fairy story theme, signed Helen Grant, *Needlecraft Magazine*. (magazine cover)

Priscilla Patchwork Book No. 1 (Revised), Boston: The Modern Priscilla. (instruction book)

Patchwork Quilts, compiled by Clementine Paddleford, New York: Farm and Fireside Inc. (instruction book)

"Old-Time Patch Work Quilts" by Carlie Sexton, *Wallace's Farmer*, January. (instruction)

"Old Time Patchwork Quilts" by Emma Gertrude Roundy, *The Country Gentleman*, January. (instructions)

"An Adorable Fairy-Tale Spread for the Littlest One's Bed" by Helen Grant, *Needlecraft Magazine*, September. (instructions)

"Applique Designs," *Comfort Magazine*, Augusta, ME, August. (instructions)

Nellie Tayloe Ross became Governor of Wyoming; first woman governor in United States.

Arrowheads discovered in New Mexico proved that America was inhabited long before the time of Columbus. ("Arrow Head" pattern, *K.C.S.*, 118–36)

The Charleston became the popular dance.

Crossword puzzles were popular. ("Crossword Puzzle" pattern, Stearns & Foster)

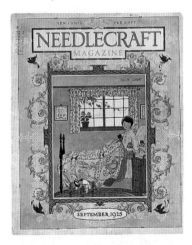

1925, *Needlecraft Magazine* cover, showing a child's embroidered quilt with a fairy story theme. By Helen Grant.

1926

"Grandmother's Red Dress" by Lois E. Brandon, *Successful Farming*, January. (fiction)

"The Patchwork Spread" by George Huse, *Hearth and Home* magazine, June. (poem)

Quilting: A New Old Art, compiled by Margaret Whittemore; edited by Florence G. Wells, Topeka, KS: Capper's Pub. (quilt contest catalog)

Series of monthly quilt block contests sponsored by the *Household Journal Magazine*, Batavia, IL.

Auction of 74 early American quilts from the collection of the late George Ketcham, Toledo, OH, at the Anderson Galleries, New York City.

Colonial Williamsburg founded.

Elizabeth Gregor Halpert opened her "Downtown Gallery" in New York City and became a renowned dealer in American folk art, including quilts.

"Mrs. Herbert Hoover's Colonial Quilt and Its History" by Nouvart Tashjian, *Needlecraft Magazine*, May. Told of wife of the Secretary of Commerce, Mrs. Herbert Hoover, commissioning a quilt made for her son's wedding gift.

"Yesterday's Quilts in Homes of Today" by Carlie Sexton, *The Country Gentleman*, July. (instructional)

"Clever and Original Applique Designs," *Comfort Magazine*, October. (photo-feature)

"A Sociable Needlecraft Is Quilting" by Anna M. Laise Phillips, *The Modern Priscilla*, September. (instructions)

"New Ways with Old Quilts" by Marcia Pallmer, *The Country Gentleman*, December. (instructional)

"Old Time Patch Work Quilts" by Carlie Sexton, *Wallace's Farmer Magazine*, January. (instructional)

"From a Little Lady's Quilt Book" by Cordelia J. Stanwood, *The Modern Priscilla*, October. (instructional)

Admiral Richard Byrd flew over the North Pole. Congress created Army Air Corps.

1927

"The Quilting" in *Black April* by Julia Peterkin, New York: Bobbs-Merrill Publishing. (fiction)

"The Patchwork Quilt" by Rachel Lyman Field. (one-act play)

"The Quilt" in *Carolling Dusk* by Mary Effie Newsome, New York: Harper's Brothers. (poem)

"Old Time Quilts" by Prudence Penny, shows quilts entered in contest sponsored by the *Seattle Post-Intelligencer*. (exhibition catalog)

Quilt block contest sponsored by *The Ohio Farmer* and Halle Brothers Co., a department store, Cleveland, OH.

Admiral Richard Byrd flew over the South Pole. ("Byrd at the South Pole" pattern, Nancy Cabot, *Chicago Tribune*)

Charles Lindbergh was the first person to fly solo, non-stop across the Atlantic Ocean in his plane the "Spirit of St. Louis." ("Spirit of St. Louis" pattern, Nancy Cabot, *Chicago Tribune*)

"Pink Dogwood in Applique" by Marie D. Webster, *Ladies' Home Journal*, September. (instructional)

"Cinderella's Own Room—A Fairy Tale Come True" by Helen Grant, *Needlecraft Magazine*, March. (instructional)

"Quilts We Rarely See" by Carlie Sexton, *Better Homes and Gardens*, February. (instructional)

"Say It with Quilts" by Carlie Sexton, *The Country Gentleman*, March. (instructional)

Cranbook Academy of Art founded.

The Academy of Motion Picture Arts and Sciences founded.

President Calvin Coolidge announced he would not run for President in 1928.

1928

Polly Patchwork by Rachel Lyman Field, New York: Doubleday & Co. (juvenile fiction)

"The Patchwork Coverlet" by Doris Wheeler Blount, *Needlework Magazine*, September. (poem)

Old Fashioned Quilts by Carlie Sexton, Wheaton, IL. (pattern catalog)

1928, *Needlecraft Magazine* cover, showing a whole cloth crib quilt, baby standing in crib. By W. Grotz.

Needlecraft Book of Patchwork and Quilting by Ethel M. McCunn, Augusta, ME: Needlecraft Publishing. (instructional manual)

Picture of girl sitting under an apple blossom tree sewing a "Nine-patch" quilt, signed Olga Hesse Bogart, *Needlecraft Magazine*, May. (magazine cover)

Picture of a woman showing a pink whole-cloth quilted coverlet to a baby standing in a crib, signed W. Grotz, *Needlecraft Magazine*, June. (magazine cover)

Picture of young woman sewing a red and white Single Irish Chain quilt, signed Mary Sherwood Wright Jones, *Needlecraft Magazine*, September. (magazine cover)

Amelia Earhart, first woman to fly as a passenger across the Atlantic Ocean.

"Wings of Victory" quilt dedicated to Amelia Earhart, Charles Lindbergh and Admiral Byrd, designed by Gretchen Heath Ageton, *The Modern Priscilla*, October. (instructional)

"Favorite Old Quilt Blocks." *The Modern Priscilla*, August. (instructional)

"Quilts" a painting by Grant Wood, private collection. (Ref. *Quilters' Newsletter Magazine*, November/December, 1983, p. 38)

"An Orchard Quilt" (made by a man), *Wallace's Farmer Magazine*, July.

There was a strong new decorative design movement in needlework characterized by straight angular lines, frequently termed "modern" or "modernistic" design. Although obviously

1928, (Left) *Needlecraft Magazine* cover, showing a woman piecing an Irish Chain quilt. By Mary Sherwood Wright Jones. (Right) *Needlecraft Magazine* cover, showing girl making quilt blocks while sitting under a blooming apple tree. By Olga Hesse Bogart.

greatly influenced by Art Deco, that term was seldom used by writers specializing in needlework.

"Quilting after the Modern Manner" by Eleanor F. Bliefling, *The Modern Priscilla*. August. (instructional)

"Modernistic Art in Shade Making" by Eleanor F. Bliefling, *The Modern Priscilla*, September. Especially valuable text explaining rationale for new "modernistic" designs.

"When You Do Your Kitchen Try This Modernistic Treatment" by Helen Carlson, *The Modern Priscilla*, October. (applique designs much like Art Deco)

Herbert Hoover elected President.

1929

"What Is Modernism? by Elsie K. Chamberlain, *The Modern Priscilla*, March. (essay)

Quilt contest sponsored by the *Chicago-American* newspaper.

Quilt Block contest sponsored by *Farm and Fireside Magazine*. Entries for this contest shown. (photo-feature)

Old Time Quilting Patterns by Emma S. Tyrrell, *Successful Farming Magazine*, Des Moines. IA. (instructional booklet)

The Book of Patchwork, Chicago: Woman's World, Manning Publishing Co. (instructional catalog)

Picture of girl in colonial dress and mob cap sewing a quilt (cover picture of *Woman's World* book listed above).

Picture titled "The Patchwork Quilt—Civil War Period," signed Reginal Ward, *Needlecraft Magazine*, December. (magazine cover)

"Patchwork Quilts" by Lenore Dunnigan, *Farmer's Wife Magazine*, October. A separate booklet was to be ordered by mail; it contained full-sized cutting patterns. (instructional)

"Beauty and Art in Quilt Making" by Gertrude Shockey, *The Ohio Farmer*, January. (instructional)

"The Lone Eagle" by Emma S. Tyrrell, *Successful Farming*, January. (instructional)

Airship Graf Zeppelin flew around the world in twenty days. ("Airship" pattern, *K.C.S.*)

"A Valiant Ship of 1840" *Ladies' Home Journal*, June. (instructional)

"Keeping Pace with Modern Movement" by Annie Davidson, *The Modern Priscilla*, February. (instructional)

"Building a Screen in the Modern Manner" by Gwendolyn Ridgeway, *The Modern Priscilla*, March. (instructional)

Various needlework items made in Art Deco style. (instructional)

"New Coverlets" by Laura Holmes, *Successful Farming*, October (new, modernistic style). (instructional)

"A Colonial Quilt Enters the White House by E. H. Jordan, *Needlecraft Magazine*, July. (illustrated essay)

"Mountain Mist," Stearns and Foster, Cincinnati, OH, printed full-size quilt patterns on its batting covers.

"An Old Applique Quilt Worth Duplicating," *The Modern Priscilla*, October (told of an exhibit of rare and old quilts at Springfield, MA) (Storrowton). Pictured quilt very similar to "Bouquet of Garden Flowers," Plate XXVI in Hall and Kretsinger, p. 158.

"The Story of Patchwork, Old and New" by Ada C. Stoddard, *Needlecraft Magazine*, April. (instructional)

Editorial "And Now We Make Quilts: An Old Fashioned Quilting Party" by Florence Yoder Wilson, illustrated with picture "The Quilting Bee" by Edward L. Simpson, *Needlecraft Magazine*, December. (essay)

"Needlework for the Children's Room" by Anne Orr, *Good Housekeeping*, September. (instructional)

"Prize-Winning Patchwork from the Homes of Our Subscribers" *Woman's World*, August. (instructional)

"Patchwork Quilts" by Eleanor Hagan, *The Handicrafter Magazine*, Feb./March. (instructional)

"The Art of Quilting and Patchwork" by Eleanor Hagan, *The Handicrafter Magazine*, April/May. (instructional)

Henry Ford Museum, Dearborn, MI established.

Stock market crash.

1930

"Polly Patchwork" by Rachel Lyman Field, adapted from short story of same title published in 1928. (one-act play)

"Quilts of the Ozarks" by Kathyrne Hall Travis, *Southwest Review*, Vol. 1, Dallas, TX: Southern Methodist University. (fiction)

Cover designed as floral quilt, signed by Alice Donaldson, *The Household Magazine*, February. (magazine cover)

Hawaiian Quilts by Stella Jones, Honolulu Academy of Art. (historical text)

Yesterday's Quilts in Homes of Today by Carlie Sexton, Des Moines, IA: Meredith Publishing. (historical and instructional manual)

"Interesting Quilt Fair" by Ruth Gordon, *Ohio Farmer*, October. (illustrated essay)

"Quilting," *The Modern Priscilla*, May. (instructional)

"Anne Orr's Suggestions for Period Decorations" by Anne Orr, *Good Housekeeping*, January. (instructional)

"The Cherokee Rose Quilt" by Marie D. Webster, *Needlecraft*, September.

"Patchwork for Quilts and Cushions in Quaint Old Time Designs" by Ada C. Stoddard, *Needlecraft Magazine*, October. (instructional)

"Patchwork Pillows" by Laura Holmes, *Successful Farming*, June (Art Deco style). (instructional)

1930, *People's Popular Monthly* cover, showing grandmotherly-type woman making a pieced quilt. By Elise D. Parks.

"Quilt Patterns" by Carlie Sexton, *Woman's Farm Journal*, November. (instructional)

"The Quaint Charm of Patchwork Pillows" by Florence Kent Crosby, *The Country Gentleman*, July. (instructional)

"Lovely Patchwork Quilts of Long Ago: Colorful Designs of Romantic Origin," *Woman's World*, January. Designs "Courtesy of Chicago Art Institute, where the original Models are on exhibition." (instructional)

Needlecraft Magazine, Augusta, ME bought *The Modern Priscilla*, Boston, MA. *Needlecraft* assumed *The Modern Priscilla's* numbering system of patterns and sold *Modern Priscilla's* quilt books until stock was depleted.

"Quilts: Handicraft of the Early American Woman" by Martin Toplitz, *Antiquarian Magazine*, July. (photo-essay)

Grant Wood painted "American Gothic," which later became almost an icon of American art.

Whitney Museum of American Art, founded in New York City.

Henry Francis DuPont Winterthur Museum founded.

Congress established the Veteran's Administration.

As a result of the 1929 stock market crash, beginning signs of the nation's depression appeared.

1931

"The Magic Patchwork Quilt" by Elizabeth Long Stewart, *Successful Farming*, December. (fiction)

"Patchwork Magic" by N. M. Bennett, *Farm Journal*, January. (poem)

"Memories of My Keepsake Quilt" by Maude Williamson English, *Woman's World Patchwork Book*. (poem)

The Patchwork Book, Chicago: Woman's World, Manning Publishing. (a pattern catalog) (also, color cover/ quilt)

One Hundred and One Patchwork Patterns by Ruby S. McKim, Independence, MO: McKim Studio. (pattern book)

Quilts by Orinne Johnson and Eleanor Lewis, *The Farmer's Wife*, St. Paul, MN. (pattern book)

Mary King's Pattern Key, Chicago. (pattern book)

Homespun Handicrafts by Ella Shannon Bowles, Philadelphia: J. B. Lippincott. (crafts text)

The Mountain Cabin Quilters, a quilt cottage industry, organized by Mrs. J. K. Stoddard of Leslie County, KY. Group later moved to Cashiers, Jackson County, NC.

"All for the Love of Quilting" by Ruth E. Finley, *The Country Gentleman*, March. (instructional)

"Linens New and Colorful" by Anne Orr, *Good Housekeeping*, July. (photo-feature)

"We Quilt from Old and New Designs" by Ruby S. McKim, *Better Homes and Gardens*, October. (instructional)

"The Very Same Patchwork Grandmother Loved" by Sadie P. LeSueur, *Woman's World*, November. (instructional)

"The May Tulip in Applique" by Marie D. Webster, *Needlecraft Magazine*, May. (instructional)

"The Story of Storrowton," editorial page, *Needlecraft Magazine*, October (in anticipation of first national quilt exhibition).

"Star Spangled Banner" officially made United States anthem.

The 102-story Empire State Building and the 77-story Chrysler Building were completed.

Unemployment estimated between 4 and 5 million; bank panic spreads as over 800 banks close in two months.

(Left) 1931, *The Patchwork Book* from Woman's World Service Library, Chicago, cover, shows woman making up a bed with quilt on it. (Right) 1932, *The Patchwork Book* from Woman's World Service Library, Chicago, cover, showing "Double Wedding Ring" quilt.

1932

"The Quilting Bee at Bascombs" by Pauline Phelps. (one-act play)

"A Heritage of the Past" by Grace Noll Crowell, in *Colonial Quilts*, Home Art Studio, Des Moines, IA, pattern catalog. (poem)

Picture of woman sewing a Double Wedding Ring quilt, unsigned. *Patchwork Book*, Woman's World Service Library. (illustrated cover)

First National Quilt Contest, Eastern States Exposition at Storrowton, Springfield, MA. (quilt contest)

"A Quilting Bee" held at Ninth Annual Women's National Exposition of

Arts and Industries, New York. Ruth Finley, judge. (quilt contest)

"We Commemorate the Washington [George] Bicentennial" by Nancy Gary and Marie Ivins, *Needlecraft Magazine*, February. (editorial essay)

"The George Washington Mount Vernon Quilt, 1732–1932," Home Art Studio, Des Moines, IA. (stamped quilt kit)

George Washington Bicentennial Quilt designed by Mary Evangeline Walker, made by Carrie Hall, shown in *Romance of the Patchwork Quilt in America*, Hall and Kretsinger, Plate CXIX, p. 256. (commemorative quilt)

Quilts. A New Book of Patterns, prepared by Orinne Johnson and Eleanor Lewis, *The Farmer's Wife*, St. Paul, MN. (pattern book)

"Patchwork Quilts That Are Genuinely Artistic" by Sadie P. LeSeur, *Woman's World Magazine*, September. (instructional)

"Favorite Quilt Designs" by Jeanette Holcomb, *Needlecraft Magazine*, August. (instructional)

"An Old Time Craft Goes Modern" by Ann Hark, *The Country Gentleman*, March. (instructional)

"Old Time Quilting Is In Again" by Ruth Finley, *The Country Gentleman*, July. (instructional)

"Nancy's Patchwork Bedroom" by Edna Guggenheim, *The Country Gentleman*, September. (instructional)

"Coverlets With Charm" by Orinne Johnson, *The Farmer's Wife*, January. (instructional)

Quilt Patterns, Minneapolis: Mrs. Curran's La Salle Quilt Co. This catalog offered handquilting services, quitting patterns and quilt patterns. (Quilt patterns were copies from *Mrs. Danner's Quilts*.) (quilt pattern catalog)

Franklin D. Roosevelt elected President.

Depression in U.S.A. reaches low point; unemployment 12 million; 5,000 banks closed. Tent camps were called "Hoovervilles." ("Depression," quilt pattern, *K.C.S.*, 3-20-37)

Broadway show, *Americana*, by Jay Gurney and E. Y. Harburg, featured the Depression-era song, "Brother, Can You Spare A Dime?"

Roosevelt's "New Deal" program stressed federal support for the economy and social reconstruction.

Charles Lindbergh's baby kidnapped from his home.

Amelia Earhart was the first woman to pilot a plane alone across the Atlantic Ocean from Newfoundland to Ireland.

Mrs. Hattie T. Caraway, AR, first woman elected to the US Senate.

1933

Second National Quilt Contest, Eastern States Exposition at Storrowton, Springfield, MA. (national quilt contest)

"A Century of Progress" quilt contest was sponsored by Sears, Roebuck & Co. at Chicago World's Fair. The quilt "Unknown Star," by Margaret Rogers Caden of Kentucky, won the $1,000 Grand Prize. The quilt was presented to Eleanor Roosevelt. "Unknown Star" quilt ("Going to Chicago" quilt pattern, Nancy Page) (national quilt contest)

The Sears quilt contest was an important stimulus for a myriad of quilt activities and publications. In the Sears building at the Fair, the *Chicago Tribune* had a counter at which were sold "Nancy Cabot" quilt patterns for 5 cents each and free pattern catalogs were offered. Some of the outgrowths of the contest were:

• Sears' *Century of Progress in Quilt Making*, Chicago: Sears, Roebuck & Co. (quilt pattern booklet) Contest quilts were also sold as kits by Sears.
• *Quilting* by Alice Beyer, Chicago, South Park Commissioners, 1934. (Contains photograph of Eleanor Roosevelt receiving Grand Prize quilt) (quilting manual with block identification)
• *Quilt Patterns* by Mae G. Wilford, Chicago. (quilt pattern pamphlet)
• *Quilt Fair Comes to You*, Kansas City, MO: Aunt Martha's Studio, ca. 1934. (quilt pattern and quilt catalog booklet)
• *Mandy's Favorite Patterns Book #1* compiled by Lillian O'Rourke, Streator, IL: Mirtie McCormick Co., 1934. (quilt pattern pamphlet)

This 1930s period marks the publication, until the end of the decade, of quilt catalogs for paper quilt patterns and cloth quilt kits, including:
• *Hope Winslow's Quilt Book*, Des Moines, IA: H. Ver Mehren, Home Art Studio, 1933 (quilt pattern catalog)
• *Old Fashioned Bedspreads-Quilts*, Bucilla No. 981, New York: Bernhard Ullman Co., Inc. 1933. (quilt catalog)
• *Quilts: "Mickey" Cut-To-Size Quilt Patches*, Chicago: John C. Michael Co. 1933. (quilt kit catalog)
• *Quilting Is in Fashion Again*, Spool Cotton Co. #575, New York 1933. (pattern leaflet)
• *Quilts, A New Book of Patterns* prepared by Orrine Johnson and Eleanor Lewis, *The Farmer's Wife*, St. Paul, MN: Webb Pub. Co. 1933. (quilt pattern booklet)
• *Royal Society Embroidery Package Outfits*, New York: The Frampton Co. (needlework kits catalog)

"The Romance of the Circuit Rider in Patchwork," *Woman's World*, January. (Original quilt in Art Institute of Chicago collection) (photo-essay)

"The Birth of Patch Quilts," *Wallace's Farmer*. (non-illustrated essay)

"Quilt Making in Old and New Designs" by Anne Orr, *Good Housekeeping*, January. ("Lincoln Quilt" shown) (instructional)

"The Prize Winners of the Quilt Contest" and "The Quilt Contest at Storrowton," *Needlecraft—The Home*

Arts Magazine, January. (A report on the First National Quilt Contest) (photo-essay)

"Rose of the Field—A Quilt Designed in Honor of President Roosevelt" [and his family] by Eleanor Madigan, *Needlecraft—The Home Arts Magazine,* August. President Roosevelt's Scottie dog, Fala, was the impetus for several quilt designs. "Scottie" pattern, Nancy Cabot quilt column; "Scottie Quilt," *Alice Brooks* #5673 syndicated pieced quilt design; "Scottie Appliqued Quilt," *Laura Wheeler* #235 syndicated quilt.

"Let's Start an Heirloom," *Ladies' Home Journal,* April. (instructional)

"Quaint and Gay" by Orinne Johnson, *The Farmer's Wife,* January. (instructional)

2,000 rural schools did not open for the fall semester; 200,000 teachers out of work; many colleges and universities forced to close.

President Franklin D. Roosevelt declared a national bank holiday; gave his first "fireside chat."

National Industrial Recovery Act to aid business enacted. ("Blue Eagle—N.I.R.A." quilt pattern, Nancy Cabot quilt column, *Chicago Tribune*)

Adolph Hitler became Chancellor of Germany; proceeded to arm the country.

Prohibition, the Twenty-first Amendment to the US Constitution was repealed.

1934

"Ma Dunaway's Operation" by Marie Mitchell, *The Farmer's Wife,* October (quilt fiction)

"The Quilt" by Dorothy McFarlane, *Woman's World,* July. (poem)

"The Patchwork Quilt of 1350," signed by Reginald Ward, *Needlecraft–The Home Arts Magazine,* December. (magazine cover)

Detroit News Quilt Contest. (newspaper-sponsored contest)

Quilting by Elizabeth King, New York: Leisure League of America. (instructional manual)

"The Elephant's Child" quilt by E. Buckner Kirk, *Woman's Home Companion Magazine* February. Adapted from Rudyard Kipling's *Just So Stories.* (instructional)

Patchwork Quilts: How To Make Them—100 Designs, Chicago: Needlecraft Supply Co. (quilt pattern and quilt kit catalog)

The Farmer's Wife Book of New Designs and Patterns by Orinne Johnson and Eleanor Lewis, *The Farmer's Wife,* St. Paul, MN: Webb Pub. Co (quilt pattern booklet)

Mrs. Danner's Second Quilt Book by Scioto banner, Emporia, KS. (quilt pattern catalog)

"The Roosevelt Rose—A New Historical Quilt Pattern" by Ruth Finley; "Pieced and Appliqued Quilts and Spreads" by Anne Orr, *Good Housekeeping,* January. (instructional)

"Franklin D. Roosevelt" quilt pattern, *Kansas City Star*, January 27, 1934, celebrated his birthday and the Warm Springs, Georgia Foundation.

"Red and Green Quilts at Home" by Carlie Sexton. *American Home Magazine*, February. (instructional)

"The New-Old Art of Quilting" by Phoebe Edwards, *Pictorial Review Magazine*, October. (photo-essay)

"Quilts for the Children," *Wallace's Farmer*, January. (essay)

"Coverlets to Cherish," by Orinne Johnson, *The Farmers Wife*, January. (instructional)

"Gay Posies on a Quilted Coverlet" by Ruth Finley, *Needlecraft–The Home Arts Magazine*, July. (instructional)

"A New Pig Quilt and Pillow for Children" by Blanche E. Hyde, *Woman's World*, September. (instructional)

Patchwork and Quiltmaking, Newark, NJ: Joseph Doyle Co. (manual and pattern catalog)

Dionne quintuplets (5 girls) born in Callender, Ontario, Canada. ("Quint Five" pattern, *K.C.S.*)

1935
"The Secret of the Patchwork Quilt" by Beryl Hubbard, *Girlhood Days*, November. (juvenile fiction)

"Peter Painter and the Crazy Quilt" by Frank Martin Webber, *Holland: The Magazine of the South*, March. (fiction)

1934, *Little Housekeepers*, a juvenile book, back cover showing child making up bed with "Rose Wreath" quilt on it.

"The Patchwork Quilt" by Inez Culver Corbin, *Home Arts–Needlecraft Magazine*, October. (poem)

"Ye Old Quilting Party of Long Ago" by Eleanor Maude Crane. (play)

How to Make a Really Different Quilt by Thelma Heath. Self-published. (quilt pattern booklet)

"The Quilts of Hawaii" by Gwenfred Allen, *Design Magazine*, November. (photo-essay)

"Color and Style Invade the Linen Closet: Quilt Making of Today" by Anne Orr, *Good Housekeeping*, January. (instructional)

Social Security Act, a federal-state program to provide unemployment compensation and a federal program of old age retirement insurance, enacted.

1935, *Comfort* magazine cover, showing sick child with quilt covered bed, doctor nearby. By Edwin John Prittie.

Soil Conservation Service set up to stop soil erosion caused by severe drought in the Great Plains ("Dust Bowl"). ("Kansas Dust Storm" quilt pattern, *K.C.S.*)

Italy invaded Ethiopia; League of Nations voted sanctions against Italy.

Persia renamed Iran.

1936
Romance of the Village Quilt by Mary McElwain, Walworth, WI. (quilt pattern catalog)

"Enchanting for Chaise Lounge or Bed" by Anne Orr, *Good Housekeeping*, February. (instructional)

"Happy Thoughts for the Nursery" by Anne Orr, *Good Housekeeping*, September. (instructional)

"Old Time Patchwork Designs" *Home Arts–Needlecraft Magazine*, May. (instructional)

"An Occupational Therapy Undertaken in 1840" by Grace Kent, Ph.D., *Occupational Therapy and Rehabilitation*.

President Franklin D. Roosevelt reelected, defeated Republican opponent Gov. Alfred M. Landon of Kansas. ("Landon's Sunflower" quilt pattern and "Peggy Anne's Special" quilt pattern for Landon's wife; both patterns were contributed to and published by the *K.C.S.* newspaper)

"Ma Perkins Flower Garden" quilt pattern for long running radio serial— forerunner of television soap operas, *K.C.S.*, 1936.

Edward VIII abdicated as King of England to marry Mrs. Wallis Warfield Simpson of the US.

Margaret Mitchell published the novel *Gone with the Wind*.

Boulder (Hoover) Dam on the Colorado River completed.

1937
"The Double Wedding Ring" by Artha V. Nelson, *Mother's Home Life and the Household Guest Magazine*, March. (quilt fiction)

"Patchwork" by Clinton Scollard in *1,000 Quotable Poems*, Harper Bros. (poem)

"New Time Quilting Goes Streamline," *The Country Gentleman*, August. (instructional)

Patchwork Quilts, How To Make Them, Needlecraft Supply Co., Chicago. (pattern and kit catalog)

New Needlework Designs for the Modern Lover of Needlecraft, "Wonder Art," Fixler Brothers, Chicago. (kits, including quilt catalog)

Handicrafts of the Southern Highlands by Allan Eaton, NY: Russell Sage Foundation.

"Rosemont Industries" by Anne Ruffin Sims, *The Commonwealth,* February. An account of a quilt cottage industry in Virginia. (essay)

"Depression" quilt pattern, *K.C.S.*

Many illegal sit down strikes.

Amelia Earhart disappeared on flight over the Pacific Ocean.

The San Francisco Golden Gate Bridge completed.

1938
"What Letty's Quilt Told" by Bessie Barker, *Home Circle,* June. (quilt fiction)

"Quiltin' Kivers" by Cecile Hulse Matschat, *Suwannee River Strange Green Land,* Ch. 8: Literary Guild of America. (quilt fiction)

American Needlework by Georgiana Brown Harbeson, published NY: Coward–McCann Pub. (needlework history text)

"All America Issue: Index of American Design," *House and Garden,* July.

Mountain Mist Blue Book of Quilts by Phoebe Edwards. Cincinnati: Stearns and Foster. (quilt pattern catalog)

"Quilts and Coverlets from New York and Long Island" by Florence Peto, *Magazine Antiques,* May. (illustrated essay)

"Let's Make A Bedspread" by Dorothy Wagner, *Woman's Day,* January. (instructional)

"Just for Fancy" by Ann Hark, *The Country Gentleman.* (instructional)

"You Might Consider Making a Bible Quilt," *Ladies' Home Journal,* August. (instructional)

"Needlework" by Anne Orr, *Good Housekeeping Magazine,* January. (instructional)

"Quilt Blocks Are Gay and Young" *Home Arts–Needlecraft Magazine,* February. (instructional)

"Old Quilts Tell a Story" by Florence Peto, *American Home Magazine,* July. (historical essay)

"Invasion from Mars," a radio play produced by Orson Welles, caused nationwide panic.

Gone with the Wind film produced.

Congress established House Committee on Un-American Activities to investigate Fascist, Communist, Nazi and other "un-American" organizations.

Pearl Buck received the Nobel Prize for Literature for her book *The Good Earth*.

1939

"Missouri Rose" by Martha Cheavens, *Good Housekeeping*, July. (fiction)

Historic Quilts by Florence Peto, NY: The American Historical Co. (quilt history text)

Lockport Quilting Pattern Book, Lockport, N.Y. (quilt pattern instructional book)

"The World of Tomorrow" Quilt Contest sponsored by Macy's Store and *Good Housekeeping* for New York World's Fair at Flushing Meadows; "Winners In Our Quilt Contest," *Good Housekeeping*, August. (photo feature)

"Eight Million Stitches," *Wallace's Farmer*, December. (essay)

"The Calico Tree" by Florence La Ganke Harris, *The Country Gentleman*, January. (instructional)

"Why Don't You Make a Quilt?" *Woman's Day*, January. (instructional)

"Birds—Quilted, Patched and Woven" by Florence Peto, *Magazine Antiques*, November. (history essay)

"Alice in Wonderland" quilt, *Home Arts–Needlecraft Magazine*, September. (instructional)

Irving Berlin releases popular patriotic song "God Bless America," sung by Kate Smith.

Nylon stockings sold for first time.

World's Fairs held in New York and in San Francisco attracted millions of visitors. ("San Francisco Fair" quilt by Bertha Stenge, Chicago)

Major attractions at the New York World's Fair were the Tryleon and Perisphere. ("World's Fair Quilt" designed by Jo-Ro Betts, 1939, incorporated those symbols. Private collection.)

1939, *Needlecraft Magazine* cover, showing woman carrying a quilt to a fair.

1940

"The Blazing Star" by MacKinlay Kantor, *Good Housekeeping*, September. (fiction)

"The Orange Quilt" by Della Lutes, *Woman's Home Companion*, October. (fiction)

New York World's Fair needlework contest, "America Through the Needle's Eye," held. Bertha Stenge, Chicago, $500 winner for her pieced quilt, "Palm Leaf, Hosannah!," one of two Grand Prizes.

"New Quilt Designs," *Ladies' Home Journal*, November. (Three quilt designs by Bertha Stenge) (instructional)

"Our Blue Ribbon Quilt" by Florence LaGanke Harris and Marion L. Dyer, *The Country Gentleman*, February. (instructional)

"The Spirit of the Hand-made: Patchwork Quilts Go Native" by Dorothy Randolph Byard, *National Historical Magazine*, May. (essay)

"Album Quilt Made in Mohawk Valley (NY)," *House and Garden*, August. (essay)

"Heirlooms of To-morrow" by Anne Orr, *Good Housekeeping*, January. (instructional)

"Just So Coverlet" (adapted from Rudyard Kipling book), *Home Arts–Needlecraft*, January. (instructional)

"America Tells Her Story in Needlework." "Patchwork Quilts" by Rose Wilder Lane, *Woman's Day*, August. (essays)

President Franklin D. Roosevelt re-elected.

Winston Churchill becomes Prime Minister of Great Britain, gives "blood, toil, tears and sweat" speech to rally the British people.

George Washington Carver Foundation for Agricultural Research established at Tuskegee Institute (AL).

1941

The Clue in the Patchwork Quilt by Margaret Sutton, NY: Grosset and Dunlap. (quilt fiction)

"Spring in Town" by Grant Wood. Sheldon Swope Art Gallery, Terre Haute, IN. (painting)

"Attractive Quilts of Today," *Wallace's Farmer and Iowa Homestead*, January.

"George Washington Slept Here, Too!" by Mary Schofield, *The Country Gentleman*, February. (instructional)

"Flower Album" quilt by Velma Mackay Paul, *The Country Gentleman*, October. (instructional)

"Needlework: Old American Designs Inspire A New Series," April, *Woman's Day*: "This Is Patchwork," May; "This Is Applique," September; "This Is Quilting," October.

"Perpetual Hope Chest" by Henrietta Murdock, *Ladies' Home Journal*, April. (instructional)

"British Empire in Patchwork" by Florence Peto, *Magazine Antiques*, September. (essay)

President Roosevelt delivered his "Four Freedoms" address. ("Four Freedoms" quilt designed and made by Bertha Stenge, Chicago, 1945)

The Japanese bombed the U.S. Naval base at Pearl Harbor. The United States declared war on Japan. ("A Salute to the Colors" quilt pattern, K.C.S.)

Top secret Manhattan Project to develop an atomic bomb began.

"Praise the Lord and pass the ammunition," said by Howell M. Forgy, the Chaplain of U.S. cruiser, the New Orleans, which was attacked at Pearl Harbor. His words later became title of popular war song.

Another war song "Don't Sit under the Apple Tree with Anyone Else but Me" was adapted to a quilt pattern offered by *Ladies' Home Journal*, 1943.

Home Arts–Needlecraft Magazine was absorbed by its sister publication, *Comfort Magazine*, Augusta, ME.

1942

"The Haste-Me-Well Quilt" by Elizabeth Yates, *Child Life Magazine*, November. (quilt fiction)

Woman's Day National Needlework Contest announced. Series of articles and instructional pamphlets published: "The Story of American Needlework," March; "To-day's Needlework," April; "To-day's Crewel," May; "To-day's Applique," June; "To-day's Quilting," July; "Today's Patchwork," September; "To-day's Cross Stitch," October; "Quilting for Christmas," December.

Ward's Quilt Design Book, published for Montgomery Ward by Lockport Batting Co., Lockport, NY. (quilt pattern booklet)

The Lockport Quilt Pattern Book: Replicas of Famous Quilts, Old and New, Lockport Cotton Co., Lockport, NY. (quilt pattern book)

Star Designs. Aunt Martha's Studios, Kansas City, MO. (quilt pattern booklet)

"Make a Mother Goose Name Quilt," *Ladies' Home Journal*, March. (instructional)

"The Age of Heirloom Quilts" by Florence Peto, *Antiques*, July. (historical essay)

"Quilts That Went to the County Fair" by Clara Belle Thompson and Margaret Lukes Wise, *The Country Gentleman*, November. (instructional)

"New Patchwork Ideas" by Dorothy Wagner, *Good Housekeeping*, August. (instructional)

Winston Churchill's two-fingered "V for Victory" sign became famous. There were Victory Bonds, Victory Stamps, Victory gardens and Victory quilts and patterns, such as: "A Victory Quilt," "Victory Quilt in Another Version" from the Kansas City Star; "Victory Quilt" from *Capper's* publication, Topeka, KS; "Victory Quilt" from *Farm Journal*, Curtis Publication, Philadelphia; and "Wings of Victory Quilt" from *American Home Magazine*.

"The Patch Quilt As a Document" by Florence Peto, *Hobbies Magazine*, January. (historical essay)

1942, *The Lockport Quilt Pattern Book* cover, showing a couple in colonial-type dress looking at a quilt.

US began strict rationing of food and materials needed for war effort.

Draft age lowered to 18. War song "This Is the Army, Mr. Jones."

Congress enacted measures to form Women's auxiliary corps of the Army, Navy, Marines, Air Force and Coast Guard.

1943

The Patchwork Quilt by Adele de Leeuw, Boston: Little, Brown and Co. (quilt fiction)

Announcement of Winners in *Woman's Day* Needlework Contest, Bertha Stenge, Chicago, Grand Prize Winner of $1,000 for her "Victory Quilt," January. Leaflets of instructions published, including: "Prize-Winning Needlework," February; "Prize-Winning Applique," March; "Prize-Winning Quilting," May; "Prize-Winning Crewel and Outline," September; "Prize-Winning Patchwork," December.

"History in the Making," *Ladies' Home Journal*, January. (instructional)

Patriotic quilt pattern "Salute to Loyalty," *K.C.S.* Meeting at Casablanca of President Roosevelt and Winston Churchill to demand unconditional surrender of the Axis powers.

Infantile paralysis (polio) epidemic swept the nation.

Salvage drives collected tin cans, newspapers, steel and scrap iron for essential industries.

Postal zone numbering system inaugurated to speed mail deliveries.

1944

Lockport Pattern Book: Anne Orr Quilts, Anne Orr Studio, Nashville, TN. (quilt pattern booklet)

"Three Generations of Quilts" by Florence Peto, *Antiques*, June. (historical essay)

"Victory Quilt" design, *Ladies' Home Journal*, April. Additional quilt patterns of patriotism appeared in the K.C.S.: "The Victory Boat," "The President Roosevelt" and "The Soldier Boy." (instructional)

Mountain Mist/Stearns and Foster, Cincinnati, OH published "Wings Over All" and "Sea Wings to Glory." (instructional)

Woman's Day inaugurated a new series "Tomorrow's Needlework" by famous designers: Ilonka Karasz, March; Norman Bel Geddes, May; Winold Reiss, June; Raymond Loewy, July; Lucite Corcos, September; William Bolin, October.

President Roosevelt elected for a fourth term; Harry S. Truman, MO, elected Vice President.

President Roosevelt signed Servicemen's Readjustment Act (GI Bill of Rights).

1945

Farm Journal and Farmer's Wife Quilt Patterns—Old and New (Silver Anniversary). (quilt pattern catalog)

"Heirlooms of To-morrow" by Pine Eisfeller, *American Home*, March. (instructional)

"Stenciled Coverlets" by Alice Winchester, *Antiques*, September. (essay)

"Newbury Quilts," *The Country Gentleman*, October. (instructional)

"The Bird and Wreath Quilt" by Velma Mackay Paul, *The Country Gentleman*, November. (instructional)

End of World War II (V-E Day) in Europe proclaimed May 8th, ("Dove of Peace," quilt kit, *Homeneedlecraft Creations*)

President Roosevelt died of cerebral hemorrhage. Vice President Harry S. Truman became President.

US dropped atomic bomb on Hiroshima, Japan and a second atomic bomb on Nagasaki. On August 14 (V-J Day) Japan announced unconditional surrender aboard US battleship Missouri in Tokyo Bay.

Footnotes

[1]Virginia Gunn, "Victorian Silk Template Patchwork in American Periodicals. 1850–1875," *Uncoverings,* 1983, ed. Sally Garoutte, (Mill Valley, CA: American Quilt Study Group, 1984), pp. 9–25.

[2]Cuesta Benberry, "Quilt Patterns of the Late Victorian Era," Part 3, *Nimble Needle Treasures Magazine,* (February 1973), p. 2.

Key to quilt pattern citations

Ladies Art Co.—Diagrams of Quilt, Sofa and Pincushion Patterns. St, Louis, MO: Ladies Art Company, various editions of the mail order quilt pattern catalog from 1895 to 1928.

Stone—Practical Needlework: Quilt Patterns Vol. III No. 3 by Clara A. Stone. Boston: C. W. Calkins, circa 1907, a mail order quilt pattern catalog.

K.C.S.—Kansas City Star, a newspaper in Kansas City, MO that published cutting-sized quilt patterns weekly from 1928 to 1961.

Nancy Page—Syndicated newspaper quilt column by Florence La Ganke (Harris) published nationally in the 1930s. Circulated by Publisher's Syndicate, NY.

Nancy Cabot—newspaper column started by Loretta Leitner in the daily *Chicago Tribune,* later syndicated nationwide. The quilt patterns illustrated were to be ordered by mail or could be purchased at the office of the *Chicago Tribune.* Circa 1932 through the early 1940s.

Woman's World—magazine first published by Currier Pub. Co., Chicago, later by Manning Pub. Co., Chicago. Patterns sold by mail, at times under the pseudonym "Helen Harper." From circa 1901 to 1940.

References

Erdang, Laurence, Ed. *The Timetables of American History.* New York: A Touchstone Book, published by Simon and Schuster Inc., 1981.

Curry, David Park, "Time Line" in *An American Sampler: Folk Art from the Shelburne Museum,* Washington, DC: National Gallery of Art, 1987.

The World Almanac and Book of Facts. New York: Pharos Books, A Scripps Howard Co.

Selected Yearbooks of the *Encyclopedia Britannica.*

Bibliography of Quilt Fiction

1844–1940

1844–1849

Stephens, Ann S. "The Patchwork Quilt," *Graham's Magazine*, January 1844: 25–31; February 1844: 63–69.

Farley, Harriet or Thompson, Rebecca. "The Patchwork Quilt," *The Lowell Offering*, Vol. 5, 1845: 201–3.

Sedgwick, Miss C. M. "The Patch-work Quilt," *The Columbian Lady's and Gentleman's Magazine*, March 1846: 123–126.

Arthur, T. S. "The Quilting Party," *Godey's Lady's Book and Magazine*, September 1849: 185–186.

Unknown. "Aunt Maguire's Visit to Slabtown," *Godey's Lady's Book and Magazine*, December 4, 1849: 425–433.

1850–1859

Gage, Frances D. "A Stray Patch from Aunt Hannah's Quilt," *The Saturday Evening Post*, July 9, 1853: Vol. XXXII.

1860–1869

May, Sophie. "Prudie's Patchwork," *Little Prudy*, 1863.

Harris, George W. "Mrs. Yardley's Quilting," *Sut Livingood's Yarns*, 1867: 134–148.

Josiah Allen's Wife (Marietta Holley). "The Quilting at Miss Jones's," *Godey's Lady's Book*, July 1868: 43–46.

Stockton, Frank. "How a Giant Managed Matters," *Hearth & Home*, January 16, 1869: 61–62; January 23, 1869: 78.

1870–1879

Unknown. "Hannah's Quilting," *Harper's Bazar*, March 5, 1870:150–1.

Austin, Jane G. "The Shadow of Moloch Mountain," *Hearth & Home*, August 27, 1870: 570; September 3, 1870: 585.

Josiah Allen's Wife (Marietta Holley). "A Axident," *Peterson's Magazine*, September 1872: 200–202.

Alcott, Louise May. "Patty's Patchwork," *Aunt Jo's Scrap-Book*, Vol. 1, Boston: Roberts Brothers, 1872: 193–215.

May, Sophie. "The Parlin Patchwork," *Miss Thistledown*, 1873: 195–205, (Chapter XV).

Stowe, Harriet B. "The Quilting," *The Minister's Wooing*, 1875: 250–260.

Thorne, Olive. "Doings of the Polly Christmas Society," *Ballou's Monthly*, 1876.

1880–1889

Unknown. "Grandma's Patchwork Quilt," *Household Magazine*, October 1881.

J. E. M. "Bessie's Silk Patchwork," *The Cultivator and Country Gentleman*, August 4, 1882.

Wilkins, Mary E. "The Patchwork School," *Wide Awake*, December 1882: 66–71.

Beard, Annie, E. S. "Grandmother's Quilt," *Soldiers Bulletin* reprinted in *Pictorial War Record*, 1883: 167.

Shepard, Sophie. "Viney's Conversion & Courtship," *Harper's Weekly*, April 21 & 28, 1883: 241, 246, 261–2.

Hamilton, Betsy. "The Quiltin' at Old Mrs. Robertson's," *Harper's Weekly*, February 2, 1884: 79–80.

Wilkins, Mary E. "An Honest Soul," *Harper's New Monthly*, Vol. LXIX, June to November 1884: 302–306.

Weir, Dulcie. "The Career of a Crazy Quilt," *Godey's Lady's Book*, July 1884: 77–82.

Caroll, Madge. "The Crazy Quilt," *Arthur's Home Magazine*, October 1885: 606–608.

Nason, Elias, A. M. "A New England Village Quilting Party in the Olden Times," *Granite Monthly*, Vol. 8, 1885: 235–239.

Chittenden, L. E. "A Story of a Crazy Quilt," *Peterson's Magazine*, December 1885: 516–518.

Dayre, Sydney. "Ruth's Crazy Quilt," *Harper's Young People*, June 1886: 526–527.

Harbour, J. L. "Mrs. Paxton's Quilting Story," *The Youth's Companion*, September 27, 1888: 457.

Rollston, Adelaide R. "Mammy Hester's Quilts," *Harper's Bazar*, August 24, 1889: 614.

Wilkins, Mary E. "Ann Lizzy's Patchwork," *St. Nicholas Magazine*, November 1889: 44–49.

1890–1899

Wilkins, Mary E. "A Quilting Bee in Our Village," *Ladies' Home Journal*, February 1897: 4.

Stemple, Antonia J. "John's Mother: The Gorgeous Quilt and Homely Socks," *Good Housekeeping*, March 1898: 99–102.

Scott, Mrs. O. W. "Aunt Bina's Quilt," *The Youth's Companion*, September 22, 1898: 434–5.

1900–1909

Vincent, Bishop John Heyl. "An Old Quilt," *The Outlook*, April 14, 1900: 873–875.[1]

Johnson, Anne Fellows. *The Quilt That Jack Built*, Boston: L. C. Page Co., 1904.

Donnell, Anne Hamilton. "The Thousand Quilt," *Rebecca Mary*, New York: Harper and Brothers, 1905: 23–43.

Robinson, Edith. "The Best Housekeeper in Banbury," *Ladies' Home Journal*, June 1905: 9–10.

Canfield, Dorothy. "The Bedquilt," *Harper's Monthly*, May 1906: 885–891.

Hall, Eliza Calvert. "Aunt Jane's Album," *Aunt Jane of Kentucky*, Little, Brown and Co., 1907.

Lee, Alice Louise. "Anne's Christmas Idea," *The Youth's Companion*, November 5, 1908: 554.

Hallett, Rosa Kellen. "The Christmas Blessing," *The Youth's Companion*, December 16, 1909: 653.

1910–1919

Weir, F. Roney. "Mrs. Hannah," *The Youth's Companion*, June 13, 1912.

Singmaster, Elsie. "The 'Rose and Lily' Quilt," *The Youth's Companion*, October 2, 1913: 508.

Baum, L. Frank. *The Patchwork Girl of Oz*, Chicago: Reilly and Lee, 1913.

Chapman, Katherine Hopkins. "The Quilt That Built A Battleship," *Southern Woman Magazine*, February 1915: 11, 29.

Wiggins, Kate D. "The Quilt of Happiness," *Ladies' Home Journal*, December 1917: 10–11, 99–100.

Glaspell, Susan. "A Jury of Her Peers," *Every Week*, 1917.

1920–1929

Hauck, Louise Platt. "Quilt Scraps," *Argosy*, April 10, 1920: 513–519.

Allee, Marjorie Hill. "The Ashley Star," *The Youth's Companion*, April 7, 1921: 210–211.

Fraenkel, H. E. "The Yellow Quilt," *Liberator*, December 1921.

Hall, Eliza Calvert. "The Horoscope," *Woman's Home Companion*, January 1922: 17–18, 80.

Gibbs, Eleanor C. "The Bible Quilt," *The Atlantic Monthly*, July 1922: 65–67.

Munro, Helen Waite. "The Wishing Quilt," *Metropolitan Magazine*, 1922: 4–5, 11.

West, Gertrude. "A Block for Friendship," *The Farmer's Wife*, June 1924: 5, 29–30; July 1924: 40, 47, 52; August 1924: 63, 76.

McQueen, Anne. "The Quilt-of-the-Cloth-of-Gold," The Youth's Companion, December 11, 1924: 821–2.

Brandon, Lois E. "Grandmother's Red Dress," *Successful Farming*, January 1926: 116–117.

Peterkin, Julia. "The Quilting," *Black April*, Bobbs-Merrill, 1927: 159–179.

Field, Rachel. "Polly Patchwork," *Rachel Field Story Book*, Doubleday, 1928: 11–41.[2]

Curtis, Helen Perry. "She Does Over Her Own Room; Patchwork," *When Sally Sews*. New York: Macmillan 1929: 90–98.

1930–1939

Stewart, Elizabeth L. "The Magic Patchwork Quilt," *Successful Farming*, December 1931: 24–5.

Mitchell, Marie. "Ma Dunnaway's Operation," *The Farmer's Wife*, October 1934: 7, 27, 29.

Webber, Frank Martin. "Peter Painter and the Crazy Quilt," *Holland: The Magazine of the South*, March 1935.

Hubbard, Mabel Beryl. "The Secret of the Patchwork Quilt," *Girlhood Days*, October 1935; November 1935: 3, 5, 8.

Nelson, Artha V. "The Double Wedding Ring Quilt," *Mother's Home Life and the Household Guest Magazine*, March 1937: 1, 2; April 1937.

Barker, Bessie. "What Letty's Quilt Told," *The Home Circle*, June 1938: 1, 8.

Cheavens, Martha. "Missouri Rose," *Good Housekeeping*, July 1939: 40–41, 82–86.

1940

Kantor, MacKinlay. "The Blazing Star," *Good Housekeeping*, September 1940: 42–43, 164–169.

Lutes, Della T. "The Orange Quilt," *Woman's Home Companion*, October 1940: 26, 27, 112, 114, 116.

Notes

[1] Bishop John Heyl Vincent, "An Old Quilt," reprinted in *The Chautauquan*, March–May 1912: 203–6.

[2] Rachel Field, "Polly Patchwork: A Play From the Story by Rachel Field," *Patchwork Plays* (New York: Doubleday, 1930): 3–27.